SANCTIONS
The Case of Rhodesia

SANCTIONS
The Case of Rhodesia

HARRY R. STRACK

 SYRACUSE UNIVERSITY PRESS   1978

Library of Congress Cataloging in Publication Data

Strack, Harry R
    Sanctions.

    Bibliography: p.
    Includes index.
    1.   Rhodesia, Southern—Foreign relations.
2.   Rhodesia, Southern—Foreign economic relations.
3.   Sanctions (International law)   I.   Title.
DT962.62.S86   327.689'1   78-2222
ISBN 0-8156-2161-2

To Eleanor

About the Author

Harry R. Strack holds a B.A. in Political Science and an M.A. in International Relations from the University of Pennsylvania. He received the Ph.D. in Political Science from the University of Iowa and is presently Assistant Professor of Political Science at Villanova University. He has conducted field research in Malawi, Ethiopia, South Africa, Mozambique, and Rhodesia under a Faculty Research Grant from Villanova University and was honored as Visiting Lecturer at Ranche House College in Salisbury, Rhodesia, in 1971 and 1976. He has testified before the U.S. House of Representatives Subcommittee on International Organizations and Movements, Committee on Foreign Affairs, on the topic "Sanctions as an Instrumentality of the United Nations with special reference to Rhodesia."

Contents

Tables

Acknowledgments

While assuming full responsibility for the contents of this book, there are several people whose assistance I found invaluable in its preparation. I would like to thank the people listed in the bibliography who were kind enough to consent to interviews. In addition, I am grateful to Mr. Ken Mew, Principal of Ranche House College in Salisbury, Rhodesia, who arranged for my residence at the College as a visiting lecturer in 1971, and again in 1976. Mr. Kenneth Towsey, Director of the Rhodesian Information Office in Washington, D.C., assisted me in obtaining primary source material and provided other information vital to this study. I would like to thank the personnel of the Bureau of African Affairs, U.S. Department of State, who shared with me information and advice during my participation in their Scholar-Diplomat programs.

I am grateful to Villanova University for supporting my research efforts. The Faculty Research Program Committee awarded a summer grant enabling me to do field research in southern Africa essential for the completion of this book. Special thanks should go to Doris Goodman for her patient typing.

Most importantly, I would like to acknowledge the assistance and advice of Professor Vernon Van Dyke, who directed my earlier research on this topic while serving as my dissertation advisor at the University of Iowa. His scholarship and integrity set a high standard which I tried to follow in the preparation of this book. My debt to Professor Van Dyke is indeed large.

Fall 1977   Harry R. Strack

Introduction

I~N~ N~OVEMBER~ 1965, Prime Minister Ian Smith, speaking for his government, declared that Rhodesia was independent and sovereign, not subject to the laws of any other country. The British government vigorously took exception to this unilateral declaration of independence (UDI) and firmly claimed continued sovereignty over Rhodesia. Ruling out the possibility of using military force, British Prime Minister Harold Wilson asked the Parliament to impose sanctions against Rhodesia to insure a "return to legality" by the Rhodesian government. The United Kingdom informed the United Nations of its actions and, eventually, the United Nations Security Council imposed sanctions on Rhodesia. These sanctions, covering Rhodesia's international economic, political, and social relations, were considered by the United Kingdom government to be the most effective and efficient instrument—short of military force— to compel the Rhodesian government to comply with the British demands. Indeed, in order to try to deter UDI, the United Kingdom government, prior to UDI, had threatened to impose sanctions and had warned the Rhodesian government of the disastrous consequences expected to flow from such sanctions.

Sanctions had been employed many times before the Rhodesian crisis—the League of Nations used them against Italy in 1935, the Arab States against Israel since 1945, the United States against Cuba since 1960 and against the Dominican Republic in 1960. Much has been written on the utility of sanctions as instruments of foreign policy and on the degree to which the objectives or goals of the sanctions policy were achieved. There seems to be a consensus among scholars that sanctions are not only an ineffective means to secure policy objectives, but may well be dysfunctional or counterproductive, producing results opposite to those desired by the initiators of sanctions. Sanctions can be counterproductive in the sense that they tend to increase the internal political cohesion of the target-state and increase its will to resist the demands being made upon it by the sanctioning agency.

Conclusions regarding the effectiveness of sanctions are clearly at variance with the initial estimation of the British government when it decided to apply sanctions against Rhodesia. According to the theory of sanctions, external economic pressure is supposed to cause internal political change. The major declared goal of the sanctions imposed against Rhodesia is to cause an internal political change which will terminate the "illegal rebellion" by the Smith régime. Such a termination will allow the United Kingdom government to discharge its perceived responsibilities as the *de jure* sovereign of Rhodesia and will allow the United Nations to end what it perceives to be a threat to international peace and security. Of course, with so many different actors involved in the application of sanctions against Rhodesia, there are different conceptions of exactly what political changes would have to occur in Rhodesia before the sanctions could be removed. This problem is discussed in Chapter 2.

The prohibitions contained in the sanctions applied by both the United Kingdom and the United Nations involve the isolation of Rhodesia from all international contacts except those concerning humanitarian needs and communications. Most of the studies done specifically on Rhodesia and sanctions have focused on the economic aspects of the sanctions and the attempt to undermine the domestic economy of Rhodesia. The focus of this book is neither Rhodesia's defense of her economy, per se, nor the domestic effects of sanctions, but rather her maintenance and development of international contacts and the avoidance of isolation during the period of sanctions. The purpose is to identify, explain, and determine how, and under what circumstances, a legally nonsovereign, sanctioned state has been able to maintain and/or establish her international relationships. The domestic effects of the sanctions are discussed to the extent that those effects have a bearing on Rhodesia's international relations. For example, sanctions affect the development of the economic infrastructure and this, in turn, affects the flow of goods to seaports for export to other countries. Foreign currency and devaluation problems are also considered because they affect Rhodesia's external trade. Also noted are the benefits which a sanctioned state can derive from being able to engage in international relations—

relations which are important for the maintenance of public morale, the acquisition of legitimacy, and the avoidance of economic deprivation. This detailed analysis of the Rhodesian sanctions case, in a context broader than merely the economic aspect, yields clues as to why sanctions programs generally produce disappointing results. Such an analysis may reveal some features or factors inherently a part of the international political system which would inevitably impede *any* sanctioning effort.

Two chapters deal with Rhodesia's international status before UDI and the nature and purposes of the sanctions imposed upon Rhodesia. The other chapters deal with the international relations of Rhodesia in political and diplomatic matters, and in the areas of economics, migration, tourism, labor, communications and transportation, and social relations.

A manifestation of the growing interdependence of sovereign states is the growth and development of what has been called "regional subsystems" or "subordinate state systems"—one of which exists in southern Africa. Three arenas of political action can thus be delineated— the global, the regional, and the national—and this provides three different perspectives or levels of analysis from which to consider the specific problem of Rhodesia and the efficacy of sanctions.

The concept of transnational relations is central to an investigation of the sanctions against Rhodesia examined from these perspectives. According to Joseph S. Nye, Jr. and Robert O. Keohane, a great deal of "intersocietal intercourse" involving transfers of money and materials, information and ideas, and people occurs without governmental control and is handled by nongovernmental elites. Karl Kaiser notes that while these elites act independently of the governments, and though the resulting transactions bypass the traditional decision-making institutions, the elites nevertheless affect the context within which these institutions have to make decisions. In other words, the transnational relations change the environment within which governmental decision-makers must act and constitute parameters on the governmental decisions and activities.

Governments may be either unable or unwilling to control these transnational relations due to a variety of reasons: difficulties in detecting the transactions; inability to set up the necessary enforcement mechanisms; or a reluctance to exercise a high degree of societal control. Governments, on occasion, may even wish to use transnational relations to enhance their economy or to give aid to another country without officially having to acknowledge the relationship.

Moreover, on the global level, some transnational actors may be immune to, or not subject to, political control by any state or group of states. Economist Jack Behrman has described how multinational corporations are skillfully able "to weave between the different requirements of national governments," thereby limiting the choices available to those governments and, in reality, challenging their national sovereignty. Another example is the International Olympic Committee which, while stressing its supposed immunity from political control, resisted for many years the political pressures to expel the Rhodesian National Olympic Committee from its membership. One may question whether, given the presence of the many and varied transnational relations, there exists—in the national, regional, or global arenas—the degree of political control and authority necessary to produce a successful sanctions program against a target state.

It is in the global arena that the problem of the lack of political control and authority is most conspicuous. Three international organizations have put sanctions on Rhodesia and have established sanctions committees to oversee their implementation; these organizations are the United Nations, the Commonwealth of Nations, and the Organization of African Unity. Because their decisions are not self-executing, these organizations must rely upon the willingness of their member-states to implement and enforce their decisions. Because there has never been a universal coalition organized against one country; because universal consensus on the legitimacy and purposes of the sanctions is lacking; and because all sovereign states are not members of the organizations applying the sanctions, it is unlikely that sovereign state compliance with sanctions against Rhodesia will ever be complete. Thus it follows that the effectiveness of an individual sanction measure will be diminished when that effectiveness specifically depends upon universal adherence and compliance. Fortunately for the target-state, many of the sanction measures do depend upon universal, or nearly universal, implementation to be effective.

Shifting the perspective to the region in which Rhodesia is located, one may inquire to what extent and in what respect Rhodesia's regional milieu or environment in southern Africa reduces her susceptibility to international isolation. Rhodesia is part of a regional grouping of states with regular interactions, mutual dependencies, and common goals. At the core of the southern African region are the white-ruled states of South Africa (with South West Africa) and Rhodesia. Portugal, although geographically distant, was nevertheless intimately involved through her two overseas provinces, Angola and Mozambique. After the April 1974 *coup d'état* in Lisbon, Portugal disengaged from the region and recognized the independence of Angola and Mozambique. Malawi, although a black-ruled state, has such intimate political, diplomatic, economic, and social ties with the white-ruled states that she may be included within the core. Peripheral members of the region—all black-ruled and at varying stages of alienation from the core—are independent Angola and Mozambique, Zambia, Lesotho, Swaziland, Botswana, Zaire, Malagasy Republic, and Mauritius. The core and peripheral states comprising the southern African region, including Rhodesia, are tied together in varying degrees by communication services, mass media, transportation facilities, interchanges of political elites, common power grids, financial dealings, trade, and institutional cooperation in the fields of tourism, marketing, soil conservation, and health, among others. Given these linkages, the effectiveness of the sanctions against Rhodesia will be lessened when they cannot be applied against the entire region. Not only could the member states reinforce Rhodesia in the face of sanctions, but Rhodesia could use the facilities of these states to gain access to the world outside southern Africa. Conversely, an increase in alienation of peripheral members from the core and/or disintegration of the core itself would threaten Rhodesia and enhance the effectiveness of the sanctions.

In approaching the problem from the level of analysis of the state, two perspectives may be identified. First, there is the perspective of Rhodesia, the target-state, and the policies adopted by the Rhodesian government to minimize, counteract, or overcome the efforts to isolate it from international relationships. Second, there is the perspective of those national and transnational actors outside Rhodesia who are engaged in relations with Rhodesia. It is useful to explore the types of arguments advanced by those actors to explain or justify their maintenance of relations with Rhodesia. From both perspectives, it is useful to investigate which aspects of the sanctions have been particularly difficult or easy to evade.

Within the above frame of reference, the validity of the following hypotheses or generalizations is investigated:

1. The effectiveness of sanctions will be lessened when national governments are unable or unwilling to bring transnational relations involving Rhodesia under their control.

2. The effectiveness of sanctions will be lessened when the enforcement of sanctions conflicts with other national interests perceived to be more important than the aims and goals of the sanctions policy.

3. The sanctioned state will pursue policies designed to induce both national governments and transnational actors to think that the application of sanctions is not in their best self-interest.

With reference to the second and third propositions, the validity of the perceptions is not of major concern; what is of concern in this book is that the perceptions do exist and influence governmental and transnational elites in their decision-making toward Rhodesia. With reference to the second proposition, transnational actors may try to identify *their* interests as being in the *national* interest.

One research problem encountered is that the struggle between Rhodesia and her enemies is current with the writing of this book. Any investigation evaluating the sanctions on Rhodesia as to their effectiveness could yield information which one side or the other might find useful in promoting their position. This being the case, Rhodesia tries to minimize or conceal the adverse effects of sanctions in order to keep public morale high and to undermine world public opinion on the efficacy of sanctions. Rhodesia has to be careful, too, not to reveal the extent to which sanctions are *not* working if that information could result in the sanctioning states taking action to correct the situation. For their part, transnational actors must keep their dealings and contacts with Rhodesia secret if disclosure could lead to legal prosecution or harmful publicity in their home countries. All these factors impede the collection of reliable data.

When one manages to gather reliable data, another problem is encountered in trying to evaluate the data, establish perspective, and provide explanation. There is a lack of explicit criteria for measuring the success or failure of sanctions because it is difficult to estimate what conditions would be like in Rhodesia without sanctions. Chapter 1 describing Rhodesia's presanction status and situation affords some basis for comparison and evaluation. Another problem is that it is difficult to disentangle the effects of sanctions from the effects of all the other factors which may be operating at the same time. Changes in Rhodesia's international relationships may be due to the effect of sanctions or they may be due to such spurious factors as guerrilla warfare, the effects of drought, devaluation of currencies, and changing patterns of world demand for minerals, among others. Indeed, as the *Rhodesia Herald* commented on October 12, 1972, business firms may be citing the adverse effect of sanctions to account for their financial difficulties when, in reality, sanctions are being used as a scapegoat to conceal a lack of ability and knowledge in marketing and management techniques.

While acknowledging these limitations, enough evidence is available to contribute to an understanding of the Rhodesian experience with sanctions. Although an investigation of the impact of sanctions on one country, this book raises broader issues such as the interdependence of states, the political influence of transnational actors, the nature of control in the international political system, and the ability of the United Nations to enforce its decisions. This provides a framework for evaluating the future potential of sanctions as instruments of control and influence in international politics.

SANCTIONS

The Case of Rhodesia

Rhodesia's International Status
Prior to UDI

O NE OF THE MAJOR POINTS of contention in the Rhodesian dispute centered around the issue of the political status of Rhodesia prior to UDI. From the standpoint of both the legal and factual situations, one may question whether Rhodesia was a British colony, a semi-autonomous state, a self-governing territory, or a dominion similar to those in the Commonwealth. The problem is complicated by the fact that, at various times in her history, Rhodesia was permitted freedom by Great Britain to act in a manner not in strict accordance with her legal status. The purpose of this chapter is to assess both the *de jure* and *de facto* status of Rhodesia in conjunction with an investigation into her formal international relations prior to UDI.

The first colonial government in the area now known as Rhodesia was provided by Cecil Rhodes's British South Africa Company under a royal charter granted to it in 1889. The British high commissioner for South Africa was charged with overseeing the rule of the company which was responsible for the legislative, executive, and judicial functions in the territory.[1] In 1898, a legislative council was formed in which the settlers and the company shared the legislative function. By 1913, the representatives of the settlers gained a majority in the council and agitation for an end to company rule accelerated. Three options were possible: Rhodesia could become a British crown colony, be annexed by South Africa as its fifth province, or acquire the status of a self-governing colony of Great Britain. The first option was most unpopular and a referendum held in 1922, gave the Rhodesians a choice between the latter two options. Despite the preference of the British government for annexation by South Africa, the vote went in favor of self-governing status.

Unlike the other British colonies at the time, responsibility for Southern Rhodesia[2] was vested in the Dominions Office rather than in the Colonial Office. According to Charles Burton Marshall, the ties between Southern Rhodesia and the United Kingdom were "quasidiplomatic in character rather than directive or executive" with the two exchanging high commissioners.[3] The Constitution of 1923 provided by Great Britain, required the approval of the British secretary of state for any legislation which discriminated against the African population. Additionally, with respect to any law passed by the legislature, the British government retained a general power of disallowance within one year of the governor's assent to that law. There is a question as to whether, in fact, these powers reserved by the United Kingdom limited Southern Rhodesia's internal self-government. Rhodesian Chief Justice Sir Hugh Beadle, claimed in 1968, that "if the chronicles of the time are examined, an accurate appraisal will show that only minimal use was ever made by the United Kingdom of those so-called 'reserved powers,' and that any influence they may have had on the internal government of the country was negligible."[4] Frank Clements, a former mayor of Salisbury, claims that Britain's authority had been "tactfully exercised by private warnings against objectionable legislation in advance of its being considered—or even presented to the local Parliament—rather than by overt disallowance afterwards."[5] Legally, the United Kingdom had power to legislate for Southern Rhodesia by Act or Order in Council, but, in fact, "in the course of time a convention was gradually evolved and accepted that the United Kingdom would not legislate for Southern Rhodesia on matters within the competence of the Legislative Assembly except with the agreement of the Southern Rhodesian Government."[6]

Under the 1923 Constitution external relations were the exclusive responsibility of the United Kingdom government. Yet, as the case with internal affairs, the factual situation was a bit more ambiguous. After 1933, the prime minister of Southern Rhodesia attended Commonwealth conferences at which all the other members were prime ministers of dominions. In the British Nationality Act of 1948, Southern Rhodesia was listed along with the dominions of Canada, Australia, New Zealand, the Union of South Africa, Newfoundland, India, Pakistan, and Ceylon. This act gave Southern Rhodesia full power to make its own laws for conferring Rhodesian citizenship—citizenship which automatically made the person concerned a British subject. Southern Rho-

desia was among the original twenty-three countries which, on October
30, 1947, signed the General Agreement on Tariffs and Trade. Aside
from Southern Rhodesia, only Burma and Ceylon, among the original
contracting parties, were not independent states, and they gained their
independence within a year after signing the agreement. Accession to
GATT was evidence that Southern Rhodesia was a separate customs
territory entirely responsible for the conduct of its external trade relations. Colonies and dependent territories, however, were included in the
General Agreement when their controlling countries acceded to the
agreement.[7]

In 1953, the secretary of state for Commonwealth relations, while
expressing Her Majesty's general responsibility for the external relations
of the colony, summarized the then-existing position of Southern Rhodesia in external affairs as follows:

1. The United Kingdom Government expressly delegated to the
Southern Rhodesia Government authority to negotiate and conclude
trade agreements with foreign governments so far as those related to
the treatment of goods.
2. In practice it had come to be accepted that Southern Rhodesia
might enter into local agreements with neighbouring territories, including
the Union of South Africa and foreign colonial territories and to make
appropriate representational arrangements with those territories.
3. In addition the Southern Rhodesia Government has, in the past,
been admitted to participation in the General Agreement on Tariffs
and Trade and to membership of certain international technical organizations which, by virtue of the terms of their constitution, Southern Rhodesia was eligible to join.
4. The acquisition by Southern Rhodesia of this delegated authority
did not, however, involve any change in the constitutional position of
Southern Rhodesia whereby Her Majesty's Government in the United
Kingdom remained generally responsible for the external relations of the
colony.
5. It followed from this that there should be prior consultation between the Government of Southern Rhodesia and Her Majesty's Government in the United Kingdom before the former entered into any commitments under sub-paragraphs one to three above.[8]

Southern Rhodesia's international personality was submerged in
the Federation of Rhodesia and Nyasaland in 1953. The federal govern-

ment assumed the immediate responsibility for the external affairs of
Southern Rhodesia, the British Crown Colony of Northern Rhodesia,
and the British Protectorate of Nyasaland. The creation of a more viable
economic unit by merging the essentially complementary economies of
the three territories was doomed from the outset by the political dominance of the Europeans of Southern Rhodesia in the federal government.
This dominance could not be reconciled with the growing African nationalism which eventually forced the dissolution of the federation after
ten years of existence. Seven months after the dissolution Nyasaland
became the independent state of Malawi, and three months later Northern
Rhodesia was granted independence as the Republic of Zambia. Meanwhile, Southern Rhodesia, which had been granted a new constitution
in 1961, reverted back to its previous legal status of "self-governing
colony."

The 1961 Constitution moved Southern Rhodesia even further
toward "dominion-like" status. More internal autonomy was gained as
the British government relinquished its theoretical right to veto certain
bills passed by the Southern Rhodesian legislature, except for those involving international obligations, stock issued under the Colonial Stock
Act, and the position of the British sovereign and her governor. The
governor, however, was to be appointed by the Queen after consultation with the Southern Rhodesian prime minister and was to act on the
advice of the Southern Rhodesian cabinet. At the official opening of the
Parliament on June 19, 1962, Southern Rhodesian Governor Sir
Humphrey Gibbs said in his speech from the Throne: "My Ministers
have received the clearest assurances from Her Majesty's Government
that they cannot revoke or amend the new Constitution."[9] This position
was reinforced further by a message from British Prime Minister Harold
Wilson to Rhodesian Prime Minister Ian Smith dated March 29, 1965,
which read: "We intend neither to impose constitutional change by
force, nor to breach the convention that the British Parliament does not
legislate for Rhodesia on matters within the competence of the Rhodesian Government."[10] Wilson acknowledged to the House of Commons,
November 12, 1965, that the governor of Rhodesia had to sign anything
which was within the Constitution and recommended to him by the
Smith régime. It should be noted that, in theory, the British Parliament
could repeal its enactment of Rhodesia's constitution and even impose
direct rule in Rhodesia. In the United Kingdom government the Parliament has absolute supremacy, and its actions are not subject to constitutional review by the British courts. While the British electorate can
hold the House of Commons responsible for any of its actions through

periodic elections of its members, this right is, of course, denied to the Rhodesian electorate.

In external affairs, Section 20(2) of the 1961 Constitution gave the Legislative Assembly the power to make laws having extra-territorial operation. According to Claire Palley, this meant that Southern Rhodesia's courts could take legal notice of Southern Rhodesian legislation governing the acts of Southern Rhodesian subjects committed outside Southern Rhodesia. Palley adds that the power to legislate extraterritorially had not previously been inserted in the constitution of a dependent territory.[11] The entrustments of external affairs to the federal government were to be enjoyed by the Southern Rhodesian government after the dissolution of the federation; the most important of these may be summarized as follows:

1. Freedom to conduct all relations with other members of the Commonwealth "direct," to exchange high commissioners with them, and to make arrangements with them of any kind.

2. Freedom to make arrangements for the treatment to be accorded within the federation to governments and organizations outside the federation and their representatives.

3. Freedom to enter into negotiations and agreements with any foreign countries—subject in each case to the need to safeguard the responsibility which the British government must have in international law.

4. Freedom to appoint diplomatic agents, or consular or trade representatives, in countries which were willing to receive them, to deal with matters within the competence of the federation, and to receive such agents or representatives from other countries.

5. Freedom to acquire, in its own right, membership in international organizations, which, by virtue of the terms of their constitutions, it was eligible to join.

These are the entrustments which guided Rhodesia in the conduct of her external relations after the dissolution of the federation and prior to UDI.[12]

A brief review of Rhodesia's formal, governmental external relations illustrates how Rhodesia put into operation these entrustments in the period immediately preceding UDI. A Ministry of External Affairs was established in Salisbury on January 1, 1964, which maintained and supervised the following external missions: the Rhodesian High Commission in London, the office of the accredited diplomatic representative in Pretoria, the office of the minister for Rhodesian affairs in Washington, and the Consulate-General of Rhodesia in Lourenco Marques. According to the 1964 annual report of the Ministry of External Affairs, its representation in Pretoria and Lourenco Marques operated independently of the British representation. The Washington mission operated under the diplomatic coverage of the British Embassy, and the staff were nominally members of the Embassy, although in practice they were permitted a wide measure of independence in conducting their activities. Symbolic of this independence was the fact that the Washington mission acquired from the British officials in 1964, the responsibility to issue visas for entry into Rhodesia and to issue Rhodesian passports. The other missions already had these responsibilities. When, however, the Rhodesian government sought to establish an accredited diplomatic representative in Lisbon, the British government strongly objected.

In July 1965 Harry Reedman was appointed to represent the Rhodesian government in Lisbon. In September 1965 Reedman presented a "letter of accreditation" from Rhodesian Foreign Minister Dupont to Portuguese Foreign Minister Nogueria; the letter was accepted. Dupont explained to Rhodesia's Legislative Assembly on September 17, 1965, that Reedman did not present "credentials" because credentials are presented on behalf of heads of state to heads of state, and, since Rhodesia was not a sovereign state, the Queen could not be represented separately in Lisbon by Rhodesia. Dupont further stated that this action was in accordance with the entrustments and did not convey the power of legation nor recognize Rhodesia as independent of the United Kingdom. It did, however, give Rhodesia independent access to the ministers of the host country. The British government objected to Reedman's appointment and demanded to have him accredited to the British Embassy in Lisbon. This demand was rejected by both the Rhodesian and Portuguese governments.

The Reedman case was important for three reasons: first, it demonstrated that there was, and might be in the future, disagreements between Rhodesia and Britain as to how the entrustments were to be interpreted, and no arrangements satisfactory to both countries existed for resolving the disagreements; second, with the talk of a Rhodesian UDI prevalent and growing United Nations and Commonwealth pressure on Britain to take firm measures to prevent it, the Reedman appointment embarrassed the British by demonstrating Britain's inability to influence or change a Rhodesian government decision; third, the form and rationale of the Reedman appointment were to serve as the model for the diplomatic representation Rhodesia maintained with South Africa and Portugal after UDI.

In the area of multilateral relations, fifteen of the federation's seventeen more important memberships or associate memberships in international organizations were obtained for Rhodesia including GATT, World Health Organization, International Wheat Agreement, International Telecommunications Union, and the United Nations Economic Commission for Africa. In 1964 Rhodesian delegations participated in approximately twenty international and Commonwealth conferences and meetings. The success Rhodesia enjoyed in this area, however, was not unqualified. Rhodesia was excluded from the Food and Agriculture Organization's African Regional Conference, the African Education Ministers' Conference in Abidjan sponsored by the United Nations Educational, Scientific, and Cultural Organization, and was not invited to the Finance Ministers' Conference at Kuala Lumpur sponsored by the Commonwealth Economic Consultative Council. These setbacks, suffered in 1964, gave the Rhodesian government a preview of the kind of rejection which it might increasingly expect to encounter in the future.

In the area of external trade relations, the Ministries of External Affairs and Commerce and Industry pursued a vigorous trade promotion program. Rhodesian trade representatives were stationed in Britain, West Germany, East Africa, South Africa, Mozambique, and Japan. Roving trade commissioners covered Africa and the Middle East, where Rhodesia had no permanent trade representation. The minister and secretary of Commerce and Industry carried out a series of trade and investment promotional visits to twelve European cities in the fall of 1964.[13] The federation's bilateral trade agreements with Australia, Britain, Bechuanaland, Basutoland and Swaziland, Canada, Japan, and Portugal were formally extended to Rhodesia. Additionally, Rhodesia negotiated a new trade agreement with Malawi (January 1964) and new five-year trade agreements with South Africa (December 1964) and Portugal (March 1965).

Finally, in the area of technical and financial assistance, lack of financing for counterpart funds impeded Rhodesia's efforts to secure multilateral aid. However, two large scale United Nations Special Fund projects for teacher training and Lake Kariba Fisheries Research, arranged by the federation, continued during 1964. United States bilateral aid supplied through the Agency for International Development was terminated in March 1964. The loss of United States aid was offset by marked increase in aid from Britain and other Commonwealth sources. In 1964, South Africa provided a loan of Rand (R)6 million for various projects in Rhodesia. The following year, South Africa lent Rhodesia another R$5 million (Rhodesian dollars) for specific infrastructure projects (dams, canals, electric power, railway, and an airport), and the South African Reserve Bank also lent R$2 million to Rhodesia to provide it with funds to meet its external obligations.[14]

On June 28, 1962, the General Assembly of the United Nations adopted Resolution 1747 (XVI) which affirmed that Southern Rhodesia was a non–self-governing territory and requested that the United Kingdom interfere with the internal political and legal structures to bring about, among other things, a "one man, one vote" system for all the people of the colony. The United Kingdom argued that the Southern Rhodesian government was *entirely* responsible for its internal affairs, and that its special autonomous status did not allow for the collection of economic and social information on the inhabitants of the territory for transmission to the Secretary-General as required by Article 73(e) of the United Nations Charter.

The evidence presented in this chapter suggests that Rhodesia's status before UDI, both *de jure* and *de facto,* resembled in many ways the status enjoyed by the British dominions before passage of the Statute of Westminster in 1931, which granted complete independence to the dominions. Power to create their own nationals, membership in international organizations, negotiation of international treaties, control of foreign commerce, internal self-government, issuance of passports, maintenance of their own armed forces, and a total absence of colonial civil and military presence are not attributes of non–self-governing territories no matter what the General Assembly may affirm or declare. The British political position *vis-à-vis* Rhodesia may be described as one which, over the years, involved a gradual devolution of authority while retaining ultimate legal responsibility without the power necessary to be able to exercise that responsibility. George Thomson, a former Labor minister for Commonwealth affairs, stated the position as follows: "Britain has responsibility for Rhodesia without power inside Rhodesia. History made Rhodesia a legal and moral British responsibility, but as history has turned out we have been denied the physical power to control events on the ground if there were an open clash of wills between London and Salisbury. Never during this century, neither before 1923 nor since, have there been soldiers, policemen or public servants in Rhodesia under the control of a Government in London. There has never been direct rule in Rhodesia."[15] Without the formal application of the Statute of Westminster to Rhodesia by the British Parliament, however, the United Kingdom was and continued to be the legitimate—but not actual—sovereign over Rhodesia.

This twilight zone between dependence and independence—being neither colony nor dominion—was viewed by the European population of Rhodesia as a most unsatisfactory position for their country. They had voted to join the Federation of Rhodesia and Nyasaland partly in the belief that it would enable their country to achieve dominion status. When the United Kingdom announced the dissolution of the federation, the European community generally felt that it had been betrayed by the British, whom they viewed as capitulating to "irresponsible" African demands.[16] The granting of independence to "the politically less mature" territories of Northern Rhodesia and Nyasaland; the intense political pressure put on the United Kingdom by the United Nations, the Commonwealth, and the Organization of African Unity to change or suspend the 1961 Constitution; the uncertainty surrounding the entrustments (especially as reflected by the Reedman case); and the feeling that Rhodesia was morally entitled to independence given the stable, peaceful political milieu which had been maintained since 1923—these were some of the reasons used to justify Rhodesian independence. These arguments influenced decision making in Salisbury; thus, on November 11, 1965, Prime Minister Ian Smith unilaterally declared Rhodesia independent of the United Kingdom.

This action was taken despite repeated warnings to Smith that a variety of sanctions would be placed on Rhodesia by other countries and international organizations in the event of UDI. At their meeting in Salisbury on October 29, 1965, Prime Minister Wilson advised Smith that "although the British government had rejected military intervention by the United Kingdom in the event of UDI, they stood by their public statements; and those meant economic war. No Rhodesian tobacco would be bought by the United Kingdom, or so far as he knew, by any other country. The fact that the United Nations were at present exerting very strong pressures in favour of the use of force made it virtually certain that the international economic sanctions would be comprehensive and severe."[17] Wilson also indicated how easy it would be to restrict oil supplies to Rhodesia. The previous year British Secretary of State for Commonwealth Relations Duncan Sandys warned that "Commonwealth and foreign Governments, with one or two exceptions, would almost certainly refuse to recognize Southern Rhodesia's independence or to enter into relations with her. Thus isolated, Southern Rhodesia would increasingly become a target for subversion, trade boycotts, air transport bans and other hostile activities."[18] These warnings had no deterrent effect. UDI was proclaimed and the response of the United Kingdom government, among others, was to place sanctions against Rhodesia.

2

The Nature and Purposes of
Rhodesian Sanctions

A REVIEW OF GENERAL THEORIES on sanctions provides a basic understanding of what is meant by the term "sanctions," the rationale behind the use of sanctions, and the intended outcome of sanctions. Such understanding serves as a framework for tracing the steps in the application of sanctions against Rhodesia. The stated reasons and objectives for the sanctions and the expected results will also be investigated as well as Rhodesia's general response to sanctions as it influences her international relations.

THE THEORY OF SANCTIONS

In the context of international relations, Johan Galtung defines sanctions as "actions initiated by one or more international actors ('the senders') against one or more others ('the receivers') with either or both of two purposes: to punish the receivers by depriving them of some value and/or to make the receivers comply with certain norms the senders deem important."[1] As Roger Fisher notes, "in international conflict as elsewhere our first reaction to somebody's doing something we don't like is to think of doing something unpleasant to them." Fisher goes on to note that the purpose of sanctions is to exert influence on the "receiver" to make some decision; "we want to cause them to change their mind."[2] Galtung defines negative sanctions as punishment for deviance and positive sanctions as rewards for compliance. After making this distinction, however, he concentrates on negative sanctions as the

instrument to induce compliance. Economic warfare, using value deprivation as a weapon, has as its end the political disintegration of the enemy
so that he gives up the pursuit of his goals.[3]

Unlike Galtung, both Margaret P. Doxey and Peter Wallensteen
clearly distinguish between economic warfare and economic sanctions.
Wallensteen defines economic warfare as a situation "where military as
well as economic measures are used to inflict maximum damage to the
economy of other nations." Examples are the blockades of the Na-
poleonic War and the world wars. Economic sanctions include general
trade bans between states without the use of military means—perhaps
as an alternative to military violence.[4] While Wallensteen focuses on the
difference in the *techniques* used, Doxey stresses that the techniques may
be similar, but the *objectives or ends* are different. In economic warfare,
the target is perceived as an enemy, and, according to Doxey, "The
objective is to hasten the enemy's defeat, to reduce or eliminate its
capacity to wage war, to undermine morale, and generally to make life
for its citizens as difficult as possible. When economic measures are used
as sanctions, the object is to deter or dissuade states from pursuing
policies which do not conform to accepted norms of international conduct. Sanctions are penalties which relate specifically to acts which the
international body condemns."[5] Doxey makes the point that perhaps the
success of economic restrictions in wartime gave rise to the widespread
belief in the efficacy of such measures as international sanctions. She
reserves the term "sanctions" for those actions which are "conformity-
defending instruments relating to behaviour which is expected by custom
or required by law," and thus in the legal system are always negative in
character.[6]

The point is that sanctions as "conformity-defending" instruments
of international legal enforcement (Doxey) may well have a better
chance of being perceived as more legitimate by the international community of actors than sanctions which are used by one state to advance
its national interests by compelling another state to do what it desires
(Wallensteen). A more legitimate threat is likely to be more effective.

Besides punishment and compliance, sanctions may serve expres-
sive or symbolic functions. Galtung states that in lieu of military action,
when doing nothing is perceived as complicity, something may have to
be done to express morality or disapproval. Galtung, however, suspects
that "economic sanctions may serve the purpose of expressing moral
disapproval best when they are of a symbolic nature and value-depriva-
tion is kept low."[7] Moreover, he notes that there are less costly ways of
expression such as declarations, resolutions, demonstrations, or non-

recognition. Anna P. Schreiber, after studying United States sanctions against Cuba and the Dominican Republic, concludes that "it is mainly its symbolic function that makes economic coercion a tempting policy to governments. Regardless of its concrete impact on the target state, a government may consider economic coercion useful if it serves to declare its position to internal and external publics, or helps to win support at home or abroad."[8]

In reviewing past applications of sanctions by states and international organizations, a high degree of consensus emerges as to the ability of sanctions to induce the targets or receivers to comply with the wishes of the senders. In short, the prevailing view is as follows: first, aside from purely punitive or symbolic considerations, sanctions have not been useful devices to induce, persuade, or compel the target to comply; second, sanctions may be dysfunctional by serving to make the target less rather than more compliant; and third, while some of the effects of sanctions may be deprivational, other effects may be very beneficial and desirable for the target, enhancing its internal political and economic situation in ways not foreseen by the senders. These conclusions are shared, in whole or in part, not only by scholars such as Doxey, Wallensteen, Galtung, and Fisher, but also by experienced diplomats such as George W. Ball and Dean Acheson.[9] All the sanctions outlined in Articles 41 and 42 of the United Nations Charter—and these include trade bans, interruption of transportation and communications, severance of diplomatic relations, demonstrations, and blockades—applied by all states against a target, would not necessarily ensure compliance by that target.

The theory of sanctions postulates that within the target there is a linkage between economic deprivation and political change. Galtung labels this as the "naive" theory of sanction which asserts a direct, positive correlation between value deprivation and political disintegration.[10] T. R. C. Curtin and David Murray claim that this theory depends on the notion that threatening peoples' incomes is as effective as threatening their lives and that, in the case of Rhodesia, a decline in real income of the country's inhabitants should lead either to the desired political changes or substantial European (white) emigration.[11] The effectiveness of a sanction, however, is dependent not only on its economic characteristics but also upon the social characteristics of the target population. The reaction to economic attack is a function of personality, culture, and social organization.

In the debate of November 15, 1965, in the British House of Commons which resulted in sanctions first being applied against Rhodesia, several Members of Parliament (MP) stressed that the Rhodesians, because of their psychological characteristics, could not easily be compelled to comply by coercive measures; as one MP stated, "Those who know the psychology of the Rhodesians will agree with me, I think, that they are not very likely to be impressed by these measures. They are men very like ourselves with, perhaps, something of a Cromwellian readiness to accept some austerity and hardship in a cause which they believe . . . to be just." "Imposing pain may not be a good way to produce a desired result," according to Fisher.[12] This is especially true if the target population perceives itself threatened with more pain by compliance than by noncompliance. For the Europeans in Rhodesia, compliance meant African majority rule sooner or later, and this was perceived as being the end of European existence in Rhodesia. British Prime Minister Wilson was aware of this attitude for, in referring to his meeting with Ian Smith in October 1965, he wrote: "Mr. Smith could not get away from his obsession, which he repeated in these talks and, indeed, on almost every occasion whenever we met. This was the assertion that the people of Rhodesia—the Europeans—knew that their country and their lives were at stake, and the situation facing them was exactly that facing Britain in 1939."[13] Even if Smith's "obsession" had no basis in reality, what is important in securing compliance is not reality, but the target's perception of reality.

Far from provoking political change or disintegration, sanctions may well do precisely the opposite—namely, enhance the solidarity, cohesion, and popular support of the target. The generalized siege mentality induced by sanctions may make dissidents or potential dissidents more susceptible to appeals for national unity. Wallensteen's research indicates that "the theory that economic sanctions would be an act of support for the opposing groups in the receiver is not validated."[14] After studying the sanctions against Italy in 1935 and 1936, George W. Baer concludes that "what was meant to be only instrumental economic pressure to elicit internal protest was transformed by the Italian government into a cause for rapid intensification of integral economic and political nationalism."[15] According to Doxey, "a siege psychosis, once engendered, can be a powerful factor in sustaining the will to resist, and it will also enable the government to take unpopular steps such as rationing consumer goods or increasing taxes."[16]

Can sanctions have any beneficial effects for the target? Keeping in mind the Italian example, if the target state had been having problems establishing or maintaining internal cohesion, outside pressure in the form of sanctions might well serve to accelerate its political integration.

In addition, Galtung notes that "a society, when worked upon by the forces of cohesion, may draw on reservoirs of strength and ability not only to resist stress but also to act creatively—qualities that lie latent in quieter periods."[17] In the case of Rhodesia, one result of sanctions has been the stimulation of an industrial revolution in manufacturing and a general economic diversification that might have taken decades to achieve naturally.

Beside the linkage between economic deprivation and political change, the theory of sanctions postulates a second linkage: that between external trade and economic deprivation. Galtung describes an ideal target for economic sanctions as a country whose foreign trade represents a sizable percentage of its gross national product (GNP), a foreign trade highly concentrated in one trading-partner, exports concentrated in one product, and the country's economy dependent on one product.[18] Placing sanctions on this ideal target should cause a reduction of incomes in the foreign trade sectors with a minimum of damage to the sanctioners. The recession engendered in the foreign trade sectors should spread to the rest of the economy, causing a large decline in the national income. This is certainly valid economic theory, however, economists or sanctioners may, on one hand, underestimate the ability of the target to adapt itself and restructure its national economy to minimize the damage and, on the other hand, may overestimate the degree of world compliance with the sanctions. There are many and varied counterstrategies available to the target, from sacrifice and smuggling to developing import-substitutes and diversifying the economy. Thus, using Galtung's criteria, Rhodesia in 1965, should have been, in theory, extremely vulnerable to the application of sanctions.

The following factors indicate the degree of Rhodesia's vulnerability to sanctions:

1. Percentage of domestic exports concentrated in one product: 33.0 percent (tobacco); in two products: 40.5 percent (tobacco and asbestos).

2. Percentage of domestic exports concentrated in one trading-partner: 25.3 percent (Zambia); in two trading-partners: 47.2 percent (Zambia and the United Kingdom).

3. Percentage of imports concentrated in one product-area: 32.0 percent (machinery and transport equipment).

4. Percentage of imports concentrated in one trading-partner: 30.4 percent (the United Kingdom); in two trading-partners: 53.3 percent (the United Kingdom and South Africa).[19]

In addition, exports earned 38 percent of Rhodesia's national income and 34 percent of it was spent on imports; according to Robert B. Sutcliffe, these are startling high figures for any country.[20] Considering this degree of vulnerability, application of sanctions against Rhodesia was the way that the United Kingdom and much of the rest of the international community of actors chose to show their disapproval of UDI.

SANCTIONS APPLICATION AGAINST RHODESIA

It is not within the scope of this study to provide a comprehensive review of United Nations' actions *vis-à-vis* Rhodesia; rather, resolutions of the Security Council imposing sanctions on Rhodesia will be examined as to their substance and purpose.[21] In addition, while sanctions were threatened by the United Kingdom and others to try to deter Rhodesia's UDI and while some actions which could be described as sanctions occurred before UDI (e.g., India's severance of diplomatic relations with Rhodesia on May 5, 1965), the sanctions program against Rhodesia will be considered to have been initiated in response to UDI which occurred on November 11, 1965.

Central to British policy after UDI were the objectives to secure universal acknowledgement of British responsibility for Rhodesia, to retain, at all times, the initiative in the United Nations regarding any action taken against Rhodesia, and to discourage the use of force against Rhodesia. Accordingly, while the debate on sanctions was taking place on November 11, 1965, in the House of Commons, the British foreign secretary was dispatched to the United Nations. Prime Minister Wilson stated: "We intend to inform the United Nations of our responsibilities and of the measures which we are taking, and we shall ask for the support of other countries in those economic measures." He stated further that he believed "the problem will be to avert excessive action by the United Nations. As for the economic sanctions, I think that it will be right for us to concentrate on trying to get other nations to follow our lead rather than seeing them get too far ahead of us."[22]

On November 11, 1965, the British government took the initiative by placing sanctions on Rhodesia; they included:

1. The British high commissioner was withdrawn and the Southern Rhodesia high commissioner in London was asked to leave.
2. Export of arms, including spare parts, were stopped.
3. All British aid ceased.

4. Rhodesia was removed from the sterling area.

5. Export of United Kingdom capital to Rhodesia was prohibited.

6. Rhodesia's access to the London capital market was halted.

7. United Kingdom Export Credits Guarantee Department stopped further coverage for exports to Rhodesia.

8. Rhodesia was suspended from the Commonwealth Preference Area and her goods no longer received preferential treatment on entering the United Kingdom.

9. United Kingdom banned purchases of Rhodesian sugar and tobacco—stopping a net total of 71 percent (by value) of Rhodesian exports to Britain.

10. United Kingdom no longer recognized passports issued or renewed by the illegal régime.

At the United Nations, meanwhile, the Security Council passed a resolution (S/RES/216) on November 12, 1965 which condemned UDI and called upon all states neither to recognize nor assist the "illegal régime." Eight days later, the Security Council passed another resolution (S/RES/217) which noted the gravity of the situation caused by UDI and determined that the indefinite existence of UDI would constitute a threat to international peace and security. Accordingly, the resolution called upon the United Kingdom to quell the rebellion and called upon the Organization of African Unity (OAU) to assist in the implementation of the resolution. It also called upon all states not to provide Rhodesia with arms or oil and "to do their utmost in order to break off economic relations with Southern Rhodesia." France abstained on both resolutions which passed without a dissenting vote.

The next batch of sanctions imposed by the United Kingdom occurred in December 1965; they included:

1. Several Rhodesian minerals (including copper, chrome, and asbestos) and foodstuffs (including maize and beef) were boycotted thus stopping a net total of 95 percent (by value) of Rhodesian exports to Britain.

2. The payments of dividends, interest, and pensions to Rhodesian citizens were put into blocked accounts in London.

3. The Board of Governors of the Reserve Bank of Rhodesia were dismissed and replaced by a British board in London; this British board assumed legal control over all Rhodesian funds outside Rhodesia. The

United States, South Africa, and Switzerland blocked the Rhodesian Reserve Bank's accounts held in their respective countries.

4. On December 17, 1965, the United Kingdom placed an embargo on the sales of oil and petroleum products to Rhodesia and asked all countries to do likewise, pointing out that she had the legal right to forbid the importation of any product into Rhodesia.

In December, the OAU also met to discuss the Rhodesian crisis. The Council of Ministers, meeting in Addis Ababa on December 3–5, adopted a resolution calling on all OAU member states to impose a total economic blockade on Rhodesia and end all economic relations, to sever all communications links with Rhodesia, and to bar the use of their air space for flights to Rhodesia. In a move designed to put pressure on the United Kingdom, the OAU also called for its member states to break diplomatic relations with the United Kingdom unless UDI was ended by Britain by December 15, 1965. Eventually, the OAU set up a Sanctions Committee on Rhodesia consisting of representatives from Egypt, Kenya, Zambia, Tanzania, and Nigeria.

During the first month of 1966, Britain escalated the application of sanctions against Rhodesia. On January 20, Britain assumed the power to embargo Rhodesia's trade in any specified product making its purchase by anyone in the world a violation of British law. The first product affected was chrome (January 20) followed by tobacco (February 7), sugar (March 17), iron ore (April 7), and asbestos and pig iron (June 3). On January 30, Britain imposed a total ban on exports to Rhodesia (except for humanitarian goods) and a total ban on imports from Rhodesia. Thus, with minor exception, all foreign trade between the two countries had been prohibited.

When the Commonwealth prime ministers convened in Lagos, Nigeria on January 11, to discuss Rhodesia, Prime Minister Wilson confidently asserted that the rebellion would be over in "a matter of weeks rather than months." The conference was marked by deep divisions with the majority urging Britain to use force against Rhodesia. Australia and Tanzania refused to even attend the conference, and those states that did were never able to agree about the means to bring down the Smith régime. The states did agree, however, on setting up a special sanctions committee under the aegis of the Commonwealth secretariat. James Barber notes that the pressure from the "militant" states at both the Lagos conference in January and the London conference in September "may have persuaded Britain to follow a tougher sanctions policy, to take the Rhodesian question to the United Nations."[23]

Commonwealth pressure notwithstanding, in April 1966, when British naval units operating in the Mozambique Channel spotted an oil tanker heading for the Mozambique port of Beira, the United Kingdom returned to the Security Council to secure authorization to use force to halt oil shipments to Rhodesia through Beira. The Security Council passed a resolution (S/RES/221) on April 19, declaring the situation a threat to the peace; calling upon all states to divert any of their vessels believed to be carrying oil destined for Rhodesia en route to Beira; asking Portugal not to receive oil destined for Rhodesia at Beria or to allow oil to be pumped through the pipeline from Beira to Rhodesia; and calling upon the United Kingdom to use force if necessary to prevent vessels believed carrying oil for Rhodesia from docking at Beira. The resolution passed without a dissenting vote; the Soviet Union, Bulgaria, and Mali abstained because they felt that the resolution was inadequate, and Uruguay abstained because her delegate was without instruction on how to vote. France abstained for two reasons; as with her earlier abstentions on S/RES/216 and 217, France claimed that the Rhodesian situation was not a true threat to international peace and that, in any event, the matter was an internal affair of the United Kingdom and therefore not within the competence of the United Nations.[24]

This was the first and only time that the Security Council authorized any use of force in the Rhodesian matter, and it was extremely limited in scope, referring only to oil shipments through the port of Beira. The British had sent naval units into the Mozambique Channel in December 1965, and they received the permission of the Malagasy Republic government to station an air reconnaissance squadron at Majunga in March 1966, to assist in the surveillance of the sea approaches to Beira. The Malagasy government asked Britain to withdraw the squadron in June 1971; Britain agreed. Upon the independence of Mozambique in June 1975, Britain formally ended the naval patrol.

At the Commonwealth conference in London in September 1966, Wilson delivered an ultimatum to Rhodesia. Unless UDI was ended by the end of the year, Britain would withdraw all settlement proposals, deny independence to Rhodesia until *after* there was majority rule, and go to the Security Council for selective, mandatory sanctions against Rhodesia. Wilson met Smith aboard the British cruiser HMS *Tiger* in December to discuss an Anglo-Rhodesian settlement. The Rhodesian government accepted the constitutional proposals set out by the British but not the British demand for abandonment of the 1965 Constitution in the interim period before the new constitution had been secured. Although she had accepted the substance of the British proposals, because

Rhodesia did not accept the means by which she was to "return to legality," Britain again went to the Security Council for more sanctions.

The resolution (S/RES/232) passed by the Security Council on December 16, 1966, for the first time declared that "the present situation in Southern Rhodesia constitutes a threat to international peace and security." Accordingly, the following measures were ordered:

1. Mandatory sanctions barring the purchase of asbestos, iron ore, chrome, pig iron, sugar, tobacco, copper, meat, meat products, hides, skins, and leather originating from Rhodesia.

2. Mandatory sanctions prohibiting the supply to Rhodesia of arms, military equipment and materials, aircraft, motor vehicles and equipment, and oil and oil products.

While the resolution reminded UN member states that failure or refusal to implement these measures would constitute a violation of their obligations under the UN Charter, it also urged non-member states to act in accordance with the resolution. The resolution passed without a dissenting vote; France, Mali, the Soviet Union, and Bulgaria abstained. The latter three countries abstained because they regarded the resolution as inadequate to end the rebellion.

When, in March 1968, the Smith régime hanged five men convicted for murder and sentenced to death prior to UDI, the African states in the UN called for a meeting of the Security Council to express their outrage and to demand further action against Rhodesia. Eventually, the United Kingdom submitted another draft resolution calling for mandatory comprehensive sanctions. This resolution (S/RES/253), passed on May 29, 1968, included a ban on:

1. All imports originating in Rhodesia.

2. All exports to Rhodesia except medical and educational supplies, publications, news material, and, in special humanitarian circumstances, foodstuffs.

3. The transportation of said banned imports and exports.

4. The provision of funds for investment or any other financial or economic resources (except payments for pensions, humanitarian purposes, or news and educational materials).

5. The entry into any country of persons traveling on a Southern Rhodesian passport or anyone who is likely to further or encourage the "unlawful actions of the illegal regime."

6. Activities designed to promote, assist, or encourage emigration to Rhodesia, with a view to stopping such emigration.

7. Airline companies from operating flights to or from Rhodesia and from linking up with any airline company constituted in Rhodesia.

The resolution also called for assistance for Zambia in order to help her solve her special economic problems associated with executing the Security Council decisions. In terms of implementation, all states as members of the United Nations or a specialized agency are called to report to the Secretary-General on measures they have taken to carry out the terms of the resolution. A committee of the Security Council was also established to gather information about the evasion of sanctions. The resolution was passed unanimously. Note should be taken that, while France did not waver from previous reservations about the role of the United Nations in the Rhodesian matter, she no longer was willing to abstain. This decision was made "taking account of the views of the administering Power [Britain] and to give Africa tangible evidence of awareness of the shocking nature of the maintenance of the regime based on racial discrimination."[25]

Between June 1968 and May 1977, the Security Council passed at least twelve more resolutions dealing with Rhodesia and sanctions. Most of the new sanctions were comparatively minor in scope. S/RES/277 (March 18, 1970) required that states "interrupt any existing means of transportation to and from Southern Rhodesia." Since air links had already been covered, this sanction was interpreted by the United Kingdom to mean road and rail links.[26] S/RES/388 (April 6, 1976) provided for a comprehensive ban on insurance for Rhodesian imports and exports and a prohibition of franchising agreements with Rhodesia involving the use of foreign trade names, trade marks, or designs. S/RES/409 (May 17, 1977) required that states prohibit the funding of any Rhodesian offices located in their territories. All the other resolutions either repeated earlier sanctions, condemned states for violations of sanction resolutions, or urged stricter enforcement measures.

Attempts were made by the Afro-Asian and Communist states to widen sanctions to include a ban on postal and telecommunications links, economic sanctions against South Africa and Portugal, and the use of force by Britain against Rhodesia. These attempts were blocked by the veto of the United Kingdom and, on two occasions, by the veto of the United States (March 18, 1970 and May 22, 1973).

Before discussing the purposes of these sanctions, special note should be taken of the timing of their enactment and their scope. Sanctions were applied gradually, escalating along three continuums: from unilateral to multilateral; from selective and partial to universal and comprehensive; and from recommendatory to mandatory. The above listing of sanctions in detail and in chronological order illustrates this escalation which took thirty months to complete (November 11, 1965 to May 29, 1968).

Whether escalation was a consciously adopted policy of Wilson, simply a result of miscalculations or a combination of both is unclear. Certainly in the debate on sanctions in the House of Commons on November 23, 1965, Wilson reflected the general feeling of the House that sanctions should be both effective and quick when he said, "Action which is speedily effective will do less lasting damage to Rhodesia's economy, and to the possibility of a reasonable settlement, than pressures which are long drawn out and inflict a continuing agony on Rhodesia." In another debate on November 12, 1965, Wilson stated: "I believe that if we are to make the maximum impact, the quickest and most painless impact . . . on the ability of the regime to survive, it is necessary to make clear now that we are not going to buy Rhodesian tobacco. The whole financial and banking structure of Rhodesia revolves round tobacco-financing in such a way that this decision will have a pretty serious and speedy effect." This prediction, combined with his "weeks not months" prediction in January 1966, at the Commonwealth conference, strongly suggests miscalculation. In his only reference to this matter in his memoirs, Wilson writes: "my phrase 'weeks not months' [was] based on advice we were receiving that the oil sanctions and the closure of the Beira pipeline would bring the Rhodesian economy to a halt. We had good reasons to believe that Portugal would not challenge the determination of the UN, nor seek to encourage sanction-breaking. We were misled but what I said to my colleagues appeared at the time to be a safe prophecy."[27] He does not mention what he believed South Africa would do regarding the oil sanctions.

Aside from possible miscalculation and despite the desire to affect the Rhodesian economy quickly, several reasons can be discerned for deliberately adopting a policy of escalation using limited means to gradually increase the pressure. Such a policy would have the following benefits:

1. It would minimize the cost to the sanctioner, and this was extremely important due to the weakness of the British pound during

1965 and 1966, which led to its devaluation in November 1967. Wilson estimated the cost to Britain of the sanctions in 1966 to be about £65 million; the Rhodesian estimate as of March 1967, was £150 million.[28]

2. Since the target was declared to be a British responsibility, it would minimize the damage to the target that Britain would eventually have to repair in the event UDI was ended.

3. It would minimize Rhodesian countersanctions against vulnerable third parties such as Malawi, Zambia, and Botswana; this was a worry expressed by several MP's in the November 1965 debates.

4. It would minimize chances of an economic and military confrontation with South Africa and Portugal which Wilson desperately sought to avoid.

5. It would minimize chances for a division in the House of Commons which Wilson wanted to avoid for two reasons: first, the Labor party had a majority of four which was extremely precarious considering the Conservatives opposed United Nations' involvement, and the Liberals and some left-wing Laborites were pressing for the use of stronger measures including force; second, Wilson wanted bipartisan support so as not to give the Smith régime false hopes that British opinion would be divided on this matter.[29]

Despite these practical reasons for adopting an escalation policy, from the standpoint of both the theory of sanctions and the specific Rhodesian case, observers have generally judged the policy unsound. Fisher notes, "the more gradual the escalation of cost the less likely that its increase will cause a change of position."[30] Furthermore, as this cost is spread out over time, the target will come to regard itself as being more committed to its course of action. But most important, a policy of escalation gives the target time to make the necessary adjustments and adaptations to cushion the effects of sanctions.

In the debate of November 12, 1965, no one in the House of Commons advocated a policy of escalation—quite the opposite, many MP's worried about the danger of "creeping sanctions" and supported Wilson in his desire that sanctions be "quick-acting." Other MP's stressed that sanctions, by their very nature, were "slow-acting." One MP remarked, "We should hit them hard straight away," and another said, "Clearly one wants to do as little damage to loyal Rhodesians as one can." These comments suggest confusion as to the tactical purposes of sanctions. Both in terms of strategy and tactics, what were the sanctions designed to achieve; what were their purposes?

PURPOSES OF THE RHODESIAN SANCTIONS

Describing or explaining the purposes of the sanctions policy is fraught
with problems. First, so many actors were involved in the formulation
of sanctions—countries, international organizations, groups, and individuals within countries—with so many diverse interests, that it would
be impossible to describe the purposes of all of them in the context of
this study. Therefore, attention will be focused upon the major actors—
the United Kingdom and the United Nations. Second, actors may not be
willing to state the actual reasons, and frequently they may not themselves be entirely aware of those reasons. This study concentrates on the
purposes as they have been declared both in formal resolutions on behalf
of the country or organization and in speeches by their officials. The
major source of the latter is selected debates of the British Parliament
and the UN Security Council. Third, for such reasons as pride and
prestige, it is sometimes difficult for an actor to extricate itself from a
policy that has failed to achieve its purposes. The actor may, therefore,
have to modify the initially stated purposes, highlight secondary purposes, or invent new purposes to justify maintenance of the policy over
time.

Knowing the purposes of sanctions enables statements to be made
regarding the termination of sanctions; presumably, sanctions cease to
apply after the purposes for which they were intended to serve are
achieved. Likewise, knowing the purposes of a policy permits judgments
to be made regarding the effectiveness of the policy. It also may be
argued that if, after a period of time, the sanctions fail to achieve the
stated purposes, they can be modified or terminated on the grounds that
they were impotent or dysfunctional. Implementation may also be
affected by the degree to which the purposes are interpreted as legitimate
and consistent with prevailing international law and morality.

The United Kingdom

In reviewing the House of Commons debate on sanctions of November 1965, there can be no question that the primary purpose of the
Labor government in asking for sanctions against Rhodesia was "to restore Rhodesia to the rule of law, to allegiance to the Crown." After
making the illegal UDI impossible and guaranteeing "untrammelled
loyalty and allegiance to the Crown," then independence could be discussed on a reasonable basis.[31] This basis for independence rested on
the famous "Five Principles":

1. The principles and intention of unimpeded progress to majority rule, already enshrined in the 1961 Constitution, would have to be maintained and guaranteed.

2. There would also have to be guarantees against retrogressive amendment of the Constitution.

3. There would have to be immediate improvement in the political status of the African population.

4. There would have to be progress towards ending racial discrimination.

5. The British government would need to be satisfied that any basis for independence was acceptable to the people of Southern Rhodesia as a whole.

These principles were endorsed by both the Labor and Conservative parties. Of course, what constitutional arrangements satisfy these principles are subject to differing interpretations. Harold Wilson added a sixth principle in 1966, which stated:

6. It would be necessary to ensure that, regardless of race, there was no oppression of majority by minority, or of minority by majority.

This sixth principle does not seem to have added much in the way of substance, and the succeeding Conservative government of Prime Minister Heath talked of reaching a settlement based on the "Five Principles." It is interesting to note that during the November debate, no MP advocated immediate majority rule in Rhodesia as a purpose to be achieved by the sanctions; quite the opposite, Wilson clearly stated on November 23, that Rhodesia was not ready for immediate majority rule.

In the November debate one MP declared that he could not imagine a rebellion less directed against British interests. Why should the United Kingdom respond to UDI in the fashion they did; why should the United Kingdom care if Rhodesia remained under British control or not? The answers to these questions may provide clues as to the secondary purposes of the sanctions. Fredrik Hoffmann concludes that by far the "most important prosanction argument is that 'we have to do this because of the reactions in other parts of the world, because other people demand action'."[32] Wilson was especially concerned about the future of the multiracial Commonwealth, British isolation at the United Nations, and the possibility of the Chinese and Soviet Communists taking advantage of the situation. Wilson spoke in the House of Commons on

November 12, 1965, of the "struggle for the soul of Africa" and worried about a "Red Army in blue berets"—a reference to the possibility that a Communist country might be invited to send an army under UN auspices to intervene in the Rhodesian crisis. He was convinced that if they failed to react strongly against UDI, "the Commonwealth, as we knew it, would break up or perhaps be reduced to a handful of the older dominions, plus Malaysia and Malawi."[33]

Two other factors figuring prominently in the November debate were the morality of opposing UDI and the image of Britain *vis-à-vis* world public opinion. Wilson viewed UDI as an offensive challenge to Britain's cherished democratic traditions. Britain could not eschew her "sacred trust" and "obligation" under the UN Charter "to promote . . . the well-being" of the Africans, as well as the Europeans, of Rhodesia. In addition, a constant theme in the debate was that Britain's reputation, honor, and credibility were at stake and had to be protected. One MP noted that since Britain had threatened sanctions against Rhodesia to deter UDI, "if we fail to make these deterrents credible now, then Britain's word in the United Nations and firmness of purpose on a whole range of other issues in the world will be torn to pieces." The same MP then proceeded to quote an editorial from the *Economist* to the effect that if Britain failed to respond to this "challenge of destiny," it would signal the farewell of "a faded and foppish" nation.[34] In a debate in the House of Commons on December 8, 1966, Labor Minister Judith Hart succinctly stated that voting for sanctions would mean voting for non-racialism, for the future of the Commonwealth, for Britain's honor and integrity in the world, and for belief in democracy and human rights.

Two final purposes can be discerned. Some MP's worried that if Britain failed to act, reprisals might occur against whites living in other parts of Africa; as one MP put it, "the sins of Mr. Smith may be visited on our fellow countrymen abroad."[35] Wilson additionally noted in his memoirs, but not in the Parliamentary debates, that economic repercussions against Britain could come from Zambia. If Britain was denied Zambia's copper, either by virtue of a Rhodesian preemptive strike against Zambia or by "a Zambia made sullen by our refusal to use force, we would have had two million unemployed within a matter of months."[36]

The secondary purposes of the sanctions against Rhodesia can be summarized as follows:

1. To forestall the use of force by other countries.
2. To maintain Britain's positive image and reputation.

3. To express morality and justice.
4. To preserve the Commonwealth.
5. To relieve pressure on Britain in the UN.
6. To reduce the chances of adverse economic repercussions from Zambia.
7. To prevent harm from coming to whites living in Africa.

These purposes are regarded as secondary precisely because they are not directly related to the ending of UDI. Actually, many of the purposes are symbolic in nature, designed to persuade third parties that Britain recognizes the gravity of UDI and that she will carry out her responsibilities in this matter.

There was widespread agreement in the November 1965 debate on what the purpose of sanctions should *not* be. Wilson stated it best when he said, "We are not going to indulge in any measures purely for the sake of recrimination, purely for the sake of inflicting punishment, purely for inflicting pain or hardship for their own sake. Every measure has been judged and must be judged against its ability to restore the rule of law and the functioning of a democratic constitution in Rhodesia."[37] One MP raised an important issue when he asked that if in the future, the efforts to discredit Smith have become hopeless and there is no further hope of altering European opinion in Rhodesia, would sanctions continued beyond that point be considered punitive? He did not receive an answer to his question, but one can deduce from Wilson's statement that the answer would be "yes."

It is interesting to note that during the entire November debate only one MP suggested the possibility of using rewards (positive sanctions). After acknowledging that threats would not work, he said, "We should start thinking about offering a little carrot to the Rhodesians who may defect from Mr. Smith, as well as merely talking about the stick."[38]

In 1972, after seven years of British sanctions and four years of United Nations comprehensive mandatory sanctions, the Conservative government's Foreign Secretary Sir Alec Douglas-Home, commented: "They [the sanctions] have been on for nearly seven years, and they have not achieved a decisive political change in Rhodesia. Those who argue that another three or four years will do so have little evidence to support their view."[39] Despite this attitude, the Heath government succeeded in renewing the sanctions order for another year in November 1972 (unlike other states, the sanctions applied by the United Kingdom must be renewed by the Parliament annually). The November Parliamentary debate can be examined to ascertain the purposes of the sanctions as of that date and if those purposes had changed since the first sanctions debate in 1965. Before examining this, however, a brief review of the 1965 to 1972 period is in order to note some of the events relevant to Anglo-Rhodesian relations.

Two major trends are discernible. First, the Rhodesian government moved to the right in domestic affairs in the sense that it hardened its attitude towards extending political and social rights to the African population. Whereas under the 1965 Constitution the Africans could theoretically gain eventual majority rule, under the 1969 Constitution the most the Africans could gain was parity of representation in the Legislative Assembly. Rhodesia also declared itself a republic in 1970, thus severing all symbolic ties with the United Kingdom.

Second, in three meetings held by Smith with Wilson aboard the HMS *Tiger* (December 1966), aboard the HMS *Fearless* (October 1968), and in Salisbury with Douglas-Home (November 1971), the British conceded point after point to the Rhodesian government in order to try to reach a settlement. Such major points as the "return to legality," the 1961 Constitution as the base for settlement discussions, the formation of a broad-based interim Rhodesian régime before independence, the external guarantee of the settlement constitution, and the right of Rhodesian citizens to appeal to the British Privy Council after independence had all been jettisoned by the British government. In addition, the rate of progression towards African majority rule had been slowed. As Smith, himself, noted in the House of Assembly, April 5, 1973, "I believe it would be appropriate to point out . . . that on every occasion on which we have held talks we have strengthened our position. We came back from HMS *Fearless* with terms which for us, were an improvement on what we had been offered on HMS *Tiger*. Then, in turn, the Constitution negotiated in 1971 . . . is an improvement on what we were offered on *Fearless*." Smith went on to say, "I must warn people who are clamouring for fresh negotiations, that if these were to take place, there would be new demands which I would make on the British Government. There would be a repetition of past performance, and we would emerge stronger than before."

The talks between Smith and Douglas-Home did result in a settlement between the two governments, but that settlement was rejected in 1972, by the African population. The test of opinion was conducted by a British commission chaired by Lord Pearce. Note that in the proposals, the British declared that they would unconditionally terminate their sanctions when independence was conferred on Rhodesia. No reference was made to the United Nations.

As British pressure on Rhodesia increased, Rhodesia moved further to the right; as Rhodesia moved to the right, the attitude of the British government as to what constitutional arrangements satisfied the "Five Principles" also moved further and further to the right.

This movement reflected a modification of the initial purposes of sanctions by the British government; no longer was the purpose to restore Rhodesia to allegiance to the Crown or to topple the "illegal" Smith régime within "a matter of weeks rather than months." The purpose seemed to have become one of trying to get the best deal possible for the Africans in a situation where, according to Douglas-Home, "very little influence and no power can be brought to bear."[40] The British objective was to keep the settlement proposals on the table and to allow time for the Africans and Europeans within Rhodesia to reflect and compromise. Sanctions were seen as the stimuli to motivate African-European contact within Rhodesia.

If these contacts either did not materialize or did not result in meaningful compromise, Douglas-Home admitted to the House of Commons, November 9, 1972, he might "be compelled by events to come to the House and to go to the United Nations and to state the case plainly for a change in policy." That change he left undefined, but he added that "sanctions were never meant to create real hardship for individuals in a way which could have no bearing on the position of the illegal régime." It is reasonable to suggest that punishment would not be seen as a valid reason to continue the sanctions once they were judged no longer able to effectively compel. The change of policy might be a unilateral termination of the sanctions and/or a transfer of responsibility for Rhodesia to the United Nations.

An analysis of the November 9, 1972, debate revals that there was much confusion regarding the original purpose of the sanctions and their effectiveness. Douglas-Home indicated that the original purpose was to induce Smith to negotiate, and then he stated: "I do not honestly think that sanctions are the main influence which brings Mr. Smith to the negotiating table." Labor and Liberal MP's claimed that sanctions were indeed effective in accomplishing this purpose. Conservative MP's joined the debate to point out that sanctions were not effective and that, in any event, negotiation was not the original purpose of the sanctions, rather it was to topple the Smith régime. The Labor and Liberal MP's wanted to strengthen sanctions to make them even more effective; right-wing Conservative MP's wanted to terminate them. This debate resulted in sanctions being renewed for one more year by a vote of 266 to 29 with many Conservative MP's avoiding the vote or abstaining.

Secondary purposes for continuing the sanctions included the

avoidance of adverse consequences to Britain's trading relationships in
Africa and the maintenance of Britain's reputation, standing and self-
respect. Preservation of the Commonwealth and the danger to whites
living in Africa were not mentioned in this debate.

Several new purposes were mentioned. Effective sanctions supported
the United Nations and the idea of being able to maintain international
order by mobilizing pressure without resorting to violence. This was not
an argument of the government ministers, perhaps because Douglas-
Home stated early in the debate that the Labor government "ought
never to have internationalized the problem by taking it to the United
Nations and asking for mandatory sanctions." Hostility to United Nations
involvement was a constant theme of the Conservative party when it
was in opposition. Citing the remarks of Bishop Muzorewa, leader of
the African National Council which opposed the settlement, Labor MP's
stated that the Rhodesian Africans were in favor of the sanctions. Support of the sanctions served the purpose of supporting the Africans and
strengthening their belief that the British would protect their rights.

Between 1965 and 1973, the British government committed itself
to a policy of sanctions which had failed to achive its primary purpose
of ending UDI. On three separate occasions during this period, the
Rhodesian government emerged from negotiations with the British
government with settlement terms—each set of terms more favorable
to European interests than the previous set. In addition, the kinds of
social and political policies affecting the African population which the
British originally objected to as a basis for independence, were precisely
the policies which the Smith régime implemented during this period.
After the negative finding by the Pearce Commission, the British government determined that it was no longer practical to negotiate with the
Rhodesian government. The initiative for a settlement had to come from
within Rhodesia through a process of negotiations and consultations
between the Rhodesians themselves.

Clearly, the Rhodesian government had been negotiating from a
position of strength derived, in part, by the degree of success achieved
in thwarting the aims of the sanctions and deflecting or muting the
adverse economic and psychological effects. But it is also clear that the
sanctioner was not fully aware of what it wished and needed to achieve
by its policy.

What emerges from the above analysis of the Parliamentary debates is that, while the Labor and Conservative parties may have been
in agreement on the need to end UDI, there was much confusion over
the years as to what sanctions were specifically meant to achieve. Should

British authority be restored in Rhodesia? Should the United Nations be involved? Should the application of sanctions be massive and immediate or should it be escalated? What conditions satisfied the "Five Principles?" How valid were some of the secondary purposes; e.g., if sanctions were not applied, would there really have been a "Red army in blue berets" in Africa? How effective have sanctions been in hurting the Rhodesian economy? Not only was there a lack of bipartisan agreement on these points, but as the balance of power shifted within the House of Commons and as third-party pressure on Britain ebbed and flowed, the answers to the questions changed over time.

In April 1974, the balance of power again shifted within the House of Commons as the Labor party was returned to power. Moreover, in that same month another event occurred which shifted the balance of power in the entire southern African region. The Portuguese government of Premier Marcelo Caetano was overthrown by a military coup and was replaced by a series of military juntas determined to end Portuguese military involvement in Africa. This event caused rapid and dramatic changes in the political situation in southern Africa as well as in the environment in which the sanctions campaign was being conducted. Within two years of that coup, Mozambique gained independence, and its new government fully implemented sanctions against Rhodesia in March 1976; a civil war occurred in Angola which featured direct intervention by Communist countries in the form of Soviet equipment and Cuban armed forces; and the South African government made a complete reassessment of its foreign policy options. These events, combined with a world economic recession in 1974 and 1975, resulted in a deterioration of Rhodesia's economic and military viability. By 1976, the Rhodesian government had very few policy options available and could no longer negotiate from a position of strength. Rhodesia's successes and failures in coping with both sanctions and the changes resulting from the Portuguese coup will be fully explored in subsequent chapters.

The annual renewal of the sanctions order was routinely approved in 1974 and 1975, by the British Parliament after debates, which, for the most part, echoed the arguments of the debates of previous years. While admitting that sanctions would not cripple the Rhodesian economy, Foreign Secretary James Callaghan expressed confidence that they would have severe economic effects on Rhodesia. He also announced that he had made direct, formal representation to the countries of the European Economic Community and Japan to try to improve the overall enforcement of sanctions;[41] a step the previous Conservative government was reluctant to take.[42] A Labor minister summarized to the House of Commons, October 31, 1975, his government's rationale for renewing sanctions by noting that the cancellation of the sanctions would amount to a virtual *de facto* recognition of the "illegal régime" in Salisbury. He concluded, "The argument for sanctions is not simply economic. It is political, and profoundly so. There is a symbolic significance about taking action that is in accordance with an international decision and with decisions taken by successive Governments."

The Labor government continued following the policy of refusing to negotiate with the Rhodesian government until the Europeans and Africans within Rhodesia arrived at their own settlement. To contribute to this end, South Africa launched a major diplomatic initiative in 1974. Concerning Rhodesia, Prime Minister B. J. Vorster stated to the South African Senate, October 23, 1974, "I believe that now is the time for all who have influence to bring it to bear upon all parties concerned to find a durable, just, and honourable solution, so that internal and external relations can be normalized. Africa, and for that matter southern Africa must not become a trouble-torn continent or subcontinent. It must . . . not become an area of conflict." Also hoping to find a peaceful solution, the presidents of the four frontline states of Botswana, Mozambique, Tanzania, and Zambia agreed to exert influence in the effort to help smooth the path of negotiations between the parties in Rhodesia. There followed intensive diplomatic activity between the five governments, the Smith régime, and the African Nationalists. Innumerable talks, meetings, and conferences occurred until March 19, 1976, when the negotiations between the Rhodesian government and the African National Council (ANC) were formally broken off. Prime Minister Smith appealed to the British government to "actively assist in resolving the constitutional issue in Rhodesia," and Joshua Nkomo, leader of the ANC in the negotiations, commented in the *Rhodesia Herald,* March 20, 1976, that Britain seemed to be "shirking her responsibility." Two days later, British Foreign Secretary James Callaghan outlined the following four preconditions—the acceptance of which would enable his government to oversee the negotiation of an independence constitution for Rhodesia:

1. Acceptance of the principle of majority rule.

2. Agreement to elections for majority rule within a period of eighteen months to two years.

3. Agreement that there would be no independence before majority rule.

4. Agreement that the negotiations must not be drawn out and the transition to majority rule would not be thwarted and would be orderly.[43]

These preconditions were promptly rejected as "hopeless" by the Rhodesian government.

The Callaghan preconditions were perhaps the most stringent demands upon the Rhodesian government since the initial demands of the Labor government immediately after UDI. All the points conceded to the Rhodesian government by the British government in their long series of bilateral negotiations were effectively negated, and a very brief transition period to majority African rule was required as a condition to be satisfied before the granting of independence. Clearly, Douglas-Home's characterization of the Rhodesian situation in 1972, as one where "very little influence and no power can be brought to bear" no longer applied. Influence was being exerted by the governments of all the states contiguous to Rhodesia—including South Africa—and the power was being applied in the form of an expanding and rapidly escalating guerrilla warfare campaign.

In April 1976, the United States launched a major diplomatic initiative through Secretary of State Henry A. Kissinger to try to find a peaceful solution to the many racial problems in southern Africa. The United States declared its strong support for the Callaghan preconditions, its unrelenting opposition to the Smith régime, and its commitment to a rapid negotiated settlement leading to majority rule.[44] On September 19, at a historic meeting in Pretoria between Kissinger, Vorster, and Smith, Kissinger presented Smith with proposals for a settlement which were fully consistent with the British position. These proposals, reported by the *New York Times,* September 25, 1976, called for the immediate establishment of a multiracial interim government in Rhodesia to plan for majority African rule within two years, the lifting of sanctions, an end to guerrilla warfare, and substantial economic support from the international community. On September 24, Prime Minister Smith announced his government's acceptance of the proposals. After nearly eleven years of sanctions, Smith agreed in principle to end UDI and accept African majority rule—an agreement the United Kingdom had never been able to secure.

The United Nations

The sanctions against Rhodesia represent the first and, so far, only application of these measures by the Security Council in the discharge of its primary responsibility of maintaining international peace and security. Article 39 of the UN Charter identifies three appropriate situations for enforcement action. "While two of them—namely a breach of the peace or act of aggression—would presumably be identifiable events, the third need be no more than a state of affairs, or set of circumstances, which is defined as threatening peace."[45] In the latter situation, sanctions can be viewed as a preventive measure against the threat to the peace from becoming an overt breach of the peace or act of aggression. The Security Council, at the initiative of the United Kingdom, declared in S/RES/232 (1966) that the situation resulting from UDI—and its challenge to Britain's sovereignty over Rhodesia—constituted a threat to international peace and security.

But the situation transcended the matter of rebellion and the challenge to sovereignty. In the Security Council debates the situation was viewed as a challenge to the entire international community because it involved the rebellion of a white, "racist régime" in a country where 95 percent of the people were black. As Ralph Zacklin notes, the international community had come to realize that "the denial of fundamental human rights, wherever it might occur, is ultimately a threat to international peace and security."[46] UDI could be viewed as a challenge to British responsibility to promote human rights in Rhodesia in accordance with her "sacred trust" under Article 73 of the UN Charter dealing with non–self-governing territories. Before UDI, the British never admitted that Rhodesia was a non–self-governing territory, but Britain did vote in favor of S/RES/253 (1968), which stated in its second operative paragraph that the United Kingdom should take all effective measures to end the rebellion *and* "enable the people to secure the enjoyment of their rights as set forth in the Charter of the United Nations." Nonetheless, prior to 1976, every attempt by members of the Security Council to bind the United Kingdom to the principle of "no independence before majority rule" (NIBMAR) was stopped by the British veto. The British position was generally supported by the United States and France and generally opposed by the other members of the Security Council—especially the African and Communist states. Recognition of this divergence of views is important in any discussion of the purposes of UN sanctions and the conditions for their termination.

The Security Council sanctions resolutions contain no provision for termination; their duration is not specified, there is no date of expiration stipulated. Presumably, they could be revoked by subsequent resolutions or they could cease to apply after the purpose for which they were intended to serve is achieved. A decision to apply sanctions or any other measure in Article 41 requires a determination of a threat to the peace by the Security Council. Therefore, the general purpose of the resolutions is to "maintain or restore international peace and security." Particular purposes or objectives of sanctions may be discovered by examining the specific clauses of the resolutions themselves. They should indicate what has to be done to restore or maintain the peace. Such an examination reveals the following purposes:

1. "In furtherance of the objective of ending the rebellion" (e.g., S/RES/253, 277); "noting with concern that the measures have failed to bring the rebellion to an end" (e.g., S/RES/217, 253, 277).
2. "Avoid assisting the illegal régime" (e.g., S/RES/217, 253, 277); "noting that measures have not brought an end to the illegal régime" (e.g., S/RES/326, 333).

Majority rule in Rhodesia is not mentioned as a purpose, but S/RES/329 indirectly acknowledges it as a purpose of one of the member-states when the Security Council commends Zambia for abandoning its southern trade route "until the rebellion is quelled and majority rule is established in Southern Rhodesia." Note should also be taken that, in the major sanctions resolutions (S/RES/232, 253, 277) when reference is made to the threat to the peace, it is the *present situation* in Rhodesia which is held to constitute the threat—presumably the situation prevailing when the resolution was adopted.

While the purposes, as reflected in the Security Council resolutions, did not change over the years, there were questions as to their interpretation. Would the purposes be achieved if Britain ends the rebellion by granting independence? Is the régime's "illegality" based on the fact that independence was not authorized by Britain, or is it based on the fact of "racist" minority rule? What conditions have to be satisfied before the sanctions can be ended?

From 1965 on, the African position in the Security Council was quite consistent; supported by the Communist states, the Africans demanded the overthrow of the "illegal régime," after which the United Kingdom must grant independence on the basis of majority rule. They believed the only effective way to accomplish this was the use of force. Hungary stated that "the sole purpose of this concerted action [application of sanctions] . . . must be to overthrow the illegal régime of Mr. Smith."[47] The Soviet Union criticized the draft resolution submitted on May 29, 1968—later to be adopted as S/RES/253—because it did not contain a provision banning negotiations with the Smith régime.[48] Needless to say, the African and Communist states vigorously condemned the Douglas-Home–Smith agreement and twice tried to get the Security Council to reject it. The United Kingdom vetoed the attempts of December 30, 1971, and February 4, 1972; Belgium, France, Italy, Japan, and the United States abstained in both instances.

With regard to the secondary purposes of the sanctions, the United States supported the British view that sanctions should not be punitive or vengeful but rather should have the sole purpose of bringing about a peaceful and honorable settlement.[49] For the Afro-Asian and Communist states, the purpose went beyond mere punishment of the Rhodesian régime; their goal was to end its existence.

Many countries recognized that the sanctions served symbolic functions. For Finland, they were "an impressive demonstration on behalf of the equality of races and the rights of man"; for Austria, they were "the indispensable complement of the heavy moral pressure that the international community exercises through international public opinion"; for Yugoslavia, the Security Council resolutions "give heart to the people of Zimbabwe to continue their struggle against oppression and colonialist rule."[50] The latter purpose was reinforced by the appearance of Bishop Abel Muzorewa, chairman of the African National Council of Rhodesia, before the Security Council on February 16, 1972, when he urged that sanctions be continued. Most importantly, sanctions are a symbol of the authority of the United Nations, and their success or failure directly affects the prestige of that organization. Sanctions thus serve the purpose of demonstrating to the world the ability of the United Nations to take effective action in a critical situation.

What emerges from the above analysis of the Security Council debates is that, while there was agreement on the need to end both the "rebellion" and the "illegal régime"—and this agreement was reflected in the various resolutions—there was no consensus on the specific conditions which would have to be present in order to declare that the above needs were satisfied. If the United Kingdom had changed the "present situation" in Rhodesia by granting independence on the basis of the 1969 Constitution, as amended by the Douglas-Home–Smith Agreement, the government of Rhodesia might still have qualified for the designation of "racist" and would definitely have been "minority." The settlement might have satisfied the British "Five Principles," but might not have satisfied some members of the Security Council that the obligations pursuant to the "sacred trust" of Article 73 were fulfilled.

While the United Kingdom denied that Rhodesia was subject to Article 73 before UDI, after UDI the United Kingdom—under the Southern Rhodesia Act 1965 of November 16, 1965—unilaterally assumed full responsibility with respect to the governing of the territory and asserted that responsibility in the Security Council. That responsibility was never challenged by any member of the Security Council and indeed was acknowledged in various resolutions dealing with Rhodesia.

If no definitive statement can be made regarding the conditions which allow sanctions to be terminated, there is moreover no agreement and much confusion on *how* the sanctions can be terminated. In the Douglas-Home–Smith Agreement, Britain formally promised to terminate sanctions when the British Parliament conferred independence upon Rhodesia.[51] No mention was made of the United Nations. British Minister of State for Foreign Affairs Joseph Godber indicated in the *Star* (Johannesburg), December 4, 1971, that his government would have granted legal independence to Rhodesia even if the Security Council had rejected a positive outcome of the test of acceptability conducted by the Pearce Commission.

Can the United Kingdom legally terminate the sanctions unilaterally? A British scholar of international law argues: "The sanctions are declared to be for the purpose of bringing the rebellion to an end, and it is for the British Government, as the constitutional authority, to decide when that event has occurred. This task cannot be assigned to the United Nations. Should the United Kingdom wish to terminate sanctions, she would declare the rebellion ended and announce that, as the United Nations sanctions had succeeded in their purpose, they were now automatically terminated."[52] U.S. Assistant Secretary of State for African Affairs David D. Newsom stated in 1971, that "the action of the Security Council would run on until the Security Council was satisfied that the conditions which have existed in Rhodesia, which brought about their original action, no longer existed."[53] Presumably, if the Security Council was responsible for determining a "threat to the peace," it—not merely one of its members—would also be responsible for determining an end to that threat. The new determination would, of course, be subject to the veto of the Soviet Union and the People's Republic of China. Responding to this point, S. M. Finger, former U.S. representative on the Security Council Sanctions Committee, stated: "Even assuming, however, that there were a veto by either the Soviets or the Chinese, it is true that under a literal interpretation of the charter and article 41 we would be bound by the sanctions. On the other hand, I think a good case could be made that, the objectives of the sanctions resolutions having been achieved, the United States would no longer consider itself bound by the results of a Soviet or Chinese veto."[54]

The operative purposes of the Rhodesian sanctions policy are muddled and confused and the termination conditions and procedures are unclear. This may undermine, from the outset, adherence to and respect for that policy. Aside from purely operational considerations, the broader issues of whether Rhodesia is indeed a threat to the peace, the competence of the UN to get involved in the matter, and the procedures followed in the Security Council are open to question.[55] Also important is the attitude of the actors involved in the application of sanctions and the attitude of the target. France, Portugal, and South Africa have questioned the competence of the UN in applying sanctions against Rhodesia. Their doubts lent credence to the Rhodesian position, discussed in Chapter 3, that such UN action is illegitimate. To the extent any policy is viewed as illegitimate, the effectiveness of that policy will be impaired. Furthermore, if the sanctioners themselves are in disagreement and confusion over purposes and termination, how can the target be expected to clearly perceive what it must do in order to comply and have the pressure removed? Finally, if the purposes are in flux and the demands on the target changeable—as was the case with the British position and the interpretation of the "Five Principles"—the target may anticipate that if it delays compliance, its position will improve over time, and its interests will be better served in the future.

These kinds of problems associated with the Rhodesian sanctions were alleviated somewhat by the announcement of the four preconditions (noted above) by British Foreign Secretary James Callaghan in 1976. The new British policy went a long way in meeting African demands in the United Nations—especially as Britain had now formally agreed to the principle of no independence before majority rule (NIBMAR). Impressive unity on the Rhodesian issue was demonstrated on April 6, 1976, when S/RES/388 became the first UN Security Council resolution ever to be cosponsored by all fifteen members. Although only a minor extension to the sanctions program, the resolution, with unanimous sponsorship, was described by UN Secretary-General Kurt Waldheim as a "welcome sign of the willingness of the international community to bring about majority rule in Southern Rhodesia."[56] That such symbols were still needed ten years after the first sanctions were applied is indicative of the failure of the sanctions program to persuade the Smith régime to end its UDI.

On the immediate, *tactical* purpose of the sanctions, there does seem to have been general agreement among the sanctioners. Since the imposition of comprehensive, mandatory sanctions (with the exceptions of communications and humanitarian needs) in May 1968, the tactical purpose has been to isolate Rhodesia from the rest of the world. While this isolation was expected to cause economic stagnation, it was also expected to cause psychological pressures in Rhodesia. For example, in the Security Council debate of May 29, 1968, (S/PV.1428), Denmark stated the sanctions are supposed to "persuade the men in Salisbury of their isolation from the rest of the world and convince them that there is no future in persisting in their illegal course"; the United Kingdom declared: "We have to convince them that their rebellion can lead nowhere but to economic stagnation and political isolation." British Lord Chancellor Lord Gardiner, in referring to the travel restrictions, said that they were not intended to operate by way of punishment, but rather to bring home to the ordinary Rhodesian "the isolation and estrangement from the rest of the civilized world which the actions of their leaders have imposed on them."[57] Such isolation also serves to prevent recognition of legitimacy in any form, political or otherwise. In the Security Council debate of February 24, 1972, Somalia stated: "Sanctions must be preserved and intensified to maintain the illegal régime's present international isolation; if there were no sanctions, the drift towards recognizing it *de jure* would follow as surely as day follows night."

RHODESIA'S GENERAL RESPONSE

Obviously, the prime consideration of the Rhodesian government is to minimize in every way possible any adverse impact the sanctions may have on their country. To that end, the Rhodesian government seeks to maintain and develop international contacts and to avoid isolation from the rest of the world. The avoidance of isolation is necessary for three reasons. First, it is necessary to avoid the economic deprivation and stagnation that would result from the inability to maintain international commercial contacts. Both the sanctioners and the target know that Rhodesia must trade with other countries in order to survive. Second, it is necessary to strengthen public morale and to avoid, what Michael Lake of the *Manchester Guardian* calls, the "psychological cancer of isolation."[58] Third, it is necessary to demonstrate to the world the legitimacy of the government's position, gain acceptance for that position, and demonstrate the illegitimacy and ineffectiveness of the sanctions.

Subsequent chapters are devoted to an investigation of how and in what respects Rhodesia has been able to avoid isolation. Political, economic, communication, transportation, migration, tourism, and social relations are discussed. Empirical evidence is presented in order to offer explanations for Rhodesia's successes and failures and to judge the effectiveness, in general, of sanctions as an instrument of the United Nations.

3

Political and Diplomatic Relations

GENERAL FOREIGN POLICY

ACCORDING TO A SPOKESMAN for the Ministry of Foreign Affairs, discussions of Rhodesia's external policies are often a very delicate matter. Faced with sanctions, Rhodesia obviously must try to conceal details of the many unofficial contacts or linkages it has maintained with other states since UDI. While sanctions remain, Rhodesia cannot afford to say anything that might alienate or embarrass a supporter or potential supporter. Nevertheless, the basic philosophy which underpins the external policies of the Smith régime is quite clear. As the bastion of anticommunism, the outpost of civilization in Africa, and the model of stability and order, Rhodesia, according to Prime Minister Ian Smith, is on the northern border of the strategic area of southern Africa holding the line there against Communist aggression. The obvious manifestation of this aggression is the Communist Chinese involvement in central Africa and the Russian threat to the freedom of the sea lanes around the African continent.[1] After the Angolan Civil War of 1975–76, Smith warned in the *Rhodesia Herald,* February 7, 1976, that the Communists aimed to establish a "Marxist-dominated saddle" across Africa from coast to coast from which they would prepare to launch their campaign against southern Africa, establish their dominance, and deny the subcontinent's vast natural resources and communication facilities to the free world. The Rhodesian government has always viewed this aggression as part of a larger Communist plan to erode Western influence, largely through indirect methods, throughout the world and particularly in those areas from which the former colonial powers were withdrawing. Those indirect methods include the training, arming, and

41

financing of "malcontents and agitators in underdeveloped territories" by the Communists in order to subvert and remove Western influence from those territories.[2] The Rhodesian government subscribes to a domino theory which suggests that if Rhodesia is subverted by the Communists, then full-scale guerrilla warfare could be launched against South Africa; should the entire region fall to guerrilla warfare, the entire civilization of the noncommunist world would be threatened. The former president of Rhodesia, Clifford Dupont, warned in the *Rhodesia Herald,* December 27, 1973, that the battle for southern Africa was part of the "third world war" which had already started and was being fought by international and commercial blackmail, by infiltration and terror. Rhodesia's Foreign Minister Pieter van der Byl explained in a private interview on August 2, 1976, that "what we are doing here and what we fully believe we're doing, is defending the western world against Communist expansion and Soviet aggression." He said he could not understand why countries like the United States and Great Britain did not appreciate this but instead actually aided Rhodesia's enemies. According to Smith, it is a great irony that Rhodesia may be undermined from within the free world, by those members who are siding with the Communists against Rhodesia.[3]

It was noted in the last chapter that the Rhodesian government needs to demonstrate to the world the legitimacy of its political position, gain acceptance for that position, and demonstrate the illegitimacy and ineffectiveness of the sanctions. By associating sanctions with the Communists and his government with anticommunism, Smith hopes to do just this. It was in this spirit that Smith, in February 1966, made an offer of tangible help in the Vietnam war against communism. The ideological orientation of a state which is a target of sanctions may prove an additional strength in its ability to resist sanctions and may provide the target with valuable support.[4] Indeed, Rhodesia's anticommunist orientation was frequently noted by those members of the U.S. Congress supporting the Byrd Amendment which permitted resumption of limited trading with Rhodesia (see Chapter 4). Moreover, the domino theory is used by the Rhodesian government to help maintain the internal solidarity of its white community by imputing a sense of "mission" to their defensive efforts against sanctions and guerrilla warfare; allegedly, such efforts will not only save their community, but also the whole of Western civilization.

The Rhodesian government maintains that the sanctions are inherently illegitimate due to the noncompetence of the United Nations, denial of due process in the United Nations, and the invalidity of the premise upon which the UN sanctions are based. According to the government, the UN is prohibited by Article 2 of its Charter from intervening in matters which are essentially within the domestic jurisdiction of any state—and Rhodesia is either a "state" or part of another "state." If the latter is true, then the United Kingdom government had no legal standing in asking the UN to intervene in an internal British political dispute. Even British Foreign Secretary Sir Alec Douglas-Home declared in 1972: "In my view the previous Government . . . ought never to have internationalized the problem by taking it to the United Nations and asking for mandatory sanctions."[5] While Douglas-Home's opinion seems based on political rather than legal considerations, it does serve the Rhodesian purpose of trying to erode the legitimacy of the sanctions.

On May 18, 1966, the Rhodesian government, claiming to be a party to a dispute under consideration by the Security Council, petitioned the UN Secretary-General for an invitation to participate in the Council's debates concerning Rhodesia as provided in Article 32 of the UN Charter. The Secretary-General reported the Rhodesian communication to the Security Council; there was no debate and the Secretary-General decided not to reply because the sender of the communication was "illegal." Justice J. A. Macdonald of the High Court of Rhodesia commented: "The consideration of Britain's application before the United Nations was conducted without regard to well-established principles of natural justice—in particular, of the right of an accused to be heard in his own defence. In the Privy Council an *amicus curiae* was appointed; before the United Nations it apparently occurred to no member to propose the appointment of such a person."[6]

Since UDI, Rhodesia has consistently disavowed any aggressive intentions toward any country and has advocated noninterference in the internal affairs of all states and expects the same treatment in return. A spokesman for the Ministry of Foreign Affairs explained to the author in 1971, that this principle of Rhodesia's foreign policy and its implementation since UDI rendered the premise upon which the sanctions were ordered by the UN Security Council invalid—namely that the situation in Rhodesia constituted a "threat to international peace and security." If other states threaten or attack Rhodesia, can it be said that Rhodesia is the threat to the peace? Moreover, would not the attacking states be in violation of Article 2 of the UN Charter which requires states to settle their international disputes by peaceful means? The Rhodesian government, of course, rejects as invalid the view that its domestic policies *vis-à-vis* its African citizens constitute the threat to the peace by provoking the sensibilities of other states on the African continent. In any event, it is an interesting question when a provocation is a threat to the peace and when the response to the provocation constitutes the threat.[7]

Rhodesia tried to establish a pattern of conduct in its foreign relations that in no way could be construed as hostile or threatening. This has been especially difficult in her relations with Zambia and Mozambique. Immediately after UDI, according to the *New York Times,* December 5, 1965, largely to deter British military intervention, Prime Minister Smith hinted that Rhodesia had the capability to blow up the Kariba Dam—an action which would ruin Zambia's economy. But in the face of sanctions, the only action actually taken against Zambia was an embargo on the supply of oil to Zambia and the levying of a royalty and export tax on coal and coke exports to Zambia. This was announced on December 12, 1965, but was lifted on January 2, 1966, as a "goodwill gesture" by Smith, who repeatedly stated that a bankrupt neighbor is no asset to Rhodesia.

Zambia, however, from the date of its independence, maintained a policy of overt hostility toward the white minority Rhodesian government. Of major concern to Rhodesia has been the use of Zambian territory for staging areas from which guerrillas can attack Rhodesia. Despite periodic forays into Rhodesia by Zambian-based guerrillas, Smith, as late as December 14, 1971, said in the *Rhodesia Herald:* "Even when we have been provoked in the past by things said and done by the Zambian Government we've not allowed this to influence our trading relations. We don't believe that two wrongs make a right." After the first landmine explosion in Rhodesia in September 1972, the Rhodesian government issued the following warning: "Since it is within the power and scope of the Zambian authorities to prevent terrorists operating from their country, the Rhodesian Government feels it must make it clear beyond all doubt that if the Zambian Government fails to recognize its responsibilities in this matter then the consequences will rest squarely on its shoulders."[8] Rhodesia was trying to project a certain threat capability to deter aggression emanating from Zambian territory while at the same time avoiding any action which could conceivably be seized upon as an excuse to impose further sanctions or enhance the legitimacy of the current sanctions.

On January 9, 1973, faced with an increase in guerrilla activity on the Zambian border and a major new threat on the Mozambique border from guerrillas infiltrating through Tete province, Rhodesia closed its border with Zambia. This action was explained as follows by Prime Minister Smith, in the *Rhodesia Herald,* January 19, 1973:

History proved conclusively that Rhodesia, in spite of political differences with Zambia, had always tried to live as a good neighbour.
Rhodesia had helped when Zambia faced a fuel shortage, during maize
shortages, and helped with the transport of new motor vehicles through
Rhodesia and movement of Zambian fertilizer. Zambia could not point
to a single request for aid which Rhodesia had not met. Our aim was,
and still is, to bring the Zambian Government to its senses and get it
to face up to its responsibilities and accept that as far as civilized
countries are concerned there is an accepted code of behaviour between nations. All we are asking is that they observe this code. What
we now ask of them is that they dissociate themselves from the indiscriminate warfare being waged against us from Zambian soil.

Smith did permit the continuance of Zambian copper shipments
through Rhodesia because copper was a strategic metal used by the
free world, and Rhodesia did not wish to prejudice this situation. In
addition, copper made up more than 90 percent of the value of Zambian
exports and Rhodesia did not want to ruin Zambia's economy. The fact
that the Rhodesian railway system earned considerable foreign exchange
from the haulage of Zambian copper was not mentioned. Nevertheless,
the Zambian government unilaterally stopped copper shipments through
Rhodesia.

After supposedly receiving a formal message from the Zambian
government pledging to do all it could to prevent terrorist incursions into
Rhodesia from Zambia, the Rhodesian government reopened the border
on February 4. President Kaunda of Zambia denied sending Smith any
message or assurances, denounced the reopening of the border as a
trick, and announced that it would stay closed. Guerrilla activities continued and were supplemented by shootings across the Zambezi River
by Zambian army troops. Several civilians were killed by the Zambian
soldiers, including two Canadian tourists at Victoria Falls, on May 15,
1973. At this point, Rhodesia's threat capability to deter aggression
seemed quite low.

Like Zambia, Mozambique, from the date of its independence,
June 25, 1975, has also maintained a policy of overt hostility toward
the Rhodesian government. This is merely a continuation of the long-
standing policy of FRELIMO (Front for the Liberation of Mozambique)
to seek the liberation of all of southern Africa from white control. Indeed, while fighting the Portuguese, FRELIMO established a working
relationship with ZANU (Zimbabwe African National Union) whose
guerrillas were permitted to use FRELIMO base camps as early as 1972.

During the tenure of the joint Portuguese–FRELIMO provisional government for Mozambique—September 1974 to June 1975—relations between Rhodesia and Mozambique were normal. Rhodesian diplomatic personnel remained in Beira and Lourenco Marques, and the Rhodesian government repeatedly stressed its desire to establish friendly relations with any new government established in Mozambique. The Rhodesian Ministry of Foreign Affairs sent R$10 thousand worth of food and medical supplies to Mozambique in November 1974. Rhodesian Minister of Foreign Affairs P. K. van der Byl officially congratulated Samora Machel on his appointment as president of the new Republic of Mozambique and assured him that Rhodesia offered nothing but good will toward Mozambique.[9] Machel, however, made it clear that his country would not establish diplomatic relations with Rhodesia and would give material and logistic support to "Zimbabwe freedom fighters."[10]

Tension between Rhodesia and Mozambique gradually escalated after Mozambique's independence. As a result of the defections of hundreds of African students from schools near the Mozambique border, Rhodesia imposed a night curfew on its entire eastern border in July 1975. Fighting along that border was sporadic, although there was a clash between FRELIMO troops and Rhodesian security forces inside Rhodesia in October 1975. The level of violence increased sharply in February 1976, with frequent raids into Rhodesia by guerrillas operating from base camps in Mozambique. Rhodesia responded by conducting "hot pursuit" operations into Mozambique. President Machel threatened to attack Rhodesia in retaliation, and the *Rhodesia Herald,* February 13, 1976, reported that he promised "unconditional support" for the Rhodesia guerrillas. On March 3, 1976, Machel placed Mozambique on a war footing with Rhodesia, closed the border, and fully applied the United Nations sanctions against Rhodesia. With the escalation of violence along the border and the massing of Rhodesian guerrilla forces in Mozambique, Rhodesia launched several preemptive attacks into Mozambique—the largest occurring in August and November 1976, and May 1977. Although officially labelled "hot pursuit" operations, the attacks were on a far larger scale than such previous operations and seemed designed to destroy guerrilla personnel and supplies before they could be infiltrated into Rhodesia. An official government communiqué, published in the *Rhodesia Herald,* August 11, 1976, explained that "in the absence of any restraining influence from the outside world, Rhodesia has had no option but to strike at centres of organised terrorism on her borders in the interests of her own self-preservation."

Rhodesia's relationships with Zambia and Mozambique have been discussed in some detail because they indicate some of the problems

Rhodesia has to face in both formulating and implementing its foreign policy. If Rhodesia is provoked into attacking Zambia and Mozambique, then the premise that Rhodesia is a threat to international peace and security is strengthened. Indeed, the UN Security Council, in S/RES/ 411 (30 June 1977), reaffirmed that the "illegal régime in Southern Rhodesia" constituted a serious threat to international peace and security; declared the acts of aggression against Mozambique constituted a serious aggravation of the situation in that area; and urged all states to intensify assistance to the "people of Zimbabwe and their national liberation movement" in their struggle to achieve self-determination. Also, as will be noted later, Rhodesia's closure of the border with Zambia strained Rhodesia's relations with South Africa.

Another major problem facing Rhodesia in the conduct of her external affairs is the fact that the Rhodesian government is not recognized by any country in the world. The denial of legitimacy and recognition to that government has been the most conspicuous success of the sanctions program. As noted above, the Rhodesian government needs to gain recognition and demonstrate the ineffectiveness of the sanctions; in the view of the government, these two tasks are closely related.

The Rhodesian government believes it deserves recognition because, according to its foreign minister, "in terms of internationally accepted standards, Rhodesia possesses all the requirements of statehood, namely: a permanent population; a defined territory; a stable and effective government and the capacity to enter into relations with other states. In international parlance, it is accepted too, that the political existence of a state is independent of recognition by other states."[11] Contrasted to this is the British position, upheld by the Judicial Committee of the Privy Council on July 23, 1968, that the United Kingdom government is the lawful sovereign in Rhodesia, and all laws and orders made by the "illegal" government of Rhodesia are without legal effect. It is the British position which is universally recognized.

The High Court of Rhodesia ruled in January 1968, that the Rhodesian government sitting in Salisbury was the *de facto* sovereign of Rhodesia because "since the revolution the present Government has been in complete legislative and administrative control of Southern Rhodesia. Not one of the British Statutory Instruments which purport to apply here has been enforced."[12] This situation has been acknowledged by the United Kingdom government which has negotiated with the Smith régime those conditions needed to confer *de jure* sovereignty upon the Rhodesian government. The High Court of Rhodesia rejected the "idealistic

Lauterpacht theory of recognition," a theory which presupposes that recognition must always depend on an objective legal appraisal of the facts. Instead, the court adopted the view that political considerations are the overriding factor, and they depend on no principle other than political expediency. To affirm *de jure* status, the High Court would have to be satisfied that the Rhodesian government was "firmly established" and would continue in "effective control." The chief justice noted that sanctions were being employed by the United Kingdom government in order to try to end the control of the Smith régime. He added that the mere fact sanctions might do great harm to the economy did not necessarily mean that they would have the political result desired—but he did not, as yet, have enough evidence to justify a finding that the Rhodesian government was so firmly established as to constitute a *de jure* government.[13]

Eight months later, the High Court ruled that the Rhodesian government had acquired *de jure* status. The chief justice noted the attempts of the British government to regain control of Rhodesia by the continued imposition of sanctions and declared: "I can now predict with certainty that sanctions will not succeed in their objective of overthrowing the present government and of restoring the British government to the control of the government of Rhodesia. This being so, it follows that I must come to the conclusion that the 1961 Constitution has been annulled by the efficacy of the change."[14] The reasoning of the High Court was similar to the Rhodesian government position that economic success, especially in international trade, would eventually lead to political recognition and *de jure* status.

On June 16, 1970, Minister of Foreign Affairs Jack Howman outlined for the Legislative Assembly five tenets of Rhodesia's foreign policy. They are:

1. To maintain and develop the security of Rhodesia.

2. To maintain and foster cordial and effective relations with all friendly countries in the world, conscious always of the fact that because of our geographical position, our closest relations will be with other countries in southern Africa.

3. To participate in regional, international, and other specialized agencies with other states on a basis of cooperation and understanding.

4. To provide such technical and other aid, within our capacity to do so, as may be sought by countries less developed than Rhodesia.

5. To consult and cooperate on a regional and bilateral basis with countries in southern Africa on problems of common purpose or interest.

As can be noted in Howman's second and fifth tenets, Rhodesia stresses her role within the southern African region. According to Ian Smith, "we are immediately part of, we live in, our whole lives and our future are inextricably bound up with, Southern Africa. This is where we must concentrate."[15] Rhodesia strives to establish linkages with, and integrate itself as much as possible into, the southern African region. Such integration would shelter Rhodesia from the more adverse effects of sanctions as well as complicate efforts to isolate her, and Rhodesia could use the facilities of the other states in the region to gain access to the outside world. A major problem frustrating efforts to secure greater cohesion with the region—especially on a formal level—is the fact that none of the states within the region recognizes the sovereignty of Rhodesia. Lack of recognition precluded Rhodesia's participation in any formal common market scheme and in a planned regional tourism organization (see Chapters 4 and 6).

With reference to Howman's fourth tenet, it is interesting to note that Rhodesia announced in 1970, that she was making a R$1 million loan to a foreign government located in Africa in response to a request for assistance. The loan was scheduled to be paid out in five annual installments of R$200,000 each, and the recipient was to be a public secret. Howman told the Legislative Assembly on September 11, 1970, that "if the country concerned is identified or if the purpose for which assistance is rendered is disclosed . . . we will immediately forfeit the confidence of that Government which would not, of course, tolerate any discussion either of its identity or of its affairs." According to the *Rhodesia Herald,* August 28, 1970, Malawi was believed to be the most likely recipient. On November 10, 1971, the author questioned Thomas S. Tull, British High Commissioner in Malawi, from 1967 to 1971, about the likely recipient of the loan; Tull replied: "I don't think there is any truth in the rumor that this [the loan] was for Malawi; I think it was for a country further to the north and on the western part of Africa." When asked to name the country, he replied: "I can't speculate. I have forgotten now whether I was told this in confidence or not—but it certainly wasn't Malawi."

Considering Rhodesia's alleged political links with Gabon (discussed later in this chapter), its alleged economic and transportation links with Gabon (discussed in Chapters 4 and 5), and furthermore noting that Gabon fits Tull's estimate of the geographical location of the probable recipient, there is a strong possibility that Gabon was the recipient of the Rhodesian loan.

On February 17, 1976, the Rhodesian minister of finance explained

to the House of Assembly that although the country concerned had
agreed to repay the loan over a period of years, it had subsequently requested that the assistance be regarded as an outright grant. The Rhodesian government agreed to write off the loan and the outstanding
interest of R$50,054 "because of the very valuable help given to Rho-
desia in many fields by the recipient of the aid."

This foreign aid program is an interesting example of the secrecy
with which Rhodesia has to pursue many of its foreign policy objectives
on the operational level because of the sanctions. It is also an example
of how Rhodesia hopes to minimize efforts to isolate itself internationally
by stressing the useful contributions it can make by sharing some of its
assets with other countries in, according to Howman, a spirit of goodwill
and good fellowship. Finally, the aid program gives credence to the
claim of the Rhodesian government that adherence to the sanctions
program is far from universal and that Rhodesia has managed to gain
unofficial acceptance, if not official recognition. In this context, Foreign
Minister Howman stated in the Legislative Assembly on July 29, 1971,
that he thought the MP's would be "astonished at the extent to which we
have established links and communications with other countries."

FORMAL AND INFORMAL POLITICAL LINKAGES

Formal and Informal Diplomatic Representation

Upon the declaration of independence in November 1965, the Rhodesian government of Prime Minister Ian Smith assumed full responsibility for the conduct of its external affairs. In the Legislative Assembly,
June 22, 1966, President of Rhodesia Clifford Dupont stated: "the
possibility of establishing formal diplomatic relations with other countries
is under constant consideration." He also noted his appreciation of the
action of foreign governments who retained missions in Salisbury after
UDI, notwithstanding that some had been reduced in size. Minister of
External Affairs Lord Graham submitted a report to the Legislative
Assembly on August 19, 1966, on the status of external missions in
Salisbury:

> There were only two diplomatic missions in Rhodesia on the 11th
> November, 1965. Of these, Britain has withdrawn its High Commis-
> sioner and various members of his staff and has closed its diplomatic
> office, but has left a residual mission. South Africa has maintained its

representation and its office. Of the consular and trade missions, the position is as follows: Australia and Canada have closed their trade missions. Finland, Sweden, and Turkey have closed their Honorary Consulates; Denmark, France, Italy, Japan and the United States of America have withdrawn their heads of mission, but have not closed their offices, and Austria, Belgium, Germany, Greece, the Netherlands, Norway, Portugal, and Switzerland have maintained their representation and their offices at the same level as before.

After UDI, the Rhodesian government maintained loyalty to the Queen and claimed that their independence was taken "within the Commonwealth." This permitted various non-Commonwealth countries to retain their consulates without recognizing the Smith régime because their accreditation was to the Queen and not to the Rhodesian government. In 1970, however, the Rhodesian government proclaimed the country a republic and severed all symbolic ties to the Queen. In light of this action, all the countries, with the exception of South Africa and Portugal, closed their consular offices in Salisbury. Both these countries maintained their consular missions in Salisbury without recognizing the Smith régime by following the Reedman formula discussed in Chapter 1. The missions are accredited to the Rhodesian Ministry of Foreign Affairs and not to the Rhodesian head of state. In any event, British Foreign and Commonwealth Secretary Michael Stewart said in 1970: "I think one must notice . . . that the maintenance of a consulate in no way implies recognition of any kind." He explained that "a consular mission is not, in the proper sense of the word, accredited. We ourselves maintain consular missions to regimes which we do not recognise—for example, North Vietnam."[16]

The South African Diplomatic Mission in Salisbury is headed by the accredited diplomatic representative and includes several trade commissioners and a military advisor. Portugal maintained a Consulate-General in Salisbury and Consulates in Umtali and Bulawayo. In March 1975, Portugal's Consul-General in Salisbury Dr. I. J. Rebello de Andrade was recalled and the mission downgraded to "Consul" status. In August 1975, Portugal closed her consulates in Umtali and Bulawayo. The only other country to maintain an official representation in Salisbury is Malawi. The office of the "Malawi Government Representative" is operated and maintained directly from the Office of the President of Malawi and is without diplomatic standing. It is headed by a European employee of the Malawi civil service. Its major task is to take care of problems which the approximately 100,000 Malawian citizens working in Rhodesia may encounter—including passports, immigration, domestic problems, documentation, repatriation to Malawi, remittance of funds to Malawi, and social welfare problems.[17] The office also frequently serves as an informal liaison between the Rhodesia and Malawi governments.

The Rhodesian European community contains many recent immigrants; in the first seven years after UDI there was a net European migration of more than 35,000. In addition, there are uncounted numbers of foreign Europeans working in Rhodesia on a temporary basis as missionaries, teachers, nurses, etc. While living in Salisbury between June and September 1971, the author was told by unofficial sources that various governments maintained members of their diplomatic service in Salisbury on a strictly unofficial basis to give aid and assistance to their nationals residing in Rhodesia. The most specific information was provided by a Dutch businessman from The Hague who said that he was told by the Dutch Foreign Office that he could contact the "Liquidator of the Netherlands Consulate-General" in Salisbury should he need assistance. This is unsubstantiated information provided here to indicate a matter for further investigation. Specifically, it would be interesting to know if any of these "unofficial diplomats" act as intermediaries between their governments and the Rhodesian government.[18]

Official Rhodesian government representation in foreign countries is quite limited. As of 1971, the Ministry of Commerce and Industry had trade representatives or commercial consuls in Angola, Mozambique, Portugal, and South Africa; the Ministry of Foreign Affairs had officers in South Africa (Cape Town, Pretoria), Mozambique (Beira, Lourenco Marques), and Portugal (Lisbon); the Ministry of Information had officers in South Africa, the United States, Australia, and Portugal; and the Rhodesia National Tourist Board had offices in South Africa (Cape Town, Durban, Johannesburg), the United States (New York), Switzerland (Basle), and Mozambique (Lourenco Marques). In addition, according to a statement of the U.S. Department of State, Rhodesia allegedly maintained an unofficial "information office" in Paris and employed a citizen of Belgium to act as the unofficial representative of Rhodesia in Belgium.[19] It is interesting to note that Accredited Diplomatic Representative Harold Hawkins in Pretoria and W. M. Knox in Lisbon traveled on Australian passports. After receiving a protest from Ghana, the Australian government declared in 1972, that it would not renew those passports when they expired. Since Rhodesian passports are accepted by only a few countries, Australian passports would allow the bearer greater mobility in international travel.

By 1976, Rhodesia's representation in foreign countries had greatly diminished. The Rhodesian mission in Lisbon was closed in April 1975, because its presence was "no longer justifiable," according to the new Portuguese government. Rhodesian diplomatic representation in Mozambique was terminated by that country when it assumed its independence in June 1975. Officials of Rhodesia's trade mission, railways, and customs remained in Mozambique until the border closure in March 1976. In 1974, the Rhodesian Information Centre in Australia was deregistered and no longer allowed to operate under that name. Rhodesia's trade representative no longer operates in Angola. Finally, upon presentation of evidence that the head of the Rhodesia National Tourist Board (Air Rhodesia) office in New York was engaged in activities which were outside the scope of his license (e.g., exporting clothing to Rhodesia for commercial use), the United States government closed that office in 1974.

Rhodesia has also been unsuccessful in maintaining her representatives to the various international multilateral organizations in which she held some form of membership prior to UDI; those included: the General Agreement on Tariffs and Trade (GATT), World Health Organization (WHO), and the International Telecommunications Union (ITU).

Official and Unofficial Visits

Excluding meetings with British officials to discuss an Anglo-Rhodesian settlement, as of 1976, Ian Smith has had meetings with the heads of only two governments—Portugal and South Africa. He met with the prime minister of Portugal in Lisbon twice—once before UDI with Salazar and again with Caetano in 1972. Smith frequently made trips to South Africa to meet Prime Minister B. J. Vorster. In addition, Vorster became the only head of government to travel to Rhodesia after UDI when he met Smith in Salisbury in May 1970, after an official visit to Malawi. The *Rhodesia Herald,* May 19, 1970, commented editorially on the significance of Vorster's visit: "It implies open condonation of independent Rhodesia, bestowed in person by the most powerful man in South Africa. Though subtly so, it is a more telling signal of acceptance than any that has gone before. In a way, the visit goes further than formal recognition which, in international practice, is seldom accompanied by the taking of pains to establish friendly contact at such a level. Having the substance of South Africa's acceptance, Rhodesia could hardly ask for the extra token of diplomatic formalities which would get South Africa's foreign relations into unnecessary trouble." Smith's visits to South Africa are usually associated with opening an agricultural show, attending a sports match, or taking a vacation. The *Sunday Mail*, June 10, 1973, asked Smith why he had taken three "holidays" in just over a year. Smith replied that he normally liked to go to South Africa once a year to "have a short break" and at the same time to discuss matters of mutual interest with his South African counterpart.

Smith's meeting with Prime Minister Marcello Caetano in Lisbon in October 1972, was also associated with a vacation to the island of Madeira. The meeting was described by Portuguese officials as a "private courtesy call." It lasted sixty-five minutes and was handled in a "low-key" style by the Portuguese—no statements were issued; no press conference permitted.[20]

Visits of cabinet level officials between South Africa and Rhodesia are routine and frequent. Less frequent, perhaps because of distance, and less publicized were the visits of Rhodesia cabinet officers to Portugal. Information on the visits of Rhodesian cabinet officers to countries other than South Africa and Portugal is virtually non-existent. Minister of Foreign Affairs, Jack Howman, told the House of Assembly on August 7, 1973, that he had been courteously received in two foreign countries—one in Africa, the other in Europe. He refused to name the countries and noted that "so long as sanctions continue there must remain this aura, this attitude of secrecy however unfortunate we may think it is." He added that Rhodesia has had "warm and positive" contacts with other countries and that he had met foreign ministers "both inside and outside Africa." Perhaps the country in Africa he visited was Malawi; Howman was in Malawi on August 10, 1971, to confer unofficially with President Banda, and it is possible he made subsequent visits to that country.[21] While Smith was in Portugal in October 1972, Permanent Secretary for Foreign Affairs Stan O'Donnell was in Malawi for "a three-day holiday," according to a Ministry of Information report in the *Sunday Mail*, October 15, 1972. O'Donnell frequently met with President Banda—the last visit occurring in 1975, before he retired from the Ministry of Foreign Affairs.

It has been alleged by Peter Niesewand, writing in the *Manchester Guardian*, August 27, 1973, that P. K. van der Byl, Howman's successor as minister of foreign affairs, made an unofficial visit to Gabon during the first half of 1971, in which he met members of President Bongo's government. Niesewand further alleges that Libreville virtually became a "posting" of Rhodesia's Ministry of Foreign Affairs. Rhodesia's interest in Gabon was related to bilateral trade and the use of Libreville as an intermediate "cover" stop for Rhodesian air freight shipments to Europe.

It was alleged in the *Sunday Times* (London), August 26, 1973, that Harry Oxley, an assistant secretary in the Rhodesian Ministry of Foreign Affairs, helped to arrange the Rhodesian connections with Gabon. Perhaps embarrassed by the publicity given Rhodesia's linkages with Gabon, President Bongo in 1975, undertook an advertising campaign in Western countries to declare his country's full support of the liberation movements in southern Africa. Bongo stated: "the majority of the member nations of the OAU, of which Gabon is a member, trade with Rhodesia. If I do not give you the list, it is out of courtesy." He further stated: "Gabon wishes to emphasize that the country has now taken all necessary steps to terminate in due course the last links between herself and Rhodesia."[22]

Another country visited by the Rhodesian foreign minister was the Ivory Coast. The author personally observed and greeted P. K. van der Byl at the Hotel Ivoire in Abidjan on August 31, 1976. A spokesman for the Rhodesian Ministry of Foreign Affairs explained to the author in August 1971, that "we have become expert undercover diplomats in maintaining good, but unofficial relations with other countries." The evidence suggests that this is not a false claim.

The Rhodesian government encourages visits to Rhodesia by prominent people from other countries; on July 6, 1966, Minister of Information Jack Howman, explained his government's policy in the Legislative Assembly: "In the field of public relations, we deliberately adopted a policy of inviting prominent opinion-formers to come to this country. We have met them and shown them what there is and whatever they wished to see. Various British Members of Parliament have, I believe, taken a different view of our affairs following visits to this country which have enabled them to see for themselves the truth of the distortions made against us."

With reference to the United States, a Rhodesian MP told the Legislative Assembly on September 9, 1966: "We must be extremely careful to see that the people who put forward our case in the United States of America are people whose opinions count. The most influential people in the United States of America are the senators and the congressmen. Every one of these people is entitled to call a press conference any time that he wishes, and they have a tremendous amount of influence. I would suggest that money would be well spent in bringing to Rhodesia, both congressmen and senators, to see for themselves what the position is here."

Legislators from several countries have visited Rhodesia since UDI, sometimes in delegations, but usually in a private capacity. In 1971,

Representative Graham Purcell (D-Texas) accepted an invitation to open the annual congress of the Rhodesia Tobacco Association, and a year later, Representative William Poage (D-Texas) accepted an invitation to open the annual congress of the Rhodesia Cotton Growers' Association; Poage at that time held the influential position of Chairman of the House Committee on Agriculture. In December 1972, Clark MacGregor, former White House advisor and close associate of President Nixon, vacationed in Rhodesia and gave an interview to Rhodesia Television Limited (RTV) stating that the presence of sanctions against Rhodesia was "unnatural," and Americans believed that "unnatural situations were subject to change."[23] In 1975, Representatives John Dent (D-Pa.), Richard Ichord (D-Mo.), and Harold Runnels (D-N. Mex.) visited Rhodesia. All three were leaders in the effort in Congress to retain the Byrd amendment which permitted limited United States trade with Rhodesia. These examples do not comprise a complete list of important visitors from the United States, but rather illustrate the fact that the Rhodesian government has evidence to reinforce *its* claim that the country is indeed *not* isolated and had friendly, if unofficial, contacts with many prominent people overseas. In a broader sense, its claim is also reinforced by the visits to Rhodesia by prominent people in the arts, music, sports, science, religion, education, and business—as well as tourists; these visits will be discussed later.

The effect of the visits on the morale and psychology of the European community in Rhodesia may be more important *vis-à-vis* the sanctions than any material benefits which might result. Nevertheless, whether the European community realizes it or not, post-UDI Rhodesia has had far fewer visible, formal, official international contacts than she had prior to UDI. The irony is that as a "self-governing colony," Rhodesia had more formal international linkages—of a type not ordinarily possessed by a colony—than she has had as a self-proclaimed independent country.

Overseas Information Offices

Another means used by the Rhodesian government to try to influence public opinion in other countries is the overseas information offices, and, on a more informal level, the Friends of Rhodesia Societies. In 1966, Jack Howman issued a report on the formation of the societies:

> Through direct action from Salisbury, there have now been created more than 60 Friends of Rhodesia Societies throughout the

United States, through whom are lobbied Senators and Members of the House of Representatives, articles and letters submitted to the Press, and full and active operation undertaken in serving our cause. In Canada we have three such societies.

In Britain, directly and also through the Anglo-Rhodesian Society, we have encouraged the formation of branches throughout the United Kingdom.

Europe follows the same pattern—societies now exist in France, Belgium, Norway, Italy, Denmark, Switzerland, Germany, Holland, Sweden, and Malta.

There now exist in South Africa 150 Friends of Rhodesia societies and to channel, control and coordinate all the various activities, we created a national trust.[24]

Howman noted the special importance of the United States: "Of course one is fully aware of the need for counterpropaganda or counterinforming the peoples of the world everywhere and indeed its particular importance in the United States."[25] The Rhodesian Ministry of External Affairs stated in 1964: "Public relations is a vast and pervasive industry in the United States, and no important institution or personality can afford to ignore its significance. By concentration of effort and purpose it has proved possible to cultivate a better understanding and a wider circle of friends of Rhodesia than would have been the case if no such effort had been made. This is an infectious process and may well prove to be of inestimable value to Rhodesia to the extent that informed and sympathetic public opinion exercises a leverage on policy making."[26]

Extensive quotations are presented here not only to document the geographical scope and the activities of the societies but also to note the Rhodesian government's expectation that perhaps its public relations efforts, especially in the United States, would result in the adoption of public policies favorable to Rhodesia. As of 1976, little is known of the activities of the societies or even if they are all still in existence. Therefore, the remainder of this section concentrates on the two information offices.

The Rhodesian Information Centre in Australia was established in Melbourne in 1966, and subsequently moved to Sydney. It was formed by an Australian citizen and headed by Denzil Bradley, a South African by birth with considerable experience in the Rhodesian government. Bradley described the operation in the *Rhodesia Herald,* January 16, 1973, as a public relations office for Rhodesia whose main concern was informing Australian politicians about developments in Rhodesia. The Centre also encouraged politicians to visit Rhodesia; Bradley noted that

58 SANCTIONS

eight members of the Liberal party traveled to Rhodesia at their own expense. The Liberal government of Prime Minister William McMahon tolerated the presence of the Centre. Within one hour after taking office in December 1972, however, the new Labor government of Prime Minister Gough Whitlam announced its intention to close the Centre. While in opposition, Whitlam had constantly attacked the Liberal government's policies regarding the existence of the Centre and the sale of wheat to Rhodesia. Deregistration of the Centre by the federal government was challenged by the Liberal government of New South Wales, under whose laws the Centre was registered. After a complex legal battle, deregistration was achieved in 1974, which effectively ended the dissemination of Rhodesian propaganda in Australia under the Centre's name.

One major difference between the office in Australia and the office in Washington, D.C., is that the latter is directly operated by, and represents, the Rhodesian government.[27] The Rhodesian Information Office (RIO) is an agency of the Ministry of Information to which Principal Information Officer H. J. C. Hooper is responsible; its director, Kenneth Towsey, is seconded to the Ministry of Foreign Affairs. The RIO, Hooper, and Towsey are registered with the U.S. Department of Justice under the Foreign Agents Registration Act (FARA). The RIO was established in February 1966, after the Office of the Minister for Rhodesian Affairs in Washington lost diplomatic status as a result of UDI.

Towsey is classified as a "lawful permanent resident alien" under the U.S. immigration law and is not deportable except for gross criminal offenses. He acquired his status on December 27, 1967—five months before the UN Security Council passed S/RES/253, which requires member states to prevent entry into their territories of persons whom they have reason to believe to be ordinarily resident in Rhodesia and whom they believe to have furthered or encouraged the Smith régime. Hooper applied for the same status as Towsey, but his application was pending when S/RES/253 was passed. The U.S. Department of State opposed Hooper's application but concluded that the resolution did not require his deportation. Action on the application was deferred indefinitely, and Hooper's status, as of 1976, was "applicant for adjustment of status to permanent resident alien." While Towsey can freely enter and leave the country, if Hooper leaves he must apply for a visa to reenter; issuance of such a visa would be unlikely in light of S/RES/253.

The RIO is financed by the Rhodesian government via "free accounts" in various New York banks. The U.S. Treasury Department licenses the transfers of funds to Rhodesia for educational, medical, and humanitarian purposes—purposes which are consistent with the exceptions listed in the various UN sanctions resolutions. The total amount of licensed funds transferred to Rhodesia from July 29, 1968, to May 15, 1973, was US$18,233,537. The Rhodesian banks make the Rhodesian currency equivalent available to the recipient of these funds in Rhodesia and deposit their U.S. dollars in the "free accounts" in New York. Rhodesian authorities can spend these dollars for any lawful purpose in the U.S.—such as funding the RIO or paying for legal exports to Rhodesia—or they can transfer these "free" dollars to foreign banks to use for whatever purpose they wish.

The purpose of the RIO is set out by that Office in its FARA registration statement as follows:

> The main purpose of the work of the Rhodesian Information Office as an agency of the Rhodesian government is to promote in the United States a better understanding of the aims and policies of the government of the Republic of Rhodesia. The office endeavours to influence public opinion to the end that United States policy toward Rhodesia will be based on a desire to reciprocate friendship. This is done by means of regular mailings of printed matter to individuals and groups, educational institutions, legislators, U.S. government officials, and the news media. The officers of the Rhodesian Information Office hold themselves available for speaking engagements and interviews. They also pay visits and discuss Rhodesian policies, political and general, with any person or persons expressing the wish to learn more about Rhodesia. Close contact is kept with members of the United States Congress and their staff members when legislation affecting the situation in Rhodesia is being debated or considered.

The U.S. Department of State has no communication with the RIO. The RIO has no official status, and its employees are private persons whose known activities do not conflict with U.S. obligations under the UN sanctions resolutions, according to Deputy Assistant Secretary of State for African Affairs Clyde Ferguson, Jr. The opposite viewpoint is held by Representative Charles C. Diggs, Jr. (D-Mich.), whose subcommittee's hearings on the RIO in May 1973, attempted to generate evidence showing the RIO to be engaged in illegal activities. The critical legal point has to do with the prohibition, contained in section 3 of S/RES/253, of any activity which would "promote" or is "calculated to promote" exports from Rhodesia or imports to Rhodesia.

Also relevant are the provisions of S/RES/253 which prohibit the entry into member states of persons ordinarily resident in Rhodesia who have furthered or encouraged the "unlawful actions of the illegal régime." Chapter 4 examines the problems surrounding the definition of the word *promotion*. Secretary Ferguson believed that *promotion* had not been interpreted to encompass general information dissemination, public relations activities, or advertisements. This view was shared by Assistant Secretary of Treasury for International Affairs John H. Hennessy, who added that there was a question as to when an activity passed from promotion information for dissemination into an actual calculation of promotion itself. Secretary Ferguson viewed the difficulty as involving the underlying constitutional problem of the exercise of free speech and the difficulty of making the distinction as to where free speech stopped and unlawful advocacy began.

To increase pressure on Rhodesia, the UN Security Council unanimously passed S/RES/409 on May 27, 1977, which decided that all member states shall prohibit the use or transfer of any funds in their territories by the illegal Rhodesian régime for the purposes of any office or agency of that régime that is established within their territories. This would mean that the RIO could neither receive funds from the "free accounts" nor use funds from any source.

In the U.S. Senate on June 16, 1977, as reported in the *Congressional Record,* Senators Jesse Helms (R-North Carolina) and James McClure (R-Idaho) took strong exception to S/RES/409 and its implementation in the United States on the grounds that the effect would be to infringe upon the First Amendment of the U.S. Constitution guarantee of free speech. As a legal entity and a law-abiding agency, the RIO is entitled to the protection of the U.S. Constitution. Senator Dick Clark (D-Iowa) argued that it was not a question simply of denying freedom of speech but rather a question of abiding by the Security Council decision for which the United States voted. Senator Clark, however, did join Senator Clifford Case (D-New Jersey) in sponsoring a "sense of the Congress" resolution declaring that any foreign country should be allowed to maintain an information office in the United States. The resolution was adopted on a voice vote. Kenneth Towsey told the author on January 30, 1978, that as of that date, "in a practical sense, the activities of my office have not been affected by S/RES/409." The RIO was still being funded via the "free accounts."

The operations of the Rhodesian offices raised fundamental legal questions in both Australia and the United States. The issue was whether the respective governments possessed the constitutional authority to fully implement the provisions and intent of some sections of the UN sanctions resolutions. Another area where this problem arises, for example, is in the area of tourism; the United States government does not have the legal authority to prevent U.S. citizens who choose to visit Rhodesia from doing so.

A broader question arises in this context. The UN Participation Act of 1945 legally commits the United States to give effect to the resolutions passed by the UN Security Council. A fundamental principle of the United Nations is that when the Security Council passes binding resolutions, the member states cannot pick and choose which resolutions or parts of resolutions they will obey. The question arises as to what happens in the event that the Security Council passes a resolution which violates the U.S. Constitution—the president not having ordered it to be vetoed. Such a question may arise over S/RES/409.

Regional Military Cooperation

A special case of political linkages involving Rhodesia concerns cooperation in military affairs within the southern African region. While the white-ruled states in southern Africa do not face a conventional military threat from the regular armies of any country, they do face a threat posed by armed personnel which are called, depending on one's political preferences, liberation movements, terrorist units, Communist bands, freedom fighters, or nationalist guerrillas.

Referring to Rhodesia, Henry Maasdorp, political analyst for the *Sunday Mail,* wrote on April 8, 1973: "What we are experiencing is undoubtedly a form of war, however debased—conducted by indigenous guerrillas using terrorism as their instrument, their actions being implicitly (at least) condoned by members of their own people for one reason or another. They are encouraged, trained, and supplied by foreign powers." He does not agree that it is a purely guerrilla war in which armed bands engage in irregular fighting with the aim of neutralizing the armed forces of the state. Yet he noted that they are trained as guerrillas and do engage the state's forces when cornered. Maasdorp added that "to call the affair simply terrorism directed by Communism to further Communism's aims in Africa is thoroughly misleading." There are numerous groups which are best characterized as African organizations which are striving to subvert or overthrow the present governments of South-West Africa, South Africa, and Rhodesia (and sought, in the past, to expel the Portuguese from Angola and Mozambique). The bulk of the financial and material assistance to these groups is being supplied by communist countries. The term "guerrilla" will be used in this study in reference to these groups.

One problem for the white-ruled states in southern Africa is the impossibility of preventing the flow of weapons to the guerrilla movements. General Antonio de Spinola, former governor and commander-in-chief of the Portuguese army in Portuguese Guinea, wrote in his book, *Portugal and the Future,* that it is not possible to deprive the guerrillas of their sources of supply indefinitely by military means: "Inexhaustible external support, together with the permeability of the frontier regions and the ideological support of neighboring countries, makes it utopian to hope for success in any attempt to isolate the guerrillas."[28]

Another problem is that while the guerrilla movements directed toward any one country may find it difficult to coordinate their efforts, guerrilla movements directed against different countries may be able to form tactical alliances. In the case of Rhodesia, the Zimbabwe African People's Union (ZAPU) and the African National Congress (ANC), a South African guerrilla organization, signed an alliance in August 1967, in Lusaka to "fight the common settler enemy to the finish." This alliance provided the excuse for South African police forces to enter Rhodesia to help the Rhodesian army fight the combined ZAPU–ANC force in northwest Rhodesia near Wankie. Beginning in 1972, large incursions were made into Rhodesia's northeast area, adjacent to the Tete district of Mozambique, by forces of the Zimbabwe African National Union (ZANU). Apparently, ZANU was acting in liaison with the Front for the Liberation of Mozambique (FRELIMO). This sparked joint antiguerrilla efforts by the Rhodesian and Portuguese military.

Faced with the dangers suggested by the domino theory within the southern African region, faced with manpower shortages in the security forces, and faced with the possibility that guerrilla movements of different countries could form tactical alliances to achieve their ends, it was perhaps natural that the Rhodesian government sought to coordinate its defensive efforts with those of Portugal and South Africa. A 1966 Rhodesian government pamphlet described the white-ruled states in Southern Africa as forming an *entente cordiale:* "Mozambique and Rhodesia are good neighbours, and our countries, along with the Republic of South Africa, form an *entente cordiale* on the southern tip of Africa which is of immense mutual benefit. Recent years have proved that our continued solidarity is vital for the survival of each one of the three countries."[29]

It would be difficult for the *entente cordiale* to become a formal defense treaty or military alliance while Rhodesia remained unrecognized, legally, by any country. Moreover, it was a cardinal principle of the foreign policies of South Africa, Portugal, and Rhodesia that a formal alliance did not exist and did not need to exist. Rhodesian Minister of Defense Jack Howman referring to military cooperation between the three countries, told the *Rhodesia Herald,* January 28, 1970, that good friends, facing a common threat, having mutual interests, do not need treaties for a careful and good understanding of one another.

Indeed, the *Rhodesia Herald,* October 12, 1972, noted that a ceaseless interchange of intelligence and practical support—on a number of levels—took place between South Africa, Portugal, and Rhodesia. Commander of the Rhodesian Air Force Air Marshall M. J. McLaren told *Rhodesian Commentary,* November 1973, that there was considerable understanding and interchange of ideas at all levels of government between Rhodesia and South Africa—including the armed services. He noted that staff courses previously undertaken by Rhodesians with the British army and the Royal Air Force were subsequently attended at the South African army colleges and the South African Air Force. James Barber, referring to defense cooperation between the three countries, aptly noted that "they have moved closer together to create an informal but increasingly integrated response."[30]

Evidence of the "moving together" could be seen in the many meetings and visits involving regional defense which took place— especially in the period 1970–1974. While these are too numerous to document here, the meeting in Salisbury in February 1971, between Prime Minister Ian Smith and the "security chiefs" of Portugal and South Africa and the meeting in Salisbury in October 1972, between Smith and the South African defense minister and the commandant general of the South African defense forces might be cited as important examples. In addition, military advisors were attached to the South African and Portuguese diplomatic missions in Salisbury.

Evidence of the "integrated response" could be seen in the joint military operations. As noted above, South African police units had been sent to Rhodesia in August 1967, in order to help Rhodesian forces combat joint ZAPU-ANC guerrilla incursions across the Zambezi River. To try to avoid international legal complications, the South African government sent its civilian police rather than its army into Rhodesia. It also officially informed the United Kingdom government of the situation on September 8, 1967, thus recognizing British sovereignty over Rhodesia. On September 14, 1967, the United Kingdom government lodged a formal protest with the South African government claiming that no foreign security forces had the right to operate in Rhodesia without the consent of Her Majesty's government. The UN Security Council, in S/RES/277 (1970), "demanded" the immediate withdrawal of South African police and armed personnel from Southern Rhodesia. These demands were repeated in S/RES/326 (1973) and S/RES/328 (1973). The South African government responded to the latter resolutions by officially informing the UN Security Council that the police would remain in Rhodesia while the threat posed to the security of South Africa by Zambian-based "terrorists" remained.[31]

Little is known of the extent of the South African involvement. Charles W. Petersen and Alan Rake both claim the initial commitment involved 300 men plus equipment such as armored cars and helicopters.[32] According to the *Rhodesia Herald,* March 6, 1968, an additional R$1,460,000 was requested in the South African House of Assembly for the police budget as a result of police presence along South Africa's borders and in Rhodesia. Included in the request were funds to buy two patrol boats for use on the Zambezi River. The *Star* (Johannesburg), November 24, 1973, quoted the South African Minister of Police S. L. Muller as saying that the police were patrolling much of the northern border of Rhodesia but the numerical strength could not be discussed. The best estimate is that the police force in Rhodesia was increased to well over 1,000 by 1973—perhaps reaching a maximum of about 2,000. The following year, Chief Deputy Commissioner of the South African Police Nolan Loxton commented that the presence of police on the borders had caused a considerable drain on law enforcement sections in South Africa.[33]

Joint military operations between Rhodesian and Portuguese security forces were far less obvious than the operations with South Africa. The first published information concerning the possibility that Rhodesian forces were conducting sweeps in Mozambique was in April 1971, with the report that three Rhodesian soldiers had been killed by a landmine explosion in Mozambique. Rhodesia's minister of defense told the *Rhodesia Herald,* August 12, 1972, that Rhodesia would help the Portuguese forces in Mozambique if asked. While he characterized the situation in the Tete province as "serious" and "difficult," he stated that he believed the Portuguese could control it themselves. Smith visited Prime Minister Caetano in Lisbon in October 1972, and the guerrilla situation in Tete was reported to have been discussed. The Portuguese were quite sensitive about any report doubting their ability to maintain security in Mozambique. On December 4, 1972, Smith affirmed that "Rhodesian security forces only operate on their side of the border." He added that Rhodesian forces would be prepared to participate, but there was no need for it as the Portuguese seemed to be containing the guerrilla situation. Just nineteen days later, a communiqué was issued from security force headquarters in Rhodesia describing "a successful operation carried out in conjunction with Portuguese forces on the Rhodesia-Mozambique border."[34]

In 1973, the Portuguese commander in Mozambique, General Kaulza de Arriaga, said that he was on the best of terms with the heads of the Rhodesian armed forces. He added: "We have an agreement with Rhodesia that troops may only cross the border from either side when they are in hot pursuit of the enemy. Otherwise, there is no involvement in each other's campaigns whatsoever."[35] While the general continued to deny that Portuguese forces were being assisted by any foreign forces in Mozambique, press reports told a contrary story of substantial Rhodesian involvement deep into Mozambique territory.[36] Peter Niesewand and Antonio de Figueiredo reproduced a report in the *Manchester Guardian*, April 27, 1974, prepared by Portuguese army officers serving in Mozambique which described the "intimate collaboration in the military field" between Portuguese and Rhodesian security forces.

To admit that Rhodesian forces were in Mozambique aiding the Portuguese forces would confirm the fact that the military situation had deteriorated. This the Portuguese government could not admit— especially since the Caetano régime was, at the time, facing mounting criticism of its African policies by elements of its own military. Exactly one month after the Caetano régime was overthrown by a military junta in April 1974, Rhodesia was asked by the junta to stop all military pursuit operations against guerrillas in Mozambique.

Denied cooperation with Portuguese security forces in 1974, Rhodesia's defense problems were further compounded by the withdrawal of the South African police in 1975 (for reasons noted below). While the South African government had repeatedly stressed that their police were not sent to Rhodesia to fight Rhodesia's war or to protect and safeguard Rhodesia, it was obvious that the police were important to Rhodesia's defense efforts. Rhodesia's minister of defense told the *Sunday Mail,* April 8, 1973, that the South African police involvement was "most welcome" and explained: "We've got a very big border—if we had ten times the number of troops we've got we'd probably still have trouble traversing the border." In the House of Assembly, August 1, 1975, the minister confirmed a report that the withdrawal of the police necessitated the redeployment of Rhodesian forces to cover the gaps and was a contributory factor to the need for escalation of the defense effort.

Rhodesian security forces were stretched to the limit in 1976, by President Machel's declaration that a "state of war" existed between Mozambique and Rhodesia. The entire 765-mile Mozambique border now had to be patrolled. Nearly every able-bodied European was subjected to military call-up, and a second battalion of the Rhodesian African Rifles was formed. In 1977, guerrillas based in Zambia increased infiltration into Rhodesia through Botswana, requiring Rhodesian forces to patrol most of that 550-mile border as well. In May 1977, President Kaunda declared that a "state of war" existed between Zambia and Rhodesia, and guerrilla raids from Zambia increased.

While qualified aliens are welcomed into the Rhodesian security forces as regular soldiers, sanctions have made any widespread overseas advertising campaign impossible. According to the *Sunday Mail,* December 17, 1972, 20 percent of the police recruits originated from foreign countries compared to nearly 80 percent before UDI. The recruiting that does occur takes place surreptitiously—often by word of mouth. Articles sympathetic to the Rhodesian military appear in such American publications as *Guns & Ammo* (June 1975) and *Soldier of Fortune* (August 1977), and these may help recruitment. In a series of equally sympathetic articles written for the *New York Times Syndicate* in 1977, Robin Moore estimated that several hundred Americans, many of them veterans of the Vietnam war, were fighting for the Rhodesian security forces. The UN Sanctions Committee noted with concern in 1977, that increasing numbers of recruits from Australia, West Germany, Greece, Italy, New Zealand, Portugal, South Africa, the United Kingdom, and the United States were joining Rhodesia's armed forces.[37] It is highly unlikely, however, that these foreign recruits could compensate Rhodesia for the loss of cooperation with the South African and Portuguese security forces.

ATTITUDES OF COUNTRIES HAVING POLITICAL RELATIONS WITH RHODESIA

South Africa

South African policy toward Rhodesia and sanctions has been most consistent during the years following UDI.[38] Four basic principles guiding that policy were enunciated by the South African ambassador to the UN in 1973:

1. We do not interfere in the domestic affairs of other countries.

2. We do not initiate boycotts, and we do not reply to sanctions with counterboycotts.

3. We are unconditionally opposed to terrorism, and we shall, in terms of our declared policy, render assistance within our means to Governments who seek it in their fight against terrorism.

4. Where and when we are directly threatened, we shall at all times take all steps to protect the life and property of our people and our territorial integrity.[39]

South Africa, in declining an invitation to be represented at the UN Security Council debates on Rhodesia in November 1965, made it clear that the Rhodesian issue was "one of exclusively domestic concern in which the United Nations was not competent to intervene." The South African government refrained from commenting in any way on the substance of the problem as its policy of nonintervention required. It also noted that "all the immediate neighbours of Rhodesia are confronted in the present situation with very practical problems arising from the need to maintain the regular intercourse which is implicit and inherent in the geographical and other essential facts governing the relationship between each one of them and Rhodesia."[40]

Prime Minister Henrik Verwoerd outlined his country's interests vis-à-vis UDI to the House of Assembly on January 25, 1966: "It was clearly in South Africa's interest not to be dragged into the conflict if avoidable. It was clearly in our interests to try to have the conflict restricted to those directly implicated, the United Kingdom and Rhodesia. It was clearly in South Africa's interests not to make enemies unnecessarily." He added that it was in South Africa's interests to consistently uphold the principles on which its whole international fight has been fought—especially the principles of nonintervention into the domestic affairs of others and nonparticipation in either boycotts or sanctions.

Also in South Africa's interests was an Anglo–Rhodesian settlement—a settlement Vorster repeatedly declared in public he would like to see. At Klerksdorp in October 1968, Vorster explained that the Rhodesian situation was preventing the building of a southern African bloc of "nations" which would be an example to the rest of the world of how people of different races and different political views could live together in peace; "all that stands in the way is the Rhodesian question."[41]

It is thus unlikely that South Africa encouraged the Rhodesian government to declare UDI; indeed, British Prime Minister Harold Wilson told the House of Commons on November 11, 1965, that he had no reason at all to suppose that either South Africa or Portugal encouraged the Rhodesian government in their course of action or were lending any form of financial or other support to the action that was taken. One wonders, however, if Ian Smith was not encouraged by the trade agreements signed with Portugal and South Africa and the South African loans which all were negotiated in the twelve months preceding UDI (see Chapter 1).

South Africa's refusal to recognize Rhodesia after UDI is best explained by South Africa's principle of nonintervention—and the Smith régime acknowledges it. On March 4, 1968, Ian Smith said in an interview: "I'm satisfied that their [South Africa and Portugal] behaviour has been absolutely correct and proper. They were placed in the most invidious position and made their decision that they would virtually be neutral. They would neither work against us or against Britain. I think it was the wisest decision in the circumstances and I certainly have no criticism whatsoever."[42] However wise the decision, the lack of recognition precludes Rhodesian involvement in any formal multilateral linkages that South Africa would like to establish within the southern African region. In this sense, Rhodesia is a source of instability within the region and an impediment to South Africa's goal of establishing greater regional integration.

Has the lack of an Anglo-Rhodesian settlement strained South African-Rhodesian relations in the years since UDI? Some scholars, such as Richard Hall, have suggested that South Africa put pressure on Smith to settle with Britain; he claims that in 1968, "Vorster had assured Wilson that he was prepared to cooperate fully in making Smith abandon his stubborn attitudes and was ready to use powerful economic levers in the process."[43] Both parties have denied such allegations. On February 21, 1967, Smith told the Legislative Assembly: "As far as the South African Government is concerned they have never at any time tried to insist that we follow any policy. I am convinced they will never try to do this." Vorster echoed Smith's views; in 1971, Vorster said that South Africa had never been prepared to twist Rhodesia's arm, but "this matter must be solved if it is possible. If an honourable settlement can be achieved we will welcome it."[44] In Salisbury, May 24, 1970, to a *Rhodesia Herald* reporter who suggested that Rhodesia was an embarrassment to South Africa's "outward policy," Vorster replied: "Rhodesia is a friend of mine, and my friends never embarrass me."

Embarrassment or not, as noted above, the South African government perceived that its interests would be compromised if it was "dragged into the conflict." Sending police forces into Rhodesia in August 1967, was consistent with South Africa's declared principles. There were other kinds of situations, however, in which South Africa might be drawn into the conflict under circumstances which *did* compromise her interests and principles. One such situation occurred in January 1973, and it led to a visible strain in South African–Rhodesian relations.

For reasons outlined earlier in this chapter, Rhodesia closed her border with Zambia on January 9, 1973. But incredible as it may seem, the Rhodesian government had no prior consultations with either South Africa or Portugal before closing the border—despite the fact that the main transportation routes for the South African exports to Zambia traversed Rhodesian territory and thus were affected. In a formal statement issued on January 19, Vorster declared that South Africa was not a party to the decision and noted that "one can expect divergent speculation as to the wisdom or otherwise of this step." He declared that he would treat the matter in accordance with the basic principles of South Africa which included the following: "We do not initiate boycotts, and we do not reply to sanctions with counterboycotts."[45] South African businessmen immediately sought alternate routes for their exports to Zambia. This move was severely criticized by Rhodesian Minister of Information P. K. van der Byl, who said that it could present the world with a picture of a divided Southern Africa; according to the *Rhodesia Herald,* February 16, 1973, van der Byl also stated that he could not understand South Africa's criticism of the border closure—especially since two South African policemen had been killed on the border.

The Afrikaans-language press, usually sympathetic to Rhodesia, was generally critical of Smith's actions. The Afrikaans-language newspaper with the largest circulation in South Africa, the weekly *Rapport,* explained: "This section of the press has always understood Rhodesia's problems. We have a great understanding and a brotherly attunement. But this cannot be a blank cheque for all Rhodesia's decisions which affect us as well. Rhodesia's interests are not necessarily ours."[46] The divergence of interests between Rhodesia and South Africa was further illustrated by South Africa's "détente" exercise—an exercise which introduced further strain in the relations between the two countries.

As noted in Chapter 2, South Africa launched a major diplomatic initiative in October 1974, designed to normalize relations between South Africa and the rest of Africa and maximize the political stability of southern Africa as a prelude to increased economic cooperation and development. Prime Minister Vorster, speaking to the South African

Senate on October 23, 1974, stated his belief that southern Africa had come to the crossroads between peace on the one hand and an escalation of strife leading to chaos, on the other. Vorster committed himself and his government to seeking peace and cooperation but admitted that there were several "stumbling blocks" or "contentious issues" or "problematical situations" which could not be ignored—Mozambique, South West Africa, and Rhodesia.

The disengagement of Portugal from Africa had brought southern Africa to the crossroads Vorster spoke of and had accelerated South Africa's long standing desire to see the Rhodesian issue settled. As long as South Africa remained the prime supporter of the Smith régime, any attempts South Africa made toward achieving *détente* with black Africa would falter. Moreover, Africa is clearly committed to use violence, if negotiations fail, to "liberate" Rhodesia and the rest of southern Africa. This option was emphasized by the OAU Council of Ministers which met in Dar es Salaam in April 1975. After the Mozambique government closed its border with Rhodesia in March 1976, and pledged itself to the "liberation" struggle, the option of using violence to achieve black rule in Rhodesia became more viable. Rhodesia's military vulnerability had been greatly increased by Mozambique's actions.

Pragmatic considerations alone would dictate a reassessment in South Africa of continued support for Rhodesia—especially if it might mean being dragged into a protracted and costly military confrontation with guerrilla forces. South Africa had intervened in the Angolan Civil War in 1975, and eventually met substantial Cuban armed forces backed by Soviet equipment. Lacking support from Western countries, South Africa had to withdraw. In 1976, South Africa faced major and continuous riots in its African townships, a decline in the price of gold, which did not help the serious deficit in its balance of payments, and the necessity for its congested rail and port system to handle *all* Rhodesia's imports and exports. Taken together, these factors made it extremely difficult for South Africa to give unconditional support to Rhodesia.

Another important consideration is that the South African government has never indicated in public that its objective in Rhodesia was to maintain a white régime. The emphasis has been on stability regardless of the color of the régime. If violence increases in Rhodesia, that would guarantee a radical régime coming into power—possibly with Communist support. Moreover, ideological and cultural differences between the white South African government and the white Rhodesian government were often cited as reasons for South Africa's unwillingness to become heavily involved in Rhodesia. The South African minister of labor explained in the *Rhodesia Herald,* September 5, 1975, that Rhodesia's "colour policy" differed radically from that of the Nationalist party; the former aimed at whites and blacks governing together in the same parliament, while the latter aimed at giving the various black nations in South Africa self-determination in their own homelands and therefore in their own parliaments. John D'Oliveira, political reporter for the Argus South African newspapers, noted in the *Rhodesia Herald,* March 8, 1976, that if South Africa became involved in a conflict aimed at maintaining the Smith régime in Rhodesia, it would mean that in theory South Africa would be fighting to defend an ideology which it had rejected itself.

While massive and obvious South African support for Rhodesia would be incompatible with South Africa's attempt to achieve *détente,* massive and obvious pressure on Rhodesia would be incompatible with long standing and deeply revered principles of South African foreign policy. Nonintervention into the domestic affairs of other countries and nonparticipation in boycotts and sanctions are two cardinal principles which constrain South African policy toward Rhodesia. South African violation of these principles might serve as the justification for other countries to violate them with respect to South Africa. Whenever the suggestion was made that South Africa was pressuring Rhodesia, there was a sharp denial from the South African government. For example, Prime Minister Vorster told the South African House of Assembly on April 21, 1975, that it was untrue that South Africa had forced Smith to negotiate with black people in Rhodesia; "South Africa's conduct in respect of Rhodesia has at all times been irreproachable."

Domestic political considerations in South Africa also constrain South African policy toward Rhodesia. While the policy of *détente* has received considerable public and press support and the Nationalist party maintains a huge parliamentary majority, there are ultraconservative elements which reject *détente.* For example, the Herstigte Nasionale party (HNP), which broke away from the Nationalist party in 1969, wants South Africa to offer Rhodesia immediate and unlimited military help. While opposition political leader, Sir de Villiers Graaff supports the general policy of *détente,* he acknowledged in the *Rhodesia Herald,* September 5, 1975, that South Africa had sentimental ties and common interests with Rhodesia which could not be forgotten or denied. Indeed, nearly 50,000 residents of Rhodesia were born in South Africa—including 20,000 Afrikaners. Prime Minister Vorster needs to be careful not to take any action which would provoke a "white blacklash" against his

Rhodesian policy, keep his Afrikaner nation together, and, above all, not be perceived as the man who "sold Rhodesia down the river."[47]

Vorster admitted to the House of Assembly on April 21, 1975, that "the Rhodesian issue is . . . a particularly delicate one." His government has to "bring influence to bear" without exerting "pressure"; it has to avoid using sanctions without making it appear that such avoidance constitutes approval and support; it has to encourage but not dictate. According to Vorster: "We have issued warnings where it was necessary, and we have given advice where it was necessary. We pointed out alternatives, but it was always in a good spirit of neighbourliness, and in that spirit we shall continue in spite of the fact that there is a world of difference between politics in Rhodesia and the policy we follow here in South Africa."[48]

While the Rhodesian issue may have been "particularly delicate" for Vorster, it would have to be resolved if *détente* was to progress. In October 1974, South Africa sought to act in concert with Zambia, Tanzania, and Botswana to create the proper conditions or atmosphere which would enhance prospects for a settlement between the Smith régime and the black nationalist leaders in Rhodesia. Serious strains developed between South Africa and Rhodesia over a number of issues related to the détente exercise. One of the more serious strains involved the issue of military cooperation.

In December 1974, Smith announced that an agreement had been reached with nationalist leaders on a ceasefire in the guerrilla war, preparation for a constitutional conference, and the release of all detained African nationalist leaders and followers in Rhodesia. According to the Zambian foreign minister, South Africa was expected to show its sincerity in the *détente* exercise by removing its police forces from Rhodesia.[49] After being pulled back into base camps in January 1975, the police were gradually withdrawn from Rhodesia—the final contingents leaving in August. Meanwhile, the talks between the Smith régime and the black nationalists were totally unproductive—agreement not even being reached on the venue or chairmanship of a constitutional conference. To settle these and other issues, an agreement was worked out in Pretoria in August 1975, to arrange a meeting between the two sides; the agreement was guaranteed by the governments of South Africa, Botswana, Mozambique, Tanzania, and Zambia. The meeting was eventually held on August 25, aboard a South African railway train on the Victoria Falls Bridge which links Rhodesia with Zambia across the Zambezi River. Despite the presence of Prime Minister Vorster and

President Kaunda, the Victoria Falls conference ended in failure. There was no cessation of the guerrilla war.

A joint communiqué issued after the meeting between Smith and Vorster in Cape Town in March 1975, stated: "It was again confirmed by the South African Government, and understood and accepted by the Rhodesian Government, that the South African Police will be withdrawn as soon as the ceasefire has become effective." Smith, in May, indicated that he understood the withdrawal was a quid pro quo for the cessation of terrorism, and if terrorism ceased, no aid would be needed from South Africa.[50] Of course, the problem was that "terrorism" had not ceased and, indeed, had increased. In September, the Smith-Vorster disagreement became more evident. Smith stated that his government felt the withdrawal was the wrong decision and that it had made a settlement more difficult. Vorster immediately reacted: "It must not be said that South Africa has let down Rhodesia or anybody else." But Smith repeated his view that the withdrawal had prejudiced rather than helped bring about a settlement.[51] South African Minister of Police J. T. Kruger outlined the rationale for the withdrawal in statements printed in the *Rhodesia Herald,* August 2, and 4, 1975: South Africa originally sent police into Rhodesia to intercept terrorists heading for South Africa, since no terrorists were moving down, the original necessity for the police presence has diminished; South Africa did not want police presence to become a disturbing factor in the process of negotiations. No mention was made of the absence of a ceasefire.

In October 1975, relations between South Africa and Rhodesia reached a new low as Rhodesian cabinet officers strongly attacked the policy of *détente.* The minister of local government indicated that terrorism would have been eliminated if it had not been for the *détente* exercise. At the Rhodesian Front party congress, Prime Minister Smith said that of all the countries involved in *détente,* Rhodesia was the only country in a worse position than at the beginning. Statements of this kind were not really new, as they had been expressed before by the minister of defense in August and the minister of roads in June.[52] But on October 12, Smith gave an interview to British television in which, according to a transcript printed in the *Sunday Mail,* he stated: "I go so far as to say that I believe that if this new initiative had not been taken by Mr. Vorster and the four northern Presidents, I believe we would have had a settlement by now."

Reaction from South Africa was immediate and vehemently critical. One critic, South African Minister of Indian Affairs Marais Steyn, stated, in a report in the *Rhodesia Herald,* October 16, 1975, that Smith's statement was a source of astonishment and shock and charged Smith with the responsibility to put matters right with Vorster. Interestingly, Steyn also noted that South Africa, in pursuance of its policy to avoid boycotts, maintained normal relations with Rhodesia despite criticism from outside. Smith requested, and was granted, a meeting with Vorster in Pretoria after which a formal statement was issued and printed in the *Rhodesia Herald,* October 21, 1975, stating that Smith did not intend to criticize Vorster; Smith had been a willing partner in Vorster's efforts; Smith formally apologized for any embarrassment caused by his remarks; Smith assured Vorster there was no inference that Vorster had in any way attempted to interfere in Rhodesia's internal affairs; and Smith appreciated Vorster's efforts to promote a more favorable climate for a peaceful settlement.

It has been said that negotiating with Ian Smith was "like trying to nail a jelly to the wall"; the Johannesburg *Star,* October 25, 1975, gave credit to Vorster for "finally nailing the jelly." After this abject apology, Rhodesian newspapers were filled with comments from Rhodesian cabinet ministers warmly praising *détente* and South African support. The incident did not seem to cause any lasting damage to Rhodesian–South African relations, although it did serve as a reminder to the Rhodesians that their freedom of action was limited by their dependence on South Africa and South Africa's determination of its own national interests. Ironically, sanctions may have forced Rhodesia into a dependent relationship with South Africa of far greater proportions than she had had with the United Kingdom prior to UDI.

Portugal

Prior to 1974, it was difficult to detect differences between the Portuguese and South African attitudes toward the Rhodesian situation. The government of Portugal announced that it had certain doubts of a procedural and juridical nature concerning the various Security Council resolutions on Rhodesia and was awaiting clarifications from the UN which might possibly explain these matters. Specifically, it asked for " . . . clarification on whether the question of Southern Rhodesia still lies within the exclusive jurisprudence of the United Kingdom, as has been affirmed by the United Kingdom . . . or whether it henceforth comes within the exclusive international jurisdiction of the Council." The government of Portugal believed that S/RES/221 of April 9, 1966, prohibiting the import of oil through the port of Beira was simply a recommendation and was not mandatory. The Portuguese believed that the resolution was not adopted because France and the Soviet Union had abstained, and, according to the Charter of the UN, decisions of the Council required the concurring votes of its permanent members. They acknowledged that it had been the practice of the Security Council not to consider the abstention of a permanent member as being equivalent to a veto, but this occurred with respect to matters not involving Chapter 7 of the Charter and at a time when the Council consisted of eleven members. The Portuguese noted that S/RES/221 " . . . constitutes a clear denial of the principles of the freedom of the seas, and of free access to the sea by landlocked countries, embodied in conventions which have the status of international law. Accordingly, if the law is not repealed, the resolution must be regarded as invalid" as the Council cannot legislate against international law.[53] If there was any difference between the Portuguese and the South Africans in their view of the UN resolutions on Rhodesia, it was one of style rather than substance— with the Portuguese raising all kinds of questions and doubts and seeking clarifications and enlightenment, and the South Africans, with minimum correspondence on the issue, simply stating their principles and affirming that the UN was not competent to inquire into the Rhodesian matter.

Certainly in terms of national interest, Portugal had as much interest as South Africa in ensuring stability in the southern African region. Prime Minister Marcello Caetano told the National Assembly in 1968, that although Portugal, South Africa, and Rhodesia maintained different racial policies, "at many points our interests in Southern Africa coincide, based on the conviction that the progress of that zone of Africa needs the stable presence of the white man, taking root there, getting used to it, taking it to his heart, and working with the natives. This is why, for example, we cannot be indifferent to the fate of Rhodesia, whose main outlet to the sea is through our harbour of Beira. In our interest, in that of Southern Africa, and on behalf of world peace, we should truly like to see Rhodesia and Great Britain agree on a formula to permit an honourable agreement which would put an end to the grave present situation."[54]

Portugal, as well as South Africa, desired an Anglo-Rhodesian settlement, and, to this end, it was reported that both Caetano and his predecessor, Antonio Salazar, sought to mediate between Rhodesia and Great Britain.[55] Like South Africa, Portugal withheld recognition of Rhodesia in the absence of a settlement. The *Rhodesia Herald,* January 10, 1967, reported that Portugal's foreign minister said his government was not contemplating official recognition of Smith's administration, adding that "the Rhodesian Government has not asked for any formal recognition."

Portugal had a far greater immediate need for a settlement than did South Africa as sanctions caused a decrease in the flow of Rhodesian transit traffic through Mozambique—particularly affecting the port of Beira. Mozambique suffered further losses when Zambia closed its border with Rhodesia, as a great deal of Zambia's imports and exports passed through Rhodesia to and from Beira and Lourenco Marques. Mozambique earned a great deal of revenue from the port, railway, and oil pipeline services provided to Rhodesia. Portugal several times pointed out to the UN that she had sustained huge losses of revenue as a result of sanctions and claimed international compensation as was her right under the UN Charter. On February 12, 1967, the *New York Times* reported that Portugal had asked the UN for US$28 million indemnification for losses resulting from sanctions.

Two sources of visible strain in Rhodesian-Portuguese relations were the security situation in Mozambique and the closing of the border with Zambia. As noted above, during the nine months prior to the Smith-Caetano meeting in October 1972, there had been a deterioration in the military situation in Mozambique's Tete province. Indeed, there was a great deal of press speculation that this situation was one reason why Smith visited Caetano. In the month following Smith's visit, Caetano declared in a major address to the Portuguese people, published in the *Rhodesia Herald,* November 16, 1972, that Portugal was in firm control of the situation in the Tete district of Mozambique and added, "but some of our neighbours with less experience do not conceal their fears and thus play the enemy's game. They have been told more than once that there is no reason for their great fright." While he did not directly name Rhodesia, the implication was clear.

There is very little information on the second source of strain. In January 1973, the Portuguese government denied that it had rebuked Rhodesia over its closure of the border with Zambia. Nevertheless, while printing the Portuguese statement, the *New York Times,* January 28, 1973, quoted sources in Lisbon as saying that the Rhodesian blockade was "both precipitate and drastic" and noted that Portugal had kept her transit facilities in Angola and Mozambique open to Zambia for imports and exports.

After the coup of April 1974, relations between Portugal and Rhodesia remained unchanged for about one year while the new government tried to stabilize its position and move its African colonies to independence. As noted above, in April 1975, the Portuguese government closed the Rhodesian diplomatic mission in Lisbon and downgraded, but did not terminate, its diplomatic mission in Salisbury. Rhodesia has a Portuguese population of between 10,000 and 20,000 and the Portuguese representative in Salisbury explained to the *Rhodesia Herald,* June 16, 1975, that his government did not wish to deprive them of consular representation.

Portugal stated, in a note to the UN Sanctions Committee dated October 14, 1976, that the new government of Portugal accepted the obligatory nature of the system of sanctions imposed against Rhodesia.[56] It was not until August 1977, however, that Portugal ceased to recognize Rhodesian passports and the Portuguese airline, TAP, did not suspend its direct flights to and from Rhodesia until November 1977. Portugal had terminated its annual participation in Trade Fair Rhodesia in 1975.

Malawi

To understand Malawi's attitude toward Rhodesia, it is necessary to understand the broader aspects of Malawian foreign policy.[57] That policy is the creation of Malawi's Life President and Minister of External Affairs Dr. H. Kamuzu Banda. Realistically, Banda is cognizant of his country's geographical position and of its economic dependence upon South Africa, Rhodesia, and Mozambique. He has consistently defied the policies of the Organization of African Unity (OAU) by maintaining close relations with those countries. As early as July 1964, at the OAU Conference in Cairo, Banda declared that while he endorsed the anticolonial philosophy of his "good friend" Dr. Kwame Nkrumah of Ghana and while he felt strongly against imperialism and colonialism in any form, he did not think that in order "to help his brothers and sisters under colonialism and imperialism a man must cut his own throat."[58] Realistically, Banda ridicules the position of those who call for the use of force against the European-controlled areas of Southern Africa on the ground that no country in Africa could hope to match the military might of the countries whose destruction they seek. Morally, he opposes violence for it would inflict suffering on the Africans as well as the whites and would kill the "many liberal white men and women who genuinely wanted justice for the Africans."[59]

Although often voicing a fear of Communist imperialism in Africa, Banda does not believe in automatic alignment with one bloc or another. Instead, he described his foreign policy to the Malawi Parliament on November 10, 1965, as being one of "discretionary nonalignment" explaining that "I will ally with any power when I think that that power is doing the right thing, and I disalign with any power when I think that power is doing the wrong thing." On the opening of the Malawi Parliament, July 2, 1971, Banda listed three primary requirements for the formation of relations between Malawi and any other country:

1. The existence between Malawi and the country concerned, of spheres of mutual interest whereby the people of both countries . . . can benefit from common association.

2. The relations between Malawi and any other country must not be determined or influenced by the race or colour of those at the moment in control of the affairs of any country concerned.

3. Relations between Malawi and any other country must not and cannot be governed by or be dependent upon our agreement with or approval of the internal policies of any such other country.

In keeping with these three requirements, Banda has advocated the policy of "dialogue" with South Africa, Rhodesia, and Portugal. A basic principle of the dialogue policy is the idea that to be an African is not necessarily to be black—there are Arab Africans, white Africans, brown Africans—and all must learn to live in peace with each other. Malawi must serve as an example of a black-ruled state where racial discrimination is absent and where white residents, in particular, have nothing to fear. In addition, by establishing full diplomatic relations with South Africa and Portugal, it will force those governments to receive Malawian officials and visitors and accord them honorable and equal treatment. By peaceful example, apartheid and notions of racial superiority can be eroded, the position of liberal whites strengthened, and the conditions created whereby peaceful change can develop within the white-ruled countries of Southern Africa.[60]

The two stable tenets of Malawi's Rhodesian policy are that the use of military force against Rhodesia is unrealistic and must be strongly discouraged and that the problem of UDI is one which must be solved by Britain. "It is Britain, and Britain alone, that can solve this problem. And the rest of us must leave it to Britain and trust her to choose the best method of solving the problem of Rhodesia," according to Banda in a speech to the Parliament, March 8, 1966. Before UDI, at the OAU meeting in Accra, Ghana, in June 1965, Banda expressed his deep conviction that Rhodesia was not a problem that could be solved by military action or economic sanctions. Once Britain chose the instrument of sanctions to try to solve the problem, however, Malawi cooperated to some extent (see Chapter 4).

As the weeks and months passed after the imposition of sanctions on Rhodesia, and it became clear that those sanctions were not achieving the result that was predicted, Britain came under increasing pressure from the African states and the OAU to use force to crush the "rebellion." Dr. Banda firmly supported the British position, and in several speeches made before the Parliament of Malawi in 1966, he cautioned against dictating to Britain that she should or must use force in Rhodesia and urged African leaders to be patient with Britain and let the sanctions have the time necessary to be truly effective.

It soon became apparent that Britain indeed could not be pressured into using force against Rhodesia and instead preferred to open negotiations with the Smith régime with a view of arriving at a settlement peacefully. From Banda's statements, it seems that he supported sanctions partly as a device to forestall the use of force. When the possibility of violence receded, the contradiction between a policy of dialogue and a policy of sanctions and isolation must have become evident to Banda, because he became increasingly critical of the latter policy. On April 23, 1969, Banda told Parliament: "You cannot solve the problem of Black and White in this part of Africa by either denunciation or by boycott and isolation." It is interesting to note that President Tsiranana of the Malagasy Republic addressed the Malawian Parliament on April 15, 1969, and fully endorsed Banda's policy of dialogue with Rhodesia, Mozambique, and South Africa (Tsiranana was ousted by a military coup in May 1972).

It is significant that in the many speeches Banda made on Rhodesia since UDI, there was a paucity of overt criticism of the Rhodesian government. He never referred to Rhodesia as a colony or used its United Nations designation (Southern Rhodesia) or its African nationalist designation (Zimbabwe). Even when Rhodesia declared herself a republic in 1969, Banda refused to criticize and said that it would be pointless for Malawi to change her attitude toward Rhodesia for such a step would help neither Malawi nor its fellow Africans in Rhodesia.

Over the next few years, Banda vigorously pursued his dialogue policy and included Rhodesia in his plans. For example, in 1970 and 1971, senior Rhodesian officials were invited to attend regional tourism conferences in Malawi (see Chapter 6). In July 1971, the commissioner of Rhodesia's British South African police attended a conference of senior police officials from Zambia, South Africa, Kenya, Uganda,

Botswana, Swaziland, and Malawi in Blantyre. According to the *Rhodesia Herald,* July 27, 1971, "Malawi is being used, to Dr. Banda's delight, as a venue for contacts between Southern Africa and several black nations." Indeed, Banda went so far as to describe Malawi's relationship with Rhodesia to the Parliament, July 2, 1971, as being "friendly, constructive, and beneficial." For Malawi and Dr. Banda, it is quite evident that the policy of dialogue and contact takes precedence over the policy of sanctions and isolation.

The Portuguese coup in 1974, and the independence of Mozambique under FRELIMO leadership in 1975, caused no fundamental shift in Banda's *policy* toward Rhodesia—only a shift in *approach.* These events obviously placed Malawi in a difficult position. Banda was never very enthusiastic about the southern African "liberation" movements and had maintained close relations with Portugal. In June 1975, FRELIMO leader Samora Machel attacked Banda for giving unconditional support to the old "racist regime" and for preventing, or hindering, FRELIMO action against the Portuguese. Machel then noted that the railway passes through Mozambique, and it helps Malawi.[61] Indeed, Malawi is vitally dependent upon the seaports located in Mozambique; Malawi's major trading routes—both rail and road—traverse Mozambique territory. When Mozambique closed the border with Rhodesia in March 1976, all direct rail, road, and air links between Malawi and Rhodesia were severed.

Banda, however, did not deviate from his policy of maintaining cordial relations with South Africa and Rhodesia—he simply stopped talking about it! In contrast to earlier parliamentary debates, those surveyed from 1974, through March 1976, contain almost no references to Rhodesia or South Africa. In one rare reference to his policy of dialogue, Banda told the Malawi Parliament on March 27, 1975: "I was being called the "odd man out in Africa.' The man out of step, the odd man out when I was preaching the gospel of contact, dialogue, contact, and discussion. Now the very people who were condemning me are talking my language. I am not going to say 'I told you so.' That's not my style. So far as I am concerned, better late conversion than no conversion at all." Ironically, Banda remained an "odd man out" as Malawi was not included as a major participant in the southern African *détente* exercise which began in 1974.

From the standpoint of Rhodesia, Malawi's friendship has the same benefits as the foreign aid program noted above. It reinforces the credibility of Smith's prodialogue policy with black Africa, and it gives credence to the claims of the Rhodesian government that it is not isolated internationally. Moreover, the Rhodesian government, when making contacts with other governments (especially in Africa), can use Malawi as an example of Rhodesian cooperation and goodwill in foreign relations on the operational level. In a very rare reference to a relationship with a specific country other than Portugal or South Africa, Ian Smith told the Legislative Assembly on June 10, 1970, that "peaceful and cordial relations have always existed between Malawi and Rhodesia, and our aim is to preserve this position."

Switzerland

While Switzerland has no known official or unofficial political relations with Rhodesia, the Swiss do permit limited trade with Rhodesia, accept Rhodesian passports, and their banks and companies are important to the Rhodesian effort to circumvent the sanctions. Since the Swiss permit these kinds of contacts with Rhodesia for political reasons, it is perhaps appropriate to document those reasons here.

Switzerland belongs to several specialized agencies of the United Nations (e.g., International Labor Organization, International Monetary Fund, Universal Postal Union, etc.). However, because it does not wish to compromise its legal status of perpetual neutrality which was established at the Congress of Vienna in 1815, the Swiss government has not joined the United Nations and has not signed its Charter. Its neutrality precludes its participation in a war or other political disputes between countries; membership in the UN could require the Swiss government to take action against a country—such as applying economic sanctions.

Nevertheless, many of the sanctions resolutions adopted by the Security Council call upon states which are members of the UN or of the specialized agencies to implement certain provisions of the resolutions (e.g., S/RES/253, o.p. 8 and 18); other resolutions "urge" states not members of the UN to act in accordance with the provisions of the resolutions (e.g., S/RES/232, o.p. 7; S/RES/277, o.p. 18). The latter resolutions cite as justification for their "urgings" Article 2(6) of the UN Charter which reads: "The Organization shall ensure that states which are not Members of the United Nations act in accordance with these Principles [of the Charter] so far as may be necessary for the maintenance of international peace and security." These resolutions, read in conjunction with Article 2(6) of the charter, may create an obligation for Switzerland to enforce the sanctions regardless of its neutrality. This is rejected by the Swiss government.

The definitive statement of Swiss policy regarding Rhodesia and the UN sanctions was presented in a note dated February 13, 1967, from the permanent observer of Switzerland to the United Nations to the Secretary-General:

> The Federal Council has concluded that, for reasons of principle, Switzerland, as a neutral State, cannot submit to the mandatory sanctions of the United Nations. The Federal Council will, however, see to it that Rhodesian trade is given no opportunity to avoid the United Nations sanctions policy through Swiss territory. It is for that reason that it decided, as early as 17 December 1965, independently and without recognizing any legal obligation to do so, to make imports from Rhodesia subject to mandatory authorization and to take the necessary measures to prevent any increase in Swiss imports from that territory. The ban on exports of war material imposed at the end of 1965 is being maintained. Similarly, the National Bank continues to block funds deposited with it by the Rhodesian Reserve Bank.[62]

On the one hand, Switzerland cannot submit to the sanctions and thus help the United Kingdom and the United Nations; on the other hand, she cannot abstain from taking any action and thus help Rhodesia. What she did decide to do was to apply some sanctions "voluntarily" which, among other things, restricted Swiss-Rhodesian trade to pre-UDI levels. Nevertheless, as will be explained in later chapters, Rhodesia does benefit by the Swiss position. In any total collective security action involving the use of sanctions against a target country, contact between a neutral third party and the target country can be interpreted as aiding the target country. The reason for this is simply that many of the sanction measures depend upon *universal* adherence and compliance in order for them to achieve a high level of effectiveness.

CONCLUSION

In this chapter some of the political relations and linkages, official and unofficial, which Rhodesia has with other countries are documented. In the following chapters, a great variety of other relations, linkages, and contacts Rhodesia has with other countries in such fields as economics, transportation, communications, tourism, labor, and social will be presented. Noting these kinds of contacts, Rhodesian Minister of Internal Affairs Desmond Lardner-Burke asked the Legislative Assembly on May 5, 1967, if they did not constitute a degree of recognition. Claiming that independence is a matter of degree for all countries, Lardner-Burke maintained that "while we may not have recognition in some fields, we have it in others." Ian Smith also claimed in the Legislative Assembly, February 10, 1967, that "practical recognition has been adopted by many countries who are continuing to trade with us and whose sympathies lie entirely with us." He avoided the question of the *de jure* aspect of recognition, however. Considering the evidence presented in this chapter on political relations, what assessment can be made of the claims of the Rhodesian government *vis-à-vis* recognition? Is it possible that certain countries by virtue of their conduct have implicitly recognized Rhodesia?

This is an important question because recognition is being withheld from Rhodesia as a sanction that has psychological, political, and economic consequences for the Rhodesian government. Anyone who has read the Rhodesian newspapers and parliamentary debates since UDI and has lived in Rhodesia for even a short period of time cannot fail to notice the longing for recognition—the reaching out for any scrap of recognition. Opposition MP C. Chipunza, noted the implications in the Legislative Assembly, June 23, 1966, as follows: "I believe this lack of recognition by the outside world, in spite of the stories we have been told that this country has many friends all over the world, is important. If we have friends why can they not recognize us as a government and a country? It is because they have no confidence in what we are doing, and they believe that what we are doing is completely wrong. When one looks at the comic side of this whole exercise one finds that certain honorable members and their staffs have been able to get people to attend their parties hoping they will get official recognition and acknowledgement."

In terms of political consequences, it has already been noted that lack of recognition precludes Rhodesian involvement in any formal multilateral arrangements within the southern African region. Economically, recognition would permit Rhodesia to establish the necessary legal relations with other countries to enable her to borrow money and buy capital goods on credit—both of which are badly needed by Rhodesia to refurbish key sectors of her infrastructure (e.g., the railroads).

One scholar has claimed that "there is such a thing as 'tacit consent' and recognition by implication in International Law—by exchanging diplomats, concluding treaties, and generally by treating a State as an international 'person.' This kind of recognition has already been given to Rhodesia by several countries."[63]

D. J. Devine carefully investigated this contention from the stand-

point of South African relations with Rhodesia and concluded that such
information that was available in 1969, favors the proposition that South
Africa had *not* implicitly recognized Rhodesian independence. The
normal trade relations which South Africa has permitted to continue
with Rhodesia since UDI comprises private trading by South African
citizens and companies. Even the supplying of oil to Rhodesia is entirely in the hands of private individuals and companies. Devine claims
that "such actions on the part of private individuals cannot compromise
the attitude of the South African Government in the matter of Rhodesian
recognition."[64] He notes that the establishment of consular relations does
not necessarily imply recognition. He further notes that although South
African police forces were present in Rhodesia, "no implication of recognition need necessarily be drawn from mere temporary arrangements
or from agreements for limited purposes."[65] Indeed, Prime Minister
Vorster said in 1972, that "South Africa has no defense agreement with
any country in Southern Africa."[66] In any event, according to Devine,
the question of recognition hinges on the intentions of the parties concerned. Rhodesia makes no claim to recognition by South Africa; the
statement of principles by the South African government—especially
concerning nonintervention and the "need for an Anglo-Rhodesian
settlement"—makes clear that government's intention not to implicitly
or explicitly recognize the Smith régime. On July 6, 1966, Rhodesia's
Minister of External Affairs Lord Graham, said in the Legislative Assembly that "just as in the past it used to be said that the flag followed
trade, so today I am quite certain that recognition will not be long in
following trade also." Lord Graham has been proved to have been quite
incorrect.

It was noted above that the viability of the economy in the face
of sanctions was one of the factors which led the High Court of Rhodesia
to rule that the Rhodesian government had attained *de jure* status. In
the next chapter a survey of the Rhodesian economy in connection with
an examination of Rhodesia's international economic relations will be
presented.

4

Economic Relations

OVERVIEW OF THE ECONOMY AND THE ROLE OF FOREIGN TRADE

General Economic Review

THE STRUCTURE OF the Rhodesian economy is such that it is highly dependent upon foreign trade. The prosperity of agriculture, manufacturing, and mining is to a significant degree dependent on exports, as are the power, transportation, and communications sectors. In 1965, these six sectors were responsible for 64 percent of the total African employment and 39 percent of the total European employment.[1] In order to better understand the importance of foreign trade, it is necessary to present a brief overview of the Rhodesian economy with special emphasis on manufacturing, mining, and agriculture.

Table 4.1 presents key indicators of the economy and how they have changed in the first decade of sanctions, 1965 to 1975. While it is hazardous to cite figures out of context and without relevant comparisons to other time periods or other countries, this cross section of indicators accurately reflects, in the words of Rhodesian Minister of Finance John Wrathall, "an economic buoyancy," outstanding considering the international restraints placed on the economy through sanctions. Indeed, these restraints have been partly responsible for the economic improvement; they have stimulated the diversification of manufacturing, making Rhodesia more self-sufficient in an ever-widening range of goods that were previously imported; new markets have been created and developed; and the traditional patterns of trade have been changed. Confidence in the economy was particularly reflected by the high level of capital investment—most of it financed from domestic savings—and the huge increase in the Index of the Rhodesian Stock Exchange. Confidence was also reflected by the fact that the net outflow of Europeans from Rho-

85

Table 4.1
Rhodesian Economic Indicators
1965–1975

Indicators	1965	1975	Percentage Increase
Population—African	4,260,000	6,110,000	43.4
Population—Non-African	230,600	308,900	33.9
Ratio—Non-African: African	1:18.47	1:19.78	
Total net European migration (1961–65)	−23,430		
Total net European migration (1966–70)	17,550		
Total net European migration (1971–75)	22,430		
Tourists from other countries	208,725	244,404	17.1
Total African school enrollment (year)	654,241	868,689	32.8
African employees	656,000	945,000	44.1
Non-African employees	89,700	119,700	33.4
European Consumer Price Index (1964 = 100)	101.7	149.2	46.7
Sales of principal crops and livestock ($m.)	124.2	305.4	145.9
European-owned cattle (m.)	1.63	2.78	70.6
Mineral output ($m.)	63.9	169.8	165.7
Index of volume of manufacturing production (1964 = 100)	108.7	204.3	87.9
Building plans approved ($m., 1966–75)	17.7	82.3	365.0
Electrical energy consumed (m. Kw. hrs.)	2028.9	6136.4	202.4
Rhodesia Railways—net tons hauled (m. tons, 1968–75)	9.886	12.800	29.5
Retail Trade Value Index	100.0	266.5	166.5
Imports ($m. 1965–72)	239.6	274.2	14.4
Exports and re-exports ($m. 1965–72)	309.2	328.5	6.2
Terms of trade (1964 = 100)	100.8	79.9	−20.7
Gross national income ($m., 1965 prices, 1965–74)	722.2	1352.6	87.3
Gross fixed capital formation ($m.)	100.0	400.0	300.0
Gross public debt ($m., central and local governments)	557.0	896.1	60.9
Rhodesian Stock Exchange Index	118.3	375.1	217.1

Source: Rhodesia, Central Statistical Office, *Monthly Digest of Statistics*, March 1973 and April 1976.

Notes: $m. = million Rhodesian dollars. 1972 was the last year that import and export statistics were made public by the Rhodesian government.

ECONOMIC RELATIONS

desia was halted and turned around in Rhodesia's favor. The sustained level of domestic demand, as reflected by the retail trade value index, was accompanied by an extremely low rate of inflation—one of the lowest rates of any economy in the world. Wrathall summarized the economic situation in the House of Assembly, July 15, 1971: "Rhodesia has emerged from the stage of being largely reliant upon primary production with a relatively unsophisticated secondary industry into a vibrant economy which is well diversified. I believe that this development may well have been achieved at a somewhat faster pace than would have been possible under free and unfettered conditions."

While the economy may have been "vibrant" and "buoyant," it was also under considerable strain. The indicators in Table 4.1 yield some clues as to the sources of the strain. The rate of growth of the African population is about 3.6 percent per year—twice the world average and well above the average rate for the African continent. Moreover, with a high fertility rate, some 46.6 percent of the African population is under the age of fifteen. This puts a heavy demand on social services— especially health and education. It also means that there has to be a rapid rate of increase in gross national product each year if living standards are to improve materially, and some 30,000 new jobs must be created each year to provide sufficient employment opportunities.[2] It is doubtful whether the economy under sanctions can expand fast enough in the long run to adequately alleviate the problems associated with the African population increase. In addition, the European increase, supplemented as it was by immigration, is still inadequate to reduce the ratio of Africans to Europeans.

Another source of strain is reflected in the deterioration of the terms of trade. This indicates a rise in import prices relative to export prices. Some of this deterioration was due to international currency instability and the depression of world base metal and agricultural prices; however, sanctions were also a major cause. As Prime Minister Ian Smith admitted in the House of Assembly, April 5, 1973: "The imposition of sanctions created many trading problems for us. We find that we are compelled to export at a discount and import at a premium. The result is that we lose out on both transactions. This has the effect of reducing profit margins internally, and at the national level, it has an adverse effect on our balance of payments and foreign reserves." He went on to note that "because our foreign reserves are depleted artificially, our natural development is prejudiced. This clearly has a serious inhibiting effect on the creation of job opportunities." Yet the creation of job opportunities is necessary in order to reduce some of the adverse effects of the African population explosion.

Table 4.1 reveals that Rhodesian exports were 6.2 percent higher in 1972 than in 1965. This was the first time since UDI that exports exceeded the 1965 figure. On July 21, 1966, Wrathall told the Legislative Assembly that "exports are Rhodesia's life blood. Our success or failure as a nation depends on our ability to make good, by whatever means possible, the loss of the export markets which have been closed by sanctions." By 1973, Rhodesia did "make good" by increasing the volume of exports while decreasing their price. In his 1972 budget statement, Wrathall declared that with the major exception of tobacco "the country is virtually exporting to the limit of its physical capacity."[3] This limit, however, was not attributable to a lack of exportable goods, but rather to the inability of the railways to move the goods to the seaports of Mozambique and South Africa.

Table 4.1 indicates that the net tons hauled by Rhodesia Railways increased by 29.5 percent between 1968 and 1975; this increase was insufficient to satisfy the demands made on the system. Not only the railways, but other sectors of the infrastructure such as roads and dams, need replacements and improvements. But the following paradox emerges: the foreign currency needed for capital equipment is generated by exports; but the ability to export is being hampered by railway congestion; and the congestion exists because of the need for replacement and additions of capital equipment. "The railways are holding up the export effort more than are the sanctions."[4]

The sustained growth momentum of the Rhodesian economy during the first decade of sanctions came to an end in 1975. Beginning in 1974, the economy received some powerful exogenous shocks whose effects became apparent in 1975 and 1976. The worldwide economic recession triggered by huge increases in the price of petroleum put a serious strain on Rhodesia's balance of payments. World market demand for primary commodities was depressed as production in the industrialized countries declined. This caused a deterioration in Rhodesia's export prices. Meanwhile, inflation in the industrialized countries caused an increase in the price of Rhodesia's imports. Price manipulation by the Organization of Petroleum Exporting Countries (OPEC) trebled Rhodesia's oil import costs between late 1973 and 1976. As a consequence, the terms of trade moved unfavorably against Rhodesia declining from 85.1 in 1973 to a record low of 74.3 in 1976 (1964 = 100).

This problem was aggravated by the severe railway and port congestion in South Africa (see Chapter 5). During the Portuguese withdrawal from Mozambique, operational efficiency dropped at Beira and Lourenco Marques inducing many Rhodesian and South African businessmen to switch to South African ports. This overloaded most main lines of the South African Railways. When Mozambique closed her border with Rhodesia, all Rhodesian imports and exports had to be moved through South African ports causing protracted delays in the movement of goods and increased shipping and freight costs. This increase in invisible expenditures further eroded the balance of payments. Stringent import controls were required in Rhodesia in order to conserve foreign exchange. But this in turn restricted the raw material imports needed by Rhodesian manufacturers to sustain production. In 1975, for the first time since 1966, the volume of manufacturing production declined. The decline, which continued into 1976, was led by textiles, clothing, furniture, printing, and nonmetallic mineral products. There was no significant rise in unemployment, however, because the increased intensity of the guerrilla war siphoned off excess manpower.

As a result of the increased war effort, the 1976 budget provision had to be increased 40 percent for the Ministry of Defense and 23 percent for the police over the previous year. Valuable foreign exchange had to be diverted from domestic allocations to buy military equipment. In the face of the expanding conflict, tourism, a significant earner of foreign exchange, declined sharply in 1976. In the same year, Rhodesia also experienced the first net migration loss of Europeans in a decade, causing a drain on vitally needed professional and technical manpower and manpower of military age—20 to 40 years of age. The emigration and foreign travel allowances had to be drastically reduced in 1976, to conserve foreign exchange.

Recovery from these adverse economic conditions depends far more on the economic recovery in the industrialized countries which are Rhodesia's main customers and on ending guerrilla warfare than on lifting the sanctions. Any recovery *must* be export-led according to the minster of finance.[5] In such a situation, sanctions are, to quote Prime Minister Smith, "little more than a nuisance."[6] The sanctions helped to create a broadly-based, diversified economic structure quite resilient to short-term shocks or challenges. Moreover, sanctions helped create a psychological atmosphere in which rigid governmental controls on the economy were accepted—however reluctantly—by Rhodesian businessmen. The control machinery was in place to facilitate swift government manipulation of such factors as import quotas, resource allocations, and prices in order to blunt the short-term effects of the world recession on Rhodesia. For example, the rate of inflation, as measured

by the European consumer price index, increased an average of 2.9 percent per year between 1965 and 1973; for 1974 and 1975, the average
annual increase was 7.6 percent. Although the latter figure represents a
sharp escalation, the ten-year, overall, record compares quite favorably
with other countries and is due partly to high productivity and to the
presence of governmental controls.[7]

Manufacturing

Manufacturing has shown remarkable expansion since UDI; by
1975, the Rhodesian index of volume of manufacturing production had
risen 88 percent above the 1965 level. The range of output expanded
from 602 products in 1963, to 1059 in 1966, to 3837 in 1970. However, 65 percent of these products in 1970, were monopoly products
which probably would not be able to survive a return to competitive
conditions. Economist Neal J. Dickinson explains: "too many products
for too small a market commits too many producers to too small a scale.
Small-scale production is costly production, and costly production cannot compete."[8] The implication of this situation for exporting to, for
example, South Africa is that there are few commodities whose production runs are long enough in Rhodesia to bring unit costs down to a
level where goods are competitive in the South African market. Where
this can be achieved (e.g., textiles), the quantities involved are often so
large that affected South African firms charge unfair competition and
ask their government for protection against the Rhodesian goods.
Six of the nine fastest growing industries are infrastructure industries such as chemicals and petroleum, construction and steel production, and these are the kinds of industries which provide the basis of
future industrial expansion. Continuation of this expansion, however, is
endangered by shortages of foreign exchange. To understand this process, it is necessary to understand that the whole strategy in Rhodesia
has been to solve short-term problems for the mere sake of survival.
But with each short-term solution, a long-term problem began to assert
itself. The short-term problem after UDI was how to maintain employment and prevent a recession. The answer was to industrialize and
diversify. The existing surplus capacity in industry and the surplus
capacity created by the drop in manufacturing exports was used. At the
same time, this expansion was directed toward import-substitution which
would offset the loss of export earnings and stabilize the balance of payments. The foreign reserves the government had on hand at UDI were

run down to stimulate the expansion—partly at the expense of replacing capital equipment. By 1969, when the surplus industrial capacity was largely absorbed, and the replacement demand for capital goods started to build, the long-term problem was beginning to appear. The government believed that a process of import-substitution would save foreign exchange, but the process of industrialization actually increases the need for foreign exchange for raw materials and machinery. In many cases, the need is greater than if the finished product had been imported initially. Much of the expansion was concentrated in primary products and their benefication (e.g., iron, tin, nickel, chrome) and in the production of finished goods. In the latter case, the problem was that the intermediate production stage between the primary stage and the finished stage was often lacking, necessitating the importation of some industrial raw materials.

For a while, according to John Robertson, "the retarding effect of Rhodesia's shortage of foreign currency has been counteracted by a vastly improved standard of efficiency that has developed throughout industry, and the more extensive use of locally produced materials."[9] Nevertheless, the long-term problem remained. One partial solution was for the import-substitution manufacturers to start exporting their finished product—but this was inhibited by the "economy-of-scale" discussed earlier. Also, as Gordon Handover, chairman of the Export Advisory Committee of the Association of Rhodesian Industries (ARnI), noted in the *Rhodesia Herald,* May 19, 1972, many manufacturers would rather content themselves with the profitable, and in many cases captive, home market.

The outlook is uncertain. John Graylin, ARnI's executive officer, warned in the *Rhodesia Herald,* August 12, 1971, that industrial expansion and development were being slowed down—and might actually decrease—because of insufficient foreign currency needed to buy raw materials and new machinery. As noted above, the 1975 index of volume of manufacturing production declined for the first time since UDI. Provided the balance of payments constraints are not too severe, however, manufacturing growth is likely to resume. It is also likely that the standard of living of the European community can be maintained and preserved for some time, but at the expense of long-term balanced growth which is needed in light of the African population increase. What is certain is, like South Africa, Rhodesia will continue to rely upon the export of the primary products of mining and agriculture for the major part of her foreign currency earnings.

Mining

Between 1964 and 1972, the value of Rhodesia's mineral production doubled, reaching R$107.4 million; four years later, in 1976, it again doubled to R$230.5 million.[10] Rhodesia has vast mineral potential to exploit. A geological formation known as the Great Dyke, 500 kilometers long and six kilometers wide, contains unbelievable mineral wealth; ore reserves of the platinum group metals are on the order of 4,000 million tons, and three-quarters of the world's known reserves of high-grade chromite ore is located there. There are vast reserves of asbestos, copper, limestone, and nickel waiting to be developed. Most of the major South African mining companies are actively prospecting in Rhodesia—including Messina, Anglo-American, Johannesburg Consolidated Investments (JCI), Gold Fields of South Africa, and South African Manganese—and Rhodesian Minister of Mines Ian Dillon estimated in the *Rhodesia Herald,* February 7, 1976, that overseas companies spent up to R$5,000,000 a year prospecting for minerals in Rhodesia.

In terms of current production, the figures for the various minerals are top secret. Estimates published by the U.S. Bureau of Mines, however, indicate that in 1974, Rhodesia ranked among the top nine world producers of lithium, corundum, chromite, gold, asbestos, and nickel. She also produces forty-five other minerals including beryllium, coal, copper, iron ore, magnesite, silver, tungsten, tin, and antimony.[11]

In 1965, Rhodesia imported about 18.5 short tons of nickel and nickel alloys; six years later, she was estimated to be the world's ninth leading producer of nickel—producing about 13,000 short tons.[12] Indeed, it has been in the minerals sector that some of the largest private expansion and investments have occurred since UDI.

On the whole, disposal of mineral exports seems to have created fewer difficulties than with tobacco and other agricultural produce. There are several reasons for this situation. First, many of the minerals found in Rhodesia are of exceptionally high quality; the metallurgical grade chromite has a chrome oxide content in excess of 48 percent, the asbestos has unusually long fibers, and the lithium ore has a low iron content. Second, it is evident that Rhodesia sells her minerals at a very attractive price—well below the world market prices. The advantages of a removal of sanctions would not be in terms of volume that could be exported but in the price realizations that could be achieved. Third, Rhodesia strives to maintain marketing standards which involve a high degree of integrity and efficiency; this means maintaining regular deliveries and assuring continuity of supplies, being honest and protecting the anonymity of the buyers.

The quality of some of Rhodesia's minerals is mentioned as an export advantage; ironically, it could also be a disadvantage in that the distinctive quality aids in the identification of origin once the mineral reaches the world market. It was also mentioned that the railways are under strain, and there is a question as to whether they can carry the growing output of the mines. Both of these problems can be eased through benefication—the upgrading of an ore mineral by the removal of unusable impurities. Once chrome ore is turned into ferrochrome, it is difficult to determine origin. In addition to the considerable value added through benefication, the tonnage shipped is much less and is rated higher than if the unrefined ore was shipped.

Agriculture

Like manufacturing and mining, agriculture has also experienced expansion since UDI with the sales of principal crops and livestock in 1975 totaling 145.9 percent higher than in 1965 (see Table 4.1) According to Mike Butler, president of the Rhodesia National Farmers' Union, quoted in the *Rhodesia Herald,* February 16, 1973, agriculture provides about a third of the country's foreign exchange earnings. Another achievement is that through diversification and increased productivity, Rhodesia today is virtually self-sufficient in foodstuffs. Aside from fish and wheat, most imports have been largely substituted; Rhodesian food processors now make such formerly imported items as condensed and powdered milk, cheese, breakfast cereals, instant coffee, biscuits, jams, and canned fruits.

But agriculture does not only involve foodstuff; the mainstay of Rhodesian agriculture and Rhodesian exports before UDI was tobacco. In 1965, Rhodesia was the world's second leading exporter of flue-cured tobacco (the U.S. was first), earning R$93,936,298 in foreign exchange. This figure represents one-third of all domestic export by value in 1965. Although the tobacco was exported to over sixty-four countries, the United Kingdom bought the largest amount—45.6 percent. Thus the sale of one product (tobacco) to one country (the United Kingdom) accounted for 15 percent of Rhodesia's total domestic exports in 1965. Because of this concentration and because the origin of Rhodesian tobacco is easily identifiable on world markets, it was difficult to evade the sanctions. The 1965 crop was 250 million pounds; by 1968, the crop had been reduced to 132 million pounds and the number of growers reduced from 2,800 to 1,700. The Rhodesian government created the Tobacco Corporation to buy the crop at a guaranteed minimum price and then to make export sales where it could and stockpile the rest.

Rhodesian flue-cured tobacco is universally regarded as the best quality in the world; the pesticide contamination levels in the leaf are the lowest worldwide; and, by world standards, production costs in Rhodesia are low. U.S. Secretary of Agriculture Earl Butz, was quoted by the *Rhodesia Herald,* May 24, 1975, as saying that Rhodesian flue-cured tobacco was as good as the American tobacco and could be produced for 25 to 30 U.S. cents a pound less. Butz estimated Rhodesia could take over 40 percent of the U.S. tobacco export market in a free trading situation. In addition, according to Rhodesian Minister of Agriculture David Smith, "Our integrity in fulfilling every contract and obligation that we enter into in trading is respected throughout the world."[13] In light of these facts, it is not surprising that the journal, *World Tobacco,* estimated in 1972, that Rhodesia still accounted for 10 percent of the world's trade in flue-cured tobacco (the pre-UDI figure was 27 percent). This meant that about one-third of the crop still reached export markets.[14]

The key to the recovery of agriculture in general from the tobacco losses was the ability to diversify and especially to convert tobacco growing areas to the production of maize and cotton—two crops with good export potential. In 1972 maize production totaled 18 million bags valued at R$26,250,000 with an average yield of 62 bags per hectare; the comparable figures for 1965 were: 5.2 million bags valued at less than R$10 million with an average of 30 bags per hectare.[15]

The greatest success story in agriculture, however, has been cotton. William Margolis, chairman of the Agricultural Marketing Authority, stated in the *Rhodesia Herald,* November 2, 1972, that the role played by Rhodesia's cotton industry was the greatest single factor enabling the economy to withstand the effects of sanctions; land and laborers used for tobacco were diverted to cotton. Between 1965 and 1972, the production of cotton expanded by 800 percent to over 200 million pounds, 80 to 90 percent of which was exported. Yields per hectare increased four-and-one-half times and were believed to be second only to those in Israel among the cotton-producing countries of the world.[16] Moreover, the cotton grown is among the best grades of hand-picked cotton available on world markets. Also, unlike tobacco, whose distinctive low nicotine, high sugar content renders it susceptible to easy chemical identification as being of Rhodesian origin, there is no chemical test available to identify the origins of cotton in the world market. The farmers sell their crop to the state-operated Cotton Marketing Board, which, for security reasons, has only one international broker with which it places its export allotment. The broker, in turn, arranges the sale of the lint to various spinners around the world, who are concerned with the quality and type of cotton, not with its place of origin.[17]

An important by-product of the cotton expansion has been the growth of the domestic textile industry. The textile output doubled between 1965 and 1971. The growth of textiles, combined with the expansion of the beef industry and the associated leather industry, means that Rhodesia is virtually self-sufficient in the essential day-to-day items of clothing and footwear—and now exports about one-half the production.[18]

Another example of achieving self-sufficiency in a formerly imported item is wheat. In 1965, Rhodesia imported wheat valued at R$3,829,610; 68 percent of it from Australia. After UDI, Australia continued to sell wheat to Rhodesia in substantial quantities on "humanitarian grounds" until 1972. The need for Australian wheat diminished as Rhodesia greatly expanded her production from 50,100 bags in 1965 (1.5 percent of domestic requirements) to 900,000 bags in 1971 (75 percent of domestic requirements). By 1975, Rhodesia produced 95 percent of its own wheat requirements.[19]

In the cases of products such as tea, coffee, beef, and fruits the trends are similar to those reported for maize, wheat, and cotton; namely: expansion of output, greater productivity, and world-wide reputation for quality.

While the agricultural sector has shown remarkable resilience and adaptability, this does not imply an absence of strain. It takes capital and time to adjust and diversify, and export commodity price realizations are often very low. Agricultural indebtedness rose by 98 percent between 1965 and 1972, and only about one in seven European Rhodesian farmers earned enough to pay income tax.[20] Most important, however, is that agriculture is at the mercy of the weather. The severe drought of 1968 brought Rhodesia closer to the breaking-point than at any time since the early days of UDI. The 1972 drought reduced the maize crop by 50 to 60 percent. The government has thus given high priority to such infrastructure developments as irrigation projects and dams and also has compensation schemes and other forms of financial assistance to help maintain farmers' incomes.

Another problem developed in 1975, when transport disruptions severely affected marketing arrangements for maize and citrus. Upon being advised that railway facilities could not be assured to market their 1976 crop, Hippo Valley Estates had to destroy 16,000 tons of citrus originally destined for export markets. Concern was also expressed by the *Rhodesia Herald,* July 29, 1976, that there might not be sufficient combines available to harvest the entire 1976 wheat crop. Clearly, capital equipment replacement and an increase in the quantity of harvesting machines to match the increase in acreage under cultivation are essential if Rhodesia is to take full advantage of its agricultural potential.

Assessment

A few final general observations are in order. After a decade of sanctions, Prime Minister Smith noted to the *Rhodesia Herald,* November 12, 1975, that Rhodesia had maintained its position as one of the most prosperous countries in Africa. He said the results Rhodesia had achieved in the face of those sanctions had been little short of miraculous. Nothing presented above suggests these sentiments lack merit, but clearly it is an economy under strain—due somewhat to natural conditions found in any relatively under-developed country which is experiencing rapid industrialization and diversification. Much of the strain is largely outside Rhodesia's control—for example, droughts, oil price increases, and decreases in world prices of primary commodities.

Sanctions create strains of their own as well as reduce the ability of Rhodesia to cope with the natural strains. The direct strains from sanctions have been reflected in the unfavorable terms of trade and the inability to secure large-scale external capital. But these strains have yet to cause *sustained* economic stagnation or recession, and this is necessary if the sanctions are to induce compliance with the wishes of the sanctioners.

In crude terms, the economy was like an automobile stuck in low gear, slowly moving forward at full engine acceleration. The economy during the first decade of sanctions moved forward (i.e., expanded) and had the general confidence of the European community in Rhodesia. The fuel to drive the engine consisted partly of import-substitution, use of excess industrial capacity, and increased productivity. By 1975, the first two elements were just about exhausted, and there were limits as to what the latter element could continue to achieve. New fuel had to consist of exporting secondary products (e.g., consumer goods), increasing mineral exploitation, and producing capital goods—all of which increase the need for foreign capital.

The capacity to export expanded greatly; manufacturing, mining, and agriculture provided a greater volume and diversity of exportable goods after UDI—yet seven years after UDI, actual exports by value had risen to only 6.2 percent over the 1965 figure. This suggests the enormous cost sanctions have imposed. Lifting the sanctions would shift the economy into high gear, for it would remove the penalties Rhodesia had to pay in order to import and export; forward movement could begin to match engine acceleration. The power of the engine would not be drained by all the unnecessary intermediaries, the circuitous trade routes, and the use of marginal markets.

Given the fact that the problem of rail and port congestion in South Africa is solvable and the world economic recession of the mid-1970s is temporary, Rhodesia ought to be able to continue in a pattern of modest economic growth—sanctions notwithstanding. Economic recovery, however, will generate demands for skilled technical and professional manpower which might not be available due to the manpower requirements of the war effort and the net European migration losses, which are likely to continue if the security situation does not improve from that which existed in the period 1974–77. The interaction effect of manpower shortages and economic sanctions will most likely constrict economic growth in the short-run. In any event, the continued lack of substantial infrastructure development and the lack of capital equipment replacement combined with the African population explosion produce a rather gloomy estimate of economic progress in the 1980s.

INTERNATIONAL FINANCE

Financial Sanctions

Among the first sanctions to be placed on Rhodesia by the United Kingdom were the freezing of the assets of the Reserve Bank of Rhodesia in London, the blocking and freezing of payments to Rhodesia of dividends, profits and interests, removal of Rhodesia from the sterling area, and exclusion from the London capital market. At the same time, in December 1965, the United States and Switzerland froze the assets of the Reserve Bank of Rhodesia on deposit in their countries. The UN Security Council Resolution 253 (1968), in effect, prohibits the transfer of all funds to Rhodesia except for humanitarian, medical, or educational purposes or for the provision of news material and, in special humanitarian circumstances, foodstuffs. There is no firm estimate of the quantity of funds frozen, but the greater part of Rhodesia's gold and foreign assets had been removed from London before UDI.[21]

What is certain, however, is that, paradoxically, these financial sanctions helped Rhodesia neutralize the adverse effects of the reduction in trade with the United Kingdom and Zambia in the first few years after UDI. The Rhodesian government replied to each financial sanction placed against it with a similar counter-sanction—outlined in the Legislative Assembly on July 20, 1967: "Firstly, private investment income due to residents of Britain and Zambia was blocked in Rhodesia following similar action by the British and Zambian Government against residents of Rhodesia; since the net flow of these transactions had previously run heavily against Rhodesia, the blocking of these payments both ways had a correspondingly favourable effect on the balance of payments. And secondly, Rhodesia ceased servicing her London market debt, except that part held by residents of Rhodesia, Malawi and South Africa and purchased on or before the 4th December, 1965; and no further payments were made in respect of debts to the British Government and British Government agencies and debt under British guarantee." Thus the Rhodesian government was relieved of making capital repayments and interest payments on an obligation of about £160 million. As noted, this amount included not only loans from the British government, but loans from the Commonwealth Development Corporation, the International Bank for Reconstruction and Development, and Rhodesian government bonds issued in the London capital market.

Since the United Kingdom froze Rhodesian assets in London, the British government had to pay the Rhodesian government's London market debt, according to Wrathall. Additionally, Wrathall stated that Rhodesia would not resume responsibility for this obligation unless and until the British government made adequate reparation for the damage done to the Rhodesian economy by sanctions.[22] Since the United Kingdom acted as guarantor for some of the loans, the British government has paid out nearly R$28 million in compensation payments to the World Bank. The British treasury indicated that it would seek to recover these funds from Rhodesia when constitutional government was restored.[23]

In addition to government liability, these are large amounts due to private sectors outside Rhodesia presently in blocked accounts in Rhodesia. J. L. Morgan, financial writer for the *Rhodesia Herald*, wrote on April 20, 1972: "I would be surprised if through frozen funds we have not enjoyed the equivalent of $25/$35m. [million] of imported capital each year." Funds are blocked to the United Kingdom, the United States, Canada, the East African community, and Zambia, and are an important source of investment funds for Rhodesia. Residents of other countries such as West Germany, Switzerland, and South Africa, may remove such funds as dividends and profits from Rhodesia.

Table 4.2 reveals that Rhodesia has had a net outflow of investment income (public and private sectors) in each year since UDI. The amount of income paid abroad, however, declined sharply after UDI and did not recover to pre-UDI levels until 1971. On balance, compared to 1965, the net savings in foreign exchange was R$6.8 million in 1966; R$12.7 million in 1967; and R$11.2 million in 1968. This decrease in net income paid abroad helped to cushion the effect of large decreases in exports relative to imports in the years immediately after UDI (see Table 4.3).

Table 4.2
Selected Rhodesian Foreign Financial Transactions
(R$m.)

| | Non-Residents Investment Income | | Net Income Paid Abroad | Net Capital Inflow |
	Received	Paid		
1965	19.5	—45.6	—26.1	4.0
1966	7.8	—27.1	—19.3	—4.6
1967	12.8	—26.2	—13.4	23.7
1968	14.1	—29.0	—14.9	39.5
1969	13.1	—31.0	—17.9	9.9
1970	14.9	—36.0	—21.1	26.3
1971	14.7	—45.1	—30.4	30.5
1972	14.3	—49.4	—35.1	—2.3
1973	16.3	—54.8	—38.5	51.6
1974	18.2	—70.9	—52.7	62.6
1975	NA	NA	—42.6	101.3

Source: Rhodesia, Central Statistical Office, *National Accounts and Balance of Payments* 1974; and Rhodesia, Central Statistical Office, *Monthly Digest of Statistics*, July 1976.

Notes: Investment income includes dividends, profits, and interest. Net capital inflow includes net borrowing from abroad.

External Capital Loans

While the financial sanctions may have provided short term benefits for Rhodesia, as the years passed and the need for large-scale development capital grew, the sanctions effectively denied access to such funds. The effect of this lack of access was commented on by Sir Keith Acutt, chairman of Rhodesian Acceptances Limited in the *Rhodesia Herald,*

April 5, 1973: "Unless access to external sources of capital is eased soon, the rate of development necessary to sustain the population cannot be achieved." Projects important for Rhodesia's development, such as the expansion of Rhodesia Railways, exploitation of the mineral deposits in the Great Dyke, and the building of a thermal power station at Wankie, would require a huge capital inflow. After the Douglas-Home–Smith Agreement in November 1971, international bankers visited Salisbury to consider plans to lend substantial amounts to Rhodesia. According to those bankers, a post-UDI Rhodesia would need a minimum of 500 million rand in short, medium, and long-term loans.[24]

On a bilateral government level, there is absolutely no firm evidence that Rhodesia has been able to secure capital loans from external sources. Because of the amounts needed, it would be most difficult for any country to avoid publicity if it did make such a loan. The most likely source for any loan would be South Africa; but South Africa is not essentially a capital-exporting country and has to regularly secure large loans on the world money markets to finance her own development. The loans that South Africa did make to Rhodesia in 1964 and 1965, were small in relation to Rhodesia's needs. J. E. Spence claims that since UDI, the South African Central Bank made several loans of foreign currency to Rhodesia, but he cites no source for this information.[25] R. B. Sutcliffe makes the same claim and adds that the Central Bank has probably provided seasonal support for Rhodesia's foreign exchange.[26]

Table 4.2 indicates that Rhodesia has experienced large net capital inflows in all but two of the years after UDI (1966 and 1972). Between 1965 and 1975, the imported capital totaled R$342.5 million—two-thirds of which was imported in the period 1973–75. The amount of the net capital inflow for these latter years (R$215.5 million) is almost equal to the heavy balance of payments deficits (total: R$219.2 million) Rhodesia incurred on invisible services—mainly external freight and insurance charges on imports and exports. The source of this capital inflow is unknown, but it could represent short-term borrowing on private international money markets (for example, see RISCO case described below).

Foreign Transnational Investment

The last reliable public survey of foreign transnational investment in Rhodesia was a government survey carried out in 1963. Of the 420 firms in the survey sample, 147 were subject to external control, either as branches, subsidiaries, or majority shareholders, and their gross profits accounted for 69 percent of the sample total. Nearly half the foreign-controlled companies were controlled from South Africa—but the profits of the South African controlled firms were only 31 percent of the total, indicating that the largest firms were subject to control from outside Southern Africa. The survey also notes that "even where the immediate control is vested in South Africa, the ultimate control is still often exercised from Britain, and it has been mainly from British industry that investment capital, entrepreneurial initiative and technical expertise have been derived, either directly or indirectly."[27] The survey noted, however, that very few firms appeared to have relied entirely on foreign sources of finance.

Four giant corporations with interlocking holdings and director-ships form the nucleus of transnational investment in Rhodesia: Anglo-American Corporation, DeBeers Consolidated Mines, Charter Consolidated, and Rand Selection Corporation. In referring to this group, Giovanni Arrighi makes the point that "it is probably right to assume that the group depend neither on British nor South African capitalism but is rather an 'independent super-state,' an economic empire centered in Southern and Central Africa."[28] The major interests of this group in Rhodesia include:

1. *Mining:* including coal, iron, nickel, and copper.
2. *Heavy industry:* including smelting and refining (copper, nickel, iron, and steel) and alloys (ferrochrome).
3. *Light industry:* including timber, mills, clay products, and diamond and carbide products.
4. *Agriculture and forestry:* including forestry, sugar, and citrus fruit.

Another giant conglomerate in Rhodesia, but based in the United Kingdom, is Lonrho—with substantial interests in mining (copper and gold), timber and agriculture, the motor industry, and the Beira-Umtali oil pipeline.

United States direct investments in Rhodesia totaled about US$57 million of which US$50 million consisted of Foote Mineral's subsidiary, Rhodesian Vanadium (chrome mines), and Union Carbide's subsidiaries, Union Carbide Rhomet (ferrochrome) and Rhodesian Chrome Mines.[29] Foote Mineral eventually sold its subsidiary when it went out of the ferrochrome business.

Aside from the substantial investments in the mining sector, South African firms have broad interests in a wide range of economic activities in Rhodesia. The Southern Sun Hotel Corporation has a R$10 million stake in tourist hotels, and, according to the *Rhodesian Financial Gazette,* June 9, 1972, it lent Rhodesian Breweries R$495,000 to assist in procuring foreign exchange. Rhodesian Breweries, itself, is a subsidiary of the South African Breweries. Indeed, of the fifteen leading profit earning companies in 1976, twelve were controlled by external groups.

After sanctions were imposed on Rhodesia, if a parent company was located in a country whose government requested that it compel its Rhodesian subsidiary to halt production or cease operations, the Rhodesian government would "mandate" the local firm, meaning that the existing local management continues to perform operations according to the demands of the government and is held accountable to the government. Because of sanctions, the Rhodesian government was forced to adopt legislation putting many activities of all Rhodesian firms under strict government regulation, such as pricing policies. One law dictates that government permission is needed in order to go out of business; this means that, for purposes of maintaining employment, a firm might well be compelled to continue operations at a loss.

What are the consequences for Rhodesian firms to be associated with external companies? One advantage is the capital inflow for investment in the Rhodesian firm from the parent company. One should not, however, overestimate the amount of this capital inflow. Edwin S. Munger claims that the capital raised for development of the Trojan, Madizwa, and Empress mines was generated internally either through the use of blocked funds or issuing stock.[30] J. L. Morgan wrote in the *Rhodesia Herald,* October 5, 1972, of "the method by which powerful external groups develop and expand local subsidiaries by the minimum introduction of imported capital and by the extensive use of locally raised loan capital."

It should be noted that the capital outflow to parent companies in the form of dividends and profits from their investment may be greater than the capital inflow. Indeed, in order to decrease this outflow Minister of Finance John Wrathall declared that as of April 1, 1973, he intended to levy a non-resident shareholders' tax and a tax on the profits of subsidiaries or branches of foreign companies operating in Rhodesia at the rate of 15 percent in order to ease the strain on foreign reserves.[31] Interestingly, in 1972, for the first time since UDI, Rhodesia permitted the repatriation of proceeds from the *sales* of Rhodesia investments by most foreign investors—but such repatriation had to be spread over a six year period. The law which formerly prohibited the export of capital derived from sales insured that mandated properties would not be simply sold by the external parent company.

Another advantage of association with external firms is that often the parent firm can provide technical information and licensing for local production. South African mining companies provide the technical expertise for prospecting and developing mineral sites and at least two firms, Anglo-American and South African Manganese, maintain sophisticated geological laboratories in Salisbury. The director of Liebigs Rhodesia, Ltd. publicly admitted to the *Rhodesia Herald,* February 1, 1973, that he received advice and policy instruction from the Liebig-Brooke Bond Group based in the United Kingdom. Among the many examples of licensing arrangements is German Puma footwear. It is manufactured under license and is of such high quality that the parent firm in West Germany wanted to export from Rhodesia.[32] *The Journal of Commerce* (New York) noted on June 19, 1972, that, while the Rhodesian firm may be officially cut off from its parent, "unofficially, contacts are kept up through South African subsidiaries or via 'chance meetings' in Lisbon hotels and elsewhere, so this has been of some trading help."

Other areas of possible advantage are help with the arrangement and marketing of exports and the supply of needed equipment. For reasons of security, there is little information in these areas but much speculation. An article in the *Rhodesia Herald,* May 24, 1973, noted that Standard Telephones purchased 75 percent of its imported requirements from non-ITT sources; therefore, by deduction, its parent company must supply it with 25 percent of its imported requirements. Confidential market reports prepared by a stock brokerage firm in Salisbury in 1975, cite the following advantages derived by some Rhodesian firms from their external parent company: Plate Glass Industries Rhodesia (parent: Plate Glass and Shatterprufe Industries of South Africa): Its efforts in export operations are materially assisted by the associated companies outside Rhodesia; Rhodesian Breweries (parent: South African Breweries): Extensive back-up is provided in areas of management, marketing, and technical expertise; Carousel Limited (parent: Edgar Stores, South Africa): Through strong ties with the South African parent, Carousel has access to know-how on the latest fashion trends and fabric usage. Despite examples, no overall conclusions can be reached as to the extent of the advantages in these areas due to a lack of reliable and systematic information.

At times, worries are expressed in Rhodesia to the effect that South African firms might be gaining too much control in Rhodesia. The chairman of Rio Tinto (Rhodesia), in calling for more local participation in the ownership of foreign-based mining companies, asked for "more tangible proof of the loyalty" of these companies to Rhodesia.[33] The managing director of A. F. Philip and Company was more explicit, stating in the *Rhodesian Financial Gazette,* May 26, 1972, that "at this stage I think to allow the South Africans to move into this country in the way they are doing and rapidly taking complete control of Rhodesian business is very unhealthy." One reason for this position was his concern that South African interests might be able to eventually exert a strong influence on Rhodesian politics.

Another area of concern is that South African controlled insurance groups manage a large proportion of Rhodesia's money resources which were generated within the country from, for example, insurance premiums. Of the 74 direct insurers and professional reinsurers operating in Rhodesia in 1974, 29 had their head offices in South Africa, 25 in Britain, 8 in other foreign countries, and only 12 in Rhodesia, according to the *Rhodesia Herald,* December 16, 1976. On the whole, however, more foreign transnational investment is sought—and since visible promotion campaigns outside southern Africa are precluded by sanctions— South Africa remains the major target for these campaigns.

One of the largest schemes to attract foreign transnational investment since UDI was revealed in 1974, by an officer of a Rhodesian merchant bank who sent documents to England where they were published by the *Sunday Times* (London). The documents revealed that plans had been drawn up in 1972, for external financing of a scheme to expand production by the Rhodesian Iron and Steel Company (RISCO) from 410,000 tons to about one million tons per year. The scheme was estimated to cost R$63.5 million, of which R$42.5 million was to be derived from external sources. Repayments, which were evidently to be derived from the proceeds of steel exports, were to be made between 1975 and 1980. Representatives from thirteen organizations (finance companies, banks, steel manufacturers) located in West Germany, Bermuda, South Africa, Austria, Switzerland, and Rhodesia met in Paris in August 1972 to make the arrangements. In brief, European-American Finance (EAF), a banking consortium with headquarters in Bermuda, was to lend money to a Swiss trading company, HGZ, which would then transfer the money to another Swiss firm, Femetco. Furthermore, to satisfy Swiss authorities, a South African company was interposed to borrow the funds from Femetco and lend them on to RISCO. HGZ would buy the steel from RISCO and resell it to two West German steel manufacturers, taking a commission in the process. The West German firms would guarantee the loan. An Austrian company, VOEST, would build the new plant for RISCO and an Austrian bank, Girozentrale, would provide an additional loan. A political risk clause was inserted into the agreements which stipulated that, should difficulties arise, RISCO could be made to repay the loan immediately. According to on-site inspection, the new RISCO construction was well under way in 1973. When the RISCO project was exposed, RISCO might have had to repay the loans, while not being able to export the extra steel which was to generate the funds for repayment. Rhodesia's minister of finance noted in his 1976 budget message delivered to the House of Assembly on July 15, 1976, that RISCO's replacement, modernization, and expansion program was completed. According to the minister, this completion coincided with the recession and a downturn in steel prices and, as a consequence, the company was experiencing "cash flow problems." As a result, it was necessary that the government guarantee "certain existing and future financial facilities" for RISCO and to provide the company with a R$5 million loan.

Preliminary reports from the Austrian government indicate that it did not find any legal relations between VOEST and Girozentrale, on one hand, and Rhodesian firms, on the other hand. The West German government noted their firms concluded sales contracts with Femetco on steel of South African origin and cited a report by the Institute of Geological Sciences in London that it was not possible to ascertain the country of origin of steel by means of chemical analysis. The Swiss government stated that it had no information that a Swiss company was involved in transferring capital to RISCO. Interestingly, in the course of the investigation, it was revealed that RISCO was a member of the International Pig Iron Secretariat, a commercial organization of users and producers.[34]

Finally, to be complete, notice must be taken of the fact that sanctions have hurt some Rhodesian foreign investment, especially in Zambia. For example, African Distillers, Art Printers, Kingston's, Premier Portland Cement, and Rothman of Pall Mall all sustained losses on their Zambian interests or subsidiaries. Rhodesia Cement controlled subsidiaries in Malawi and Botswana. Generally, Rhodesian interests in Malawi have not been affected since there is no blocking of transfers of funds between the two countries. Johnson & Fletcher had to write off its R$600,000 investment in Mozambique when transfers of funds between Rhodesia and Mozambique were blocked in March 1976. This was Rhodesia's only significant foreign investment in Mozambique.

No Currency Involved Deals (NCI)

Some attention must be paid to a special kind of foreign investment in Rhodesia for it helps explain Rhodesia's problem with her balance of payments. There are two types of NCI deals. The first type involves the importation of goods without any foreign currency leaving the country. Rhodesian businessmen learn of foreign currency about to be brought into the country (e.g., by an immigrant). They buy that currency from the immigrant while it is still in a foreign bank and pay a premium for it; payment is made in Rhodesian currency. The immigrant thus sells his currency before reaching Rhodesia, where he will only be able to sell it at the official exchange rate and earn no premium. The businessmen then use the currency to import goods—usually luxury consumer goods which have difficulty in qualifying for foreign currency allotments from the government. "Reported premiums of 25%–40% on foreign held currency indicate how great the demand for such luxuries (and currency) was. Inevitably, transactions so profitable for middlemen created tremendous potential for abuse and fraud."[35] This was the case despite regulation of the NCI deals by the Reserve Bank. The Bank first accepted the NCI concept because it recognized the "morale-boosting effect" of having adequate supplies of imported goods available. Once the luxury goods reached Rhodesia, the businessmen offered them for sale at prices up to three times their selling price in their country of origin. Governor of the Reserve Bank Noel Bruce told the *Rhodesian Financial Gazette,* May 14, 1971, that these transactions "were starting to have an effect on the rating of the currency since quite clearly if an item sells for, say, the equivalent of $10. in the country of manufacture appears on our shelves at $30., outside observers, including foreign bankers are justified in arriving at the conclusion that we are suffering from a massive inflation, that our currency is losing its internal purchasing power and, consequently, that its parity value is unrealistic." Therefore, in 1971, the Reserve Bank began to exercise greater scrutiny over the first type of NCI deals by requiring applicants for NCI permits in Rhodesia to clearly prove that the financial transaction being considered did not violate the exchange control laws. The first type of NCI deals accounted for 2 percent of total imports in 1969 and 1970, according to the *Rhodesia Herald,* October 8, 1971.

The second type of NCI deal involves the importation of plant and equipment by Rhodesians from South Africa industrialists in exchange for equity interests. In many cases, the South African would take obsolete equipment, written down to "nil" asset via depreciation, and donate it to a Rhodesian firm or in order to start a new project in Rhodesia in return for an interest in that firm or project. The South African would determine the capital value of the equipment and inflate it to an excessive amount from "nil." This type of NCI deal is a short-term solution for the Rhodesian businessman who might have difficulty in obtaining a foreign currency allotment from government. It was difficult to get an allotment to start a new business, since the first priority of government after UDI was to use its foreign reserves to maintain existing production. But this process creates a long-term liability because the Rhodesian businessman is industrializing via the use of obsolete equipment which might have to be replaced in only a few years. At that time, in addition to the problem of reequipment, there was the problem of having to continue to pay the South African foreign currency for the original equipment. Because the value of goods imported on NCI permits had often been exorbitantly inflated before being brought into Rhodesia, the Reserve Bank, for the most part, stopped these types of NCI deals in October 1975.

The inflow of foreign currency is decreased by the first type of NCI deal; outflow of foreign currency is decreased—but only temporarily—by the second type of NCI deal. The NCI process also illustrates the vulnerability of Rhodesia to exploitation by profiteering and black market operations.

Foreign Exchange Position

The shortage of foreign exchange started to reach critical proportions in 1970, in the sense that the rate of development was beginning to be affected. Ian Smith warned that "in trying to keep up with the rate of growth we have in Rhodesia outstripped the foreign exchange that is available to us. Something has to be done to reduce this fantastic tempo of development. Our foreign exchange just cannot keep pace with it."[36] The strain on foreign exchange, combined with the need to expand and develop the infrastructure, led to restraints on foreign currency allocations to the private sector. If the allocations did not increase, in real terms, they decreased due to inflation in countries from which Rhodesia imported.

These restraints on foreign currency allocations plus the restrictions on NCI deals led to increasing shortages of imported goods; scotch whiskey, wine, facial tissues, photographic equipment, and automobiles were the first items to be mentioned in the press as being in very short supply. In addition, in certain instances, it has been necessary to divert

locally produced goods from the internal market to the external market
in order to preserve the derived inflow of foreign exchange and to maintain export contract integrity. For example, between June and November
1971, rationing of butter was imposed because of shortages due partly
to the need to meet export commitments. Such shortages give rise to
strong inflationary pressures.

Another complication arises from the fact that with virtually no
reserves, and quota periods of only six months, it is difficult for the
businessman to plan ahead since he is uncertain what future foreign
currency allotments are going to be, and he has to have the allocation
before the import license is issued—he cannot order imports on credit.
When the businessman can place his overseas import orders far in advance and present the South African agent with documents that the
agent can show at the port of entry, then the imported goods can pass
through South Africa "in transit" subject only to Rhodesian import
duties and sales tax. But when a shortage develops suddenly, the ten-
dency is to order goods "ex-South African stock," which means that the
goods have been subject to South African import duties and sales tax,
and must now be subject to Rhodesian import duties and sales tax. In
addition, the supplier takes a healthy commission for handling the
transaction knowing his buyer is so dependent on his services. This
process also adds to inflationary pressures.[37]

The shortage of foreign exchange has stimulated a black market in
Rhodesia of unknown dimensions. Periodically, Rhodesian citizens are
prosecuted for illegally buying foreign currency. Methods of circum-
venting the ban on private foreign exchange transactions include con-
tacting visitors and offering to buy their foreign currency at a premium
or paying the visitor's bills while he is in Rhodesia with the visitor either
reciprocating when the Rhodesian travels or transferring monies to an
external bank account accessible to the Rhodesian.

Currency smuggling is also a problem. An official of the Reserve
Bank of Rhodesia estimated that R$2.5 million was smuggled to South
Africa in 1974, and the figure for 1975 was estimated to be R$4.0
million. When Rhodesian dollars, exported illegally, were repatriated,
foreign currency of equivalent value had to be released by the Reserve
Bank.[38]

A major weapon used to combat inflationary pressures was the
maintenance of the gold parity of the Rhodesian dollar until September
1975. As the U.S. dollar, sterling, and rand have been either devalued
against gold or sent floating against other currencies, especially during
the world monetary crises of 1971–73, Rhodesia resisted the temptation

to devalue as well; thus her currency appreciated against those currencies, keeping her imports cheap and making her exports more expensive. In June 1971, one Rhodesian dollar exchanged for US$1.40 and rand 1.00; in June 1973, the rates were US$1.77 and rand 1.19. The rand was devalued 12.28 percent in December 1971 and 4.20 percent in June 1972; the U.S. dollar was devalued 8.5 percent in December 1971 and 10.0 percent in February 1973. When South Africa again devalued the rand in terms of the U.S. dollar by 17.9 percent in September 1975, Rhodesia devalued her currency 8 percent against nonrand currencies. This meant that it would only appreciate (or be revalued) by 10 percent against the rand (instead of the full 17.9 percent). One Rhodesian dollar then exchanged for US$1.60 and South African rand 1.34.

The arguments against devaluation revolve around the fact that such a move increases the Rhodesian dollar cost of imports and thus increases the current inflationary pressures. In light of the stringent import controls as well as the sanctions and resulting policies of import substitution and replacement, the Rhodesian demand for the goods still imported is fairly inelastic. Thus devaluation would not be accompanied by a significant reduction in the volume of imports. Devaluation does help a country to stimulate exports by making them less expensive, but Rhodesia's problem is not that her exports are uncompetitive for price reasons.

Also, since Rhodesia's imports from South Africa far exceed her exports, and since South Africa's rate of inflation has been higher than Rhodesia's, Rhodesia has been importing some of this inflation in the form of increasing prices. When the rand was devalued in 1971, Rhodesia was in a position to re-export most of this inflation by taking advantage of the dollar's increased buying power in South Africa. One problem, however, is that South African businessmen take advantage of their "captive" market in Rhodesia by raising their prices on exports to Rhodesia immediately after a rand devaluation. Indeed, after the currency rate adjustments of September 1975, South African exporters to Rhodesia raised their prices by the full extent of their own devaluation against the U.S. dollar, in spite of the devaluation in terms of the Rhodesian dollar being only 10 percent. This provoked bitterness in some Rhodesian financial circles.[39]

Despite the advantage of nondevaluation, there have been problems. Obviously, exporters of manufactured goods to South Africa have been hurt—especially in furniture and textiles. This was a major consideration for not permitting the full 17.9 percent revaluation to stand in September 1975. Rhodesia's tourist trade has been hurt as South

Africans find that their fixed rand travel allowance does not buy as much in Rhodesia as before devaluation; South Africa is the largest single source of tourists for Rhodesia. But the sector of the economy that has been hardest hit by the nondevaluation of the Rhodesian dollar has been mining.

The serious position of the mining sector is due to the fact that, traditionally, copper, tin, and silver are sold in sterling; gold, chrome, and nickel in U.S. dollars; and asbestos in Canadian dollars. Therefore, while contracts written in those currencies bring into Rhodesia the same amount of foreign exchange, the mining companies receive fewer Rhodesian dollars for that foreign exchange thus reducing profits. With the advent of sanctions, long-term contracts were favored. These contracts do not usually have currency fluctuation clauses; the *Rhodesia Herald* commented editorially, March 21, 1973, that with a settlement and the ability to trade openly, Rhodesia might be in a stronger position to demand forward mineral contracts with devaluation clause inserted. Obviously the 8 percent devaluation in 1975, provided some assistance to the mining sector.

One benefit to the mining sector and to Rhodesia's foreign exchange position derived from the world monetary crises has been the substantial rise in the free market price of gold. Gold is one product which Rhodesia was able to sell above the world market price; in 1972, the average price received for gold was US$59.50 per ounce (the world market average was US$58.50).[40] Between 1965 and 1972, Rhodesia's gold production averaged R$13.1 million per year; between 1970 and 1972, France imported Rhodesian gold for industrial purposes valued at US$40 million.[41]

International Payments

Before turning to international trade, it is necessary to discuss the international financial arrangements that make such trade possible. The Africa Bureau (London) reports that "Swiss with South African banks are the main means whereby foreign capital is channelled into Rhodesia. Current Swiss laws permit the banks to export up to SFr. [Swiss francs] 10 million; thereafter a permit is required. Furthermore, money is paid into Swiss accounts on behalf of Rhodesian interests and is subsequently transferred to Rhodesia."[42] A Salisbury company executive told the *Rhodesia Herald,* January 6, 1972, that "Rhodesia could not have survived and circumvented sanctions without Swiss banks, and holding companies in Switzerland, Luxembourg, and Liechtenstein." Moreover, the four Rhodesian commercial banks, Grindlays Bank, The Standard Bank, Rhobank (Rhodesian Banking Corporation), and Barclays Bank International all have world-wide connections and facilities for arranging the international transfer of funds. There are, in addition, many other institutions in Rhodesia which can handle international payments; for example, merchant banks such as Rhodesian Acceptances Limited (a part of the Anglo-American Group).

The following is a list of some of the ways in which payments can be made to Rhodesia for goods and services:

1. Send payment in convertible currency notes by registered mail.

2. Send personal check to a company; it will be processed through company's external bank account in South Africa or Switzerland. If the name of the company is easily recognized as being Rhodesian, complications can be avoided by making the check payable to an individual—usually an officer of the company.

3. American Express traveler's checks are freely accepted in Rhodesia. The checks should be countersigned, as usual, but the place and date of cashing should be left blank.

4. Payments to the Rhodesian government may be made in banker's draft in most Western European currencies (except sterling), in United States dollars or South African rand. South African postal and money orders are acceptable. British postal orders are accepted if left blank.

A Salisbury company executive, writing on banking in Rhodesia, noted in the *Rhodesia Herald*, January 6, 1972: "Pecunia non olet—money has no smell—this old Roman proverb still applies today, probably more so than ever before."

INTERNATIONAL TRADE

Table 4.3 indicates that the largest decrease in Rhodesia's international trade occurred in 1966—the first year after UDI. Despite the escalation of sanctions between 1966 and 1972, the value of Rhodesia's imports and exports showed a steady recovery to the point that imports exceeded their 1965 value in 1971, and exports did the same in 1972. Moreover, there is some evidence that Rhodesia continued to penetrate a wide geographical spread of export markets; the Export Credit Insurance Corporation of Rhodesia (ECIC) insured goods sold to sixty-six different

Table 4.3
Summary of Balance of Payments of Rhodesia
1965–1972
(R$m.)

Year:	1965	1966	1967	1968	1969	1970	1971	1972
Visible Trade:								
Domestic exports	278.4	170.2	169.7	167.5	212.2	247.5	270.8	322.3
Re-exports	30.8	17.0	12.1	8.5	6.8	6.1	6.5	6.2
Gold	13.6	12.7	12.6	11.9	12.9	11.1	11.2	12.9
Imports	−239.6	−169.4	−187.1	−207.0	−199.4	−234.9	−282.4	−274.2
Adjustments	−6.1	−3.5	5.0	−6.9	−4.8	−6.7	−6.9	−8.3
Visible net balance (merchandise)	77.1	27.0	12.3	−26.0	27.7	23.1	−0.8	58.8
Invisibles, net	−50.9	−31.3	−28.9	−24.1	−24.2	−37.1	−55.8	−58.5
Current account balance	26.2	−4.3	−16.7	−50.1	3.6	−14.0	−56.6	0.3
Capital transactions, net	4.0	−4.6	12.1	39.5	9.9	17.7	30.5	0.9
Total transactions (net inflow)	30.2	−8.9	−4.6	−10.5	13.4	3.7	−26.1	1.1

Source: Rhodesia, Central Statistical Office, *Monthly Digest of Statistics*, February 1974.

countries in 1972.[43] In addition, between 1966 and 1971, only thirteen claims, amounting to R$102,439, were paid as a result of political interference by foreign governments.[44] Such interference includes the prevention of successful importation into the buyer's country and the prevention of transfer of payments to Rhodesia. Note that in 1972, only about one-third of Rhodesia's exports were covered by ECIC insurance, therefore actual total losses due to sanctions may be greater than indicated by ECIC figures. These comments are not meant to imply that without sanctions Rhodesia's international trade would not have been in a much better position than it was; what they do suggest, however, is that there was little evidence that sanctions had the kind of constricting effect on Rhodesia's international trade that many of the sanctioners thought would be necessary in order to produce compliance.

For security reasons, the Rhodesian government stopped releasing detailed balance of payments statistics after 1972. The summary figures that were released for the years 1973 to 1976, shown in Table 4.4, reveal

Table   4.4
**Summary of Balance of Payments of Rhodesia
1973–1976**
(R$m.)

	1973*	1974*	1975*	1976
Visible net balance (merchandise)	96.0	68.2	47.6	176.1
Invisibles, net	−113.3	−150.9	−165.6	−158.5
Net Current Account balance	− 17.4	− 82.8	−118.0	17.7
Net Capital transactions	51.6	62.6	101.7	25.7
Total transactions (net inflow)	34.2	− 20.2	− 16.3	43.4

Source: Rhodesia, Ministry of Finance, *Economic Survey of Rhodesia* 1976 (Salisbury: The Government Printer, 1977), p. 10.

* Revised figures.

the visible (merchandise) balance continued to show surpluses but was offset by large net outflows on current account invisibles due to higher freight costs for imports and exports, loss of revenue from transit traffic, higher dividend payments to foreign investors, and a net outflow on the foreign travel account due to a decline in the number of tourists visiting Rhodesia. Figures compiled from the relevant annual reports of the ECIC suggest that exports continued to expand during the period 1973–1976, with a slight decrease occurring in 1975. The value of exports

114   SANCTIONS

covered by ECIC was: 1973, R$136 million; 1974, R$202 million;
1975, R$192 million; 1976, R$233 million. The huge increase in the
visible (merchandise) balance between 1975 and 1976, was due to the
fact that exports increased by 6 percent in volume and by 10 percent in
value while imports fell by 27 percent in volume and by 18 percent in
value. The drop in imports was caused by the drastic reduction in
foreign exchange allocations to Rhodesian commerce and industry
in 1975 and 1976.[45]

Acknowledged Trade

Table 4.5 lists Rhodesia's major trading partners for the two years
prior to UDI. Of these countries, several admitted they continued trading
with Rhodesia after the imposition of the UN sanctions. For essentially
political reasons, the rationale of which was discussed in Chapter 3,
South Africa and Portugal permitted normal trade with Rhodesia, and
Switzerland and Malawi permitted trade with some restrictions.

South Africa

In February 1967, Rhodesia introduced a single column customs
tariff which ended all preferences granted to Commonwealth countries
and henceforth enabled countries to compete in the Rhodesian market
on equal terms—with the exception that the advantages enjoyed by
Rhodesia's southern Africa trading partners were preserved in their
entirety. For South Africa, these advantages are reflected in the bilateral
trade agreement negotiated on December 1, 1964. The introduction of
the new customs tariff, in conjunction with the trade agreement, virtually
entrenched South Africa as the major exporter to Rhodesia. The trade
agreement provides for preferential tariff treatment for trade in both
directions between the two countries. A wide range of South African
goods are accorded either the preferences formerly accorded the Commonwealth or more favorable preferences. At the same time, a wide
range of Rhodesian products are accorded duty-free or preferential entry
into the South African market. In addition, a number of Rhodesian
exports are allowed entry into South Africa under a restrictive quota
system which was designed to maximize the diversity of the Rhodesian
entry while minimizing the disruptive effect on South African industry.
The trade agreement had an initial five-year term and is automatically
extended on a yearly basis unless either government gives twelve months
notice of termination.[46]

Table 4.5
Main Trading Partners of Rhodesia
1964–1965
(R$m.)*

Country	Imports from		Exports to	
	1964	1965	1964	1965
Australia	4.76	5.23	3.17	2.31
Belgium	1.83	4.56	5.15	3.19
Botswana	0.66	0.14	2.10	3.18
Canada	3.13	3.94	2.93	1.64
France	3.31	4.01	1.47	1.58
Germany, West	8.31	9.73	15.82	25.62
Iran	6.46	7.57	0.38	0.10
Italy	4.03	5.06	2.61	4.50
Japan	8.77	13.21	11.12	14.80
Malawi	3.26	2.79	11.04	15.48
Mozambique	2.75	2.74	1.37	1.90
Netherlands	4.80	5.91	4.54	7.45
South Africa	52.73	54.92	17.06	25.59
Sweden	2.16	3.05	1.13	1.26
Switzerland	1.24	1.43	2.76	3.60
United Kingdom	65.61	72.71	60.88	62.30
United States	14.71	16.39	7.93	6.99
Zaire	0.05	0.08	2.98	3.47
Zambia	10.38	8.64	60.47	72.18

	Re-exports to	
	1964	1965
Botswana	1.81	1.47
Malawi	3.22	3.47
South Africa	3.04	3.28
Zambia	18.72	19.65

Source: Rhodesia, Central Statistical Office, *Annual Statement of External Trade* 1965.
* The countries listed accounted for approximately 93 percent of the total international trade of Rhodesia in 1964–65.

Despite the agreement, trade between the two countries has generated a few problems. In 1968, some South African manufacturers complained that their products were being undercut in their domestic markets by cheaper Rhodesian goods. This led to the two governments agreeing to impose ceilings on the export to South Africa of a small range of products not formerly covered by quotas—mainly radios and clothing articles. Theodore Bull points out that the economies of the two countries in the products of light industry are generally competitive rather than complementary, and P. B. Harris mentions that some South African firms have felt the "cold winds of competition" as Rhodesian manufacturers increased their output and sought to sell in South Africa.[47] Worries are periodically expressed in the *Rhodesia Herald* that South African businessmen will succeed in pressuring their government to increase duties or decrease quotas in order to counter the Rhodesian export drive. This is exactly what happened in 1976, when Rhodesian textile manufacturers were forced to agree to a limited quota ceiling as an alternative to increased duty which might have priced the manufacturers out of the South African market altogether. The Rhodesian minister of commerce noted in the *Rhodesia Herald,* February 7, 1976, that competition was keen in the South African market, and in the case of some Rhodesian exports the high protective duties imposed by the South African Government "have hit us hard."

Another problem was generated by the several devaluations of the South African rand. Lionel Disler explains that under the trade agreement, quotas are expressed in rand, thus the devaluation caused an immediate drop in the volume which could be exported to South Africa. In addition, those exported goods would cost more and, since the Rhodesian market in South Africa is an elastic one, a price increase could cause a disproportionate drop in sales.[48] In Rhodesia, South Africa has a largely inelastic, captive market, and evidence abounds that South African businessmen are prepared to take advantage of the situation. For example, as noted above, many South African exporters raised their prices to Rhodesia by the amount of the devaluation thereby denying Rhodesia at least the benefits of buying devalued imports from South Africa.

The volume of the bilateral trade since UDI is, of course, secret. The UN Sanctions Committee estimates are in Table 4.6. South Africa probably accounts for about one-third of Rhodesia's exports and nearly one-half of Rhodesia's imports. These proportions are indicative of the importance of South African bilateral trade to Rhodesia's overall trade picture. Aside from providing an opportunity to earn vital foreign exchange, the availability of the South African market makes feasible longer production runs for some Rhodesian goods; this, in turn, holds down unit costs and reduces prices on the domestic market. South Africa is Rhodesia's main export market for manufactured goods.

From a different perspective, Rhodesia is a relatively minor trading partner of South Africa—accounting for between 2 and 3 percent of all imports and between 7 and 8 percent of all exports. Rhodesia, however, is one of the few markets in which South Africa has a favorable balance of trade.

Table 4.6
Rhodesian Trade with Selected Countries
1965–1975
(US$m.)

	1965	1966	1967	1968	1969	1970	1971	1972	1973	1974	1975
Exports to:											
South African Customs Union	41.0	60.0	80.0	80.0	85.0	95.0	105.0	130.0	200.0	250.0	302.0
Switzerland	5.7	4.2	3.9	3.5	3.6	4.3	4.5	4.6	7.7	7.4	7.3
Malawi	20.8	17.3	14.7	12.6	12.5	18.6	16.1	21.2	21.3	24.1	29.5
Zambia	99.5	64.9	45.1	31.6	30.5	30.5	28.9	29.6	16.2	12.0	nil
West Germany	35.1	30.5	16.0	13.3	1.1	0.6	0.5	0.4	0.5	0.5	0.7
Australia	3.3	0.8	nil	nil	nil	nil	nil	nil	nil	nil	nil
Imports from:											
South African Customs Union	78.0	110.0	135.0	150.0	155.0	180.0	215.0	182.0	220.0	230.0	270.0
Switzerland	1.6	1.9	1.9	2.5	1.5	2.0	2.9	3.2	3.8	4.5	2.8
Malawi	4.4	3.0	2.7	2.9	3.8	5.0	5.3	5.8	7.2	8.4	8.5
Zambia	15.3	7.0	2.9	1.3	0.6	0.5	0.7	0.5	1.5	0.5	0.8
West Germany	10.9	11.2	12.3	12.9	1.2	1.2	1.6	2.0	2.2	2.6	2.5
Australia	4.5	4.1	5.7	5.9	3.5	4.9	4.8	4.1	nil	nil	nil

Source: U.N. Security Council, *Official Records of the Security Council, Thirty-second Year, Special Supplement No. 2* (S/12265), annex VI.

Portugal

Trade between Rhodesia and Portugal and her overseas provinces of Angola and Mozambique was governed by the bilateral trade agreement concluded in March 1965, which provided for "most-favored-nation" treatment to be accorded by each party to the other's products. In addition, the trade agreement established a permanent Joint Trade and Economic Liaison Committee whose task it was to examine matters relating to the implementation of the trade agreement and to the development of trade between the Portuguese area and Rhodesia. The committee held twelve meetings through 1972, alternating between Lisbon, Salisbury, Lourenco Marques, and Luanda. In November 1967, a Rhodesian delegation, headed by the secretary of transportation and power, went to Lisbon to negotiate a separate agreement for the supply of power from Mozambique to the eastern districts of Rhodesia through 1975.

Rhodesia's trade with the Portuguese area immediately before UDI was insignificant. The volume of trade, while expanding after UDI, accounted for only 2.2 percent of Rhodesia's imports and 4.5 percent of her exports by 1967. Figures on trade after 1967 are not available. Yet a report given to the UN Security Council by Mozambique at the time of the border closure in March 1976, revealed that Mozambique annually imported goods worth about US$18 million (excluding maize) from Rhodesia and exported goods worth about US$5 million to Rhodesia. In addition, Mozambique imported 30,000 tons of Rhodesian maize each year. These figures indicate that Rhodesia's export market in Mozambique expanded considerably since UDI (1966–67 annual exports to Mozambique averaged US$5 million).[49] A UN mission estimated Mozambique's losses from the border closure in export earnings at approximately US$3 million per year and the increase in the price of imports at US$10 million. Mozambique, deprived of such essential products as maize and cement which will have to be imported from other countries at increased transport costs, will also have to find alternative markets for the exports normally sent to Rhodesia. The total financial loss resulting from Mozambique's application of sanctions against Rhodesia will be between US$110 and US$135 million per year.[50]

Switzerland

The Swiss government has adopted the policy that, in the interest of maintaining its neutrality, it cannot comply with the mandatory sanctions of the United Nations. Neither does it want Swiss territory to be used by any party in order to circumvent the sanctions. Therefore, trade with Rhodesia in any given year is limited to a quantitative level not exceeding the annual average of such trade for the three years from 1964 to 1966, as determined by the Swiss Federal Council.

The insignificance of Rhodesian-Swiss trade in terms of Rhodesia's total trade is obvious from the statistics of Table 4.6. The Swiss Federal Council in a note to the UN Secretary-General in 1971 pointed out: "During the preceding years, those imports represented only 1 percent of total Rhodesian exports, while Swiss exports amounted to only 0.7 percent of Rhodesian imports. These figures show that as far as the United Nations sanctions policy against Rhodesia is concerned, the traditional trade relations between Switzerland and Rhodesia are of little importance."[51] Although under the present Swiss policy, there is no potential for expanding trade with Rhodesia, in 1976, the UN Sanctions Committee did express concern that the current level of Swiss trade with Rhodesia was far in excess of the average voluntarily undertaken by Switzerland not to be exceeded annually.[52]

Swiss imports from Rhodesia consist primarily of meat and tobacco; Swiss exports to Rhodesia consist mainly of machinery, watches, and pharmaceutical products (the latter item is exempted from UN sanctions).[53]

Malawi

In January 1965, the governments of Rhodesia and Malawi concluded a trade agreement with the intention of promoting trade between the two countries. After UDI, Malawi terminated the trade agreement while according Rhodesian goods, on entry into Malawi, the same treatment as those from South Africa and the Commonwealth. Rhodesia continued to admit all imports of Malawi goods free of import restrictions and custom duties, with the exception of cement and a few items which are liable to excise duty.[54] Malawi, however, was deprived of a net fiscal payment from Rhodesia based on the trade agreement which averaged Malawi kwacha (MK) 805,000 per year.[55] On January 7, 1967, in response to the UN Security Council's Resolution 232 of December 16, 1966, calling for selective economic sanctions against Rhodesia, Malawi prohibited the importation of tobacco, asbestos, hides and skins, leather, chromium ore, copper and pig iron. Malawi informed the UN Secretary-General that, due to special economic problems, she would have to continue to import from Rhodesia meat, meat products, and sugar, but such imports would be restricted to the absolute minimum necessary.[56]

An examination of the trade figures in Table 4.6 illustrates the extent of the bilateral trade between Rhodesia and Malawi. Upon the dissolution of the Federation of Rhodesia and Nyasaland and the cancelling of the trade agreement, Rhodesia's percentage share of the Malawi import and export markets first fell sharply and then stabilized. Nevertheless, between 1965 and 1975, Rhodesia was one of Malawi's leading trade partners behind the United Kingdom and South Africa. In terms of Rhodesia's total trade, Malawi's share was quite small—accounting for about 5 percent of Rhodesia's exports and 1 percent of her imports. Rhodesia did enjoy a trade surplus with Malawi that averaged about US$14 million per year between 1965 and 1975.

Despite sanctions, there did not seem to be much hesitancy in Malawi over trading with Rhodesia. Although, as noted above, Malawi prohibited the imports of certain primary goods such as tobacco, mineral ores, and leather, at the time of the prohibition, Malawi imported virtually none of these goods anyway. Malawi continued, however, to import materials made from these goods; for example, Rhodesia was Malawi's largest supplier of cigarettes, iron bars and rods, and materials made of asbestos and asbestos cement. Delegations of businessmen and trade delegations from Malawi regularly visited Rhodesia and the president of the Salisbury Chamber of Commerce told the *Rhodesia Herald,* September 3, 1971, that Malawi was "an important export market in which I am sure we could expand."

Unfortunately for Rhodesia, ideas of expanding exports to Malawi were stifled by the closure of the Mozambique border in March 1976, which cut all direct rail, road, and air links between Rhodesia and Malawi. As a result, according to the annual financial and economic review for 1976 published by the Reserve Bank of Malawi, Rhodesia's exports to Malawi declined about 65 percent between 1975 and 1976 (estimated R$18.6 to R$6.6 million), and Rhodesia's imports from Malawi declined about 63 percent (estimated R$6.1 to R$2.2 million). Rhodesia had been Malawi's leading export market for rice and second leading market for raw cotton.[57] Rhodesia obtained most of her rice from Malawi, and by July 1976, with rice prices in Salisbury increased, the commodity was being rationed until alternative sources of supply could be found. Goods destined for Malawi have to be routed via South African ports by rail, shipped by sea to either Beira or Nacala in Mozambique, and then transported by rail into Malawi. Such routing is difficult, time-consuming and expensive.

Malawi claimed, in a report submitted to the United Nations in September 1976, that its economy was being eroded by the consequences of the border closure. Malawi estimated that net annual revenue losses of US$1,664,000 would be suffered by Air Malawi and Malawian road transporters; US$294,000 would be lost by the Malawian tourist industry; loss of export earning would total US$2,175,600 per year; and the additional cost of imports would be US$20,342,000 per year (including higher transport costs for South African imports which formerly traversed Rhodesia). Malawi estimated the minimum financial assistance required from the international community to avoid the most damaging consequences of the border closure in 1976, would be early US$25 million.[58]

Malawi's adherence to UN sanctions had been largely *pro forma;* her notes to the UN which cited economic difficulties as the extenuating reasons for the formal trade linkages were incomplete at best and misleading at worst. As noted in Chapter 3, President Banda fashioned a foreign policy doctrine of dialogue with South Africa and Rhodesia and this specifically included trade relations. In future chapters, further evidence of systematic cooperation between Malawi and Rhodesia covering many different areas of mutual interest will be discussed.

A second group of countries whose governments are politically hostile to Rhodesia and who endorse the UN sanctions yet continued to trade with Rhodesia after UDI for essentially economic reasons includes Botswana and Zambia, both of which border Rhodesia. Zaire was also quite dependent on Rhodesia and trade continued after UDI. West German and (discussed in a separate section) American trade with Rhodesia is also largely a consequence of economic dependence— albeit of a more limited scope than the dependence of Botswana and Zambia.

Botswana

Botswana is a landlocked country surrounded by South Africa, South-West Africa, and Rhodesia. Its only rail connection to the outside world is owned and operated by the Rhodesia Railways. In referring to Rhodesia and South Africa, President Seretse Khama commented in a report in the *Rhodesia Herald,* May 22, 1968, that "these two countries are our neighbours and our existence in Botswana is inseparably bound up with theirs."

The extent of trade bewteen Rhodesia and Botswana is unknown;

the imports and exports are included in the statistics for South Africa, as Botswana is part of the South African Customs Union. The Botswana goverment has released details of the 1965 trade with Rhodesia, and it reveals that Rhodesia supplied 23.4 percent of Botswana's total imports, and Botswana shipped 17.1 percent of its exports to or through Rhodesia. Botswana was heavily dependent on Rhodesia for sugar, cigarettes, fertilizer, clothing, beer, and ale.[59] For Rhodesia, this trade was an infinitesimal part of its total imports and exports. In recent years, however, mining has become an important element in the economy of Botswana and with the development of the Selebi-Pikwe project (copper and nickel) and the Orapa project (diamonds), Rhodesia is well-placed to service orders for materials and equipment; thus there may have been an expansion of the bilateral trade since 1965. The Botswanan government acknowledged to the United Nations that it may not be possible to avoid limited contacts with Southern Rhodesia in connection with development projects and notes that "as an integral part of the southern continent whose economy is bound up with that of her neighbours, Botswana would be hard put to it to develop her economy in vacuo."[60]

Botswana has cooperated with the UN sanctions by monitoring the railway to ensure that it is not used to transport petroleum, arms, and ammunition into Rhodesia. As of March 1, 1970, the importation of beer and cigarettes from Rhodesia was prohibited in all areas of Botswana except in the northern Chobe district. These actions support Botswana's political position "that it is utterly opposed to the policy of the illegal régime in Southern Rhodesia and is anxious to take all reasonable steps to contribute to the downfall of the illegal régime."[61]

The Botswanan government does not think it reasonable to cripple or destroy its own economy in order to comply fully with the UN sanctions. Specifically, the government noted:

1. Shifting the source of supply for such items as sugar to South Africa would increase transportation costs, which would, in turn, cause a significant rise in the cost of living and, due to the high level of poverty existing in Botswana, cause hardship.

2. If Botswana applied more severe sanctions, Rhodesia would retaliate by: banning all exports from Rhodesia to Botswana; prohibiting the shipment of commodities from Botswana to or through Rhodesia; preventing the transshipment of petroleum from Lourenco Marques to Botswana; and causing the withdrawal of equipment and staff from the railway.[62]

The government realizes that any Rhodesian retaliation restricting trade would be extremely harmful to Botswana, but any retaliation affecting rail operations inside Botswana could be disastrous.

Zambia

Unlike Botswana, Zambia was a major trading partner and the largest market for Rhodesia prior to UDI—accounting for one-quarter of all Rhodesia's exports and two-thirds of all Rhodesia's re-exports. More important is the fact that Rhodesia's trade with Zambia produced a huge trade surplus in Rhodesia's favor which helped offset Rhodesia's trading deficit with South Africa. In 1965, for example, Rhodesia had a visible net balance of R$83.2 million with Zambia while its *total* visible net balance was R$77.1 million. In 1965, Zambia received 33.7 percent of all her imports from Rhodesia; these included clothing and footwear, motor vehicles, sugar, mineral fuels, electric energy, coal, and coke.

Like Malawi, Zambia had been included with Rhodesia in the Federation of Rhodesia and Nyasaland between 1953 and 1963. One result of this ten-year linkage was that the economies of the three territories became highly interdependent; for example, the federation established common services for air and rail transportation and for the supply of electricity. The trading patterns established during the federation period became rather fixed and, as Hawkins notes, "It was more convenient as well as economic . . . for a wide range of Zambian importers, by force of habit, if nothing else, to continue to buy from Rhodesia unless physically prevented from doing so."[63]

Unlike Malawi, however, the government of Zambia, upon achieving independence under its president, Kenneth Kaunda, adopted a policy of disengagement from the white-controlled countries in southern Africa. This disengagement policy was accelerated after UDI. Zambia's goal was to ultimately sever all economic and trade connections with Rhodesia while giving maximum cooperation in the implementation of UN sanctions resolutions. Table 4.6 reflects the decrease in Rhodesian-Zambian trade since UDI; note the large trade surplus in Rhodesia's favor through 1973, when the border was closed.

The gradual rate of the decline in trade indicates the time it took Zambia to develop alternative sources for those goods which Rhodesia formerly supplied. One example is coal; in 1965, Rhodesia supplied 100 percent of Zambia's coal, vitally needed in the production of copper upon which the entire Zambian economy rested. By 1968, as a result of the development of Zambia's own poorer-grade coal deposits, Rhodesia had to supply only 59 percent of Zambia's coal needs.[64] It was not until 1971 that Zambia could stop the import of Rhodesian coal entirely. Thus Rhodesia's Wankie Colliery had nearly six years in which to make contingency plans, such as finding alternative markets, raising the price of coal, and investigating the feasibility of having a large thermal power plant built near its collieries, to offset the loss of the Zambian market.

The 1971 maize deal with Rhodesia is another example of the difficulties Zambia faced in implementing its disengagement policy. Despite the fact that Rhodesia could, at that time, supply Zambia with maize, Zambia, for political reasons, imported maize from as far afield as Albania, El Salvador, and the United States. Naturally Zambia had to pay far higher transportation costs than if she imported from Rhodesia. Nevertheless, in August 1971, Zambia was forced to turn to Rhodesia for 1.5 million bags of maize at an estimated cost of R$17 million. Serious Zambian shortages as a result of congestion at the port of Beira and on the railways and a slump in the home production of maize prompted President Kaunda to make "the painful decision." It was estimated by the *Sunday Mail,* August 15, 1971, that if Zambia had had to import the 1.5 million bags from the United States, it would have cost an additional R$6 million.

One area in which the two countries are extensively interdependent is in the supply of electricity. The Central African Power Corporation (CAPC) is a statutory corporation jointly owned by Rhodesia and Zambia which generates and transmits most of the electricity used in those countries. The Higher Authority for Power, composed of Rhodesia and Zambian government officials, supervised the operations of the corporation but was suspended after UDI. It was replaced by a committee of four Rhodesians and four Zambians which met alternately in Salisbury and Lusaka. In 1970, about 70 percent of the power generated for the CAPC system came from the Kariba Dam, whose power station is located on the Rhodesian (south) side of the Zambezi River; another 17 percent came from other power stations located in Rhodesia; and about 3 percent was imported from Zaire.[65] It has been a major goal of the Zambian government to achieve self-sufficiency in power and not to have to rely on the generating facilities over which the Rhodesian government has *de facto* control. To this end, it has started work on the Kafue Dam and on the Kariba North Bank Power Station. Ironically, since Rhodesia's demand for electricity has been growing more rapidly than Zambia's, by the time the two Zambian projects are completed, Rhodesia may be dependent on imports of power from Zambian-controlled facilities. It should be noted that most of the revenue derived from sales of electricity by Rhodesia to Zambia, while recorded in Rhodesian export and Zambian import statistics, is actually paid to CAPC which uses it to defray operating costs, to retire debts and pay interest on outstanding loans, and to develop new power facilities.

The Zambian effort at disengagement from Rhodesia reached its zenith in the early part of 1973. Because of alleged terrorist incursions from Zambia, the Rhodesian government closed the border with Zambia on January 9, exempting only personal travel and copper traffic. After supposedly receiving assurances from Zambia that it would do all it could to prevent terrorist incursions, the Rhodesian government re-opened the border on February 4. Zambia's official position was that it had given no assurances and that in any event, the border would remain closed, and no copper shipments would be sent through Rhodesia. President Kaunda said that the future of Zambia was too important to be dependent on the Rhodesian leader and asked, "How do I know Smith will not turn the blockade on again? It would be stupid of us to depend on some abstract assurances."[66] Zambia appealed to the United Nations for help and the Security Council sent a special mission to Zambia to assess the needs of that country in light of the border closing. On March 10, the Security Council appealed to all states to give Zambia immediate assistance.

Despite the fact that the Security Council had made similar appeals in the past, it was not until 1973, that Zambia received substantial help from the member-states of the UN. In 1968, the Zambian government claimed that it had incurred contingency expenses amounting to US$241 million of which US$46 million was repaid by the British government. In July 1976, UN officials estimated that the closing of the border with Rhodesia had cost Zambia about US$450 million.[67] President Kaunda cited the figure of US$500 million and commented that the "International Community, more generous with moral support than material support, gave us a total of about $20m of which $10m came from the People's Republic of China."[68]

Article 50 of the UN Charter provides that states confronted with special economic problems arising from the implementation of Security Council measures such as sanctions shall have the right to consult the Security Council with regard to a solution of those problems. Neither Zambia nor Botswana were censured by the UN for trading with Rhodesia. Yet, despite UN understanding for Zambia's need to maintain some trading links with Rhodesia, and despite Zambia's stated policy of reporting such links to the UN, as required by the UN Sanctions Committee, there is evidence that Zambia had secret dealings with Rhodesia which she was not willing to report. Specifically, the dealings involved transshipments of Rhodesian goods via Malawi and South Africa into Zambia.[69] The extent of such trade is unknown (see Chapter 5).

Finally, it would be a mistake to assume that Zambia's participation in the sanctions program has received universal acceptance in Zambia. The most prominent critic has been Harry Nkumbula who, until the promulgation of a one-party state in December 1972, was the leader of the opposition African National Congress party. Following a position similar to that of President Banda of Malawi, Nkumbula stated: "I'm a Pan Africanist and I probably hate racialism and apartheid more than most, but Kenneth [Kaunda] is cutting off his nose to spite his face. If we can buy food cheaper in South Africa and Rhodesia then we should buy it there. And if we can transport our copper more cheaply through Beira than through Dar es Salaam, then we should do so."[70] In 1976, three Zambian MP's, led by former Minister of Finance Arthur Wina, called for the reopening of the Zambia-Rhodesia border to relieve Zambia's economic problems. Such opposition has not had much impact on the disengagement policy yet illustrates that even in the most militantly anti-Rhodesian African country there is not unanimity among the political elite for participation in the sanctions program.

Zaire

Before UDI, Rhodesia supplied over 87 percent of Zaire's meat and coal requirements. Trade between the two countries continued after UDI and, despite the border closure, Zambia permitted transshipment of Rhodesian goods destined for Zaire over the Zambian railway system. Details of that trade are scarce, but it is known that Rhodesia supplies maize and coal to the Gecamines copper mining complex in the southern Shaba region of Zaire. In March 1976, officials of the railways of Zaire, Zambia, and Rhodesia met in Lusaka and agreed to stabilize the flow of traffic on their lines. Under the agreement, 120 wagons of coal and coke and 80 wagons of maize will be sent from Rhodesia to Zaire each week. Gecamines, in return, exported 200,000 tons of minerals through Zambia and Rhodesia to South African ports, according to the *Star* (Johannesburg), March 20, 1976. Gecamines also bought power from the Central African Power Corporation.

West Germany

Another country which has admitted limited trading with Rhodesia for reasons of economic necessity has been West Germany. The British government in 1969, brought to the attention of the UN Sanctions Committee that the Federal Republic of Germany (West Germany) was importing graphite from Rhodesia in violation of the sanctions. The West German government admitted the violation and stated the following:

> A German graphite mining company, Kropfmuhl, established a graphite mining company in Rhodesia in May 1965 and agreed to buy the total production of the new company. The product mined in Rhodesia is crystalline natural graphite which is obtainable in only a few countries in quantities sufficient for purposes of large-scale industry. Kropfmuhl's research has shown that it is at present not possible, nor will it be possible for the foreseeable future, to obtain the necessary quantities elsewhere. Kropfmuhl cannot mix their own product with any other kinds of graphite because of their different qualities vis-à-vis flake structure, grain size, softness, and ash composition. Since Kropfmuhl is one of the world's largest producers of natural graphite, any embargo on their imports of Rhodesian graphite would not only lead to the closure of the Federal Republic's only graphite mine but would also have world-wide repercussions.[71]

There are several interesting points about this specific case: first, it illustrates the problem of vertical integration where an overseas secondary producer integrates with a Rhodesian primary producer in such a fashion that if the arrangement is broken, the secondary producer is badly hurt financially; second, it illustrates the point that secondary producers may have to become reliant on a Rhodesian primary product because of the unique physical and technical properties of that product. Kropfmuhl was not alone in facing these kinds of problems. The British firm, Turner and Newall, was dependent upon their Rhodesian mines to supply the raw asbestos for their manufacturing plants. Both Foote Mineral and Union Carbide, based in the United States, relied upon supplies of chrome ore from their mines in Rhodesia to make ferrochrome. In the case of Union Carbide, its domestic ferroalloy plants were specifically designed and built to use the high-grade, lumpy Rhodesian ore.

The West German government, while adopting legislative and executive measures to comply with the UN sanctions, did permit trade contracts existing with Rhodesia in February 1967, to continue subject to nonrenewal. There were reports that West German businessmen hurried to negotiate longterm contracts prior to the UN mandatory sanctions.[72]

Australia

A final reason for trading with Rhodesia, different from those already discussed, is offered by Australia. Australia had been exporting an average of 65,000 long tons of wheat each year to Rhodesia since UDI on humanitarian grounds. The Australian government, in a note dated February 19, 1971, to the Secretary-General, declared: "It is the Australian Government's view that the application of sanctions was never intended to deprive the Rhodesian population—of whom the over-whelming majority are black Rhodesians—of basic foodstuffs. Australia supports the application of sanctions against Rhodesia. It has permitted the export of wheat to that country on humanitarian grounds, as pro-vided for in paragraphs 3 (d) of Security Council resolution 253 (1968)."[73] This position was met with some skepticism on the part of several members of the UN Sanctions Committee. They expressed doubts that the wheat exports were of a humanitarian nature since Rhodesia was known to be a net exporter of maize. Also since wheat had been exported in nondrought years, it appeared to those members that it was not a case of humanitarian assistance but one of normal trade relations which would be at variance with the spirit of the Security Council resolution. Other delegations stated that since the resolution did not clearly define what constituted a humanitarian exception, there was room for doubt as to this matter.[74]

The Sanctions Committee did not pass any judgement on the wheat case, leaving it for consideration by the Security Council. In December 1972, however, the Labor party of Gough Whitlam defeated the ruling Liberal party of William McMahon in the Australian general elections. The Labor party had had a long history of anti-Rhodesian sentiment and had frequently criticized the Liberal party for its handling of the issue. Upon taking office, Prime Minister Whitlam acted swiftly to end the wheat exports.

Secret Trade

Rhodesian trade with nine countries has been examined in order to, among other things, discover the kinds of reasons or rationale offered to justify such trade in light of the UN sanctions. That trade, however, along with other minor trade which has been reported to the UN, accounts for only a part of Rhodesia's total trade picture. Unreported and unacknowledged trade increased after UDI to the extent that, by 1972, it represented over one-half of Rhodesia's imports and exports. While it is interesting to investigate reasons for such trade, since the trade is secret, the reasons are not readily discernible. Of course, there is no logical reason why the motives for engaging in secret trade should be radically different from the motives associated with acknowledged trade. Factors such as the opportunity to obtain high quality, low cost Rhodesian products stimulate both types of trade. One difference, however, may be that unacknowledged trade remains unacknowledged partly because the reasons (such as profit considerations) for that trade are perceived as less defensible in light of a country's obligations to uphold the UN Charter and the Security Council resolutions. Moreover, there is the possibility that a portion of the unacknowledged trade cannot be explained because the Rhodesian origin (or destination) of the goods remains unknown to the foreign trader and/or his government. In any event, the emphasis in this section is on how such trade can take place, including a discussion of some techniques of sanction evasion and the difficulties associated with the detection of Rhodesian trade.

Clearly the role of South Africa and Mozambique (until the border closure) is pivotal in the Rhodesian effort to sustain and promote its international trade. Rhodesian products are sent to these two countries and then are reshipped to buyers all over the world. The records of the importing countries show these goods as having originated in South Africa or Mozambique. If any government challenges a buyer, the buyer can produce false declarations and certifications of origin. With the Rhodesian linkage to the product thus obscured, the buyer is protected from possible prosecution and forfeiture of the product. This method is also used to shield the ultimate destination of goods which Rhodesia imports.

The UN has amassed quite a bit of circumstantial evidence to document this method of thwarting the sanctions, for the method gives rise to a disparity in the trading figures of Rhodesia's neighboring countries and *their* main trading partners. Table 4.7 shows the excess of reported imports of twenty-three countries over reported exports of South Africa, Mozambique, Zambia, and Malawi. Notice that the disparity increased as Rhodesia's indirect trade increased. The annual reports of the UN Sanctions Committee contain a great deal of statistical evidence regarding discrepancies between exports of specific products

Table 4.7
Summary of Rhodesian International Trade
1966–1975
(US$m.)

	1966	1967	1968	1969	1970	1971	1972	1973	1974	1975
TOTAL DOMESTIC EXPORTS	238	238	234	297	346	379	474	625	600	640
To countries reporting to the United Nations	181	96	68	48	50	48	72	68	60	93
To South African Customs Union*	60	80	80	85	95	105	130	200	250	302
To world markets via indirect trade	-3	62	86	164	201	226	272	357	290	245
Indirect trade as a percentage of total	—	26	37	55	58	60	57	57	48	38
Excess of reported imports of twenty-three countries** over reported exports of South Africa, Mozambique, Zambia, and Malawi	-3	102	122	195	317	243	298	398	333	261
TOTAL IMPORTS	236	262	290	278	329	395	404	480	515	588
From countries reporting to the United Nations	79	63	44	15	16	18	18	18	20	18
From South African Customs Union	110	135	150	155	180	215	182	220	230	270
Unaccounted trade	47	64	96	108	133	162	204	242	265	300
Unaccounted trade as a percentage of total	20	24	33	39	40	41	50	50	51	51

Source: U.N. Security Council, *Official Records of the Security Council, Thirty-second Year, Special Supplement No. 2* (S/12265), annex VI.
* Estimates derived from published data for South African trade with "Africa" less trade with South Africa reported by African countries.
** Market economy countries in Western Europe, Canada, Japan, Australia, and New Zealand; similar statistics are not available for imports.

reported by South Africa and Mozambique and reported imports of those products by other countries from South Africa and Mozambique. For example, with respect to tobacco, there is reasonably good agreement on the reported imports and exports for 1965 and 1966. In 1967, however, imports of tobacco from South Africa and Mozambique were recorded as 17,300 metric tons, while those countries only reported exporting 10,100 metric tons—a difference of 7,200 metric tons. This discrepancy increased to metric tons 15,800 in 1969; 22,800 in 1971; 33,800 in 1973; and decreased to 16,600 in 1975. The UN Sanctions Committee concludes that these discrepancies may represent Rhodesian tobacco reaching world markets through false declarations of origin. These trends are present also in the analyses of other major Rhodesian exports such as asbestos, chrome ore, and maize. In the case of maize, countries importing maize received 1,155,000 tons from Mozambique during the period 1967–69, despite the fact that Mozambique reported exporting only 17,000 tons. Indeed, after reviewing production yields and consumption figures for Mozambique, to have exported what importing countries claimed, consumption of maize in Mozambique would have had to virtually cease! In the case of chrome ore, it would have been nearly impossible for the reported South African production 1967–70, to be sufficient to meet the expanding domestic requirements for the ore and the reported exports. This leads to another possibility regarding the disposition of Rhodesian products. South Africa and Mozambique may have directly imported some Rhodesian products, allowing themselves to release abnormally large quantities of the same products from their own production into the export market. This would be a useful method in cases where chemical or other tests could prove transshipped goods were of Rhodesian origin, or where it was difficult to use falsified certificates of origin.

It should be noted that discrepancies between import-export figures routinely occur and are due to errors in recording trade data, differing methods of calculating value, time-lags between origin of shipments in one country and receipt in another, transshipments among countries, and rerouting of goods while in transit. What is compelling in the Rhodesian case is that the discrepancies escalate sharply after 1967, involve the major products of Rhodesia's export trade, involve South Africa and Mozambique, and are consistent with Rhodesian export estimates.[75]

Various reports emanating from Southern Africa tend to corroborate the circumstantial evidence of the UN. Less than a year after UDI, the Rhodesian periodical, *Property and Finance*, October 1966, noted that South Africa imported consignments of Rhodesian beef for domestic consumption and, in turn, exported its own beef. An influential economic study group in South Africa, the Afrikaanse Handelsinstiuut, was reported in the *Rhodesia Herald,* June 19, 1966, to have made several recommendations to aid Rhodesia; the first was that "the South African firms should undertake to market Rhodesian products to the world in a way that the country of origin cannot be traced." It was also reported in the *Bulawayo Chronicle,* March 8, 1966, that a firm, Export Sales Ltd., was formed in 1965, to sell Rhodesian products outside the country. It had entered into an arrangement with the South African firm, Imex, which had worldwide contacts and purchased South African goods from producers for resale to outside interests, as well as serving as an agency for exporters. Export Sales claimed that this arrangement allowed it to offer the same kinds of services to Rhodesian producers. The Rhodesian government subsequently established various central trading and buying agencies, such as UNIVEX, which coordinated exports.

A study of the oil embargo on Rhodesia further underscores the critical role of South Africa and Mozambique and enables examination of some techniques of sanctions evasion. Britain imposed an embargo on oil shipments to Rhodesia on December 17, 1965, and the United States government urged American companies to observe the boycott. The Rhodesian government began rationing petrol and diesel fuel on December 28. On March 4, 1966, the *New York Times* reported that major oil companies operating in South Africa agreed to limit their sales in South Africa to ten percent more than they sold there in 1964, in order to discourage re-exports to Rhodesia. Rhodesia's only oil refinery, at Umtali, had to close on January 16, due to a lack of oil in the Beira-Umtali pipeline. The UN Security Council ordered a stop to the importation of oil destined for Rhodesia through the Mozambique port of Beira on April 9, 1966, and authorized the United Kingdom to use force, if necessary, to ensure no oil destined for Rhodesia was unloaded at Beira. Finally, in December 1966, the UN placed a general mandatory oil embargo on Rhodesia.

W. J. Levy, Inc. of New York prepared a report for the UN Secretary-General on the economics and logistics of an oil embargo on Rhodesia. Levy concluded that Rhodesian oil consumption was concentrated in road transportation where possibilities for substitution were minimal and that oil shortages would cause a major upset in the Rhodesian economy and society directly affecting the mobility of people and goods. An oil embargo, therefore, would be the most direct and potent manifestation of international sanctions. The governments of South Africa and Portugal could effectively support the Rhodesian oil economy.

However, if the South African government compelled oil companies to re-export oil to Rhodesia in defiance of the policies of the governments of their parent companies, it could lead to serious repercussions on the future availability of supplies to South Africa from these sources. The key consideration is the fact that South Africa itself is almost entirely dependent on imported oil to support its own requirements.[76]

Levy correctly noted the potency of an oil embargo to directly and quickly affect the population, he further stated that South Africa and Portugal could frustrate an oil embargo on Rhodesia but doubted that they would do so in the face of their own dependence on imported oil and susceptibility to outside pressure. Levy further noted indirect methods of getting oil to Rhodesia yet doubted their efficacy:

It is not uncommon, owing to practical problems of programming, for a tanker to take on an oil export cargo consigned to "sea-for-orders," subsequently to be routed to the desired destination. This practice could be invoked in an attempt to disguise procurement for Rhodesia. Brokers have a role in the oil trade, buying and selling when and as they can serve the commercial interests of individual oil producers and oil customers; and Rhodesia could attempt to get oil through established brokers or other intermediaries. Finally, crude might be sought by purchase from resellers who might be induced by price offers above the going price, even in countries which have no oil production of their own but depend on imports.

The likelihood that such oil supplies would readily be identified is great—as to producing country or refinery, commercial intermediary, and tanker or general cargo ship carrying the oil. To find a supplier, to get a ship, and to accomplish delivery and transit for Rhodesia— each poses separate problems. Each, in itself, may not be beyond possibility; but the compound probabilities tend to get relatively slim. And the prospects of disclosure would obviously have to be considered by individuals or companies who might be potential participants in oil trade with Rhodesia—having to balance the quick profits of a clandestine transaction against the subsequent commercial and political repercussions which could threaten their whole operations in the future.[77]

The Levy Report demonstrates the kinds of miscalculations which were initially made regarding sanctions. It also contains some valuable insights on the methods which have probably been used to thwart the oil embargo, such as the use of intermediaries and brokers, methods which may be applicable to products other than oil.

In the actual situation, as early as February 15, 1966, the *Rand Daily Mail* (Johannesburg) reported that at least 35,000 gallons a day of petroleum products were crossing the border from South Africa into Rhodesia in a regular road shuttle arrangement; one month later, the same newspaper reported, on April 18, 1966, the quantities to be between 140,000 and 160,000 gallons of oil per day—*double* Rhodesia's needed quantity. According to Young, "by the autumn of 1966, most of Rhodesia's petrol came from the Sonarep refinery of Lourenco Marques. Sonarep was involved with the French Total group, and new storage tanks were built at the Rutenga railhead."[78] On November 23, 1967, Foreign Minister of Portugal Dr. Franco Nogueira stated at a press conference that Portugal made no secret of the fact that oil products were passing through Lourenco Marques to Rhodesia, but that these products were the property of non-Portuguese firms and were carried in non-Portuguese ships. Rhodesia began to ease the petrol rationing in 1967, allowing extra allowances for flying clubs, for schools training commercial pilots, and for Rhodesians going outside Rhodesia on holidays. Under the rationing system motorists, in addition to their ration quota, could buy as much "off ration" petrol as they could afford at an extra cost of two shillings per six pints.[79] On May 12, 1971, The Rhodesian government abolished all petrol rationing. It is significant that, according to the *Rhodesia Herald,* November 30, 1973, motor vehicle registration in Rhodesia climbed from 135,000 in 1965, to 182,000 in 1972, showing no depression due to the oil embargo or shortages of petrol.

In late 1973, the Organization of Petroleum Exporting Countries (OPEC) began dramatically increasing the price for its oil exports. On November 28, 1973, fifteen Arab heads of state, meeting in Algeria, announced an embargo on oil exports to Portugal, South Africa, and Rhodesia alleging that those countries had aided Israel. These developments led to a reimposition of fuel rationing in Rhodesia in February 1974. The increase of oil prices contributed substantially to Rhodesia's inflation and balance of payments problems in succeeding years; in the three years ending in January 1976, the cost of fuel had trebled in Rhodesia, according to the *Rhodesia Herald,* January 1, 1976.

Levy's figures showed in 1965, a Rhodesian consumption of 9,000 barrels of oil per day compared to South Africa's consumption of 111,000 barrels per day.[80] It would be relatively simple for South Africa to increase her imports of petroleum and petroleum products and re-export some to Rhodesia. Coincidentally, according to UN statistics, South Africa increased her 1966 imports 25.4 percent over 1965 levels, and Mozambique increased her 1966 imports 55.7 percent over 1965 levels.[81] In neither country were the percentage increases in the years after 1966 nearly so large as the increase for 1966.

The mechanics of the reshipment of oil has been described by the Africa Bureau (London): "Oil was supplied by Shell (Middle East) through the Shell/BP refinery in Durban to Shell/BP (South Africa) who sell it through independent dealers to the Rhodesian government purchasing agency (GENTA) who sell it to Shell/BP (Rhodesia)."[82] The March 1966 agreement whereby oil companies in South Africa were reported to curtail expansion of their sales seems inoperative. Munger explains that "to relieve themselves of liability for penalties under American and British law, the American and British companies in South Africa do not inquire when and where their petrol is finally resold. But even so, as long as they do not sell directly to Rhodesia, there is no follow-through."[83] This is a point Levy overlooked in his report. Moreover, it is an interesting example of how two governments use transnational actors as intermediaries in an economic relationship that might otherwise prove to be politically embarrassing were it conducted on a direct government-to-government basis.

Meanwhile, in light of the demonstrable failure of the oil embargo to deny supplies to Rhodesia, Britain maintained the Beira "blockade" until Mozambique assumed her independence in June 1975. In the House of Commons on March 6, 1972, Sir Alec Douglas-Home was asked: "What vital British interest is served in having Rhodesian oil imported through Lourenco Marques instead of Beira?" Douglas-Home replied: "This is one [question] which is not very easy to answer. But it is part of the sanctions bargain which we made. We are sticking to it until conditions are changed." This is a good example of a government committed to a policy which proved to be unsuccessful but had to be maintained for symbolic reasons; the policy's mere existence became a justification for its continuance.

While the role of South Africa and Mozambique has been extensively discussed, it should not be assumed that other countries have not also been engaged in the effort to thwart the sanctions, although there is less information available on these cases. One case discussed here is interesting partly because it involves an African state not contiguous to Rhodesia and partly because it sheds some light on the motives behind trading with Rhodesia.

It has been alleged that Rhodesian aircraft flew thousands of pounds of meat, fruit, and vegetables weekly into Libreville, capital of the West African state of Gabon. The *Rhodesia Herald* reported on March 1, 1972, that the operation had the blessing of the Gabonese president, Albert Bongo. President Bongo has been one of Africa's strongest supporters of dialogue with South Africa. A local Gabonese importer explained that "the plain truth is that we realize the geographical advantages of importing cheaply from sources close at hand. The country would pay more than double by bringing the same things in from, say, Europe."[84] Rhodesian beef was the cheapest and best in French-speaking West Africa, selling in Libreville for about 20 percent less than beef in other French-speaking states of West Africa. A note from the United Kingdom dated December 8, 1969, brought the Gabon case to the attention of the UN Sanctions Committee.

Reports in the *Sunday Times* (London), August 26, and September 2, 1973, and the *Manchester Guardian,* August 27, 1973, suggested that Gabon's role was far more important to Rhodesia than merely accepting Rhodesia's beef exports. It was alleged that the Rhodesian air freight firm, Air Trans-Africa, established a Gabonese subsidiary, Compagnie Gabonaise d'Affrètements Aériens (Affretair), whose DC8F Model 55 jet freighter carried consignments of Rhodesian beef several times a week to Athens using Libreville as a refuelling stop. The *Sunday Times* reported that the Greek importer paid Affretair at least US$200 less per ton than legitimate importers had to pay for meat but that the entire operation still earned Rhodesia up to UK £4 million per year. On the return flight from Athens, the plane stopped either at Amsterdam (Schiphol Airport), Cologne, or Paris (Le Bourget Airport) to load freight destined for Libreville. Since the destination of the freight was not Rhodesia, this specific activity did not violate UN sanctions. The carrying charges paid to Affretair, however, constituted foreign exchange for Rhodesia, and this was a violation.

In June 1974, Greece decided to deny Affretair landing rights and not to accept any more certificates of origin issued by South African authorities on merchandise suspected to be of Rhodesian origin. Greek importers had produced such certificates for the Rhodesian beef. Over 30 people were put on trial in Athens including the trade minister of the former Papadopoulos régime and one of Greece's biggest meat importers, Stavros Tsonis. Tsonis claimed that he was doing a favor to the state, offering the best meat, and the cheapest, at a time when the meat shortage was an international phenomenon. He also claimed that he acted on direct orders from the Trade Ministry. A total of 23,000 tons of meat was imported from May 1971, to the end of 1973, according to the *Rhodesia Herald,* June 14, 1975.

In 1975, the United States indefinitely denied all U.S. export privileges to Affretair because that company had falsely represented to the U.S. government that the plane in question (the DC8F purchased in the U.S.) would not be utilized in any traffic with Rhodesia. Advertisements signed by the "Presidency of the Gabon Republic" were placed in London newspapers in July 1975, affirming that Gabon recognized the legitimacy of sanctions against Rhodesia and had taken all necessary steps to terminate in due course the last links between herself and Rhodesia. Gabon subsequently announced that Affretair had been dissolved and its assets incorporated into the national airline, Air Gabon.

A perusal of the annual reports of the UN Sanctions Committee reveal that some of the arrangements made by multinational corporations to secure Rhodesian trade are unbelievably complex and intricate and involve difficult questions of where legal jurisdiction and responsibility reside for such trade. One case cited illustrates this point—*UN Case No. 112: Sugar-"Evangelos M."* On January 22, 1971, the United Kingdom submitted information to the Sanctions Committee about the importation of sugar by Kuwait. A ship owned by a Panamanian company, registered in Greece, and managed by a Greek firm, loaded sugar suspected to be of Rhodesian origin at a port in Mozambique for transport to a firm in Kuwait, which bought the sugar from a firm in Switzerland which declared the sugar originated in Malawi. Payment transfer was made from a Lebanon branch of a Russian bank to a Swiss bank. The Kuwaiti government said that the Kuwaiti buyer, who acted in good faith, could not be held responsible and moreover, it was the seller who must be held accountable for the invoice. The invoice was issued by the Swiss firm, certified by the Geneva Chamber of Commerce, and stated that the sugar was of Malawian origin. The Malawian government noted that at no time was sugar exported from Malawi through any firm in Geneva. The Swiss government noted that the transaction took place entirely outside Swiss territory. The concluding of contracts for the delivery of goods which were not to be shipped to or did not originate in Swiss territory was beyond the control of the Swiss government, which had no legal means of preventing operations of this kind. Regarding the actual shipment, the government of Panama stated that the primary responsibility rested with the country under whose flag the vessel sailed. For two years Greece did not respond to the inquiries from the Sanctions Committee, however, in 1974, several Greek citizens were arrested and tried in the Court of Piraeus. All defendants were acquitted on the grounds they did not know the Rhodesian origin of the merchandise.[85] Given the complexity of the transaction, it is remarkable that it was even documented in the first place. Note also that it took the UN nearly four years to conduct the investigation without any responsibility or penalty being determined.

The ease with which Swiss territory was used to circumvent the sanctions against Rhodesia may be greatly diminished by a Swiss law which took effect January 1, 1978. According to a report in the Johannesburg *Star,* December 17, 1977, the law prohibits any company or private person in Switzerland from arranging, on behalf of third parties, the sale of goods to Rhodesia or the purchase of Rhodesian products.

The Gabon case and the Kuwait sugar case are fairly representative of the mixed degree of success which the UN Sanctions Committee has had in attempting to establish responsibility for alleged breaches of the sanctions. This committee was established by Security Council Resolution 253 of May 29, 1968, as a committee of the Council charged with the function of coordinating and gathering information on matters related to the implementation of the various sanctions resolutions and reporting such information, along with any recommendations, to the Security Council. Through 1976, the Committee considered about 340 suspected breaches of the sanctions, most of which were brought to its attention by the United Kingdom. Only a handful of countries (including the United States and the United Kingdom) have successfully prosecuted their nationals for violating the sanctions. According to the Africa Bureau: "Prosecutions depend upon the provision of information on the one hand and a political willingness upon the part of the country to whom the information is provided to take action against its nationals on the other hand. What emerges clearly from the UN reports of suspected violations of sanctions is the fact that even when information is provided, governments respond at a minimum rather than at a maximum level."[86] It is clear that the cases considered by the Committee represented a miniscule proportion of Rhodesia's international trade since 1968.

On May 22, 1973, the Security Council passed Resolution 333, which set forth the following measures, among others, to try to strengthen sanctions enforcement:

1. Requests states to provide that trading contracts with South Africa and Portugal contain legally enforceable provisions prohibiting

purchase of goods of Rhodesian origin or resale or re-export of goods to Rhodesia.

2. Calls upon states to inform the Sanctions Committee on their present sources of supply and quantities of those products which are known to constitute the major Rhodesian export items.

3. Documentation emanating from South Africa, Angola, and Mozambique in respect of products and goods that are also produced by Rhodesia should be considered *prima facie* suspect.

4. The Sanctions Committee should publish a list of experts who would be available to be called in at short notice by the government of any importing country to make appropriate investigation.

5. The Committee should encourage individuals and nongovernmental organizations to report information regarding sanctions-breaking operations.

6. The Committee should periodically request member states to draw the attention of their public to the importance of the UN resolutions relevant to the sanctions policy.

7. The Committee recommends that member states should seize, in accordance with their domestic regulations, cargoes established to be of Rhodesian origin and should put the proceeds from the sale of those cargoes into a special fund to pay the expenses associated with the implementation of the sanctions—especially the expenses of the experts referred to above in paragraph four.[87]

Whether Resolution 333 will be successful in diminishing Rhodesia's trading linkages remains to be seen. Clearly it, as well as the past resolutions, depend upon the political willingness of the governments of the member-states for enforcement. It does, however, raise an interesting new possibility—it encourages nongovernmental transnational actors to report directly to the Sanctions Committee bypassing their own governments, which might be reluctant to provide information. Since the passage of that resolution, the Sanctions Committee has dealt severe blows to several transactions important to Rhodesia; e.g., the RISCO case (cited above), a tobacco smuggling operation in the Netherlands, and the Air Rhodesia interline agreements with other air carriers (see Chapter 5). Vital information relating to these cases was developed by nongovernmental actors. The *Sunday Times* (London), the Anti-Apartheid League of the Netherlands, various church groups, trade unions, the Carnegie Endowment for International Peace (United States), and various pro-United Nations interest groups, among others, have been most helpful with information regarding sanction-breaking operations.

Transnational actors have obviously played a critical role in thwarting the sanctions. In a surprisingly candid statement to the Legislative Assembly on April 26, 1967, Rhodesia's minister of transportation remarked: "whatever any particular government says, of course, is quite different to what their businessmen do and this is precisely how Rhodesia . . . is winning the war. It does not matter a hoot . . . what the government says; it is precisely what the people within that country do." Prime Minister Ian Smith, in an interview in the November 1971 issue of the British journal, *Industrial Management,* said: "I think the attitude of most of the governments is that their companies can get on with it [trading with Rhodesia], so long as the governments themselves don't know about it."

It is probable that without more rigorous enforcement and effective policing, Rhodesia will not realize much more adverse economic consequences from the sanctions than she has already experienced. In addition to the difficulties in detecting breaches of the sanctions already discussed, there is the added problem of the allocation of resources that would be needed to increase the efficacy of the enforcement and policing. According to Marshall, economic sanctions "require much administrative and technical perseverance. Talent must be recruited from financial institutions, metallurgical and petrological industries, manufacturing, merchandizing, and so on, and deployed into consular and embassy staffs abroad, placed strategically in corporate structures abroad and in dummy companies, and supplied with adequate funds for buying information and for bribing. Money has to be spent lavishly on preclusive buying of goods destined for the target country, and in subsidizing alternate sources of supply for its products. I have seen no signs that the game was played that way in this instance. With but a few notable exceptions governments have been content to subscribe to resolutions and let the matter go at that."[88]

U.S. Ambassador William Schaufele, senior advisor to the U.S. representative to the UN, has commented that "every country, if it is to observe the sanctions, will have to make sure that it has the procedures, the laws, the statutes, and the surveillance to make sure that sanctions work." He further noted that most members of the UN "will in effect not do the work which many of them think is properly the work of the UN." The United States proposed that more nations might consider doing chemical analyses of minerals to establish their origin but "some nations plead that they are unable to allot the resources and money to carry out such chemical analyses. We, in fact, do carry out such analyses in this country, but ours is a rare case."[89] Perhaps the "special fund" envisioned in S/RES/333 will help to remedy the problem of inadequate resources.

Trade Promotion

While the United Nations is trying to diminish Rhodesian exports, Rhodesia is obviously trying to promote them. In doing this, Rhodesia has available a number of devices to aid promotion; those devices which rely upon international relations are discussed here. Note, however, that because of the lower profit rates associated with exporting, Rhodesian secondary producers are constantly being exhorted to export and various incentive schemes have been initiated by the government to aid this process. It is interesting that in the many discussions of export incentives, attention is paid to not violating any of the articles of the GATT— although Rhodesia's membership in the Agreement is suspended.[90]

The importance of export promotion is self-evident; it is even important in southern Africa, where Rhodesia's export drive is not without its complications and problems—as noted earlier in this chapter. An absolutely essential prerequisite for export promotion is that the promoters be able to travel and communicate with the world outside Rhodesia. In calling for tighter security in Rhodesia's international business, Peter Lowe, president of the Associated Chambers of Commerce of Rhodesia (ACCOR) said in the *Rhodesia Herald,* June 7, 1973: "The communications network built up over the past few years is vital to Rhodesia and if the economy is to expand, it is essential that this network remains intact."

Foreign Visits

To successfully match product with market, information must be gathered. In 1972, ARnI launched "Operation Magpie" whereby every businessman who traveled outside Rhodesia was asked to bring back any information he felt might help the country's export effort. In addition to individual business trips, delegations were sometimes sent to various international commercial meetings. For example, in 1971, ACCOR sent a delegation of twelve business executives to the Congress of the International Chamber of Commerce in Vienna. An ACCOR spokesman told the *Rhodesian Financial Gazette,* April 23, 1971, that they found these congresses very useful in keeping up with international business trends and making informal contacts with businessmen from other countries. A similar delegation was also sent to the 1973 Congress in Rio de Janeiro and the 1975 Congress in Madrid.

In addition to information gathered by traveling Rhodesians, the Rhodesian Promotion Council (RPC) is in the forefront of arranging visits to Rhodesia by foreign economic and business elites. In 1971–72, more than 100 people from twelve countries came to Rhodesia under the auspices of the RPC. The RPC hosted Professor Milton Friedman, Nobel Prize economist at the University of Chicago, for five days in 1975. C. G. Tracey, chairman of the RPC, noted that Friedman's writings and broadcasts about Rhodesia after his return to the U.S. "have probably done more to correct false impressions about this country than any man has done during the last ten years."[91] Specialists are often invited to Rhodesia to hold seminars and consultancies. Export market research is also provided by various international consulting firms, such as Associated European Consultants, which have established offices in Salisbury.

Foreign Advertising

Despite the fact that the UN Security Council decided in 1968, in S/RES/253 that all member-states shall prevent any activities by their nationals "which would promote or are calculated to promote the export of any commodities or products from Southern Rhodesia," the following major advertisements have appeared under the aegis of the Rhodesian Promotion Council:

1. Three full-page advertisements in the *International Herald Tribune* of August 9, 1971. This newspaper is published in Paris jointly by the *New York Times* and the *Washington Post*.
2. An advertisement of unknown length in the West German daily commercial newspaper, *Handelsblatt*, issue of May 2, 1972.
3. A sixteen-page special supplement to the *Journal of Commerce* of June 19, 1972, published in New York and to its international edition of June 26, 1972. Various shorter advertisements have appeared in this newspaper subsequently.
4. A thirty-two page supplement to the French financial and economic review, *Agence Economique et Financiere,* in 1974 and 1976.

C. G. Tracey hailed these advertisements as being among Rhodesia's major breakthroughs in penetrating sanctions. Tracey also stated to the

Rhodesia Herald, June 27, 1972: "I believe that we must take advantage of the opportunity to take space and utilize supplements in economic and financially oriented journals throughout the world to take the story of Rhodesia and its opportunities to a far wider range of influential people that we could ever manage to bring to Rhodesia." The 1971–72 *Annual Report* of the RPC states that Tracey made arrangements for the *Journal of Commerce* supplements while visiting the United States.

It was alleged that the *International Herald Tribune* advertisement did not violate French law but did violate a British Order in Council specifically forbidding any advertising designed to help Rhodesia.[92] In the case of the *Journal of Commerce,* the U.S. Department of State advised:

> We have interpreted the term "promote or calculated to promote" as encompassing only those activities which facilitate the accomplishment of transactions unlawful under the sanctions. Certain general activities, not related to a particular transaction which is prohibited under the sanctions program, may nonetheless indirectly contribute to such transactions. Under the interpretation set forth above, such an indirect relationship would not fall within the meaning of the terms "promote or calculated to promote," especially if the ultimate violation can be prohibited directly. Furthermore, a general prohibition against all activities which might conceivably have the effect of "promoting" violations of Rhodesian sanctions could involve fundamental constitutional questions.[93]

Here is a case where a state may be unable to give statutory or legal effect to a provision of a UN sanctions resolution because it conflicts with its constitution—specifically, in this case, with the freedom of speech and press contained in the Bill of Rights.

Trade Fairs

To exhibit its products to potential foreign buyers, Rhodesia, until 1975, regularly participated in the FILDA (Luanda) and FACIM (Lourenco Marques) trade fairs and continues its participation in the Windhoek Agricultural and Industrial Show. In 1971, tobacco and soft drink manufacturers exhibited at the Lisbon Trade Fair. Rhodesia also participates in various shows and exhibitions in South Africa. Rhodesian products are occasionally entered in international competitions; for example, a Rhodesian variety of maize won championship awards at the

Royal Canadian Winter Fairs 1970–73 and 1975; a Rhodesian cereal, "Honey Krunchies," won a gold medal at the Monde Selection international cereal competition in Geneva in 1973; and a Rhodesian cigarette won a gold medal at the International Exhibition of Tobacco Products in Brussels in 1974. Commenting on the maize prize, the *Rhodesia Herald* noted on December 8, 1972, that "the good performance in this world event is expected to increase international interest in Rhodesian varieties."

Rhodesia organizes two major trade fairs each year: Trade Fair Rhodesia in the spring in Bulawayo and the Salisbury Agricultural Show in August. Portugal (until 1975) and South Africa maintained regular pavilions at both shows. At the 1972 Trade Fair Rhodesia, for the first time since UDI, foreign firms from outside southern Africa exhibited; they were: Guido Oberdorfer of West Germany (cleaning machines) and Hausammann Textiles of Switzerland.[94] To further improve Trade Fair Rhodesia, its general manager, Peter Roach, was sent on a tour of trade fairs in Europe in 1972, to examine their methods and operations.

Trade Missions

The Rhodesian government maintained trade missions in Johannesburg and, until 1975, in Lisbon, Lourenco Marques, and Luanda. There are persistent reports that one unofficial trade mission is maintained in Paris. Little is known of the activities of these missions. The minister for commerce and industry explained to the Legislative Assembly on September 7, 1967, that "to open an office or agency anywhere would only draw attention to our activities. It would be a focus on which to concentrate the sanctions effort. We could not expect to be able to open any office with the agreement or blessing of a government which does not recognize us as a country, so we do have that particular problem." Nevertheless, the Export Promotion Section within the Ministry is active in arranging selling missions to external markets and buying missions to visit Rhodesia.

It might be argued that the overseas contacts, associate companies and branches of transnational firms in Rhodesia act as informal "trade missions" gathering information, trade intelligence, and matching products with markets for communication to Rhodesia. There are four major banks (discussed earlier in this chapter) claiming to have worldwide contacts, several accepting and confirming firms, and several trading companies. With respect to the banks, J. T. Gilbert notes that "the exporter is fortunate that the banking sector as a whole has moved with the times in Rhodesia and is able to offer or obtain specialized advice on export markets and on the peculiarities relating to individual countries."[95] An advertisement of the Manica Trading Company in the *Rhodesia Herald*, March 23, 1972, stresses their international contacts and fast communications (both essential to export promotion): "Our 'hot-line' is your fastest link with overseas markets. The Manica network of offices and world-wide communications through our associate companies is there for the asking."

The Case of Cotton

Certain unique aspects to the promotion of Rhodesia's cotton industry warrant special mention. In 1970, various cotton growers established the Cotton Promotion Council (CPC), a nongovernmental body. The CPC then approached the International Institute of Cotton and asked to be allowed to register the international cotton emblem and be responsible for its administration in southern Africa. The emblem is the executive property of the International Institute of Cotton (IIC) and is an internationally recognized symbolic guarantee of quality. The IIC acceded to the CPC's request in 1971. The CPC thus has the responsibility to award the emblem to manufacturers throughout southern Africa whose fabrics measure up to the international quality standards required. Peter Johnston, chief executive of the CPC, told the *Sunday Mail*, November 14, 1971, that "the granting of the cotton mark franchise to Rhodesia . . . is a tremendous step forward for our industry." As noted above, this is the industry that the chairman of the Agricultural Marketing Authority said was "the greatest single factor that enabled the Rhodesian economy to withstand the effects of the sanctions." The marketing, either for domestic or export consumption, of the cotton goods bearing the cotton emblem will be facilitated by the presence of that emblem.

The IIC is headquartered in Brussels, and its membership comprises thirteen of the leading cotton producing countries. For political reasons, Rhodesia is not a member, and the IIC cannot help the CPC financially. But where the IIC can help without it necessitating the establishment of official records, it does. The reasoning of the IIC is that if it encourages or promotes the consumption of cotton fabrics in southern Africa, less fabrics will be exported to Europe and hence Europe will be a less competitive market for other cotton and textile producing countries. The assistance the IIC gives to the CPC is in the form of technical information, general market reviews, and research data on the latest chemicals and machinery. A CPC official notes that "technical data is not subject to sanctions."

Of major help to the CPC is the establishment in Salisbury of a cotton fabrics library containing information manufacturers need about world trends in cotton textures, fashions, styles, colors, and designs. It contains samples of cotton fabrics from all over the world. It is only the fourth such library to be established in the world, and the Paris library renders assistance by providing some samples and literature, as well as displaying Rhodesian manufacturing samples.[96]

This is a clear example of two transnational actors (IIC and CPC) engaging in an international relationship that has mutual economic benefits, however indirect, which in turn affects the political milieu in which governments have to operate.

THE BYRD AMENDMENT: A CASE STUDY

In the study of economic sanctions against Rhodesia, the United States holds an unique distinction—it is the only member-state of the UN to vote in favor of sanctions and then, afterwards, enact domestic legislation that directly violated part of those sanctions. The legislation is popularly referred to as the Byrd Amendment.

The focus of this section is on the history of the legislation, the stated reasons for its passage, and the kinds of interests which were involved in lobbying in support of its enactment. Neither the arguments against its enactment nor the validity of the supporting arguments are examined. It is sufficient to note that the supporting arguments were considered valid enough to warrant its passage. Some of the reasons offered in support of the legislation to contravene the sanctions are unique to the United States; others may have more universal application. Finally, as far as can be determined, it was clear to all the actors involved that this piece of legislation did indeed contravene the UN sanctions.[97]

Legislative History

In 1971, several resolutions were introduced in the U.S. House of Representatives designed, in one way or another, to end or restrict United States sanctions against Rhodesia. One resolution, H.R.5445 introduced by Representative James Collins (D-Texas), sought to amend the United Nations Participation Act of 1945 to prevent the imposition of any prohibition on the importation into the United States of any strategic and critical material from any free world country for so long as the importation of like material from any Communist country was not prohibited by law. Senator Harry F. Byrd (Ind-Virginia) introduced S.1404, companion legislation to the Collins resolution, in the Senate.

H.R.5445 was referred to the Subcommittee on International Organizations and Movements of the House Committee on Foreign Affairs, and S.1404 was referred to the Subcommittee on Africa of the Senate Committee on Foreign Relations. After holding Hearings on the resolutions during the summer of 1971, both subcommittees refused to report the resolutions out for House and Senate consideration.

Since it seemed that direct approaches to ending or modifying the Rhodesian sanctions could and would be frustrated by the antagonism of the foreign relations committees of the House and Senate, Senator Byrd then used an indirect method. In August 1971, Byrd approached the Senate Armed Services Committee, of which he was a member, and offered for consideration an amendment to the Defense Procurement Bill which was identical in wording to S.1404. The committee unanimously adopted the amendment as section 503 of the defense bill. It has been claimed that Byrd purposely timed his introduction of the amendment to coincide with the absence of the three liberal members of the committee, Symington (D-Missouri), McIntyre (D-New Hampshire), and Hughes (D-Iowa), thus ensuring the unanimous approval.[98]

When Section 503 reached the Senate floor for debate on September 23, 1971, an amendment to delete the section from the defense bill was introduced by Senators Gale McGee (D-Wyoming) and Edward Brooke (R-Massachusetts); it was defeated by a vote of 36–46. Sen. J. W. Fulbright (D-Arkansas) offered an amendment on September 30, giving the president discretionary authority to ignore Section 503, and it passed by a vote of 45–43. A series of motions, however, tied up the amendment in procedural knots, and when the final vote was taken on October 6, Fulbright's amendment was defeated 38–44. An amendment to delay implementation of Section 503 until January 1, 1972, was passed by a voice vote. The defense bill went to conference, and the only change that was made in Section 503 was to have it amend the Strategic and Critical Materials Stock Piling Act rather than the United Nations Participation Act. The conference report, issued on November 5, concluded: "Continued observance of the UN-imposed embargo against the importation of chrome ore from Rhodesia adversely affects the national interest of the United States."[99] When the conference report went to the House on November 10, Representative Donald Fraser (D-Minnesota), chairman of the subcommittee which had earlier killed the Collins resolution, demanded a separate vote on Section 503, since it was nongermane to the bill as a whole. The House voted 251–100 to keep Section 503 in the Bill. The conference report then passed the House and the Senate and was signed into law by President Nixon on November 17, 1971.

A general license was issued by the Department of Treasury on

January 25, 1972, authorizing imports of chromium ore of Rhodesian origin, ferrochrome produced in any country from chromium ore of Rhodesian origin, and any other material of Rhodesian origin determined to be "strategic and critical." The only proviso was that the price paid for the materials could not exceed the prevailing world market price.[100] Senator Byrd *repeatedly* said the only commodity that would be affected by his legislation would be chrome ore; "the reason for singling out this commodity is clear and simple: it is the one item which could and should be imported from Rhodesia that is vital to the national security of the United States."[101] All the congressional hearings and debates referred only to chrome imports from Rhodesia. "Chrome," however, was not mentioned in either H.R.5445, S.1404, or Section 503. When the general license was issued, S. N. Muus, president of the Chamber of Mines of Rhodesia said in the *Rhodesia Herald,* January 27, 1972: "the industry did not realize that any mineral other than chrome was affected, and this is a very pleasant surprise." Rhodesia produces 22 of the 72 metals, minerals or mineral products listed by the United States as "strategic and critical."

Table 4.8 records the United States imports from Rhodesia for the six years (through August 1977) after the license was issued. Nonchrome commodities represented 56 percent of the total imports by value in 1972 and 1973. In both years, the largest single import by value was nickel. In 1972, the imports of raw chrome ore and processed ferrochrome were approximately equal by value; in 1973, however, U.S. importers started to import far more processed ferrochrome than raw chrome ore. Total imports from Rhodesia during the six years the Byrd Amendment was in effect totaled US$211,975,000—of which 50 percent represented ferrochrome, 7 percent represented chrome ore, and 28 percent represented nickel.

With respect to chrome ore, U.S. import patterns changed little during the six year period; the Philippines remained the leading supplier of low grade ore; South Africa remained the leading supplier of medium grade ore; the Soviet Union remained the leading supplier of high grade ore. Indeed, between 1972 and 1976, the Soviet Union supplied 52 percent, by volume, of all high grade ore imported; Rhodesia supplied only 11.2 percent. Rhodesia was able to capture a large share of the expanding import market for high carbon ferrochrome—ranking first in 1973 and 1975, and second in 1972, 1974, and 1976.

A group of people led by the chairman of the Black Congressional Caucus, Representative Charles Diggs (D-Michigan), brought a suit in the U.S. District Court to stop the Rhodesian imports, because Section

Table 4.8
United States Imports from Rhodesia
1972–1977
(US$ in thousands)

Commodity	1972	1973	1974	1975	1976	1977*
Asbestos, crude and fiber	99	423	1,011	2,271	2,307	2,368
Chrome ores	2,751	1,483	2,531	7,181	1,399	0
Miscellaneous ores**	20	0	373	73	574	406
Ferrochrome, low carbon	1,114	1,871	2,258	5,369	8,098	7,496
Ferrochrome, high carbon	1,548	7,904	6,520	33,160	15,131	16,109
Miscellaneous Ferroalloys	2,246	2,936	1,053	1,631	6,323	5,132
Copper, unwrought	0	62	0	0	217	0
Nickel, unwrought	4,521	10,977	5,629	9,880	11,773	17,459
Miscellaneous	57	14	40	38	6	133
TOTAL	12,356	25,670	19,415	59,603	45,828	49,103

Source: U.S., Bureau of the Census, *U.S. General Imports*, Report FT135, December 1972, 1973, 1974, 1975, 1976; August 1977. Value cited excludes all freight and insurance charges incurred in shipping.

* January–August 1977.
** Including antimony, beryllium, copper, and tungsten.

503 conflicted with the treaty obligations of the United States under the UN Charter. The District Court dismissed the suit in April 1972, commenting that it is settled constitutional doctrine that Congress may nullify, in whole or in part, a treaty commitment. The Diggs' group then appealed to the U.S. Court of Appeals claiming, among other things, that the United States commitment to the UN has more force than an ordinary treaty. The U.S. Court of Appeals rejected this contention, dismissed the appeal, and concluded in October 1972: "Under our constitutional scheme, Congress can denounce treaties if it sees fit to do so, and there is nothing the other branches of government can do about it. We consider that this is precisely what Congress has done in this case; and therefore the District Court was correct to the extent that it found the complaint to state no tenable claim in law."[102] The Diggs' group tenaciously continued to seek judicial relief; this terminated when the U.S. Supreme Court refused to consider an appeal in April 1973.

Meanwhile, Representative Fraser and Senator McGee introduced new legislation to attempt to negate Section 503; both attempts were ultimately defeated; in the Senate, on May 31, 1972, by a vote of 36–40; and in the House, on August 10, 1972, by a vote of 140–253. The following year another attempt was made to negate Section 503; in May 1973, Fraser and Senator Hubert Humphrey (D-Minnesota) introduced identically worded resolutions to amend the UN Participation Act to restore the sanctions on Rhodesia. The House Committee on Foreign Affairs delayed action until the Senate had acted. On December 19, 1973, the Senate passed the Humphrey bill, S.1868, by a 54–37 vote. Six months later the House Committee ordered S.1868 reported favorably by a 25–9 vote. Four times the measure was scheduled for House consideration, and four times it was withdrawn by its sponsors, who were unsure of majority support. Finally, on December 19, it was withdrawn permanently. Rather than risk defeat, it was decided to introduce a new measure in the next Congress which presumably would be more favorably disposed to the legislation given the net Democratic gain of forty-three House seats in the 1974 election.

The third attempt to negate the Byrd Amendment was launched early in the Ninety-Fourth Congress. In January 1974, H.R.1287 was introduced by Congressmen Fraser and Diggs and was referred to the House Committee on International Relations. That committee added an amendment to the bill which required that all imports of steel mill products would have to be accompanied by certificates of origin stating that they contained no Rhodesian chromium. Proponents of the amendment hoped to allay the fears of the domestic specialty steel producers, who felt they woud face unfair competition from foreign producers who might have access to cheap Rhodesian chromium after the Byrd Amendment was negated. H.R.1287, as amended, was reported favorably by the Committee on International Relations by a 17–8 vote in July. In that same month, the bill was sequentially referred to the more conservative House Committee on Armed Services which promptly reported it unfavorably by a 29–7 vote. Finally, on September 25, 1975, the bill was brought to the floor for debate. The amendment was deleted by a 108–119 vote; the original bill was defeated by a 187–209 vote.

While the State Department vigorously opposed the enactment of the Byrd Amendment, the attitude and actions of the White House were deemed critical to the outcome of the Senate votes. For example, Senator McGee, referring to the 1972 vote, stated: "I asked the spokesman at the White House if they would simply lift the telephone and call. I gave them the names of six Senators, all Republicans, who said they could only switch their vote if they received urging from the White House. As it turned out, it would only have taken three phone calls instead of six to win. But the response was, 'Sorry, we have gone as far as we can go.' "[103] Why was the White House not more active in support of the State Department? According to Assistant Secretary of State for African Affairs David D. Newsom, during the 1971 vote, the overriding consideration of the White House was to neutralize Senator Mike Mansfield's attempt to amend the defense bill to require withdrawal of all U.S. troops from Vietnam. The White House was thus not anxious to alienate conservative senators on the Rhodesian issue. During the 1972 vote, President Nixon was preparing for his trip to the People's Republic of China, and the White House was concerned about the possibility of vocal opposition to the trip from conservative senators and therefore did not wish to risk alienation by pressure against Senator Byrd's position.[104]

The foregoing explanation illustrates the fact that in the hierarchy of political problems with which a government has to deal, the Rhodesian problem may not rank very high. Furthermore, it is difficult to mobilize public pressure on a government regarding a particular issue if that issue lacks salience in the public's mind. That certainly was the case of sanctions and Rhodesia; as Senator McGee candidly noted: "They [sanctions] are not very sexy, I mean that they don't hold Cronkite's attention for a very long time in the evening news, and certainly no more than once. Thus, it is difficult to sustain a public interest and a public concern in what is taking place through sanctions."[105] In addition, while the United States was repeatedly condemned at the United Nations for the enactment of the Byrd Amendment, according to Secretary Newsom, only two African countries formally protested to the U.S. government, Kenya and Nigeria, and they were verbal protests.

As the Rhodesian issue gained importance for the United States in 1975 and 1976, repeal of the Byrd Amendment became an important device to exert pressure on the Smith régime to arrive at a settlement with African nationalist groups. In his April 1976 speech in Lusaka, Zambia, U.S. Secretary of State Henry Kissinger specifically pledged to seek the repeal of the Byrd Amendment. The new Democratic administration of President Carter moved almost immediately, upon assuming office in 1977, to urge Congress to repeal the Byrd Amendment.

On January 11, 1977, Congressmen Fraser and Diggs introduced H.R.1746, which amended the UN Participation Act of 1945 by requiring enforcement of Executive Orders which applied measures against Southern Rhodesia pursuant to any UN Security Council Resolution, notwithstanding the provisions of any other law. This would not repeal the Byrd Amendment, it would simply negate its provisions *vis-à-vis* Rho-

desia. H.R.1746 also contained a section requiring that all imports of
any steel mill product containing chromium (e.g., ferrochromium, stainless steel—but not including finished goods) be accompanied by certificates of origin issued by the government of the foreign producer
specifying that the chromium contained therein did not originate in
Rhodesia. Also, on January 11, Senator Dick Clark (D-Iowa) introduced S.174, companion legislation to H.R.1746, in the Senate.

House and Senate subcommittees held hearings in February, and
the new Secretary of State Cyrus Vance and U.S. Ambassador to the
UN Andrew Young vigorously lobbied on behalf of the president in
favor of the legislation. Secretary Vance stated that the Byrd Amendment was a symbol of ambivalence in American policy toward Rhodesia
and toward international law, and its repeal would not only restore U.S.
adherence to obligations under the UN Charter but would also persuade
the Smith régime to find a peaceful settlement. He noted that "the
Carter Administration attaches the highest importance to repeal."[106]

The Congress responded quickly. The House Committee on International Relations reported H.R.1746 favorably on March 2 by a 27–
5 vote, and the full House passed the bill on March 14 by a 250–146
vote. The Senate Committee on Foreign Relations reported S.174
favorably on February 22, by a 14–1 vote. To save time by avoiding
a conference committee, the Senate voted on H.R.1746 in lieu of S.174
on March 15; it passed, 66–26. President Carter signed the bill into law
on March 18. Exercising the discretion given to him by the new law,
the president exempted from the provisions of the law all shipments of
chromium which were in transit to the U.S. on March 18, 1977.

Arguments Supporting Contravention of the
Rhodesian Sanctions

This section is based upon an informal content analysis of the
speeches of the participants involved as reported in the *Congressional
Record* from January 10, 1966 through September 25, 1975. The Byrd
Amendment did not appear in Congress as the first manifestation of
antisanction sentiment. Considerable empathy with the Rhodesian
government and its plight had been expressed prior to Senator Byrd's
efforts.[107]

Ten major arguments supporting contravention of Rhodesian sanctions can be discerned; each is presented with subarguments, if any,

along with a representative quotation from one of the actors involved. For the sake of simplification, when reference is made to the *Congressional Record* (*CR*), only the date of the speech is cited.

1. *Illegality of UN action on Rhodesia.* The UN Charter prohibits interference into the domestic affairs of sovereign states and, in any event, Rhodesia is not a "threat to the peace."

> It is most sad that our nation has been maneuvered into supporting a United Nations declaration that maintains Rhodesia, which is surrounded by a number of nationalistic and rather hostile neighbors, constitutes a "threat to world peace." Under such an assumption the intended victim now becomes the threat to peace because someone else may attack him. This is like saying the store owner is to blame for being robbed because if he had not opened his business in the first place, this would have never happened. (Langen, House, R-Minnesota, *CR*, July 1, 1970)

> The initial sanctions were imposed in the United Nations either by simple error or by fraud. If we want to consider Rhodesia as a colony of Great Britain, then this sanction interferes with the internal affairs of a given member; that is illegal. If we want to consider Rhodesia as an independent state, clearly it never was a threat to world peace and, therefore, sanctions can not legally be applied through the Security Council. (McDonald, House, D-Georgia, *CR*, September 25, 1975)

2. *Double standard.* Great Britain traded with North Vietnam and Cuba against the wishes of the United States, but asked the United States not to trade with Rhodesia. The United States and Great Britain have not sought sanctions against countries in which there is either more chaos and violence or in which there is minority, unrepresentative government.

> The British carried on unlimited trade with Communist China, Communist North Vietnam, and Communist Cuba. Whenever it is possible to make a fast dollar, there the unscrupulous British are to be found and it seems to make no difference whether the source of profit is friend or foe. (Gross, House, R-Iowa, *CR*, May 2, 1966)

> Fewer than half of all the 122 UN members have governments clearly based on majority rule. Will Mr. Goldberg [U.S. Ambassador to the

UN] endorse and take part in UN actions to bring majority rule to these nations? I doubt it. (Fannin, Senate, R-Arizona, *CR,* January 12, 1967)

3. *Usurpation of power by the president.* The United States gave legal effect to the UN sanctions through the issuing of two executive orders by President Johnson, Executive Order 11322 of January 5, 1967, and Executive Order 11419 of July 29, 1968. This is in accordance with the procedures established by the UN Participation Act of 1945. It is argued, however, that the regulation of foreign commerce is the prerogative of Congress.

No power is vested in the Executive to block foreign trade except under laws which control trading with the enemy, and Rhodesia has not been designated as an enemy. (Gross, House, R-Iowa, *CR,* March 1, 1966)

President Johnson usurped and exercised a power which he did not possess under the Constitution, when he ordered an embargo on shipments to Rhodesia. (Ervin, Senate, D-North Carolina, *CR,* December 12, 1969)

4. *Rhodesia is a friendly country and is anti-Communist.*

The Rhodesians have been our good friends, they have fought beside us in two world wars and have supported us in Vietnam. Surely, our friends are deserving of better treatment. (Pelly, House, R-Washington, *CR,* July 1, 1970)

The people of Rhodesia always have been friends of the United States. There is no more dedicated nation on earth in the struggle against Communist aim of world conquest. (Sikes, House, D-Florida, *CR,* September 28, 1971)

5. *Sanctions against Rhodesia cause economic harm to the U.S.* The economic argument has four major components: the United States loses a bilateral trade whose balance was in favor of the United States; U.S. companies with investments in Rhodesia are hurt; sanctions have forced up the price the United States must pay for chrome; and, the United States is losing economic benefits to other countries who informally trade with Rhodesia. Unemployment and inflation will be stimulated in the United States as a result of the sanctions.

American business, as well as our own balance of trade with Rhodesia, have suffered because of sanctions. Before Rhodesia proclaimed her independence, the United States enjoyed a most favorable balance of trade in the ratio of about 2 to 1. (Eastland, Senate, D-Mississippi, CR, January 19, 1967)

It is worth noting that the United States, in refusing to buy chromite ore, is helping to destroy the investments which American firms have poured into the Rhodesian mining industry. (Eastland, Senate, D-Mississippi, *CR*, March 10, 1970)

It makes no sense, in fact, it is utterly insane for the United States to deprive itself of a free world supply of a strategic mineral and to pay a ridiculously inflated price for an inferior substitute from Russia, in order to comply with UN sanctions requirements while other countries are flouting those requirements for a commercial advantage. (Gross, House, R-Iowa, *CR*, November 18, 1969)

The availability of Rhodesian chrome ore has had and, hopefully, will continue to have a stabilizing and moderating effect on ore prices. Re-imposition of the ban on imports of Rhodesian chrome would . . . stimulate higher prices and discourage employment in the ferroalloys and stainless steel industries. (Derwinski, House, R-Illinois, *CR*, September 25, 1975)

6. *Sanctions against Rhodesia endanger the national security of the U.S.* The security argument has two major components; sanctions force the U.S. to depend upon the USSR for chrome, a strategic mineral, vital to defense production, for which there is no substitute; and, sanctions increase the possibilities for instability in southern Africa thus aiding Communist penetration into this strategic area.

The domestic policies of Rhodesia should not be our primary concern here. Rather we must consider the consequences of a foreign policy that makes a nation dependent on its enemies rather than its friends for strategic defense material. (Biaggi, House, D-New York, *CR*, October 14, 1971)

The United States must look upon the nations of southern Africa as holding the true balance of power and as being the only pro-western influence of any consequence in sub-saharan Africa and on the western shores of the Indian Ocean. Rhodesia in a very real sense holds the key to southern Africa. Let Rhodesia fall and every other nation will follow directly. (Watson, House, R-South Carolina, *CR,* October 12, 1967)

7. *Sanctions are contrary to American principles and heritage.* It is asserted that the United States, which was the first country to uni-laterally declare its independence from Great Britain, ought not to now aid and abet British colonialism. To a lesser extent, it was also argued that the United States, by supporting the sanctions, violates the tradi-tional principle of free trade by all in peacetime.

> Our nation, I feel, has acted in a most unprincipled way toward Rhodesia. After all, that country has followed a course which the United States itself took in 1776—namely, sought its independence from Great Britain. (Byrd, Senate, Ind-Virginia, *CR,* March 10, 1970)

> The interdependence of nations for economic product raises a basic question of using economic sanctions to create foreign policy changes. We must be careful not to deplore the Middle Eastern nations for using economic sanctions against the United States, while applauding our own efforts to use economic sanctions against other nations. (Murtha, House, D-Pennsylvania, *CR,* September 25, 1975)

8. *The Rhodesian system of government has merit.* This argument notes that the Rhodesian government provides effective peaceful control and promotes economic growth and stability. The indigenous people are not yet capable of governing in a civilized manner as can be noted by reviewing the developments in "independent, Black Africa." It is rare, but nevertheless, once in a while, this argument is stated using overtly racist (anti-black) language, most notably by Representative John R. Rarick, D-Louisiana.

> The record in the Congo, Nigeria, Tanzania, Chad, and other nations has been one which would prima facie give credence to the Rhodesian thesis that majority rule should come through merit and not by waving some mystical wand, pronouncing tribesmen sovereign with the result that everything is turned over to them, lock, stock and barrel. (Ash-brooke, House, R-Ohio, *CR,* March 8, 1966)

> The natives of Africa are simply not capable mentally nor, unfor-tunately, morally to conduct good government. (Rarick, House, D-Louisiana, *CR,* February, 6, 1967)

It was obvious to me that the educational and cultural advancement of the Africans was in such a primitive stage that he could not govern himself, nor operate the ordinary machinery of organized society, at least in the American or European sense. (Ellender, Senate, D-Louisiana, *CR*, June 24, 1966)

9. *Sanctions are not effective.* Concern is expressed that sanctions do not harm Rhodesia because many countries do indeed trade with her covertly. Why then should the United States risk economic harm by *not* doing what so many other countries *are* doing?

The record shows the futility of sanctions. Rhodesia has not been harmed by the sanctions. In fact, Rhodesia has prospered throughout the duration of the sanctions. Sanctions are not effective. The hypocrisy of the argument is exposed when we see . . . practically all of the other nations of the world trading with Rhodesia covertly. (Ichord, House, D-Missouri, *CR*, September 25, 1975)

On the political side, it is pertinent to observe that, while a resumption of the embargo would hurt the United States badly, it would not seriously affect Rhodesia. The government which prompted the United Nations embargo 7 years ago is the same government that is in power today. (Spence, House, R-South Carolina, *CR*, September 25, 1975)

10. *Contravention of the sanctions will express hostility towards the United Nations.* Explicit denunciation of the United Nations *as an organization* or advocacy of the Byrd Amendment as a means to weaken that organization was *not* a feature of the debate on the Byrd Amendment. There was, however, an implicit hostility towards the UN in some of the debate; for example, Senator Byrd was worried about having the U.S. Congress be subordinated to the UN (*CR*, August 15, 1972), and Representative Sikes talked about the "meddling" of the UN and how Congress "allows that organization to lead us around by the nose" (*CR*, September 28, 1971). John Donahey of Foote Mineral Company, who lobbied intensively for the Byrd Amendment, claimed that the decision by the UN General Assembly to reject the two-China policy of the U.S. and to oust the delegation from Nationalist China was a very important factor in increasing the size of the favorable vote on the Byrd Amendment—especially in the House.[108]

The sentiment that the national interest was more important than the interests of the United Nations was also expressed.

The United States must pursue policies which are in the best interest of our Nation—not the UN. Continued trade with Rhodesia, one of the few friends we have left in Africa, is certainly in the best interests of the United States. (Dickinson, House, R-Alabama, *CR*, September 25, 1975)

It was a combination of these kinds of arguments, especially those involving the national security and economic well-being of the United States, plus the vagaries of the legislative process—especially in the Senate, where Senator Byrd's adroit parliamentary maneuvering and brilliant timing were evident—that led to the passage of the Byrd Amendment. Certainly the fact that the White House was preoccupied with more important political issues also contributed to its passage.

Interests Supporting Contravention of the Rhodesian Sanctions

By and large, the conservative press supported the Rhodesian cause and decried the sanctions; this would include newspapers (*Chicago Tribune, Indianapolis News, Cincinnati Enquirer, Journal of Commerce, St. Louis Globe-Democrat, Richmond News-Leader,* and many southern newspapers), magazines (*U.S. News & World Report, National Review*), columnists (Philip Wagner, John Chamberlain, William F. Buckley, James J. Kilpatrick), and radio commentators (Fulton Lewis, III, Gardner Ted Armstrong, Carl McIntyre). Ideological interest groups such as the Liberty Lobby, American-Southern Africa Council, American-African Affairs Association, and the American Legion also lent support. Various political scientists made public statements or testified before Congressional committees in favor of ending the sanctions on Rhodesia including Walter Darnell Jacobs (University of Maryland), Charles Burton Marshall (School for Advanced International Studies), and David N. Rowe (Yale University). Influential support was also provided by the late Secretary of State Dean Acheson and the Nobel Prize economist, Milton Friedman.

Industry support came primarily from those sectors most affected by the boycott on Rhodesian chrome—the ferroalloy and specialty steel producers (Allegheny Ludlum Steel, Colt Industries, Carpenter Technology) and the ferrochrome producers (Union Carbide and Foote Mineral). The former were adversely affected by competition from foreign steelmakers who, using the low-cost Rhodesian chrome, were able to penetrate the U.S. market with their ferroalloys at prices the

U.S. producers could not match. The latter were hurt by not having access to their Rhodesian chrome mines. The American Iron and Steel Institute and the Tool and Stainless Steel Committee supported the efforts of these companies.

Ironically, while the adoption of the Byrd Amendment made higher quality, lower cost Rhodesian chrome available to U.S. ferrochrome producers, it also made available *lower cost Rhodesian ferrochrome*. According to an official of Allegheny Ludlum Steel, between 1969 and 1971, Rhodesian ferrochrome production went from almost zero to almost 300,000 tons of capacity—equal to the U.S. capacity—due to the infusion into Rhodesia of Japanese capital and European equipment.[109] This was one of several factors which led Foote Mineral Company, in 1973, to decide to go out of the ferrochrome business and sell their Rhodesian mining properties; Foote Mineral did not actively lobby in favor of the retention of the Byrd Amendment in 1973, because it no longer had a commercial interest. Union Carbide continued to lobby because it owned both mines and ferroalloy plants in Rhodesia.

Central to a discussion of the supporting interests is the role of the Rhodesian Information Office (RIO) in Washington. Kenneth Towsey and Henry J. C. Hooper, its principal officers are employees of the Rhodesian government. Towsey, deputy secretary in the Rhodesian Ministry for Foreign Affairs, stated, "My office did not engage in what I would regard as lobby activity. Certainly, we were not in the business of seeking to solicit votes from Members of Congress in support of the Byrd amendment. We were disseminating in our regular literature a good deal of background information about chrome. Certainly, my office had an interest in the outcome of the Byrd amendment. We are pleased that it succeeded. From our point of view this was a move in the direction of normalization of relations between the United States and Rhodesia."[110] According to U.S. Assistant Attorney General Henry E. Petersen: "In its review of the correspondence files, financial records and records relating to Congressional activity the Bureau [F.B.I.] did not observe any material dealing with lobbying activity on behalf of the Byrd amendment by the RIO."[111]

Representative Charles Diggs, chairman of the House Subcommittee on Africa, in his 1973 hearings on the activities of the RIO, tried very hard to prove that Towsey was involved in the lobbying but failed. The hearings did establish the following: Towsey developed social relationships with U.S. legislators; his office helped finance a trip to Rhodesia by Fulton Lewis, III; Towsey knew some of the officers of Foote Mineral and Union Carbide; and his office mailed between 25,000 and 31,000 copies of various Rhodesian publications between August 1, 1972, and January 31, 1973.

Rhodesian newspapers credited Towsey with playing an important role in the efforts to secure passage of the Byrd Amendment. The *Rhodesia Herald,* December 11, 1971, noted that only gradually did Towsey and Hooper build up new circles of friends and political allies after UDI. "It was a task that required skill to foster all alliances without falling entirely captive to the far, far Right-wing groups, whose friendships can sometimes be the kiss of death to relations with more important Americans." The *Sunday Mail,* January 9, 1972, commented that "it is thanks to the efforts of Towsey and Hooper, and the skilled lobbying of big U.S. firms, that Congress voted to breach the UN embargo." The Senate vote establishing the Byrd Amendment, "represented many months of painstaking work by Mr. Towsey, Senator Byrd, and by a battery of other opponents of sanctions," according to the *Rhodesia Herald,* September 25, 1971.

After several interviews with Towsey between 1971 and 1973, the author concluded that, despite what one thinks about his political views, Towsey presents himself as an intelligent, well-informed, incisive, thoroughly charming diplomat. These personal characteristics assisted him in his task of supplying information to those who sought it—sometimes that included Congressmen. Often those Congressmen inserted that information into the *Congressional Record.* To the extent that that information was not easily refuted by those confronted by it, such activities may have constituted an annoyance. The symbolic significance of having paid employees of the Rhodesian government working on American territory may be an annoyance to those that consider it an "illegal régime," whose continuance in time should not be aided or abetted by anyone. It may be questioned whether Towsey, an alien, would wish to endanger the presence of the RIO by engaging in the act of lobbying when such an act could be performed more effectively by American citizens—such as those listed at the beginning of this discussion. That the RIO may supply political ammunition for the lobbyists and that Towsey may know some of the lobbyists and Congressional supporters of the Byrd Amendment is not in question; it also does not constitute violations of U.S. law.[112]

Restoration and Extension of the Rhodesian Sanctions

When the Rhodesian sanctions issue was debated in the Congress in 1977, there was virtually no change from the previous debates in the arguments supporting U.S. trade with Rhodesia. What had changed were the political and economic circumstances under which the Byrd Amendment was being debated. Politically, Rhodesia had obviously become a far more salient international problem due to the escalation of the guerrilla war and the direct involvement of the U.S. government in the efforts to seek a peaceful resolution to the problems confronting southern Africa. A new Democratic administration, whose foreign policy from the outset stressed vigorous promotion of human rights throughout the world, actively lobbied on behalf of the restoration of sanctions. Beset by worsening economic and military problems, the Smith régime's viability had deteriorated, and many congressmen wondered how a future majority government of Zimbabwe might view countries which had failed to apply the UN sanctions against the Smith régime yet continued to seek access to the country's mineral wealth.

Moreover, the economic reasons for the enactment of the Byrd Amendment in 1971, had been largely vitiated. Technological innovations in the steel industry permitted the replacement of high-quality ferrochromium with lower-quality ferrochromium smelted from ore available from sources other than Rhodesia or the Soviet Union. There was also increased capacity in South Africa and other non-Communist states for smelting enough high-quality ferrochromium to satisfy the needs of the non-Communist world. A former strong advocate of the Byrd Amendment, E. F. Andrews, vice president of Allegheny Ludlum Steel, testified on behalf of the Tool and Stainless Steel Committee and admitted that, while he still favored American access to Rhodesian chrome, U.S. reliance upon that chrome was less than when the Byrd Amendment was adopted in 1971. One of the principal supporters of the Byrd Amendment in the House, Representative John Dent (D-Pennsylvania), stated: "Now that the American industry and workers no longer need the economic protection of the Byrd Amendment, and since the existence of the Amendment might hamper American diplomatic initiatives in Africa, I believe that the Byrd Amendment should be repealed."[113] The testimony of both men was critical in defusing the argument that U.S. industry would suffer if sanctions on Rhodesia were fully restored.

Both men noted, however, that the U.S. specialty steel industry could face unfair price competition from imports of foreign steel containing low-cost Rhodesian chrome. Hence, the new law contains an *extension of sanctions* which goes beyond the previous Executive Orders; it bans the imports of foreign steel products containing Rhodesian chrome. In effect, this represents a secondary boycott against those countries who are lax in applying sanctions against Rhodesia and who import Rhodesian materials and export the final product to the U.S. Indeed, the report on H.R.1746 of the House Committee on International Relations comments that notice is served on our world trading-partners that "the United States expects them to take the necessary steps for assuring their own adherence to the sanctions in accordance with their stated policies"; failure to do so could result in the loss of premium trade with U.S. "The direct result should be more effective worldwide adherence to the UN sanctions."[114] When the amended Rhodesian sanctions regulations appeared in the *Federal Register,* a technical amendment was added requiring U.S. Customs to subject samples of *all* imports of chrome ore and ferrochromium from South Africa to laboratory testing to insure that it is not of Rhodesian origin.[115]

Effect of the Byrd Amendment on Rhodesia

A review of the Rhodesian press for the year ending June 1, 1972, reveals that the Rhodesian government's comments on the issue were kept to a minimum. Eleven days before the first vote on Section 503 in the Senate, Prime Minister Smith told the editor of the American magazine, *Plain Truth* (as reported in the *Sunday Mail,* September 12, 1971): "I have a suspicion, indeed more than a suspicion that quite a lot of it [chrome] is actually going behind the Iron Curtain to Communist Countries." This had been a major argument of the proponents of Section 503, and Smith's statement might have been designed to reinforce that argument. Soon after President Nixon signed Section 503 into law, Smith, in an interview with *U.S. News and World Report,* November 29, 1971, said that resumption of chrome exports to the U.S. would help Rhodesia to meet its foreign exchange problems. He added: "We would be able to buy certain equipment that we would like to have from America, which is at present denied to us while it is readily supplied to Communist countries. Unlike so many other countries of the world— particularly the underdeveloped countries of the world—we don't ask for things to be given to us. We have always paid our way in the past, and we are happy to pay our way in the future. We're prepared to do the task, whatever it is—prepare the land, produce the food, fight against Communism—if we have access to the tools. And we will pay for these. Our main opponents—the people who are trying to trip us up, who are trying to pull us back—are members of the free world, who are proving a far greater impediment to our progress than the members of the Communist world, and we would like to bring this incredibly stupid position to an end." Notice the appeals in Smith's statement to "traditional American cultural orientations"—the fear of communism, the Protestant work-ethic, the idea of the double-standard and fair play, and the disparagement of debators who "can't pay their own way."

Secretary of Mines K. K. Parker emphasized another angle in the *Rhodesia Herald,* November 25, 1971: "We have obligations to meet the requirements of all the customers who have been purchasing chrome from us during the past five or six years. Once we have met these obligations we will be delighted to consider the practicability of meeting any request from the United States for chrome." This statement reinforces Rhodesia's reputation for dependability in marketing—a virtue the industrial countries may not always find in primary producing countries. The economic effects were deemphasized by Towsey who told the author that it was widely known that Rhodesia did not have any difficulty in disposing of her chrome production on the world markets; therefore, the removal of sanctions on Rhodesian chrome was not likely to have any significant effect on the economy of Rhodesia. In 1973, a Union Carbide official explained that the adoption of the Byrd Amendment did not result in a large volume of Rhodesian chrome shipments to the United States because most of the output was already committed to customers in other countries. He stated that his firm had to plead with UNIVEX, the Rhodesian state trading company, for supplies of ore.[116] Yet just two years later, Rhodesian Minister of Mines Ian Dillon claimed in the *Rhodesia Herald,* May 12, 1975, that loss of exports to the United States would result in closure of chrome mines and 60,000 people would be affected, directly or indirectly, by loss of income. It would seem that judgments about the economic effect of the Byrd Amendment on Rhodesia are varied, sometimes contradictory, and probably mixed with propaganda.

According to the *Rhodesia Herald,* January 27, 1972, one of the more important effects of the Byrd Amendment might be an increase in confidence among buyers of Rhodesia's mineral exports which, in turn, could put Rhodesia in a better position to demand higher prices for her products. In any event, in 1972, United States imports from Rhodesia represented, at most, only 3 percent of Rhodesia's total domestic exports for that year. Although reliable statistics are not available, the best estimate is that the U.S. imports in succeeding years never accounted for more than 8–10 percent of Rhodesia's annual domestic exports by value.

Whatever the economic consequences, of far greater significance were the political and psychological considerations. Passage of the Byrd

Amendment reinforced the basic contention, indeed, doctrine, of the Rhodesian government that sanctions would eventually "wither away" in the face of the resolve of the Rhodesian people. The *Rhodesia Herald* editorialized on September 25, 1971, that the lifting of the embargo on chrome ore "would be a wonderful boost for Rhodesian morale and a bitter setback to those who still seek the country's collapse." While warning on November 6, 1971, that "the accelerated erosion of sanctions that is foreshadowed could not take place overnight, and in the meantime lack of foreign capital, and other consequences of the absence of international recognition, would continue to sap the country's vitality for an indefinite period," the *Rhodesia Herald* concluded: "All the same, the American move is at the least a signal to the world that sanctions are not important enough to warrant serious sacrifices; and at the most that their usefulness has lost its credibility in American eyes."

REGIONAL ECONOMIC COOPERATION

One of the most frequently discussed economic topics in South Africa and Rhodesia is the idea of promoting regional economic cooperation. The states most often mentioned for inclusion into such a scheme are: South Africa, Rhodesia, Malawi, Zambia, Angola, Botswana, Mozambique, Lesotho, Swaziland, and South West Africa. Lombard's matrix of total trade flows for 1964 (the last year for which reliable statistics are available) shows that interregional trade accounted for 27.9 percent of the total exports to all countries and about 25.0 percent of the total imports from all countries. According to Lombard, "of all the states concerned, Rhodesia's reliance on trade within the subcontinent seems to be much greater than any of the other states concerned."[117] This reliance may be assumed to have increased greatly since UDI. Other states that have been mentioned for possible inclusion into the scheme are Malagasy Republic, Mauritius, and Zaire. Rowan Cronje, Rhodesian MP, who has written a great deal on the topic, included Gabon in a report for the *Rhodesia Herald,* December 10, 1971. This is interesting considering the earlier discussion in this chapter of Gabonese-Rhodesian linkages.

The promotion of regional development, with Rhodesia as a participant, is a key tenet of Rhodesian foreign policy. The plea for greater economic cooperation in southern Africa was the main theme of Prime Minister Ian Smith's speech opening the Cape Agricultural Show at

Goodwood, South Africa, in March 1972 (carried in the *Rhodesia Herald,* March 2, 1972). Smith claimed that the smaller states might have no chance of survival unless they created economies larger than their own boundaries—even at some cost to their sensitive national pride. "This calls, among other things, for the breaking down of artificial barriers which separate countries in Southern and Central Africa from their neighbours," according to Smith. Closer economic cooperation between respective countries was an essential first move. "Maybe in time this could lead to an all-embracing common market. But that is a decision for the future. Initially some form of economic agreement along lines of improved inter-regional marketing of goods and services would be advantageous." Smith urged that the existing bonds between southern African countries be woven into a closer-knit association for the common good. Successful economic integration would also require increased degree of political cohesion.

Smith's speech was welcomed by spokesmen of South Africa's two main political parties, the United party and the National party.[118] South African Prime Minister John Vorster, speaking at a symposium on co-operation in southern Africa at Potchefstroom University in 1971, said: "It is clear to everybody that there should be the closest possible economic co-operation in Southern Africa. We already have that co-operation in embryo. I think South Africa is prepared to support any practical proposal that will facilitate that co-operation."[119]

Despite favorable sentiments expressed by South African leaders, one month after Smith's Goodwood speech, the South African accredited diplomatic representative to Rhodesia, G. Stewart, made reference to Smith's views and stated in the *Sunday Mail,* April 30, 1972, that South Africa realized that the time was not ripe for such a system of multilateral economic co-operation in this area. Just three months after that speech, Smith was asked by a *Journal of Commerce* reporter if there were any concrete initiatives underway "to get the ball rolling" on a southern Africa trading association, to which Smith replied (as reported by the *Journal* on June 19, 1972): "It's a little different for an 'illegal' man like myself with an unconstitutional tag around my neck to stick my neck out too far at the present moment, as far as this sort of issue is concerned."

There seems to be some ambivalence in the preceding statements regarding economic cooperation. Depending on the type of economic arrangement being contemplated, it is recognized that economic problems do exist—for example, the overwhelming dominance of the South

African economy in the region, and the fact that most of the economies are competitive rather than complementary.[120] However, note the following statements (emphasis added):

1. "Initially some form of economic agreement along the lines of *improved inter-regional marketing of goods and services* would be advantageous." (From Smith's Goodwood speech)

2. "What South Africa should do, government spokesmen maintain, is to take every opportunity of encouraging a *more effective intraregional marketing system of goods* and greater economic cooperation among all countries."[121]

3. "I am not persuaded that the present is an opportune time to establish a common market. But I am firmly of the opinion that every effort should be made . . . *to improve the inter-regional marketing of goods and services,* to step up the inter-regional investment of capital resources and, generally, to move in the direction of ever closer economic cooperation."[122]

The resolution of the above confusion may be as follows. Smith may have been on solid ground *vis-à-vis* the economists and South African officials when he suggested initial steps of economic cooperation "along the lines of improved inter-regional marketing of goods and services." However, when Smith talked about "integration," "closer-knit association," and "common market"—even in tentative terms—it may have worried South African officials for political, if not for economic, reasons. South Africa resists any suggestion of overt, formal linkages with Rhodesia; sanctions are viewed as a barrier to the establishment of such ties. Smith evidently realized this as well, as his later comments to the *Journal of Commerce* suggest. Through a formal economic arrangement, Smith might indirectly be able to claim political recognition for Rhodesia as well as weaken the effects sanctions are having on Rhodesia—psychologically as well as economically.

Communication and Transportation

COMMUNICATIONS

IT OUGHT TO BE MADE CLEAR that the UN Security Council has *not* imposed sanctions on communications with Rhodesia. Twice, in fact, resolutions containing such sanctions were vetoed by both the United Kingdom and the United States—on March 18, 1970, and on May 22, 1973. The reasoning behind the U.S. veto was outlined by U.S. Ambassador to the UN Charles W. Yost,

> We in the United States have consistently attached the greatest importance to the maintenance of communications with other states, even those with whom our relations were greatly strained and in some cases even when hostilities were in progress between us. The United States has a long history and tradition of freedom of movement and speech and would view most seriously the prospect of leaving United States citizens anywhere in the world without the means to travel or communicate. Furthermore, we do not believe that the cutting off of communications, the stemming of a free flow of information, would contribute to a solution of the difficult problem with which we are faced. Rather, it might tend to further harden the attitude of the white minority.

Yost added that he did not believe that cutting off Rhodesia's communications with the rest of the world would have any decisive effect on the "illegal minority régime."[1] Nevertheless, some international organizations have called for precisely such action. The Organization of African Unity (OAU) has called upon all states to break off all means

167

of communication and transportation with Rhodesia. According to the *Times* (London), January 21, 1971, the Commonwealth Sanctions Committee called on all Commonwealth governments unilaterally to cut postal and telegraphic communications with Rhodesia. Additionally, as noted below, many countries have unilaterally imposed communications sanctions on Rhodesia.

Telephone, Telegraph, and Telex Services

In 1965, Libya, Tunisia, Algeria, Morocco, Kenya, Poland, Hungary, the Sudan, and Tanzania suspended telecommunication services with Rhodesia. The following year, Jordan, Uganda, USSR, Albania, Bulgaria, the Congo, Yugoslavia, Egypt, Ethiopia, the Dominican Republic, and Syria suspended services. Subsequently, Burundi, Nigeria, Cuba, and Pakistan took similar action bringing the total to twenty-four countries which imposed the sanction unilaterally.[2] Regarding the suspensions, the Rhodesian Postmaster-General noted in his 1968/69 annual report that "with little or no community of interest with the countries concerned, the effects of the suspension are negligible." Indeed, most of the countries were members of either the Arab or Communist blocs, and Rhodesia probably had little intercourse with those countries before UDI. The suspension of services by the East African Community (Kenya, Uganda, and Tanzania) did, however, have an effect, a spokesman for the Rhodesian Posts and Telecommunications Corporation told the author on June 30, 1971, but he declined to state the nature of the effect. Zambia suspended automatic telephone, telegraph, and telex service to Rhodesia in 1973, but operator-controlled telephone service remained available on a restricted basis. Mozambique suspended service in 1976.

International telephone service was established to Northern Rhodesia (now Zambia), South Africa, and the United Kingdom (via South Africa) in 1933. In the decade after UDI, Rhodesian telecommunication services were extended to many new countries, and, by 1975, telephone service was available to 114 countries, permitting access to over 95 percent of the world's telephones.[3] Ships at sea fitted with radiotelephones could be reached via South Africa and the United Kingdom.

There were extensive interregional telephone linkages with direct dial or trunk service from Rhodesia to Mozambique (until 1976), Zambia (until 1973), South Africa, Botswana, south Zaire, Lesotho, South West Africa, Malawi, and Swaziland. Some of Rhodesia's telecommunication links with overseas countries are routed through South

Africa; Rhodesia rents one channel of the submarine cable connecting Cape Town with Lisbon. In 1974, a new international direct telegraph link was opened between Rhodesia and Europe, and this link carried South African telephone calls to Europe when the submarine cable was temporarily out of service in 1975.

As of 1975, Rhodesia maintained reciprocal telex service with ninety-nine countries enabling subscribers to communicate by means of teleprinters. The number of telex subscribers in Rhodesia more than doubled between 1966 and 1975, to a total of 672. Those subscribers could be dialled direct from the United States, Canada, and several European countries beginning in 1972. Fully automatic telex service was introduced with South Africa and South West Africa in 1969, and later extended to Botswana, Malawi, Zambia, and Mozambique. Rhodesia was very much involved in regional cooperation in the telecommunications field and provided transit facilities for telex calls between South Africa and both Malawi and Zambia. All Mozambique's communications with Zambia passed through Salisbury as well as the telecommunication circuit between Beira and Nairobi.[4]

Postal Services

In 1965, Kenya, Uganda, and Tanzania suspended postal service with Rhodesia. The following year, Libya, Algeria, USSR, Poland, Ethiopia, and India (parcels only) suspended service. Subsequently, Nigeria, Ghana, Pakistan, Somalia, and Mozambique took similar action. Comments on the effects of the telecommunications suspensions may be applied to the postal suspensions as well. As the following figures indicate, foreign mail volume remained rather constant in the decade following UDI. In the period 1964–66, Rhodesia received an average of 23.7 million articles of mail matter from foreign countries each year and sent an average of 16.8 million articles to foreign destinations each year; the comparable figures for the 1973–75 period were: 22.6 million received; 16.7 million sent.[5]

It should be noted that the United Kingdom government declared that the definitive decimal stamps issued by Rhodesia after the declaration of republican status were not valid for the prepayment of postage. The United Kingdom informed the Universal Postal Union of this fact and reaffirmed that Her Majesty's government remained responsible for the international relations, including postal relations, of Southern Rhodesia. As of April 1, 1970, all mail matter received in the United Kingdom bearing those Rhodesian stamps was subjected to a surcharge similar to postage due mail. That surcharge was abolished on October 8, 1970. There is no evidence that any other country followed the British practice.

The Rhodesia Posts and Telecommunications Corporation (PTC) maintains a Philatelic Bureau from which stamp collectors from all over the world may purchase Rhodesian postage stamps as they are issued. The Bureau maintains a mailing list of 16,000 names and sends out regular bulletins and order forms. An officer of the PTC noted in the *Rhodesia Herald,* April 3, 1973, that postage stamps were a valuable source of foreign currency to Rhodesia.

Importance of Communication Linkages

Contrary to Ambassador Yost's assessment, cuttting off Rhodesia's communications with the rest of the world could very well have a decisive effect on Rhodesia's efforts to maintain the viability of its economy. Communications are indispensible for developing and maintaining the kinds of economic linkages described in the previous chapter. A spokesman for the PTC told the author in 1971, that "telecommunications are most vital in the economic war." The fact that Rhodesian businessmen can telex, telegraph, and telephone all over the world seeking markets for their goods and sources of supplies with a minimum expenditure of time and resources is an important reason for the success Rhodesia has had in neutralizing the effects of sanctions.

Communication linkages are also important in that they boost public morale and lessen the psychological effects of isolation. For example, referring to the British action of 1970, declaring the Rhodesian decimal stamps invalid, the *Sunday Mail,* September 3, 1972, claimed that "it was a great victory for Rhodesia when the stamps were accepted by most countries of the Universal Postal Union after Britain had refused to accept Rhodesia's stamps after UDI." The newspaper added that apart from the money they earn, "the stamps are tiny envoys for Rhodesia going to every part of the world; permanent reminders and colourful advertisements."

As important as the communication linkages are, a question may be raised as to the practical consequences of imposing sanctions on communications. Such sanctions would complicate Rhodesia's efforts to contact the outside world but probably would not make the task impossible— given the degree of integration of the communications network in Southern Africa. Rhodesian companies could contact friendly firms and parent, branch, or subsidiary firms located in South Africa or Malawi, and they could relay or retransmit the information abroad. As with so many of the sanctions, their impact is lessened by their not being applied against Rhodesia's neighbors within the southern African region; Rhodesia's regional linkages help her gain access to the outside world.

Moreover, some governments claim they do not have the authority under their existing constitutional framework to prevent their citizens from communicating with residents of another country. Japanese and French representatives to the UN cited such constitutional limitations in their arguments against communications sanctions. The representative of Italy noted the postal service essentially involved individuals rather than countries and therefore would be difficult for his country to impose sanctions on that service.[6]

TRANSPORTATION

Unlike the situation *vis-à-vis* communications, the UN Security Council did apply specific sanctions against Rhodesia in the area of transportation. In 1968, the Security Council in S/RES/253 called on members of the UN to ban air transportation to and from Rhodesia and to forbid any airline or aircraft from linking up with any Rhodesian airline or aircraft. Two years later, the Security Council in S/RES/277 decided that all existing means of transportation to and from Rhodesia should be interrupted. One of the first mandatory sanctions placed on Rhodesia was an embargo, in 1966, on the supply of aircraft and motor vehicles and all related materials and equipment (S/RES/232). Along with the sanctions on trade with Rhodesia, the Security Council also called on members in S/RES/253 not to provide facilities for the transportation of any goods to and from Rhodesia. When the latter sanction did not prove successful in stopping or even decreasing the shipments of Rhodesia's imports and exports, the Security Council, in 1973, called upon all states to forbid their insurance companies from covering air flights into and out of Rhodesia and to require that marine insurance contracts contain provisions that no Rhodesian imports or exports could be covered. The Council also called upon states to enact and enforce legislation providing for the imposition of severe penalties on persons that provide any facilities for the transport of goods to and from Rhodesia (S/RES/333). A resolution sponsored by Guinea, Kenya, and Somalia requesting states to deny or revoke landing rights to national airlines continuing to operate in Rhodesia was defeated by the vetoes of the United States and the United Kingdom on May 22, 1973. Despite

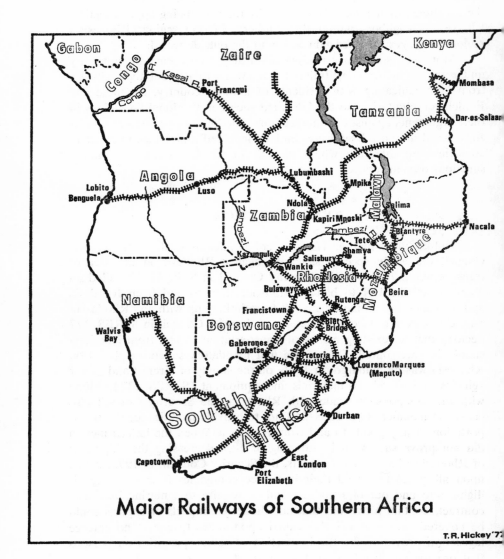

Major Railways of Southern Africa

T.R. Hickey '7?

the vetoes, the sanctions dealing with transportation are rather comprehensive, covering not only the linkages themselves, but also related equipment and insurance.

Railroad Linkages

Politics, economics, and geography all determined the course of the building of the railroads in central Africa during colonial rule. The most significant geographical fact is that Rhodesia is landlocked and thus dependent upon transit facilities through Mozambique and South Africa in order to reach the sea. But Botswana and Zambia are also landlocked, and the transportation patterns that developed under British rule made these states largely dependent upon transit facilities through Rhodesia for access to the sea. To a lesser extent, Zaire and Malawi also use Rhodesia transit facilities.

Mozambique

Rhodesia established direct rail links with the ports of Beira in 1899, and Lourenco Marques in 1955. Rhodesia, Mozambique, Zambia, and Malawi served on the Beira Port Traffic Advisory Committee— which resulted from the Beira Convention signed in Lisbon in 1950 by Portugal, the United Kingdom, and Southern Rhodesia. The convention was designed to prevent any discrimination in the use of Beira as a port, and the committee served to advise Portuguese authorities on matters regarding the operation of the port.[7] Before UDI, Beira had been Rhodesia's main outlet to the sea, but its importance declined after the Beira blockade was established in April 1966, after which Rhodesia shifted much of her trade from Beira to Lourenco Marques and various South African ports.

Serious problems with the Mozambique routes began in 1974, after the Portuguese coup and the ascendancy of FRELIMO in Mozambique. Traffic was impeded on the Salisbury-Beira line by sporadic guerrilla activity, and labor problems and strikes in Lourenco Marques forced interruptions in Rhodesian traffic several times in 1974. Increasing inefficiency, lower productivity, and a shortage of skilled labor at the Mozambique ports resulted in a 50 percent decrease in the volume of Rhodesian traffic flowing through those ports in the first year after the Portuguese coup, according to the *Rhodesia Herald,* May 15, 1975. The private sector in South Africa also shifted export traffic from Lourenco Marques to South African ports causing massive congestion on the South African Railways. Employees of that Railways were sent to Maputo (formerly called Lourenco Marques) in 1975, to help maintain operations. Maputo was vital to South Africa as it carried 40 percent of the imports and exports of the Transvaal—the heartland of South African industry and mining.

In March 1976, Mozambique closed the border with Rhodesia ending Rhodesia's use of Beira and Maputo. These ports had once handled 80 percent (by volume) of Rhodesia's foreign trade, but this was estimated by the Rhodesian minister of transport in the *Rhodesia Herald,* March 6, 1976, to have declined to about 25 to 30 percent at the time of the border closure. Most of the traffic consisted of low-rated, high-volume, low-density exports such as mineral ores and agricultural products. This traffic, very expensive to transport, had to be diverted to South African ports and carried over rail routes nearly three times longer than the routes through Mozambique. It is interesting to note that the border closure left Mozambique without rail connections between Beira and Maputo, as the only north-south link passed through Salisbury.

South Africa

In 1897, the railroad reached Bulawayo from South Africa. Instead of following the most direct route, the British-built railroad veered towards the west and then swung north through Bechuanaland (now Botswana) to bypass the Boer republics of the Orange Free State and Transvaal and entered Rhodesia from the southwest. Until 1959, South African Railways operated the railroad up to Bulawayo. In that year, Rhodesia Railways took over operation of the Bulawayo-Mahalapye section, and in 1966, it took over operation of the Mahalapye-Mafeking section of the line. In 1976, it was estimated that this line carried 15 to 20 percent of Rhodesia's foreign trade.[8]

South African Railways built a railroad from Pretoria to the Rhodesian border at Beit Bridge, but linkage to the Rhodesian rail system was deemed not to be economically viable until the Botswana link reached full capacity.[9] In 1974, however, anticipating possible disruption of rail service to Mozambique when the Portuguese left, Rhodesia began a crash program to complete the link. The 90-mile link between Rutenga and Beit Bridge was completed September 10, 1974, after only ninety-three days under construction; the first train carrying goods used the line on October 1.

Initially the new link handled 3,000 to 4,000 tons a day. In 1975, the track was strengthened to handle heavy ore shipments which raised the capacity to 12,000 tons a day. Central Train Control and crossing loops were also being installed which could eventually raise the gross line capacity to 30,000 tons a day (or a net ton capacity of around 7 million tons a year). Such a capacity for the Rutenga link alone could take care of Rhodesia's foreign trade requirements for at least a decade.[10] Rhodesia's imports and exports were estimated to average 5 to 6 million tons a year, and there seemed to be little doubt that the two rail links to South Africa could handle the tonnage involved after the Mozambique border closure.

One major problem, however, was the ability of the South African Railways (SAR) to handle the increase in Rhodesian traffic in light of their own massive congestion. An SAR official warned in June 1975, that "insurmountable problems" would be created if Rhodesia sent all her goods through South Africa; another official stressed that the SAR would not refuse any Rhodesian traffic but warned of delays.[11] South African Minister of Transport Louwrens Muller stated in a report in the *Rhodesia Herald,* March 5, 1976, that the SAR could absorb some of the trade diverted from Mozambique but admitted it could not absorb all the traffic. Muller said: "There are certain things we are not equipped to handle; the real problem lay in capacity on the rail links to the ports." He pledged that "within the limits of physical capability, we will continue to make our services available." As evidence that South Africa was willing to handle as much Rhodesian traffic as possible, the SAR spent R1.5 million on improvements to facilities on the line from Pretoria to Beit Bridge in the two years prior to the completion of the Rutenga link, and it was planning to spend another R5 million on improvements to the line in 1976.[12]

Rail congestion is real and seasonal in nature, peaking between June and October—the winter season. There is, at this time, heavy internal movement of coal for thermal power stations, and the bulk of the citrus and maize crops begin to move to the ports for export. In 1976, the congestion was aggravated by South African exporters rerouting their goods from Maputo to South African ports for reasons explained above. Rhodesia's main exports also start moving in June and, in 1976, faced severe congestion. The Rutenga link operated at less than half its actual capacity, and one Rhodesian firm had to destroy 16,000 tons of citrus due to the inability to export because of railage difficulties. The South African policy seemed to be that Rhodesian exports would not be given preference at the expense of their own and would simply have to take their place in the rail queue.

Beginning in 1975, sporadic guerrilla sabotage threatened both rail links to South Africa. Should such sabotage succeed in disrupting service, it would have grave consequences for the Rhodesian economy.

Botswana

As noted above, the only railroad in Botswana is owned and operated by Rhodesia Railways, itself a statutory corporation subsidized by the Rhodesian government, a corporation which operates all public rail service in Rhodesia. The Rhodesia Railways pays the government of Botswana R$350,000 per year in "way leave" for the Rhodesian trains traveling to and from South Africa. Botswana collects an additional R$175,000 in mail transit fees. Rhodesia Railways maintains and improves the line and employs a local work force numbering several hundred.[13] Despite the fact that there are occasional charges of racial discrimination against Botswanan citizens by railway officials, the government of Botswana has done nothing to prejudice Rhodesia's operations. President Seretse Khama was reported in the *Rhodesia Herald,* October 3, 1969, to have declared that his government had no intention of exercising its option to take over the Botswana section of the Rhodesia Railways; the option was due to expire in 1970, and he said that "we will just let it expire." In 1974, Khama stated that his government must plan to run the railway line as soon as arrangements can be made. The "arrangements" which would have to be made, however, are expensive and complex and would mean a loss of revenue from Rhodesia. Rhodesia Railways valued the stationary facilities at R$20 million and would claim reimbursement.[14] Lacking any rolling stock of its own, Botswana would need about US$50 million to buy locomotives, wagons, and coaches. Lacking trained personnel, Botswana would have to hire up to 550 expatriates to operate the railway. The overall cost to nationalize the railway could reach US$77 million (excluding reimbursement to Rhodesia).[15] Rhodesia Railways started courses to train Botswana railway workers in 1975, but it would take many years before there would be sufficient trained personnel to operate the railway. Indeed, after the Rutenga link was completed, the *Rhodesia Herald,* March 10, 1976, reported that Botswana government officials acknowledged that the railway was vital to Botswana but not to Rhodesia, and if Botswana closed the border, the line would have to be abandoned unless the South African Railways agreed to operate it.

Botswana is making an effort to expand its limited transportation options by building a road to Zambia financed by a long-term, low-interest loan from the United States. This road assumes greater importance in light of the closure of the border between Rhodesia and Zambia, as it provides an alternate route for Botswana goods destined to Zambia and Zaire. Note also that the Mozambique border closure effectively denied Botswana the use of the port of Beira.

Zambia

After the railroad reached Bulawayo in 1897, mining exerted a dominant influence in determining future construction. That construction swung west through Wankie and Victoria Falls in 1904, crossed the Zambesi River into Northern Rhodesia, and turned northeast reaching Broken Hill in 1906, stopping three years later near the Congo border. A link was eventually completed joining the railway system in the Congo. The railroad thus connected the Wankie coalfield, the "Copper Belt" region of Zambia, and the rich mining areas of Katanga. Almost all of Katanga's copper was shipped over the Rhodesian rail network to Beira until the railroad was extended in the Congo to Port Francqui on the Kasai River in 1928. Another branch, the Benguela Railway, was constructed in 1931, across Angola to the port of Lobito.[16] For Zambia, the railway through Rhodesia remained the dominant carrier of Zambian imports and exports until the border closure in 1973. Both because coal and coke from Wankie were needed for mining, and because the capacity of the Benguela line was limited and transportation costs were higher on that line, Zambia was dependent on the Rhodesia Railways. During the Federation, the railways of both countries were joined in a unitary system. UDI strained this arrangement and the operational division of the unitary system was effected on June 30, 1967.

While Zambia was dependent on Rhodesia's transit facilities, Rhodesia was dependent on Zambia's use of those facilities. That use helped Rhodesia to offset her expenditure on transit facilities through Mozambique and South Africa. Rhodesia's international transportation payments were balanced by payments from Zambia and from receipts from services rendered in Botswana. Roger Hawkins describes Rhodesia's "invisible exports" as follows: "These comprise two categories. First, there are the goods which move across Rhodesia between two neighbouring countries. The most profitable is Zambian copper but there is a heavy volume of other items such as wheat and fertilizer from Beira to Zambia and clinker and fertilizer from South Africa to Zambia. The second category of invisibles is the net earnings from the part of the Rhodesia Railways system which operates in Botswana. This includes goods of Botswana origin such as cattle (and soon will include copper and nickel), goods transitting Botswana, goods imported into Botswana and large numbers of passengers."[17]

Hawkins notes that Zambian copper is the most profitable item in the transit traffic. This is because copper is a high-rated rail commodity; it helps the Rhodesia Railways to offset the cost involved in moving low-rated Rhodesian products such as maize, chrome ore, and iron ore. Rhodesia's minister of transport and power explained to the Legislative Assembly, July 7, 1966, that "under normal circumstances, about two-thirds of the Rhodesia Railways' expenditure is incurred in Rhodesia and Bechuanaland, but half of their revenue is derived from Zambian traffics." This explains why Rhodesia Railways diverted wagons to carry Zambian copper exports when there were not enough wagons available to carry Rhodesian products.

After UDI, the government of Zambia tried to apply transportation sanctions against Rhodesia and to bankrupt the Rhodesia Railways. In April 1966, Zambia prohibited the transfer of funds to Rhodesia to pay for freight costs incurred on the Rhodesia Railways. The Rhodesian government threatened to block all Zambian freight unless payment was made in advance in U.S. dollars or Swiss francs. The price of British copper imports from Zambia soared. An arrangement was worked out with the British government whereby payments would be made to Rhodesia through various European countries. Zambia then tried to divert her high-rated copper traffic away from the Rhodesia Railways to other routes while expecting the Railways to continue to carry the low-rated imports and exports. Rhodesia responded by placing various surcharges on the Zambian traffic and allowing one wagon to enter Zambia for every wagon that came from Zambia into Rhodesia. In 1968, Zambia guaranteed to export a minimum of 25,000 tons of copper per month through Rhodesia. Whenever exports fell below this figure, a surcharge was introduced on Zambian traffic until Zambia fulfilled its guarantee for two consecutive months. Zambia also tried to restrict the carriage of her imports from South Africa to road transport firms based outside Rhodesia. This move was designed to deny revenues to the Rhodesia Railways while producing stress on Rhodesia's highways from Beit Bridge to the Zambian border. The Rhodesian government responded by restricting road permits to foreign-based vehicle operators from June 1, 1972.

Despite this harassment, Zambia continued to make demands on the Rhodesia Railways. For example, Zambia continued to expect the workshops at Bulawayo to repair and maintain their locomotives until October 1971, when the Zambian workshops were opened at Kabwe.

After exhausting all other possibilities, Energoprojekt, the Yugoslav construction firm building the Kafue hydroelectric project, approached the Rhodesia Railways and asked them to organize and transport heavy equipment to the Kafue site.[18] Zambia's demands ceased with the decision by the government not to reopen the border with Rhodesia in February 1973.

Prior to the border closure, Zambia had sought to develop alternative routes for her imports and exports. An oil pipeline and an improved road were built to the Tanzanian port of Dar es Salaam, and greater use was made of the Benguela Railway to the Angolan port of Lobito. In 1969, the People's Republic of China started to build the Tan-Zam (later called Tazara) railroad linking the Zambian Railways at Kapiri Mposhi with the port of Dar es Salaam 1,130 miles away. Statistics reveal that Zambia sent 13,000 tons of copper monthly by rail to Lobito, 16,000 to 20,000 by road to Dar es Salaam, and 25,000 to 30,000 by rail through Rhodesia to Beira.[19]

After the border closure, Zambia sent 30,000 tons of copper monthly by rail to Lobito, 20,000 by road to Dar es Salaam, 10,000 by road to Mombassa, and 7,000 by road and rail through Malawi to Nacala.[20] Initially, the rerouting exercise seemed successful. In the first year after the closure, vital copper exports increased 40 percent by value and total exports increased 35 percent.[21] This success was largely due to the logistical support provided by Portugal, South Africa, Malawi, Tanzania, and Kenya and to international financial support in the form of loans and grants to help cover increased freight rates and to buy transportation equipment. South Africa airlifted vitally needed imports into Zambia; Malawi offered her rail facilities between Balaka and the Mozambique port of Nacala to Zambian freight hauled by road to Balaka; Portugal kept her ports of Lobito and Nacala open to Zambian traffic and offered to increase the flow of traffic on the Benguela Railway; Tanzania declared Dar es Salaam a "transit port" from February 1, 1973, open only to traffic destined for and coming from Zambia, Rwanda, Burundi, and Zaire while diverting her own traffic to the smaller port of Tanga; and Kenya took Zambian traffic at the port of Mombassa.

While Zambia seems to have finally been able to sever her transportation links with Rhodesia, some logistical problems have occurred. Most of the time between July 1975 and August 1976, the Benguela link to Lobito was inoperative due to the civil war in Angola. The Tazara railroad was pressed into emergency service in September 1975, and ships were diverted from Lobito to Dar es Salaam. The latter port, however, suffered massive congestion and, at one point, 119,000 tons of Zambian imports and exports were stranded.[22] The minister of transport and power of Rhodesia promised in the *Rhodesia Herald,* August 21, 1975, that his country would do all it could to accommodate Zambian railway traffic if the Zambian government would reopen the border. Zambia kept the border closed but had to cut copper exports by 30 to 40 percent until the Benguela link was reopened.

The economic effect on Rhodesia of the cessation of Zambian traffic was discussed by Prime Minister Ian Smith, who remarked to the *Rhodesia Herald,* January 29, 1973, that it would release more rail transport facilities to Rhodesian companies enabling them to increase exports and actually benefit Rhodesia's balance of payments. Since Rhodesia stopped releasing detailed balance of payments statistics after 1972, it is not known whether an increase in export earnings offset the decrease in earnings from the Zambian transit traffic. What is known, however, is that Rhodesia Railways annual deficit soared from R$1.9 million in 1971–72 to R$11.0 million in 1972–73 while its revenue-earning tonnage actually increased by 100,000. The earning capacity was not equivalent to the increased tonnage hauled because of the loss of the considerable high-rated traffic from Zambia. This pattern continued; the annual reports of Rhodesia Railways showed that each year the revenue earning tonnage increased, and each year the annual deficit increased— reaching a record R$29.1 million in 1975–76. Also the net balance of payments loss on "invisible" transactions—which include transportation items plus expenditure on foreign travel and insurance—nearly doubled between 1972 and 1973 (−R$57.4 million to −R$100.5 million). The loss continued and reached a record −R$161.1 million in 1975.[23]

Zaire

The Zambian minister for transport and works stated in a report carried in the *Rhodesia Herald,* February 9, 1973, that his government would continue to permit the transit from Rhodesia of several hundred thousand tons of goods a year bound for Zaire. Zaire imported coke, coal, and maize from Rhodesia and shipped copper exports through Rhodesia to the port of Beira. After Mozambique closed its border, Zaire shifted its copper exports to the South African port of East London. The railway administrations of Rhodesia, Zambia, and Zaire concluded an agreement in March 1976, to stabilize the flow of Zairian transit traffic on their lines. Zaire agreed to ship 200,000 tons of minerals annually through Zambia and Rhodesia to South African ports. The three railway administrations also agreed to meet periodically to review the situation.[24]

Malawi

Unlike Zambia, Malawi has direct rail links with the Mozambique ports of Beira and Nacala which do not traverse Rhodesian territory. Consequently, Malawi is far less dependent on Rhodesia Railways than Zambia. Dr. H. Kamuzu Banda, president of Malawi, advocated to the Malawian Parliament on July 29, 1969, the linking of the Mozambique State Railways with the Rhodesia Railways at Shamva, Rhodesia, via either Tete or Cabora Bassa. This would have provided Malawi with a direct rail link with Rhodesia through the potentially prosperous Cabora Bassa Dam area. This idea never reached the planning stage, and the only land transport links between the two countries remained the rail link through Beira and the road link through Tete.

Malawi was dependent on Rhodesia for coal for Malawian steam engines, and there was a system of interchange of railway wagons between the two countries. Referring to the interchange, the Malawian government told the United Nations that "if this was interrupted, Malawi would have to obtain a considerable increase of rolling stock from other countries, at great expense."[25] When Mozambique closed the border with Rhodesia, all transportation links between Rhodesia and Malawi were severed. The Malawi Railways estimated that they would suffer a net revenue loss of Malawi kwacha (MK)927,000 in the first full year following the border closure.[26]

It should be noted, however, that when Zambia closed the border with Rhodesia, Malawi benefited. Revenue earned by Zambian traffic on Malawi Railways enroute to Mozambique ports increased from MK89,000 in 1972 to MK1,243,000 in 1973.[27] To facilitate this traffic, Malawi signed a loan agreement with South Africa in November 1974, for rand (R)19 million to extend the rail line from Nacala by linking Lilongwe with Mchinji near the Zambian border.

Malawi Railways also served to transship Rhodesian goods into Zambia which the latter country did not want to import directly from Rhodesia. Although Zambia denied such traffic existed, the *Malawi Directory of Trade* for 1972 notes that Rhodesian maize was imported in 1970, and subsequently exported to Zambia. According to the *Directory:* "a significant trade in re-exports has been one of the spin-offs

Malawi has gained from UDI with an increase from MK1.7 m. [million] in 1965 to MK9.6 m. in 1971."[28]

Railroad Equipment

The inability of Rhodesia Railways to fully meet the demands placed upon it has been alluded to in the previous chapter. The railways are severely congested and are unable to always move goods when required. When these goods are exports, it is particularly serious, since exporting is the main source of foreign currency needed to purchase new equipment and upgrade the basic infrastructure. The 1970 annual report of the Industrial Development Corporation of Southern Rhodesia noted: "The recent evidence of serious lack of carrying capacity on our national railway system has pointed to a need for immediate and drastic action. For years the shortage of rail transport has been an inhibiting factor in the expansion of base mineral exports." On August 27, 1965, three months before UDI, a Rhodesian MP told the Legislative Assembly that it was a shocking state of affairs that the exports of the country were governed by the tonnage the railways could carry to the ports.

Thus, while the problem predated UDI, the solution of it has been complicated by UDI and the imposition of sanctions. Basically what is needed is more rolling stock such as motive power units and wagons and ancillary equipment such as heavier rails, signalling and wagon control systems, and goods handling devices. The wagon situation, up to the time of the Mozambique border closure, had not been especially critical due to the fact that, since UDI, Rhodesia became largely self-sufficient in the manufacture of wagons. Between 1967 and 1974, over 3400 new wagons built in Rhodesia were placed in service, according to figures compiled from the relevant annual reports of Rhodesia Railways. When Mozambique closed the border, two diesel locomotives, three steam engines, and *one-third* of Rhodesia's railway wagons were trapped inside Mozambique.[29] Since the routes to the South African ports are nearly three times longer than the routes to Beira and Maputo, the average turnaround time for wagons carrying imports and exports was greatly increased making the loss of wagons in Mozambique even more critical.

According to Minister of Transport and Power Roger Hawkins, Rhodesia was short of traction.[30] Of the 317 locomotives in service in 1970, 89 were diesel and 228 were steam—and many of the steam engines were built between 1912 and 1930. There was a recorded increase of only six locomotives during the period 1968–70. In 1970, Rhodesia Railways had to lease six steam and six diesel locomotives

from South African Railways.[31] Hawkins told the *Rhodesia Herald,*
July 15, 1972, that he believed by 1980, steam engines would be entirely
replaced by diesel and perhaps electric. Evidence that diesel traction
is becoming more important than steam is reflected by the statistics on
locomotive mileage reported in Rhodesia Railways' annual reports. In
1968, diesel accounted for 45 percent of the mileage; by 1975, 76
percent.

In 1971, the British government warned the UN Sanctions Committee that Rhodesia Railways was endeavoring to obtain up to sixty
new diesel electric locomotives and had approached a South African
company to undertake manufacture. South Africa, however, does not
produce traction machinery and therefore would have to approach suppliers in other countries. The British wanted the Secretary-General to
inform the governments of the twelve countries which produce diesel
electric traction machinery to be alert to any enquiries or orders from
South Africa. Despite this vigilance, the British government stated in a
note to the UN Sanctions Committee in 1973, that it had reliable information that up to fifteen locomotives and spares had been delivered
to Rhodesia by an Austrian firm through a South African intermediary.[32]

The difficulty in obtaining locomotives is due to the limited supply
area—only twelve countries produce the machinery; the machinery itself
is large and hence highly visible, making detection of possession and
origin comparatively easy; and the locomotives are expensive—new
diesel locomotives cost two to three million dollars apiece. Yet the
statistics on locomotive mileage seems to indicate Rhodesia did manage
to acquire some additional diesel units.

Airlines

Rhodesian Airlines

The main airline and national carrier of Rhodesia is Air Rhodesia.
It was organized in 1967, upon the dissolution of the Central African
Airways, which had been the national carrier for Southern Rhodesia,
Northern Rhodesia, and Nyasaland since 1946. Air Rhodesia provided
extensive service to South Africa (Johannesburg, Durban), Mozambique
(Beira, Lourenco Marques, Vilanculos), and Malawi (Blantyre). The
Zambian government stopped the Air Rhodesia service into Lusaka from
January 1, 1968. Those who wished to fly from Salisbury to Lusaka
could travel through Blantyre which provided connecting flights to
Lusaka; Blantyre also served as a connection point for flights to Mauri-

tius, Dar es Salaam, and Nairobi. As a result of a significant decline in traffic, Air Rhodesia suspended its service into Lourenco Marques in April 1975. The Mozambique government stopped all Air Rhodesia service into that country from March 3, 1976. Since flights between Salisbury and Blantyre overflew Mozambique's Tete district, these flights were suspended on the same date. Those who wished to fly from Salisbury to Blantyre could travel through Johannesburg which provided connecting flights to Blantyre. The cost of flying via Johannesburg, which served as a connection point for virtually every major city in the world, was five times higher than the cost of flying direct.

To help make connections for its passengers, Air Rhodesia enjoyed interline relationships with eighty-seven air carriers throughout the world as of 1971—an increase of twelve over the previous year. Air Rhodesia commented in its 1971 annual report that: "Interline relationships in general continue to be excellent and the co-operation received from our Interline partners has been of considerable assistance." These eighty-seven carriers apparently acted in violation of the UN Security Council Resolution 253 of May 29, 1968, which forbids any airline from linking up with any Rhodesian airline. The author made reservations in April 1971 for an air flight involving Philadelphia–London–Cairo–Nairobi–Johannesburg–Salisbury–Johannesburg–Rio de Janeiro–New York. British Overseas Airways Corporation (BOAC) made all the arrangements. At the time payment was to be made, however, a BOAC official noticed that the Salisbury–Johannesburg link was on Air Rhodesia and therefore, "because of sanctions," he could not accept any payment. He suggested that another airline involved in the trip might accept payment and hence validate the entire ticket; VARIG, the Brazilian airline, agreed.

This transaction apparently violated Executive Order 11419 (July 29, 1968) which implements S/RES/253 for the United States. This order forbids "coordination" with airline companies in "Southern Rhodesia," and a regulation of the Federal Aviation Administration (September 18, 1968) defined "coordination" as "connecting flight, interline agreement, block booking, ticketing, or any other method of linking up." This FAA regulation applies to U.S. travel agents, foreign airlines operating in the U.S., and domestic airlines.[33] Airline companies, if they issue tickets for Air Rhodesia, eventually must transfer payment to Air Rhodesia and such transfers of funds constitute violations of several Security Council resolutions.

It was not until 1974, that the attention of the UN Sanctions Committee was drawn to the interline agreements of Air Rhodesia. The

Committee was informed not by a government, but by the Center for Social Action of the United Church of Christ. Although Air Rhodesia claimed not to be a member of the International Air Transport Association (IATA), it evidently was allowed to associate itself with the IATA multilateral interline traffic agreement in March 1968.[34] This agreement facilitates international payments for traffic and cargo between airlines. Most airlines seemed to have offered routine concurrence with the agreement vis-à-vis Air Rhodesia. The IATA disassociated itself with Air Rhodesia effective July 1, 1974, and requested all airlines to withdraw their concurrence; most airlines did so in 1974.

The author found it impossible to make reservations involving Air Rhodesia in May 1976. Advice was offered to fly TAP Portuguese, South African Airways (SAA), or leave the Johannesburg–Salisbury link open and contact SAA in Johannesburg who could schedule an Air Rhodesia flight. SAA maintains both an interline agreement and pool arrangements with Air Rhodesia.

An independent Rhodesian airline, Afro-Continental Airways, maintained cargo and passenger service from Salisbury to Windhoek, South West Africa, between 1971 and July 1973, using a Super Constellation airliner. Captain J. Malloch is the managing director of the airline, according to the *Rhodesia Herald,* October 5, 1971. Very little information is available about this company; however, Malloch was listed as the diretcor of another Rhodesian airline, Air Trans-Africa (ATA). ATA was responsible for establishing a subsidiary in Gabon, Affretair, which maintained an extensive worldwide air freight service for the benefit of Rhodesia until it was dissolved by the government of Gabon in May 1976 (see Chapter 4).

Foreign Airlines

Before UDI, among the international airlines, BOAC, British United Airways, East African Airways, UTA (France), Alitalia, and South African Airways (SAA) held landing rights in Rhodesia. Of these companies, only SAA continued to operate after UDI. It was joined in November 1967, by TAP Portuguese Airways. As of 1973, SAA and TAP provided six weekly round trip flights to Europe; two terminating in London, three in Lisbon, and one in Paris (via Madrid). In 1976, SAA provided two weekly round trip flights terminating in London, and TAP provided one weekly round trip flight terminating in Lisbon (via Kinshasa). Referring to the SAA stop in Salisbury on its Johannesburg-Paris flight, the French representative on the UN Sanctions Committee said that his country believed the stop to be a technical necessity and did not regard it as "transportation to or from Southern Rhodesia"—which implied a flight beginning or ending in Southern Rhodesia. The fact was not mentioned that for many years the TAP flights originated and terminated in Salisbury. The British representative noted that as long as passengers experienced no difficulties in getting connecting flights to Rhodesia (e.g., from Johannesburg), it would be pointless to extend sanctions by requesting states to deny landing rights to flights which included stopovers in Rhodesia on their route schedules. The Swedish representative, who had pressed for such an extension, noted that there were divergent interpretations of the Security Council resolutions on the subject.[35] In any event, in November 1977 the Portuguese government ordered TAP to suspend its direct flights to and from Rhodesia.

Several international airlines maintain offices in Rhodesia in order to promote tourism; they are (as of 1976): Lufthansa, Sabena (Belgium), TAP Portuguese, Alitalia, UTA (France), and BOAC. The British government reported to the UN Sanctions Committee that BOAC did not pursue any activity contrary to the sanctions because BOAC did not sell tickets for Air Rhodesia and did not transfer funds to Rhodesia.[36]

On the regional level, Zambia halted all flights to Salisbury on January 1, 1968, and Botswana National Airways withdrew their twice-weekly return service between Francistown and Bulawayo on September 30, 1968. Rhodesia, however, continued to be serviced by SAA, DETA Mozambique Airlines, and Air Malawi. The latter two airlines withdrew service on March 3, 1976, as a result of the Mozambique border closure. According to the Malawian government the withdrawal of service would cost Air Malawi a net annual revenue loss of US$1,392,384. In 1968, Malawi noted that the Salisbury route was the only route to produce substantial income and, additionally, the Viscount airliners of Air Malawi were totally dependent upon Salisbury for all servicing facilities.[37] The Mozambique government estimated its annual revenue loss at US-$1,750,000 which included the cost of rerouting DETA airlines to serve other cities and the loss of service charges, airport taxes, and landing fees.[38]

Equipment and Services

The division of the assets of Central African Airways (CAA) left Air Rhodesia to start service in 1967 with five Viscount 700D and three DC3 airliners. The UN Sanctions Committee received information that

Middle East Airlines of Lebanon sold a Viscount in April 1970, to Mervyn E. Eyett, an "aircraft agent headquartered in Lourenco Marques." Delivery was made in Nampula, Mozambique. M. E. Eyett actually was the deputy general manager of Air Rhodesia. The government of Lebanon investigated and was assured by Middle East Airlines that it had no knowledge of the intentions and motives of the purchaser. The aircraft was subsequently registered by Air Rhodesia.[39] The *Sunday Mail* reported on March 12, 1972, that Air Rhodesia had bought another Viscount which had "logged thousands of flying hours for at least two other airlines before arriving in Salisbury," and the *Star* (Johannesburg) reported on April 21, 1973, that Air Rhodesia had acquired still another Viscount for a grand total of eight.

Although Air Rhodesia prospered financially with the Viscounts, there were problems. The *Rhodesia Herald,* September 2, 1971, reported Air Rhodesia pilots were frustrated because they could not operate jet airliners, and there was increasing competition from the jet aircraft flown by SAA and DETA on the regional routes that Air Rhodesia serviced with the slower Viscount turboprops. Jet aircraft were needed. But a jet airliner is probably one of the most visible products that a country can import. Like locomotives, they are very expensive, and extensive records are kept on every jet airliner produced so ownership is easily traced. This accounts to a large extent for the difficulty Rhodesia had in obtaining such equipment in the face of sanctions. On April 14, 1973, however, three Boeing 707 Model 720 jets arrived at Salisbury airport flying the Air Rhodesia colors. The aircraft were flown by Rhodesian crews, who had been training on jet aircraft for over a year. The 720s had been owned by a West German charter firm, CALAIR, which went bankrupt in 1972. The planes were stored at the Basle, Switzerland airport which is actually in French territory. The Swiss firm, Jet Aviation, purchased two planes outright and one plane by auction via a French court. It then resold all three planes to a Liechtenstein company, IAC. Jet Aviation prepared the planes for a flight from Basle to Lisbon. From Lisbon, the planes flew, perhaps via Luanda, to Salisbury. The government of the Federal Republic of Germany noted that it could not be proved that the persons involved in the sale of the planes to Jet Aviation knew of a subsequent resale to Rhodesia; therefore, it could not be established that any law was violated. The government of Switzerland claimed that it had no legal means of taking action against Jet Aviation since the aircraft were sold to a Liechtenstein company and bore German registration markings when they left Basle en route for Lisbon; the papers of the aircraft and crew were issued by German authorities and were in order. The government of Liechtenstein reported that a company named IAC was established in 1957, liquidated in 1958, and that no company of that name had been registered in Leichtenstein since 1958; the government stated that it was "keen" on obtaining documentary evidence about the "alleged" involvement of a Leichtenstein company in the transaction.[40] Clarence C. Ferguson, Jr., deputy U.S. assistant secretary of state for African affairs, pointed out the difficulty in enforcing provisions of export licences "particularly if you have instances in which you are dealing with collapsible corporations who may be in the chain of title. There is simply no one against whom to enforce the provisions. Substantially the only sanction is the refusal to license in the future."[41]

The arrival of the Boeing jets in Rhodesia reportedly had a favorable impact on the public morale. The *Rhodesia Herald* commented editorially on April 16, 1973: "Jet aircraft for Air Rhodesia. What an accomplishment; what a boost for the country's morale at a time when it can do with one!" Ian Smith told the *Star* (Johannesburg), April 21, 1973, that the arrival of the airliners had "thrilled Rhodesians and been quite a boost to our morale." Before entering regular service, a number of demonstration flights were conducted over Rhodesia's main population centers. Aside from the psychological benefits, the planes provide economic benefits in terms of greater carrying capacity and faster service. There are also benefits in terms of the haulage of air freight; the 720s can be converted from passenger to full cargo configuration within thirty minutes. Pat Travers, general manager of Air Rhodesia, stated that the company had spent R$250,000 on equipment for handling containerized freight and had sent staff to Europe and the United States for training in handling container traffic.[42] Rhodesia's minister of transport told the *Rhodesian Financial Gazette,* November 28, 1975, that Air Rhodesia was not suffering from any shortage of equipment. Indeed, Air Rhodesia even leased one of their Viscounts to Air Malawi.

Air Trans-Africa also had success in obtaining aircraft during the period of sanctions. Between 1970 and 1972, five DC-7 aircraft were sold to Affretair, the Gabonese subsidiary of ATA. In 1972, Aerodyne International of Chicago sold Affretair the DC-8F jet freighter described in Chapter 4 as the aircraft involved in the Rhodesia-to-Europe freight service. Affretair obtained one CL-44 aircraft from Cargolux of Luxembourg in 1975 and another DC-8 from Pomair of Belgium.[43]

The sophisticated aircraft owned by Rhodesian air firms and by SAA and TAP airlines, which operate through Salisbury, require sophisticated servicing. Until April 1972, the servicing of jet aircraft was handled by SAA staff stationed in Rhodesia. Air Rhodesia sent engineering and traffic staff to South Africa for training and, after April 1972, Air Rhodesia serviced all aircraft landing in Salisbury. Special training was required for the Boeing 747 jumbo jets which SAA uses, and it was reported by the *Sunday Mail,* March 19, 1972, that key staff members of Air Rhodesia were sent to the United States to observe how to service the 747s. In this context, it should be noted that Salisbury airport was elected a member of the International Civil Airports Association (ICAA) at the association's annual meeting in Venice in 1971. Salisbury's membership was sponsored by Schiphol airport (Amsterdam) and Maastricht airport (Limburg, West Germany). Members of the ICAA exchange ideas on airport planning and development.[44] Such membership may help Salisbury airport in coping with the problems associated with handling jet aircraft.

Roads

Rhodesia's exports move almost entirely by rail, since legislation favors the use of railways where long distance and bulky traffic is involved. Nevertheless, for an African country, Rhodesia has a well-developed road network—with slightly more miles of road per unit area than South Africa. A certain amount of exports to South Africa move by road through Beit Bridge. The Salisbury-Blantyre road via Tete carried much of the trade between Malawi and Rhodesia as there existed no direct rail link between the two countries. In 1970, Portugal provided a loan of MK5 million to Malawi for the construction of a new tarred road from Blantyre to the Malawi-Mozambique border. At the time, Malawian government officials considered the road links from South Africa through Rhodesia to Malawi vital in developing Malawi's tourist industry. Of course, those links were severed when Mozambique closed the border with Rhodesia in 1976.

Rhodesia's international road links were also important to Rhodesia's tourist industry. The great bulk of foreign visitors arrived in Rhodesia by road; in the period 1966–71, 72.3 percent of total tourist arrivals was by road, 21.3 percent by air, and 6.3 percent by rail.[45]

6

Tourism, Labor, and Migration

T HE THEME OF THIS CHAPTER is the movement of people to and
from Rhodesia whether it be for pleasure (tourism), employment
(labor), or for establishing permanent residence (migration). The sanctions affecting transportation discussed in the previous chapter are designed, in part, to discourage such movements of people. In addition,
the UN Security Council Resolution 253 of May 1968, required member
states to prevent the entry into their territories, save on "exceptional
humanitarian grounds," of any person travelling on a Rhodesian passport and of persons resident in Rhodesia who furthered or encouraged
or are likely to further or encourage the activities of the "illegal régime."
The same resolution calls upon member-states to prevent the transfer
of financial and economic resources to tourist enterprises in Rhodesia.
Any activity which promotes, encourages, or assists emigration to Rhodesia is also prohibited.

TOURISM

Travel to Rhodesia

Rhodesia is fortunate to have many and varied tourist attractions, including Victoria Falls, Kariba Dam and Lake, the Eastern Highlands,
Zimbabwe Ruins, Sinoia Caves, and many game reserves—the largest
is Wankie National Park. Attractions such as these, coupled with many
fine hotels and reliable transportation, have made Rhodesia one of
Africa's leading tourist countries.

Table 6.1 details the origin of visitors to Rhodesia for 1964 and 1965—the last year these statistics were published. It shows that, by far, the countries contiguous to Rhodesia supplied the most tourists with only about 10 percent originating overseas. The Rhodesia National

Table 6.1
Origin of Visitors to Rhodesia
1964–1965
(Thousands)

Area	1964	Percentage	1965	Percentage
Africa	263.7	89.5	230.8	89.4
Europe	20.6	7.0	18.4	7.1
Americas	8.2	2.8	6.5	2.5
Asia and Oceania	2.3	0.7	2.3	0.9
Total	294.8	100.0	258.0	100.0

Countries	1964	Percentage	1965	Percentage
Zambia	133.0	45.1	107.2	41.5
South Africa	94.8	32.2	95.8	37.1
United Kingdom and Ireland	15.7	5.3	13.5	5.2
Mozambique	14.5	4.9	10.6	4.1
Malawi	11.4	3.9	9.7	3.8
United States	7.3	2.5	5.7	2.2
Other	18.1	6.1	15.5	6.1
Total	294.8	100.0	258.0	100.0

Source: Rhodesia National Tourist Board, *Annual Report for the year ended 30th June* 1966 (Salisbury: The Government Printer, C.S.R.48–1966).

Tourist Board claimed that between 1966 and 1969, the growth rate of tourist traffic from overseas countries had been more than 21 percent per annum. The South African proportion of visitors was estimated to have increased to nearly 50 percent by 1968 and stayed at that level through 1972.[1] The Zambian proportion decreased, and the border closure in 1973, effectively ended Zambian tourist traffic to Rhodesia.

Table 6.2 outlines the numbers of visitors to Rhodesia and the per annum growth rate. After suffering a 16 percent decline in 1966, it took three years for the number of visitors to recover to the 1965 level. Increases were recorded in every year between 1967 and 1972. Of course, it is not possible to estimate what the increases would have been without sanctions, but the increases compared favorably with the percentage increase of world tourist traffic and the percentage increases of visitors to South Africa.

Table   6.2
Visitors from Other Countries: Arrivals by Reason for Visit
1964–1976

Year	In Transit	On Business	For Education	On Holiday	Total**	Change (percent)*
1964	126,933	30,292	5,581	162,248	325,054	—
1965	103,816	25,194	5,643	208,725	343,378	+ 5.6
1966	88,806	29,194	5,773	163,222	286,995	−16.4
1967	70,470	27,256	5,859	193,707	297,292	+ 3.6
1968	72,401	22,864	6,417	217,542	319,224	+ 7.4
1969	68,908	24,648	7,493	254,441	335,490	+11.4
1970	59,336	25,951	8,124	270,659	364,070	+ 2.4
1971	47,208	22,146	7,175	317,381	393,910	+ 8.2
1972	37,354	20,978	7,943	339,210	405,485	+ 2.9
1973	15,557	21,105	7,631	243,812	288,105	−28.9
1974	12,498	22,878	7,758	229,570	272,704	− 5.3
1975	14,668	20,368	5,257	244,404	284,697	+ 4.4
1976	7,615	16,909	4,907	140,423	169,854	−40.3

Source: Rhodesia, Central Statistical Office, *Monthly Digest of Statistics,* March, 1977.
* Percent change from previous year total.
** Includes visitors staying less than one night.

In 1973, the oil crisis manifested by petrol shortages, the closure of the border with Zambia, devaluation of the South African rand, and the increase of guerrilla activities dealt a severe blow to Rhodesia's tourist industry. The number of visitors to Rhodesia in 1973, declined by nearly 29 percent compared to 1972. There was a considerable drop in visitors from South Africa and, in the *Rhodesia Herald,* March 1, 1973, Rhodesia's minister in charge of tourism blamed the English-language South African press for a "degree of hysteria in articles on terrorism which put a lot of South Africans off coming to Rhodesia." During 1973, events such as the kidnapping of two German tourists and a Rhodesian railway worker from the Victoria Falls Bridge by Zambian police, the murder of two Canadian tourists by Zambian troops firing across the Zambezi Gorge at Victoria Falls, and the killing of a Rhodesian fisherman on the Zambezi River by machine gun fire from the Zambian bank certainly made South Africans interested in visiting those tourist areas wary.

An intensive effort was made to promote tourism to Rhodesia in the South African market, which, according to the Rhodesia National Tourist Board (RNTB), offered the greatest potential at the least cost. The board (RNTB) is the major Rhodesian organization responsible for the promotion of tourism. It accomplishes its task in a variety of ways. In conjunction with Air Rhodesia, it provides educational tours of Rhodesia for travel agents from all over the world. Also in conjunction with Air Rhodesia, the board maintains foreign offices in Johannesburg, Durban, and Cape Town. Their offices in New York and Lourenco Marques were closed in 1974 and 1975, respectively. Dr. F. Kachelhofer of Basle, Switzerland, was listed as the board's "honorary representative" in Europe and was cited for his valuable assistance in promoting traffic from his area.[2] Partially through these offices, the board yearly distributed over a million pieces of printed matter which eventually reached seventy-five countries. The board also distributed promotional films. Although expelled from the International Union of Official Travel Organizations in 1969, after a twenty-two year membership, the board claimed to derive much value from its long-standing membership in the American Society of Travel Agents.[3] In December 1973, the Association of Rhodesian Travel Agents became the sixty-third member of the Universal Federation of Travel Agents' Associations.

The director of the RNTB, Michael Gardner, told the *Rhodesian Financial Gazette,* April 14, 1972, that in promoting tourism to Rhodesia, "personal contact with the airlines . . . has helped tremendously." The international airlines which serve Salisbury obviously want to increase their traffic there. TAP Portuguese Airlines and South African Airways provide information on Rhodesia from their international offices; they include Rhodesia in some of their packaged African tours, and in advertising those tours, indirectly help to promote tourism to Rhodesia. In addition, airlines which fly to South Africa also cooperate in promoting travel to Rhodesia. For example, the *Rhodesia Herald,* September 24, 1971, reported that Lufthansa, the South African Tourist Corporation, the RNTB, and Air Rhodesia hosted and sponsored a study tour for fourteen American travel agents which included a five-day tour of Rhodesia.

"Inclusive tour passengers are the bread and butter of the Rhodesian tourist industry," according to Captain Pat Travers, chief executive of Air Rhodesia.[4] In the effort to organize group tours to Rhodesia, the airlines, foreign travel agents, and international touring companies are very important. The United Touring Company of Rhodesia, part of an international company, carries out extensive advertising throughout the world. The RNTB assists overseas tour promoters, and it commented in its 1970 *Annual Report* that "the numbers of inclusive tour programmes with a Rhodesian content currently being marketed abroad probably exceeds a hundred, and these 'package tours' would have accounted for over 20,000 tourist arrivals this year."

The Rhodesian government assists tourists in two ways. First, it does not require visas of nationals of Britain and the Commonwealth countries, or of Belgium, Denmark, Ireland, Iceland, Italy, Liechtenstein, Luxembourg, the Netherlands, Norway, San Marino, South Africa, Sweden, Switzerland, and the United States. Visitors from countries other than the iron curtain countries, Egypt, and Israel may be issued temporary permits in lieu of visas when they arrive in Rhodesia. Second, upon arrival in Rhodesia, it is customary for the Rhodesian passport control officers to ask if the visitor wishes to have his passport stamped. If the visitor declines, the officer will place the entry stamp on a piece of cardboard and insert it in the visitor's passport; the cardboard is surrendered upon leaving Rhodesia. Thus, no record will appear in the tourist's official documents that he ever visited Rhodesia. These measures make control of travel to Rhodesia difficult. Additionally, some countries like the United States openly acknowledge that they lack the legal authority to prohibit their citizens from traveling to Rhodesia. A memorandum from the legal advisor of the U.S. Department of State notes that "the U.S. does not have the legal authority under current domestic law to prevent U.S. citizens who choose to visit Rhodesia from doing so. However, the Department of State does try to discourage Americans from traveling to Rhodesia." The memorandum also notes that "nowhere in Resolution 253 is there any decision that member nations should not allow their nationals to visit Rhodesia as tourists. Travel not being precluded by the Resolution, it must be assumed that travel expenditures are likewise not precluded."[5]

What is precluded by Resolution 253, however, is the transfer of funds to tourist enterprises in Rhodesia. The UN Sanctions Committee concluded that the organizing of any tourist activity to Rhodesia for individuals or for groups on a package tour basis must entail such a transfer—directly or indirectly. The committee started to investigate such tours in 1974 and called upon member states of the United Nations to prohibit or discourage organized travel to Rhodesia.[6] The termination of most of the IATA interline agreements Air Rhodesia had with other airlines hurt Rhodesia's ability to attract tourists.

In his Lusaka speech of April 27, 1976, U.S. Secretary of State Henry Kissinger promised that the U.S. government would carry out its responsibility to inform its citizens that the U.S. had no official representation in Rhodesia nor any means of providing them with assistance or protection. American travelers would be advised against entering Rhodesia; Americans resident there would be urged to leave. In May, the U.S. Department of State issued a "travel advisory" on Rhodesia to all

U.S. diplomatic and consular posts and all passport issuing agencies in the United States. Citing "unsettled conditions," "potential for increased violence," and "inability to provide assistance or protection," the advisory urged American citizens not to travel to or within Rhodesia and urged Americans there to exercise "extreme caution." This advisory, with its wide publicity, was detrimental to Rhodesia's efforts to attract tourists.

While exaggerated in tone, the advisory did reflect the deterioration of the security situation in Rhodesia. The guerrilla war had increased in intensity, prompting several major roads to be closed to travel at night; on a few roads military convoys were provided for daylight travelers. In addition, five out of eight border posts had been closed in a country whose tourist industry depended heavily on road travelers from contiguous countries.

These events began to affect Rhodesia's tourist industry in late 1975. Beginning in November 1975, the number of visitors to Rhodesia each month was less than the corresponding month in the previous year.[7] As noted in Table 6.2, the total arrivals in 1976, declined by a drastic 40.3 percent. Fewer people visited Rhodesia in 1976, than in any year since the breakup of the federation.

Foreign Travel by Rhodesians

Table 6.3 lists the numbers of Rhodesian residents (non-African) who travel to other countries. After a small decrease in 1965, the number of travelers increased each year until 1971. Decreases occurred each year thereafter. The number of residents absent for one night or more—perhaps a better reflection of Rhodesian tourist travel—remained fairly steady between 1967 and 1973 (varying by no more than about 10 percent in any given year); between 1973 and 1976, there was a steady annual decline totaling about 20 percent for the entire period. Keeping in mind that the total non-African population varied between 230,600 in 1965, and 308,500 in 1976, this table is indicative of a highly mobile population.

Selection of destinations to which Rhodesians can travel is influenced or limited by several factors, namely: acceptance of a Rhodesian citizen (or resident) on a non-Rhodesian passport, acceptance of a Rhodesian passport (officially or unofficially), and the travel allowance set by the Rhodesian government.

The effort to impede the international travel of Rhodesians is complicated by the fact that one may hold dual citizenship in the Common-

Table 6.3
Rhodesian Residents Returning from Visits to
Other Countries (non-African)
1964–1976

Year	Absent for less than one night	Absent for one night or more	Total
1964		251,470*	251,470
1965		250,968*	250,968
1966		365,655*	365,655
1967	255,589	199,595	455,184
1968	278,971	207,349	486,320
1969	289,745	199,681	489,426
1970	298,202	220,896	519,098
1971	239,066	225,792	464,858
1972	144,873	212,983	357,856
1973	91,316	230,312	321,628
1974	43,766	204,491	248,257
1975	31,271	202,504	233,775
1976	23,491	185,665	209,156

Source: Rhodesia, Central Statistical Office, *Monthly Digest of Statistics*, March 1977.
* Separate statistics not kept before 1967.

wealth and thus be a citizen of both Rhodesia and some other country, such as Great Britain. In such a case, a person may be a Rhodesian citizen and carry a British passport or, perhaps, both a Rhodesian and a British passport. The 1969 census of Rhodesia indicates that of the 228,296 Europeans, 7.7 percent held dual citizenship, 7.0 percent were citizens of South Africa, 10.3 percent were citizens of the United Kingdom and colonies, and 6.0 percent were citizens of other countries; 69.0 percent were citizens solely of Rhodesia.[8] S/RES/253 specifies that member-states shall prevent entry into their territories of persons whom they have reason to believe to be ordinarily resident in Rhodesia and whom they have reason to believe to have furthered or encouraged the illegal régime, or are likely to do so. Thus, the United Kingdom government confiscated the British passport of Sir Frederick Crawford, former governor of Uganda, when he arrived in Britain in May 1968. Commonwealth Secretary George Thomson explained that this was done because Sir Frederick had adopted since UDI, "a course of behaviour which certainly gave every appearance of lending full support to the claims of the régime to have achieved legality and independence."[9] Presumably, an ordinary Rhodesian resident with no history of political activities, carrying a non-Rhodesian passport, would not encounter such difficulties.

As of 1976, South Africa, Portugal, Malawi, and Switzerland recognized and accepted Rhodesian passports. South Africa was, by far, the most popular destination for Rhodesians traveling outside their country. In 1965, 94,752 Rhodesians visited South Africa; by 1975, this figure had doubled to 183,020. Although the Rhodesian proportion of total visitors to South Africa declined from 42 percent in 1965 to 26 percent in 1975, Rhodesia still constituted the largest single source of visitors to South Africa.[10] South African Airways maintains large offices in Salisbury and Bulawayo and frequently advertises in Rhodesian periodicals and newspapers.

Before the Portuguese coup in April 1974, Portugal, Mozambique and, to some extent, Angola were popular destinations for Rhodesian tourists. Although reliable statistics are lacking on such travel, it was reported in the *Rhodesian Financial Gazette,* November 27, 1970, that TAP Portuguese Airlines carried 3,000 Rhodesians a year to Portugal. Until November 1977, TAP maintained offices in Salisbury and Bulawayo and provided a weekly flight between Salisbury and Lisbon. DETA Mozambique Airlines also maintained offices in Rhodesia, and the economy of Beira was highly dependent on the tourist trade from Rhodesia. The Mozambique government estimated 50,000 tourists coming from Rhodesia annually. As a result of the border closure in March 1976, the Mozambique government estimated it would lose US$4.5–5.5 million each year from loss of tourist trade.[11]

Tourism in Malawi is in its infant stages with detailed records dating from only 1970. In 1970 and 1971, Rhodesia was the largest single source of visitors to Malawi with an annual average of 5,100, but was second to Zambia as a source of tourists due to the fact that more than one-half of the Rhodesian visitors traveled for business reasons.[12] In a note to the UN Secretary-General, Malawi claimed that prohibiting entry into Malawi of Rhodesian passport holders would have a serious effect on the private sector as many commercial and industrial concerns were dependent upon expatriate staff domiciled in Rhodesia and, in addition, relied upon visiting Rhodesians for specialist advice and technical services.[13] The policy of the Malawian government was to encourage greater tourist traffic from Rhodesia. To this end, Malawi frequently sent tourist teams to Rhodesia to promote Malawi as a tourist attraction, teams which sometimes contained officials of ministerial rank. Prior to the Mozambique border closure in 1976, it was estimated that 9,000 Rhodesians visited Malawi annually.[14] Of course, travel between Rhodesia and Malawi was made extremely difficult by Mozambique's action. All Air Rhodesia and Air Malawi flights between the two countries were suspended.

Air Malawi based its first representative in Rhodesia in 1970, and one year later it opened a full reservations and booking office in Salisbury. Besides promoting tourism to Malawi, it offered its facilities to enable Rhodesians to gain access to other countries. In 1971, it introduced, in conjunction with Air Rhodesia, package holiday tours to Mauritius. In 1972, it launched a nationwide promotion campaign for its tours to the Seychelles islands. Also in 1972, Air Malawi, in conjunction with BOAC, offered flights to Cyprus. A spokesman for Air Malawi told the *Rhodesian Financial Gazette,* May 12, 1972, that, provided Rhodesian residents stopping at Cyprus were not staying longer than five days and were in possession of an onward ticket, they would not require a visa. Air Malawi advertising in Rhodesia, from 1971 to 1973, boasted passage for Rhodesians to Nairobi with direct connections to Athens or Bombay without passport problems because "Air Malawi have the right connections."

Unofficial acceptance of Rhodesian passports is difficult to document. As a Rhodesian Ministry of Foreign Affairs spokesman commented to the author on August 20, 1971, "some countries say one thing and do quite another; it is a delicate subject." Advertisements in the Rhodesian press promoting travel to certain countries seem to constitute *prima facie* evidence of acceptance, or at least tolerance, of Rhodesian visitors. Frequent advertisements appeared promoting individual and tour visits for Rhodesian passport holders to Portugal, Switzerland, Greece, and the Greek Islands. In 1973, Cyprus was added to the list. In 1971, Air Rhodesia, in conjunction with Air Madagascar, announced all-inclusive tours to the Malagasy Republic. It was explained in the *Sunday Mail,* July 25, 1971, that the vistitors' air tickets would serve as passports if they were Rhodesians. The *Rhodesian Financial Gazette* commented editorially on July 16, 1971, that the step of establishing travel connections with the Malagasy Republic was an indication of Rhodesia's widening outside contacts. The travel connection quickly evaporated, however, when Tsiranana's régime was overthrown by a military coup in 1972, and the leaders of that coup opposed contact with South Africa and Rhodesia.

Paul Berenger, leader of the Mauritian Militant Movement, a Marxist-oriented, anti-South African political party, promised in 1974, if he were elected, to halt the little-known practice of allowing Rhodesians holding post-UDI passports to visit the island.[15] Mauritius was a popular destination for Rhodesian tours, and officials of Rhodesia's tourist industry even attended a congress of travel agents meeting in Mauritius in 1975.

Both Mauritius and Greece are good examples of "countries saying one thing and doing quite another." Mauritius told the UN: "Passports issued or renewed by the illegal régime of Southern Rhodesia are not recognized as valid travel documents."[16] Greece told the UN: "After thorough investigations on the matter, it was found out that no citizen of Southern Rhodesia . . . has entered Greece since the adoption by the Security Council of prohibitive provisions in this regard."[17] Of course, these governments might argue that they do not recognize Rhodesian passports, but instead regard Rhodesians' air or sea tickets as acceptable travel documents (the "Malagasy ploy")—an approach certainly contrary to the intent and spirit of the travel sanctions.

Rhodesian travel agents interviewed by the author in August 1971 and August 1976, noted many discrepancies between the theory and practice of travel sanctions. For example, some foreign airlines with offices in Salisbury, guarantee entry into their home country if the Rhodesian passport holder books passage with their airline on a flight from Johannesburg. This was the case with UTA French Airlines in 1971. Also, because passport control at rail border crossings is often less strict than at airports, a Rhodesian passport holder may be advised to fly to a "safe" country like Switzerland and then board a train to his final destination in western Europe. Another ploy is the use of "humanitarian" grounds to gain entry into a country; some custom officers accept "flimsy humanitarian" stories as qualification for entry. Travel agents, however, stressed that the only "guaranteed" countries they could book passage to for Rhodesian passport holders in 1971 were: Cyprus, Mauritius, Malawi, Seychelles, Portugal, Angola, Mozambique, Greece, Switzerland, Botswana, and South Africa; in 1976: Mauritius, Seychelles, Portugal, Spain, Greece, Switzerland, Botswana, Malawi, and South Africa. The latter five countries did not require visas of residents of Rhodesia according to the *Travel Information Manual* of July 1976.

Sea cruises seem to be exempt from the effects of the travel sanctions. Several cruise lines, including the British Union-Castle Line, advertised cruises to Australia, South America, and Indian Ocean ports in the Rhodesian newspapers. The ploy in this case was that the ship's captain held the passengers' passports and a composite or "blanket" visa was granted to the vessel; landing cards were issued at each port for the purpose of going ashore with the sole condition that a passenger could not sleep ashore or effect a break of journey.

Regardless what type of passport a Rhodesian carries, his travels may be restricted by the foreign currency travel allowance and this, in turn, is influenced by Rhodesia's balance of payments situation. Before UDI, the travel allowance was equivalent to R$600 per year. This was reduced to R$200 in November 1965, and later increased to R$300. Conservation of foreign currency and the fact that Rhodesia has long had an adverse balance of payments in the tourism area prompted the decreased allowance in 1965. In 1974, the travel allowance was raised to R$400 and made cumulative over a two-year period for travel beyond Africa. This was interpreted by the *Rhodesia Herald,* December 22, 1973, as a major stimulant to foreign travel and reflective of a healthy overall balance of payments situation. Two years later, however, the balance of payments situation had deteriorated to such an extent that the minister of finance was forced to lower the allowance to R$250 per year. It would be difficult for Rhodesians to finance an overseas vacation on such a small amount even if the amount was allowed to accumulate for two years to a total of R$500.

Regional Tourism: The Case of SARTOC

The major markets for tourists for any country in southern Africa are clearly the countries contiguous to it. It is natural, therefore, that the countries of southern Africa should want to cooperate in the tourism field. As apparent in the case of Rhodesia, bilateral cooperation existed— especially with South Africa and Malawi.

The Malawian government initiated promotion of regional coopera- tion by inviting ministerial delegations from Angola, Botswana, Lesotho, Madagascar, Mauritius, Mozambique, Portugal, South Africa, Swaziland, and Zambia to a regional tourism conference in Blantyre in August 1970. Lesotho, Mauritius, Portugal (including Mozambique and Angola), South Africa, and Swaziland accepted the invitation. This conference was an important step in President Banda's policy of dialogue, and he stated in his opening address that "as far as Malawi was concerned, regional co-operation meant co-operation by all countries in this part of Africa, regardless of their political differences, political ideologies or the colour of those in control of the governments concerned."[18] The six countries attending the conference accepted President Banda's philos- ophy and issued a joint communique which recommended, among other things, that a Southern African Regional Tourism Council (SARTOC) be established. The southern African tourist region was defined as in- cluding Botswana, Lesotho, the Malagasy Republic, Malawi, Mauritius,

Portugal, South Africa, Swaziland, and Zambia, and "any other country which would fall within the geographical region of Southern Africa."[19]

Rhodesia was represented at this conference by two observers, Alex Inglesby, director of the RNTB, and Captain Pat Travers, general manager of Air Rhodesia. No official notice was taken of the Rhodesian delegation. Inglesby confirmed to the author on August 17, 1971, that he and Travers attended after receiving an invitation by telephone; he also claimed that Rhodesia had a vote at the conference.

Six months later, in February 1971, the Second Conference for Regional Tourism Cooperation met in Malawi to draw up a constitution for SARTOC. The same countries invited to the first conference were again invited, and, in addition, invitations were extended to the Indian Ocean islands of Comores, Reunion, and Seychelles. The original six countries sent ministerial delegations and were joined by delegations from Botswana and the Malagasy Republic. The French ambassador to Malawi attended as an observer on behalf of Comores and Reunion. A listing of other observers failed to note anyone from Rhodesia.[20] As this was a drafting conference, each of the eight official delegations had officers of their foreign ministeries present. Despite the lack of official acceptance, Rhodesia again was invited, this time by letter from the Malawian director of tourism, to send a delegation. The four-man Rhodesian delegation included L. S. "Tim" Hawkins, Rhodesia's Under-Secretary for Foreign Affairs.[21] The conference concluded with the official delegations from Botswana, Lesotho, the Malagasy Republic, Malawi, Mauritius, Portugal, South Africa, and Swaziland agreeing to recommend to their respective governments that a Southern African Regional Tourism Council—to be known as SARTOC—be established.

On April 17, 1971, representatives of the governments of Malawi and Portugal signed the Articles of Agreement of SARTOC in Blantyre. A Malawian government press release stated that "now that the initial signing has taken place, the documents will be taken by courier to those Governments in Southern Africa that elect to join SARTOC."[22] SARTOC was designed as an international organization which would come into being as soon as four governments signed the Articles of Agreement. Alex Inglesby told the author in August 1971, that Rhodesia was given the articles to sign and "the Rhodesian Government is considering the document and is interested in signing." But he added, "touristically, it is not exciting; tourism is a commercial affair—not governmental. Governments are not the best people to increase tourism." At the Ministry of Foreign Affairs, a spokesman remarked that the articles which had been given to Rhodesia to sign, constituted an international treaty and that Rhodesia could sign them. He added that Rhodesia liked the idea, felt it had merit, and "we would like to be in it." A. H. Mell, senior tourism officer for Malawi, said, however, that Rhodesia would not be asked to sign the articles as long as sanctions continue; "they can't be admitted as a state, but could attend meetings as an organization."[23]

The only newspaper report on this confusing situation came in connection with the RNTB's annual tourism conference held in May 1971. This conference was attended by, among others, Malawi's director of tourism, the Mayor of Blantyre, the secretary-general of the Tourist Alliance of the Indian Ocean (ATOI), Reunion's director of tourism, and representatives from twelve airlines. Prime Minister Ian Smith opened the conference by praising regional tourist cooperation in general terms: "Rhodesia has an important part to play in regional tourism, and our policy is wholeheartedly in favor of co-operation in this field and of participation to the full measure of our resources."[24] Malawian Director of Tourism T. J. Muwamba told the *Rhodesian Financial Gazette,* May 28, 1971, that the question of Rhodesia's membership has not been discussed yet, but that it would appear that whoever signs the Articles of Agreement would become a member of SARTOC. "Rhodesia are in possession of the articles of agreement and they have attended all the meetings," he said. The newspaper headlined the story: "International breakthrough for Rhodesia."

In April 1971, Mauritius decided not to join SARTOC yet in November 1972, reversed its earlier stand and decided to join. On December 7, 1972, Alex Inglesby acknowledged to the *Rhodesia Herald* that Rhodesia had been excluded from SARTOC, observing that "promoting Southern Africa without Rhodesia is like running a wheel without a hub." In February 1973, the State President of South Africa, Jacobus Fouché, announced to his Parliament that an international tourist council for southern Africa, comprising South Africa, Portugal, Malawi, Swaziland, and Mauritius, had been established to promote and coordinate tourism in southern Africa. As of 1975, Lesotho had joined SARTOC and the status of Portugal (Angola and Mozambique) was in question due to the Portuguese coup.

SARTOC is important for South Africa as it reflects one success for its policy of dialogue with African states. It is important because it represents an element of formal integration in the southern African region—a region that has seen few formal multilateral linkages established. It is important because the absence of Botswana, the Malagasy

Republic, and Zambia may be indicative of the problems and limitations of such regional integration.

Moreover, from the standpoint of this book, it is important because it clearly demonstrates the penalties which Rhodesia incurred because of its "illegal" international political status. SARTOC is an international organization; if Rhodesia had signed—or been invited to sign—the Articles of Agreement, the Rhodesian government would have had a compelling case for claiming *de jure* recognition of its independence. It would have, indeed, been an international breakthrough for Rhodesia. Perhaps the Malawian government, or some if its officials, failed to grasp this point; this may explain the confusion in 1971, as to whether or not Rhodesia was eligible to join; it may also explain the delay in launching SARTOC after the second conference in 1971. Perhaps Rhodesia's ambiguous standing *vis-à-vis* SARTOC explains why Mauritius changed its policy and signed the articles—after Rhodesia's exclusion from SARTOC was acknowledged. It is the author's opinion after reviewing the public statements and private interviews, that Rhodesia wanted to join SARTOC—but did not want to appear to be too anxious to join. Perhaps the Rhodesian government wanted to minimize publicity on the subject until after something definite could be worked out in private with the other governments. Malawi's handling of the issue may be questioned. It wanted to incorporate Rhodesia into SARTOC—at least unofficially—but developed SARTOC as a formal international organization which would prelude Rhodesia's participation as a signatory, dues-paying government with voting rights. In any event, threaded throughout a study of SARTOC are details and evidence of Rhodesia's extensive *sub forma* regional contacts in the tourism field and some of the ploys used to develop and maintain those contacts.

Importance of Tourism for Rhodesia

Tourism is economically, politically, and psychologically vital to Rhodesia. It is a major earner of foreign currency; in 1965, tourism was Rhodesia's fourth largest source of foreign exchange after the export of tobacco, asbestos, and copper. Rhodesia's foreign exchange earnings from tourism increased from R$10.3 million in 1965, to R$27.3 million in 1975 and, between 1965 and 1975, she earned a total of R$48.4 million from international fare payments and R$177.8 million from other tourist expenditures.[25] Moreover, tourism is an efficient source of foreign exchange because of its small import content. Most of the infrastructure (airports, roads, and hotels) can be built with local ma-

terials, while the food, drink, souvenirs, and services needed by tourists
can also be supplied locally. Furthermore, tourism as a service industry
is labor-intensive and a source of many new jobs.

Despite the earnings in foreign currency, in balance of payments
terms, Rhodesia incurred a net deficit on foreign travel. In 1965, Rhodesians spent R$24.6 million on foreign travel; in 1972, they spent
R$33.2 million; and between 1965 and 1972, the total spent on inter-
national fare payments was R$49.0 million and R$169.0 million on
other tourist expenditures. Rhodesia did manage to reduce the "travel
gap" (deficit) from −R$14.3 million to −R$5.7 million between 1965
and 1972.[26]

In 1976, the Rhodesian government, out of necessity, drastically
reduced the allocation of foreign currency for its citizens' travel, thus
narrowing the "travel gap." The *Rhodesia Herald,* July 17, 1976, described the reduction as costly to public morale, and the *Sunday Mail,*
July 18, 1976, stated, "for a nation hemmed in by politics, sanctions,
terrorism and a heap of irksome restrictions it is no morale booster."
The newspaper added that other countries had forced Rhodesians into a
"physical and psychological laager," and the minister of finance, by reducing the travel allowance, aided them, to some extent, in their
objectives.

Travel into and out of the country decreases the sense of isolation
and boosts public morale. Rhodesia's minister of foreign affairs told the
Legislative Assembly on September 1, 1967: "We are not in a state of
isolation. I have already said it is only the State Department, the Civil
Service in Britain and the same sort of people in other places who treat
us in a manner as if we were isolated. I think . . . we have had more
tourists this year from all parts of the world than in any other year."

Tourism also serves a political function. Prime Minister Smith, in
a speech at the opening of Rhodesia's first Holiday Inn, reported in the
Sunday Mail, December 16, 1973, said that he had long regarded
tourism as one of the most important industries in Rhodesia, not only
because of its importance as a foreign currency earner but also because
it earned "an untold wealth of good will" for Rhodesia. In another
speech, Smith said: "I never cease to be amazed at the way our case is
distorted overseas. The majority of our tourists go away converted to our
cause and this assists us in putting the record straight."[27]

While the government has not provided any empirical evidence to
support their case regarding the political value of foreign tourists, it
seems to be reasonable. The average white tourist, unschooled in the
principles of Rhodesian politics, is unlikely to encounter anything during

his stay in Rhodesia to convince him that the hostility meted out to Rhodesia by the international community has been either reasonable or just. Probably occupied with visiting the tourist areas, a visitor is unlikely to engage any Africans in a discussion of racial discrimination. If the government did not feel its case was reasonable, it would presumably have erected barriers to travelers originating overseas—especially from the United States and the Commonwealth.

LABOR

In the southern African region, comprising the countries of Angola, Botswana, Lesotho, Malawi, Mozambique, Rhodesia, South Africa, South-West Africa, Swaziland, and Zambia, there is a large interchange of African peoples. The Africa Institute of South Africa estimated in 1970, that approximately 1.4 million Bantu were not living in the country were they hold citizenship, but rather in one of the other countries of the region.[28] The 1969 Census of Rhodesia recorded 337,840 foreign-born Africans living in Rhodesia distributed as follows: 163,440 (48.4 percent) from Malawi, 109,110 (32.3 percent) from Mozambique, 44,150 (13.2 percent) from Zambia, and 20,780 (6.2 percent) from other countries.[29] Rhodesia's Central Statistical Office estimated that there were 223,000 alien African *workers* in Rhodesia in 1972—representing 27 percent of the total African labor force in Rhodesia.[30] To look after the interests of their workers, Malawi maintains a labor office in Rhodesia; Mozambique maintained a similar office between 1914 and 1975.

Table 6.4 shows a per annum breakdown of the statistics on the migration of foreign African *men* since UDI.[31] Although the source of this table does not refer to these migrants as workers, there is little doubt that the overwhelming majority are indeed workers. The table reflects a steadily diminishing immigration of alien African men into Rhodesia with the total net migration showing a deficit for each year between 1965 and 1975, with the exception of 1973 and 1974. Rhodesia reduced her alien African work force by a total of 57,970 men between 1965 and 1975. This continues a trend which was well established before UDI.

Table 6.4 also shows that most of the immigrants originated in Malawi. Almost one-third of the entire work force was employed in countries outside Malawi, and the net capital inflow derived from this labor was important to Malawi's economy. Indeed, African labor was

Table 6.4
Migration of Foreign African Men
1965–1975

Year	Immigrants	Percentage From Malawi	Emigrants	Total Net Migration	Malawi Net Migration
1965	26,920	68.4	30,300	− 3,380	− 800
1966	17,430	78.5	33,630	−16,200	− 6,170
1967	16,280	77.8	20,960	− 4,680	− 1,050
1968	19,350	74.4	21,910	− 2,560	+ 420
1969	15,880	63.4	18,020	− 2,140	+ 1,290
1970	13,000	54.3	22,270	− 9,270	− 5,230
1971	10,500	60.7	20,250	− 9,750	− 4,890
1972	8,640	63.0	16,290	− 7,650	− 2,420
1973	11,310	55.7	7,360	+ 3,950	+ 1,310
1974	6,990	49.2	6,460	+ 530	− 990
1975	6,320	47.3	13,150	− 6,830	− 1,540
Total 1965–75	152,630	66.0	210,600	−57,970	−20,070

Source: Rhodesia, Central Statistical Office, *Monthly Digest of Statistics*, April 1976.

Malawi's third largest export following tobacco and tea. Besides providing foreign currency for Malawi, the export of labor helped provide employment opportunities for Malawians unable to find work in their own country. One of the most densely populated countries in Africa, Malawi had, in 1973, a labor force in excess of 1.6 million, of which 216,000 were in domestic wage employment, and another 140,000 were working in Rhodesia and South Africa on contract. Remittances from migrant labor in that year were Malawi kwacha (MK)21.1 million—92 percent earned in South Africa and only 8 percent earned in Rhodesia; by contrast, in 1965, 76 percent was earned in South Africa, 15 percent in Rhodesia, and 9 percent in Zambia.[32] Rhodesia's importance to Malawi as a source of capital from labor emigration diminished in the years after UDI.

Malawian labor entered Rhodesia in two ways; first, there was the free flow labor entering without a contract of employment; second, there was the labor recruited in Malawi and put under contract by the Rhodesia African Labour Supply Commission (RALSC). The RALSC worked in close cooperation with the Malawi Ministry of Labor, maintained an office in Blantyre, and recruited only in Malawi and Rhodesia.

With an indigenous African population of six million in 1975, only 16 percent of which were in wage employment, and a yearly population increase of 3.6 percent, Rhodesia seemingly had an ample domestic labor reservoir from which to fill job vacancies. Yet there are both cultural and economic reasons why Rhodesia imports labor. K. A. Vanderplank, general manager of the Chamber of Mines of Rhodesia, explained in the *Rhodesia Herald,* February 18, 1972, that despite higher wages for underground work in the mines, indigenous Africans generally were not interested in such work because of superstition and tribal background. Likewise, there is also a reluctance on the part of some indigenous Africans to accept farming jobs. In addition, the Malawian has a far better reputation than does the Rhodesian African for hard work and reliability, and the former is often preferred over the latter by Rhodesian employers.

Clarke, however, believes that white farmers are unwilling to offer sufficient wages to attract indigenous peoples away from the tribal trust lands where it is relatively easy for them to meet necessary subsistence as well as "discretionary" consumption needs. Clarke claims that RALSC reinforced an artificial labor shortage by recruiting labor in Malawi, thus exploiting underdevelopment in that country as a means of maximizing employer welfare in Rhodesia.[33] Rhodesian Secretary of Labor R. Dawson told the author on July 30, 1976, that the wages offered to Malawians by RALSC were "pathetic," and Rhodesian Africans were fully prepared to work "if they think it is worthwhile to work." Indeed, the 1971 chairman's report from RALSC noted that although cooperative, the Malawi Ministry of Labor made it clear to RALSC that it was difficult for them to give full support to RALSC so long as the minimum wage remained at the rate of 20 cents per day. The Mine Labour Organizations (WENELA) of South Africa recruited in Malawi and offered a minimum of 38 to 40 cents per shift; Malawi's minimum agricultural wage was also raised from 20 to 23.5 cents per shift.[34]

It has been the Rhodesian government's policy since before UDI to progressively reduce, by various controls, the number of alien African workers in Rhodesia. Since 1964, foreign migrant workers newly arrived in Rhodesia were not permitted to seek work in urban areas; since 1966, the "free flow" labor was restricted to employment in the eastern districts of Rhodesia; since 1976, foreign migrant labor was prohibited from seeking employment anywhere in Rhodesia except on mines or farms. In 1966, the Rhodesian minister of labor said that RALSC was expected to recruit as much indigenous labor as possible, and in 1973, he called upon mine owners to substantially reduce their numbers of foreign African employees.[35] RALSC, however, failed to attract very many Rhodesian Africans, and Rhodesia never closed her borders completely to foreign African workers because of the strength of the agricultural and mining lobbies, according to Dawson. Ending the need for foreign migratory labor in Rhodesia would have eased the unemployment problem among indigenous Africans and would have reduced the net capital outflow—especially important in light of foreign currency shortages in Rhodesia. Some help in solving these problems came from an unexpected source in 1974.

After a WENELA aircraft crashed in Botswana in April 1974, killing 74 Malawian mine workers returning from South Africa, President Banda suspended all recruitment of contract labor. Although the crash occurred because of incorrect refuelling, the responsibility of Shell (Botswana) Limited, both RALSC and WENELA were prohibited from recruiting, and, as of 1977, no Malawian contract labor remained in either South Africa or Rhodesia.

Although no definitive reasons were provided by Banda himself, political considerations did not seem to play a role in his decision. Malawian relations with both Rhodesia and South Africa remained cordial after the ban was announced. The ban, therefore, should not be construed as an application of sanctions. A more likely explanation is that Banda used the plane crash as an excuse to stop recruitment until more favorable economic benefits could be obtained for the migrant workers. In Parliament on October 7, 1975, Banda explained that he had been "begged" by various South African officials to reconsider the ban, and, because he believed in "cooperation and friendship," the South African minister of labor had been invited to Malawi to inform Banda "what changes they were willing to make to meet our demands." The demands remained unspecified. Banda also reported that Malawi's economy was not collapsing as a result of the ban, and the workers who returned from South Africa were not giving the government trouble.

Reasons for his action may have as much to do with Banda's impetuous personality as with any calculated rational motive such as economics. Extensive interviews conducted by the author in 1976, with Rhodesian businessmen and government officials—some who knew Banda personally—provided the following alternative explanation. Banda impulsively ordered the ban upon learning of the air crash. Vanity precluded him from reversing the decision, especially after the Malawi Congress party eagerly passed resolutions supporting it. There does not seem to have been any compelling economic reasons for Banda to reconsider the ban as the Malawian economy—at least in the short-run— was not seriously harmed by the loss of earnings from migrant labor.

The economic effect on Rhodesia was also not great. Although the chairman of RALSC claimed in the *Rhodesia Herald,* June 30, 1975, that the suspension of recruitment was having a serious effect on the tobacco and cotton farmers, the number of Malawian contract laborers was not large compared to the total African work force. A few farmers who had become heavily dependent on recruited labor suffered difficulties due to a shortage of labor. Banda's decision did lead to an unexpected benefit for Rhodesia—the recruitment of Rhodesian labor by WENELA.

Foreign migrant workers, comprising only 13.3 percent of the total African labor force in South Africa as of June 30, 1974, were heavily concentrated in the mining and quarrying industry where they composed 65.2 percent of the African labor force.[36] WENELA, the leading supplier of contract labor to this industry, obtained about 30 percent of its workers in 1972–73 from the "tropicals" (i.e., Rhodesia, Angola, and Malawi)—most of these from Malawi. By 1975, the tropicals accounted for only about 4 percent of WENELA's total—a drop of 112,429 workers. This loss was partially offset by increased recruiting of indigenous labor and Mozambique labor.[37] But in 1976, the flow of labor from Mozambique also diminished, creating serious strains in the South African mining industry.

To compensate for the loss of workers from Malawi and Mozambique, WENELA approached the Rhodesian government for permission to recruit in Rhodesia. The labor agreement negotiated permitted WENELA: to initiate recruitment January 1, 1975; to recruit unlimited numbers with the right of review should the numbers exceed 20,000 per year; to offer one-year contracts to workers with the option of renewal; to recruit only in the Salisbury, Bulawayo, Fort Victoria, and North-East areas in the first year; and to remit, after three months work, 60 percent of the workers' earnings to their accounts in Rhodesia. The total number of Rhodesians recruited in 1975, was 8,619; between January and October 1976, 27,700. The total foreign exchange injected into Rhodesia from South Africa in the form of remittances of workers' earnings was estimated to be R$4.8 million per year—increasing to R$7.8 million in 1977.[38]

Rhodesia's Chamber of Mines protested the agreement with WENELA fearing that it would create a labor shortage in Rhodesia. According to the *Star* (Johannesburg), February 1, 1975, the starting pay for a mining novice in Rhodesia was 31 to 36 cents per shift in 1975; in South Africa, it was 154 cents per shift. WENELA's success in attracting Rhodesian labor and RALSC's failure seems to confirm Clarke's thesis that inadequate wages offered by employers created an artificial labor shortage in Rhodesia. Rhodesian government officials told the author in 1976, that the farming and mining lobbies hated the agreement, but Rhodesia's relations with South Africa had higher priority than satisfying internal lobbies.

Thus, by 1976, the net capital outflow due to earnings of foreign migration labor was turned into a net capital inflow. Remittances to Malawi ended as a result of President Banda's ban on RALSC recruitment, and remittances to Mozambique were halted as a result of the application of sanctions against Rhodesia by Mozambique. Remittances to Rhodesia from South Africa commenced in 1975. All this contributed support to Rhodesia's balance of payments at a time when they were under considerable strain.

One political implication of this reduced dependence upon external sources of labor is that the Rhodesian government loses political hostages. On December 8, 1965, the *New York Times* reported that Ian Smith warned he might have to order the deportation of alien workers if economic sanctions created unemployment in Rhodesia. Minister of Justice Desmond Lardner-Burke explained the argument in its crudest form prior to UDI, perhaps hoping it would act as a deterrent preventing the imposition of sanctions: "If pressure were brought to bear on the Rhodesian Government, they might have to do unpleasant things. If economic measures created a recession, they would first get rid of the half million alien Africans in the country. In such circumstances Europeans could pull in their belts; but Africans would lose their livelihood and might even be without food. External opinion should consider these harmful effects which might follow action against Rhodesia."[39] Although several British MP's expressed worry about the fate of the alien Africans in Rhodesia when sanctions were debated in the House of Commons in November 1965, Lardner-Burke's arguments did not act as a deterrent, and the sanctions were voted against Rhodesia.

MIGRATION

A critical priority of the Rhodesian government is to encourage the immigration of whites (Europeans) to Rhodesia because they possess the skills and experience which are prerequisites to the employment of workers in the lower echelons of the skill hierarchy. Rhodesia's economic expansion after UDI required a corresponding expansion of skilled laborers—engineers, technicians, scientists, doctors. The Smith régime believed that in order to develop the country it was better, at least in the short-run, to import the needed skills and expertise rather than trying to train indigenous Africans. It was believed this would help the Africans, for it was the European who created employment opportunities for the African people. The 1967 Sadie Report on economic planning for Rhodesia estimated one European worker was needed for the employment of each 7.4 Africans in the modern sector of the economy. The more Europeans in Rhodesia, the more Africans that can be given jobs. Sadie recommended that there be a net inflow of 10,000 immigrants per year by the early 1970s.[40] Creation of employment opportunities for the Africans and the additional immigrants would also increase purchasing power and Rhodesia's domestic market for goods and services. Financial assets which the immigrants bring to Rhodesia are another economic benefit from immigration. In 1974, for example, the assets and capital brought to Rhodesia by immigrants was in excess of R$24.5 million.[41]

In addition to the economic benefits of immigration, there are also political and psychological benefits. Ian Smith, in a press statement released on June 28, 1972, described the buoyant immigration figures for the previous year as tangible evidence of confidence in Rhodesia's future. In an interview for a South African periodical, Smith described Rhodesia's vigorous immigration policy as "not purely an exercise to try to alter the ratio of Black to White. It is a practical exercise which will develop the country but which will also, at the same time—I don't deny it—give more confidence to the White man if we can increase the White population."[42] Altering the ratio of black to white might very well be an underlying purpose of immigration promotion as reflected by fears continually expressed in the Rhodesian press about the quality of the immigrants. Smith, himself, conceded in the *Sunday Mail*, May 13, 1973, that immigrants for the previous seven years had not reached, in some instances, the high standards of the past. In 1974, proposals by leading Asian businessmen in Rhodesia encouraging colleagues in other countries to immigrate with several hundred thousand dollars in assets were rejected by Rhodesia's Department of Immigration, which stated: "A policy of not encouraging Asian immigration has been pursued by all Governments since 1923."[43] This indicates that race is at least as important as skill *vis-à-vis* the government's immigration policy.

Table 6.5 presents statistics related to the migration of Europeans to and from Rhodesia both pre- and post-UDI. After an initial net loss of Europeans in 1966, there was a steady increase in immigrants and a decrease in emigrants culminating in 1971, with the largest net migration increase since 1956. Clearly the Rhodesian government had stopped the massive outflow of Europeans that had characterized the early sixties. But the average net migration per annum never reached Sadie's recommendation of 10,000. The total net increase between 1965 and

Table   6.5
RHODESIA: Migration of Europeans

Period	Immigrants	Emigrants	Net Migration	Net Migration with South Africa
1955–59	74,000	39,000	+35,000	
1960–64	38,000	62,710	−24,710	
1965–69	49,957	36,470	+13,487	
1970–74	60,018	33,193	+26,825	
1965	11,128	8,850	+ 2,278	− 730
1966	6,418	8,510	− 2,092	−3,496
1967	9,618	7,750	+ 2,048	−1,498
1968	11,864	5,650	+ 6,214	− 321
1969	10,929	5,890	+ 5,039	− 802
1970	12,227	5,896	+ 6,331	− 621
1971	14,743	5,336	+ 9,407	+ 488
1972	13,966	5,141	+ 8,825	+ 444
1973	9,433	7,751	+ 1,682	−1,126
1974	9,649	9,069	+ 580	−3,016
1975	12,425	10,497	+ 1,928	−4,042
1976	7,782	14,854	− 7,072	−6,899

Sources: Rhodesia, Central Statistical Office, *Monthly Migration and Tourist Statistics for June,* 1976 and *Monthly Digest of Statistics,* March, 1977. South Africa, Department of Statistics, *Bulletin of Statistics,* March 1969; December 1973; September 1977.

1976, was 35,168; the yearly average was only 2,931. The trends began to sharply reverse themselves in 1972. The diminishing effect began in August 1972—for that month and every month thereafter through July 1974—the net migration was lower than the corresponding month in the previous year. September 1973 showed a net loss of Europeans—the first month since 1966. There was a partial recovery in 1975 when 12,425 immigrants arrived. But many of these people were Portuguese refugees from Mozambique and Angola. The immigration rate for 1975, seemed to be caused more by push conditions in other countries than by pull conditions in Rhodesia as the number of people leaving Rhodesia was the highest since 1964. In 1976, the number of refugees from Mozambique and Angola dwindled while the emigration rate increased by a record 41.5 percent over the previous year. The result was a disastrous net loss of over 7,000 Europeans. According to Rhodesia's official *Monthly Digest of Statistics,* December 1977, this loss continued at an accelerated rate into 1977. In the first eleven months of that year, there was a net loss of 9,871 Europeans; the comparable figure for 1976 was 5,914. Interestingly, in the years after UDI, Rhodesia had an overall negative migration balance with South Africa. South Africans did not flock to Rhodesia after UDI. Moreover, the official South African statistics in Table 6.5 reveal a very large net migration loss to South Africa—over 13,000 people for the three years 1974–76.

Describing the composition of the migrants is complicated by the fact that the Rhodesian government does not publish countries of origin or destination. Table 6.6 lists the country of birth of Rhodesian whites recorded in the 1969 census. Of the grand total of 228,296, 40.7 percent are *not* settlers—having been born in Rhodesia; another 27.4 percent were born elsewhere in Africa—the largest group coming from South Africa. The remaining 31.9 percent originated outside Africa—the largest group coming from the United Kingdom.

Table   6.6
RHODESIA: Country of Birth of Europeans, 1969

Country	Number	Percentage
Rhodesia	92,934	40.7
South Africa	49,585	21.7
Zambia	8,130	3.6
Other Africa	4,683	2.1
Total Africa	155,332	68.1
United Kingdom	52,468	23.0
Portugal	3,206	1.4
Ireland	1,833	0.8
Greece	1,658	0.7
Germany	1,602	0.7
Other Europe	6,202	2.7
Total Europe	66,969	29.3
Other	5,995	2.6
Grand Total	228,296	100.0

Source: Rhodesia, Central Statistical Office, *Census of Population 1969* (Salisbury: The Government Printer), p. 72.

Analysis of migrants in terms of age and skill is beyond the scope of this study. Many articles, however, appeared in the Rhodesian press describing severe shortages in skilled labor existing throughout the professions and trades in Rhodesia. As early as November 23, 1973, the *Rhodesia Herald* declared that "Rhodesia's manpower shortage is reaching crisis proportions in some industries and is causing concern to leaders in all sectors of the economy." These shortages in skilled labor are partially caused by the decrease in net European migration between 1972 and 1976. The president of the Rhodesian Institute of Architects said in the *Rhodesia Herald,* September 11, 1975: "I do not think there is a mass migration of people yet, but we are very close to suffering a grievous loss of technical people." In 1975, Rhodesia suffered a net loss of 254 physical scientists, engineers, physicians, accountants, administrative and managerial workers; in the first six months of 1976, the net loss for the same occupations was 239.[44]

There are several reasons for the decrease in European net migration: the intensified guerrilla war, military duty requirements, general political uncertainty, and sanctions. With respect to the latter, if tourism was largely insulated from the effects of sanctions, the opposite is true in the case of immigration promotion. In 1970, a government minister described immigration promotion as "badly hit" by sanctions. He noted that immigration could not be disguised by "arranged certificates of origin"—it had to be open and clearly defined.[45] The 1971 annual report of the secretary of information, immigration, and tourism described the job of publicizing Rhodesia overseas as "exacting"—but claimed that in 1971, promotional literature in seven languages was sent to 20,000 people in forty-five countries. Prime Minister Smith stated in the *Rhodesia Herald,* May 29, 1973, that it was virtually impossible to advertise for immigrants overseas, and when immigrants were found it was difficult to screen them. Arrangements had to be made through third parties which made it very difficult to get the "correct type" of immigrant. Besides the UN Security Council resolutions, a British Order in Council provides heavy penalties for anyone who promotes emigration to Rhodesia; Britain had been a major source of immigrants prior to UDI. One major method used to encourage immigration is postal communications—a medium free of sanctions.

On January 1, 1974, the Rhodesian government launched a massive campaign to promote immigration. It started by asking Rhodesian Europeans to submit the names of one million people residing overseas who might be interested in coming to Rhodesia. The Ministry of Immigration then mailed promotional literature to those people with the view of eventually achieving a net migration increase of 8,000 to 9,000 per year.

Allan Savory, a leader of the opposition Rhodesia party, told the *Sunday Mail,* May 19, 1974, that the government's immigration campaign was a "dismal failure," an "absolute farce which served no useful purpose." The statistics in Table 6.5 seem to confirm Savory's judgment. According to official Rhodesian statistics, between 1965 and 1976, the

African population increased by 1,960,000, and the European population increased by only 67,000. Immigration was certainly unable to mitigate the fundamental imbalance between the European and African populations. Moreover, given the economic rationale of the immigration program, the failure to even approach Sadie's recommendation of 10,000 net migration gain per year may well seriously compromise the continued economic growth and development of Rhodesia.

7

Social Relations

THIS CHAPTER is concerned almost exclusively with transnational relations—in sports, agriculture, education, entertainment, and broadcasting. While Rhodesian participation in international conferences is also mentioned, activities not ordinarily subject to sanctions, such as church and medical linkages, and other humanitarian activities, such as those involving the Salvation Army and the Red Cross, are not considered.

SPORTS

Sports are a major example of multiracial cooperation in Rhodesia. Africans, in the past, have preferred athletics, soccer, and boxing and have more recently started to compete in swimming and golf. The first multiracial athletic meet was held in December 1958, and the following year a multiracial team of athletes visited from the United States to take part in local meets and to help coach the Rhodesians.[1] Since that time, Africans have regularly been included in all aspects of athletics in Rhodesia, and in 1970, Artwell Mandaza, an African sprinter, was elected Rhodesian sportsman of the year. Before the formation of the Football Association of Rhodesia in 1965, separate European, African, and colored teams competed against each other; after 1965, the teams were integrated. Rhodesia's 1970 World Cup Soccer Team was comprised of thirteen Africans, seven Europeans, and two coloreds. In 1971, African professional golfers were allowed to play on the Rhodesian circuit for the first time and were extended full use of the facilities of the Royal Salisbury Club.

There is absolutely no interference into sports by the Rhodesian government outside of education institutions. Unlike South Africa, there is no ministry of sport. In 1968, the Ministry of Education did ban multiracial sport at government schools. European school teams still played against Asian or African schools teams as long as the matches were not held on European school lands. The ban provoked considerable opposition from the public, and Brian Streak, sports editor of the *Rhodesia Herald,* commented on January 1, 1974, that "the good faith of multiracial sport must be carried through every level of sport in Rhodesia— including the schools."

Many areas of Rhodesian sport are tied to South Africa. For sports such as cricket, rugby, and women's hockey, Rhodesia is a "province" of South Africa. Alan Peden, Rhodesian sports writer, explained in the *Rhodesia Herald,* November 10, 1972, that "finance plays the biggest part in welding Rhodesian sport to South Africa—it is hardly likely that cricket and rugby would want to break away when they reap monetary benefits." Pegen goes on, however, to ask: "Can we afford South Africa's sporting policies which are slowly eroding their international status?" While some Rhodesian sports have benefited financially and improved their caliber of play through competition against South Africa, there is resentment against international public opinion which often fails to discriminate between South Africa's apartheid approach to sports and Rhodesia's multiracial approach. South Africa, however, remains a major source of international competition for Rhodesian teams, and competition is avoided only if prohibited by some international sporting body in which Rhodesia is a member. Since sports competition with South Africa is so prevalent, it is not documented in this chapter.

Rhodesians, especially whites, generally consider sports an important part of their life. The *Encyclopaedia Rhodesia* notes that "much of the adult social life is centered around sports clubs, while school children have ample opportunity to play organized sport throughout the year."[2] Besides maintaining and increasing athletic performance and morale, international competition also serves to foster a sense of Rhodesian national identity separate from either South Africa or the United Kingdom. For example, regarding Rhodesian participation in the Olympic Games, the sports editor of the *Sunday Mail* wrote on October 15, 1967: "We like to consider ourselves a proud nation, a country which has achieved wonders with few resources. Competing in the Olympics is as essential a part of this nation-building as any political or economic development." Prime Minister Ian Smith commented in the *Rhodesia Herald*, January 13, 1968, that "it is a wonderful thing that Rhodesia is able to take its place alongside other nations of the world at the Olympic Games." David Butler, the late Rhodesian Olympic yachtsman, told the *Rhodesia Herald*, May 8, 1968, that it was imperative to have a team in Mexico City attending under the Rhodesian flag "for the purpose of establishing the point which Rhodesians wished to prove to the world—that Rhodesians were running their own affairs, and doing it very well." These statements indicate that, although international sporting relations are transnational relations, they nevertheless have important consequences for the internal—if not external—political milieu in which the Rhodesian government operates. At a minimum, such contacts reduce the sense of isolation of the European community from the rest of the world and, at a maximum, enhance the subjective perception of the legitimacy of the political system resulting from UDI.

Although Rhodesia's international sporting contacts bring little, if any, actual financial benefits to Rhodesia or the Smith régime, the UN Sanctions Committee is nonetheless concerned with preventing such contacts. Rhodesian participation in sporting events outside her territory might ostensibly violate S/RES/253 (1968), which requires that all states prevent entry into their territories of any person travelling on a Rhodesian passport or any person who has encouraged the "unlawful actions of the illegal régime." This is the basis, for example, of the committee's complaint regarding Rhodesian participation at the 1972 Olympic Games in West Germany and the 1973 Maccabiah Games in Israel. In addition, the presence of non-Rhodesians in Rhodesia in any capacity may involve a transfer of funds to that territory, and this would also violate S/RES/253. Possibly a more important reason for the UN concern over sporting activities involving Rhodesia is symbolic. Participation in such activities by national teams or teams of a representative nature is regarded with particularly grave concern by the Sanctions Committee. Even if the participation is undertaken in a private capacity, it may accord representative status to the participants involved and should be discouraged. Participation in sports with Rhodesia and Rhodesian membership in international sports organizations "tend to enhance the status and promote the international recognition of the illegal régime" and must therefore be frustrated, according to the committee.[3] Regarding the Olympics, the British government explained that admission of the Rhodesian team into West Germany might enable Rhodesia "to improve her status and progress towards the international recognition she forfeited at UDI in 1965."[4] Both the United Nations and the United Kingdom evidently believe that Rhodesia's international sporting relations may have important consequences for the *external* political milieu in which the Rhodesian government operates.

The following discussion of Rhodesia's successes and failures in maintaining or developing international sporting linkages since UDI focuses on six major sports and culminates with an examination of the Rhodesian experience with the Olympic Games.

Soccer

With its 532 clubs, 11,000 registered players, and large following, soccer must be classified as Rhodesia's national sport.[5] Prior to 1965, Rhodesian soccer teams rarely engaged in international competition. Rhodesia beat the Israeli World Cup team in Salisbury in 1954, for its first international victory and made its first tour when a national team went to Mauritius in 1963. Under the sponsorship of Sir Stanley Rous, chairman of the International Football Federation (FIFA), the Football Association of Rhodesia (FAR) was formed in 1965. It was admitted into FIFA on May 21, 1965, as a football association established in a British colony. George Kerr, secretary-treasurer of the FAR, explained that under FIFA rules, a country is merely a geographical boundary; it is not a political entity. Thus colonies can apply for membership in their own right or be a member via their parent organization. Prior to 1962, Rhodesia was a provincial member of South Africa. A Mauritius national team visited Rhodesia in 1967, and Malawi sent a national team in 1969. The Lesotho government, however, refused to permit its team to tour Rhodesia in 1968. Rhodesia sent delegates to the 1966 FIFA Congress in London and the 1968 Congress in Guadalajara without encountering any difficulties. Rhodesia could not play South Africa during this time, for that country's football association was suspended from FIFA on the grounds that it practiced racial discrimination.

In 1969, Rhodesia made preparations to enter one of the most prestigious sporting events in the world—the World Cup Soccer competition. The African countries did not want Rhodesia placed in their zone and threatened to leave FIFA if their demand was ignored. Rhodesia was thus matched in a group that included Israel, Australia, Japan, North Korea, and South Korea. North Korea immediately withdrew because of the presence of South Korea. FIFA decided that Rhodesia, South Korea, Japan, and Australia would play first round matches in Seoul, with the winner to meet Israel. The South Korean government announced on September 17, 1969, that it would not issue the Rhodesian team visas because of the UN sanctions. FIFA reaffirmed Rhodesia's right to play in the competition and asked Japan to stage the matches. The Japanese declined. FIFA then arranged for South Korea, Japan, and Australia to play in Seoul with the winner meeting Rhodesia at a neutral venue. Australia won the initial round and agreed, after much argument, to meet Rhodesia in Lourenco Marques. On November 27, 1969, the Israeli government announced that if the Rhodesian team won, it would not be issued entry visas "in accordance with the UN sanctions." After holding Australia to ties in two matches, Rhodesia finally was defeated—that match proved to be Rhodesia's last international competition in soccer.

At the 1970 FIFA Congress in Mexico City, Rhodesia was suspended from membership for two years. According to Kerr, the grounds were purely political since the FAR did not breach any statutes, rules, regulations, or orders of FIFA, nor did it fail in its duties to FIFA. The Ethiopian delegate who proposed the action did so on the grounds that Rhodesia had no legal international standing and many countries refused to recognize Rhodesian passports. No rule violations were cited. The Afro-Asian and Communist organizations comprise the majority in FIFA and were able to vote the suspension. Technically, the suspension was to last two years while the FIFA executive committee prepared a report on the state of the game in Rhodesia. The anti-Rhodesian bloc could not muster the three-fourths vote by the congress required for expulsion—hence the tactic of calling for a suspension which requires only a simple majority.

The FIFA executive committee endorsed the decision of an ad hoc committee which had investigated Rhodesia's membership and had recommended that the suspension be lifted. But the Afro-Asian bloc again commanded enough votes to continue the suspension at the 1972 congress in Paris.

During suspension, Rhodesia is not allowed to play any international soccer matches. The only international soccer Rhodesia has been involved with during the suspension has been a yearly match between the British South Africa Police (BSAP) and the Malawi Police. These matches were arranged on a government-to-government basis when the BSAP commissioner visited Malawi in 1971 as President Banda's guest, according to the *Rhodesia Herald*, September 10, 1971. A group of sixteen leading English soccer player-coaches visited Rhodesia in June 1973, and played a series of demonstration matches under the name Lexington Internationals.

Hockey

Rhodesia has been much more successful in maintaining international linkages in hockey than in soccer. Rhodesian (men's) hockey broke away from South Africa in 1962, and is a full member of the International Hockey Federation. A Rhodesian national hockey team made major tours of Europe in 1967, 1970, and 1975. In the latter tour, the team played nineteen matches—including matches against the Belgian, French, and Austrian national teams and club teams from West Germany and Spain. The Rhodesian Shumbas, a private touring team, played thirteen matches in England in 1972. As is the case with most Rhodesian overseas tours, the itineraries were kept secret until after the tours were completed to avoid trouble—such as demonstrations—in the countries visited.

In recent years, many teams have visited Rhodesia. In 1971, a Welsh national team toured Rhodesia under the name Dragons; the name change was made to avoid complications in Wales. Also in 1971, a top West German hockey club, the Deutscher Hockey Club from Hanover, toured Rhodesia. In 1972, Rhodesia played several matches with both South Africa and Malawi. In 1973, Rhodesia was one of five national teams competing in the South Africa Games, playing Ireland, Malawi, South Africa, and West Germany. Before the games, the West German team, which had won the 1972 Olympic Gold Medal, played three matches in Rhodesia, and after the games, Ireland played three matches in Rhodesia. In 1974, Rhodesia again played in the South Africa Games.

Despite these successes, the secretary of the Rhodesia Hockey Association told the *Rhodesia Herald,* November 26, 1971, that "we hockey people welcome a settlement because it will make our task so much easier to meet and visit overseas countries."

Rugby

Rhodesia is affiliated with the South Africa Rugby Union, and Rhodesian rugby teams are subject to its control. As with the case of cricket, Rhodesian citizens have played on the South African teams. Whereas Rhodesia has never sent a representative team outside Africa, she has received visits from national teams from Australia in 1969 (the Wallabies), New Zealand in 1970 (the All Blacks), and Italy in 1973. In addition, club teams from England (the Penguins and Lions) and Wales (Cardiff and Newport) have toured Rhodesia.

In 1971, after all arrangements had been made, the Argentine government refused to allow their national team, the Pumas, to play in Rhodesia while it was on a tour of South Africa. In 1973, the Argentine government refused to allow a club team "loaded with Pumas" (San Isidro) to play in Rhodesia. In this case, San Isidro decided to defy their government and did play three matches in Rhodesia. In doing so, they forfeited their financial help from the Argentine Ministry of Sport, and the Rhodesia Rugby Union paid their expenses. The Argentine government also retaliated by appointing a state administrator to take control of the private Argentine Rugby Union because the union supported the tour. This experience illustrates the determination of some sportsmen outside Rhodesia to play Rhodesian sporting teams even if it involves penalties. It also illustrates the massive political and governmental interference in sports that does take place in some countries.

Polo

Rhodesia has staged international polo matches with Uruguay (1969), Argentina (1970), Peru (1971), and New Zealand (1972). On August 30, 1971, Colin Black, leading Rhodesian sportsman and sports promoter, was asked if he could explain the lack of consistency in, for example, Argentina's approach to sporting ties to Rhodesia; their rugby teams were forbidden to visit Rhodesia, but the Argentine polo team did play in Rhodesia. Black replied that one factor which determines whether a team visits Rhodesia or not is whether the top executives of the foreign sporting association can exert enough influence to resist or overcome negative governmental pressures.

Golf

At the professional level, the Rhodesian Professional Golf Association (PGA) is affiliated with the South African PGA. Aside from frequent matches with South African teams, an annual match has been played with the Malawi Golf Union since 1967. The International Golf Association invited Rhodesia to compete in the World Cup Tournament in Florida in 1971, and in Australia in 1972. Australia, however, refused entry to the Rhodesian team. Many famous professional golfers have played in Rhodesia as individuals, including Arnold Palmer, Tommie Bolt, and Doug Casper.

At the amateur level, Rhodesia is a member of the World Amateur Golf Council, which has always invited Rhodesia to participate in the

Eisenhower Trophy Tournaments held every two years. At the Melbourne Convention of 1968, all member countries of the council agreed formally to accept teams from all other members. Despite this agreement, Rhodesia was prohibited from competing in the tournaments by the governments of Australia (1968), Spain (1970), and Argentina (1972). When the Malaysian government refused to guarantee entry to South African and Rhodesian teams for the 1974 tournament, the World Amateur Golf Council switched the tournament to the Dominican Republic. There a Rhodesian team did compete, and as a result of its performance, Rhodesia was invited to send a team to the 1975 world pairs championship in Bogota, Colombia. When the Colombian government initially refused to issue visas for the Rhodesian team, the prestigious Royal and Ancient Golf Club of Great Britain withdrew their entry. Tournament officials then threatened to cancel the tournament unless visas were issued, and the Rhodesian team subsequently won the championship. Rhodesian golf officials noted in the *Rhodesia Herald,* February 26, 1976, that "sport could on occasions reverse a political decision by a government."

Tennis

Rhodesia is a member of the International Lawn Tennis Federation and holds frequent matches with South Africa and Malawi. In 1972, the French Davis Cup Team and a West German team played matches in Rhodesia. Unlike South Africa, Rhodesia was permitted to compete in the Davis Cup tournaments because Rhodesia allows nonwhites to compete in their national championships. Rhodesia's participation in the Davis Cup tournaments, however, has been fraught with problems.

Rhodesia first competed in the Davis Cup tournament in 1968—drawing Sweden as its first-round match. After protests in Sweden, the venue for the match had to be changed to France. In 1969, Rhodesia's match with Spain had to be staged in a neutral venue—Portugal. In 1970, Rhodesia drew Israel and the Israeli Foreign Ministry, on March 26, 1970, refused the Israeli Lawn Tennis Association permission to stage the match in Israel, Rhodesia, or any other place "because of sanctions which are aimed at increasing the isolation of Rhodesia."[6]

On January 19, 1971, Basil Reay, secretary to the Davis Cup Nations, analyzed the situation in a report in the *Rhodesia Herald:* "The unfortunate fact about Rhodesia playing in the Davis Cup tennis competition was that, because of the UN ruling, it was extremely difficult for a European country to play against her. The result is that we could have the ridiculous position of Rhodesia going through to the challenge round without striking a ball. How can any team play in the Davis Cup if that team isn't allowed to travel freely around the world and go in and out of countries?" Because twenty-three of the twenty-six European countries were not able to give the Rhodesian team visas, the Davis Cup Nations Committee decided to exclude Rhodesia from the competition in 1971; and again in 1972.

In July 1975, Rhodesia was readmitted to the Davis Cup competition after the United States and several other countries threatened to withdraw from the competition if any nation was expelled for political reasons. Rhodesia was scheduled to play Ireland in the first match with the winner then scheduled to meet Egypt. The latter country joined several African states in protesting Rhodesia's presence in the competition, and the British Foreign and Commonwealth Office started an investigation. Eventually, the Irish government refused to permit its team to play the match with Rhodesia. Rather than pressing the matter and "to ensure satisfactory competition for all nations," Rhodesia's LTA withdrew from the Davis Cup competition in September 1975.[7]

The Olympic Games

The Olympic Games are undoubtedly the most prestigious and publicized sporting events in the world. Rhodesia's post-UDI attempts to participate in those games set the stage for a significant collision between divergent transnational and governmental aims. The historical fact that political differences were to be put aside for the playing of the games is legendary and is not documented here. Rule 1 of the Olympic Games Charter is explanation enough: "The Olympic Games are held every four years. They assemble amateurs of all nations in fair and equal competition. No discrimination is allowed against any country or person on grounds of race, religion or political affiliation."

Rhodesia was admitted into the International Olympic Committee (IOC) in 1960, as a separate country; prior to that time, it had been treated as part of South Africa. Rhodesian teams participated in the 1960 games in Rome and the 1964 games in Tokyo. For ten years after UDI, Rhodesia remained a member in good standing of the IOC and received invitations to participate in all subsequent winter and summer games. Not having any winter sports, Rhodesia did not seek to participate in the winter games. The problems arose, however, when Rhodesia accepted the invitations to the 1968 summer games in Mexico City and the 1972 summer games in Munich.

In May 1967, a member of the Mexican Organizing Committee for the Olympic Games declared that "all the nations recognized by the International Olympic Committee are being invited. We have no knowledge of any situation prevailing in Rhodesia that would put Rhodesia in question."[8] A personal representative of the president of the committee flew to Rhodesia in November to hand deliver Rhodesia's official invitation. On May 27, 1968, Rafael Solana, committee spokesman, said that the Union Jack would be flown for the Rhodesians, and the British National Anthem would be played if Rhodesia won an event. Solana added that, to overcome the passport problems for the Rhodesian team, all athletes would travel to Mexico on Olympic credentials, which would act as passports to overcome any suggestion that Mexico had given Rhodesia *de facto* recognition as an independent republic. On May 28, Ossie Plaskitt, secretary of the Rhodesia National Olympic Committee (RNOC), issued a statement indicating acceptance of the conditions. But the next day, the UN Security Council passed S/RES/253 containing the mandatory sanctions relating to travel by Rhodesians. The substance of the resolution was transmitted to the Olympic Organizing Committee which issued a press statement on June 8, 1968, carried in the *Rhodesia Herald,* stating that, as a result of the resolution, "the sports delegation of Southern Rhodesia, which was invited to participate in the sports competitions of the month of October next, will find it impossible to participate in them." This communication was not sent to the RNOC.

The Organizing Committee, in effect, used communications to disrupt Rhodesia's plans to travel to Mexico City. IOC Chairman Avery Brundage wrote to the RNOC stating that he would insist on the Mexican authorities undertaking their obligations. But the Organizing Committee equivocated on the status of the Rhodesian entry. It delayed sending identity cards and entry forms while acknowledging Rhodesia's request for them. On August 30, the Organizing Committee issued two lists of countries—one list of those countries which sent entry forms; one of those countries which had not. Rhodesia was not on either list. The RNOC pleaded for a communication advising whether their entries had been accepted; the committee replied by stating that they were sending a reply—which never arrived. Faced with fulfilling a financial obligation to the airline which was to carry the team to Mexico City and lacking a clear communication from the Organizing Committee, the RNOC issued a statement "deprecating the lack of direct and official communication from the Mexico Olympic Authorities" and "accepting the enforced exclusion from the 1968 Mexican Olympics."[9] To send the eighteen-member team, which included two Africans, and face the possibility of not receiving permission to leave the plane in Mexico City involved a financial risk which the RNOC felt it could not accept. Technically, Rhodesia was not formally excluded from the 1968 games; Rhodesia was maneuvered into withdrawing.

At the 1970 meeting of the IOC Executive Committee in Amsterdam, Rhodesia faced charges of "nonexistence." The argument was that because the UN did not recognize Rhodesia, the IOC should also not recognize Rhodesia as a member. Objections to Rhodesia's IOC membership were dropped because, according to some observers, the African countries concentrated their efforts on having South Africa expelled. Abraham Ordia, president of the Supreme Council for Sport in Africa (CSSA), told a press conference that the Council was not concerned about Rhodesia since it did not practice discrimination in sport.[10]

Thus, by maintaining its membership in the IOC, Rhodesia was, of course, eligible to receive an invitation to compete at the 1972 games in Munich; the invitation was issued and accepted in March 1971. From that date, a concerted international effort developed, featured by United Nations involvement, to exclude the Rhodesians from the games. The UN Secretary-General, on behalf of the UN Sanctions Committee and the UN Special Committee on Decolonialization, made representations to both the government of the Federal Republic of Germany and the IOC. A note dated June 10, 1971, from the West German government explained that, while abiding by the UN sanctions on Rhodesia, the Federal Government had, in March 1966, pledged to the International Olympic Committee that "it would grant unrestricted entry, regardless of racial or political affiliations, to the representatives of all national olympic committees recognized by the International Olympic Committee at the time of the Olympic Games in 1972—an undertaking which had been a precondition for holding the Games in Munich. The Federal Government was in no position to influence the instructions of the IOC, which were binding on the Organizing Committee, nor to prevent the Organizing Committee, which acted independently of the Government, from extending the invitation."[11] A letter dated May 29, 1971, from the chairman of the IOC stated: "For your information, the International Olympic Committee deals only with National Olympic Committees, and not with Governments. The National Olympic Committee of Rhodesia has been recognized for many years—and, so far as we know, conforms to Olympic regulations."[12]

When the IOC Executive Committee met in Luxembourg in September 1971, it considered the problem of Rhodesia and ruled that Rhodesia could compete under the exact same terms as it competed under in Tokyo in 1964. This meant that the Southern Rhodesian flag (incorporating a Union Jack) and the British National Anthem must be used. There would be no passport problems as the Olympic identity cards would suffice as travel documents. A senior official of the IOC committee was quoted in the *Rhodesia Herald,* September 10, 1971, as saying: "We cannot conceive of the Rhodesian Government allowing the team to compete under such conditions. It would effectively negate the Rhodesian declaration of independence from Britain." Abraham Ordia, speaking for the African Sports Council (CSSA), stated that "we are very pleased that the IOC executive committee accepted this solution because we are sportsmen."[13]

But the political pressure continued to mount. Diallo Telli, secretary-general of the Organization of African Unity, rejected the IOC solution: "The so-called Rhodesian Government is completely illegal and has not been recognized by anyone, and all that Rhodesia is trying to do is to obtain some sort of quasi-recognition by taking part in the Games. We will never accept a decision such as that taken by the IOC which goes against Africa's interests."[14] On December 10, 1971, the UN General Assembly adopted Resolution 2796 (XXVI), which, among other things, deeply regretted the IOC decision and "called upon all States to take all appropriate steps to ensure the exclusion of the so-called National Olympic Committee of Rhodesia from participating in the XXth Olympic Games."

Some Rhodesians expressed the opinion that Rhodesia ought not degrade their independence by accepting the IOC conditions. The editor of the *Rhodesian Financial Gazette* wrote on September 17, 1971: "It is inconceivable that Rhodesia will accept such a recommendation, and it is difficult to understand why the Rhodesian authorities—political and sporting—have not made this clear yet." But the sporting ethic prevailed, and the Rhodesian government upheld the Olympic rule of noninterference in sporting matters. Consequently, a forty-four member team (including six Africans) was announced in June 1972.

On August 10, 1972, a meeting was arranged between a delegation from the African Sports Council (CSSA) and the Olympic Organizing Committee to discuss the Rhodesian problem in light of the threats by several African governments to withdraw their teams if Rhodesia competed. A new compromise was worked out which included the following points:

1. Rhodesia will participate as a British colony known as "Southern Rhodesia" under the terms of their participation at the 1964 Olympics in Tokyo.

2. The Southern Rhodesian flag which incorporated a Union Jack will be flown.

3. In the event of a Rhodesian victory, the British National Anthem will be played.

4. The Olympic identity cards will describe the nationality of the Rhodesian athletes as British subjects.

5. Any nationality examinations carried out by the IOC will be made on the "basis of these official documents."

Secretary of the CSSA Jean-Claude Ganga was satisfied with the agreement and urged all the national olympic committees in Africa to compete in the Games.[15] Five days later the Rhodesian team arrived in Munich and the official flag-raising ceremony took place in the Olympic Village—in accordance with the above agreement.

The president of the IOC, Avery Brundage, warned that any national olympic committee which allowed their team to be withdrawn by their government could have their IOC recognition withdrawn and be prohibited from participating in future Olympic games. Despite this warning, the Ethiopian and Kenyan governments ordered their teams home on August 17, and by August 22, a total of twelve African countries as well as Guyana, Cuba, Haiti, and Yugoslavia had threatened to withdraw from the games. A group of black American trackmen also threatened a boycott.

Faced with this kind of pressure, the IOC Executive Committee met on August 22, four days before the opening ceremonies, and voted to withdraw Rhodesia's invitation to compete in the games by a 36-31-3 vote. According to the *New York Times*, August 23, 1972, the technicality cited to support the decision was that the Rhodesian team could not produce British passports and thus had no "official documents" to prove that they were British subjects as indicated on their Olympic cards. The day before, the British Embassy in Bonn issued an announcement stating that the British government officially recognized the Rhodesian Olympic sportsmen as British subjects. This announcement was consistent with the British government's view that UDI was illegal, and the citizens of Rhodesia were indeed British subjects. In an ironic vein, the *Rhodesia Herald* noted editorially on August 24, 1972 that, by rejecting Britain's claim that Rhodesians were British subjects, "the

African states have recognized our independence . . . but a rush of ambassadors is unlikely." Clearly, the thirty-six members of the IOC voting against Rhodesian participation had to invent some reason to justify their vote—no matter how devious and hypocritical (especially *vis-à-vis* Rule 1 of the Olympic charter). When asked for his personal view of the outcome, Avery Brundage stated in a report in the *Rhodesia Herald,* August 23, 1972, that he thought Rhodesia had complied with the agreement. But the alternative facing the IOC was the potential collapse of the games. Approximately US$700 million spent by the West Germans to prepare for the games would have been wasted. Moreover, Rhodesian participation in the Olympic Games under any terms probably would have been a morale-booster for the European population. It may well be that politics and the Olympics have become inseparable.

Yet, the Rhodesian experience with the 1972 Olympic Games is a good example how the application of sanctions may well be dysfunctional. A great deal of sympathy was generated internationally for the Rhodesian Olympic team. The team stayed on at the games as spectators at the invitation of the Organizing Committee; they were invited to visit several towns in the vicinity of Munich and were the guests of the Salzburg, Austria, tourist bureau. Even the Vatican Radio indirectly criticized the IOC decision and wondered "whether all the nations scheduled to participate in the Munich Olympics were free from the plague of racism or other evils that undermine the freedom, the dignity of man and the respect for the individual."[16] Glen Byrom, sports editor of the *Rhodesia Herald,* wrote on November 18, 1972, that "we must be realistic—politics are entwined with sport and there is hypocrisy and double standards everywhere." The IOC decision simply reinforced a view widely held by Rhodesian Europeans that they are the special victims of a double standard. Part of the legitimacy of any law or principle lies in the consistency of its application. There is little if any published evidence that any part of the European community in Rhodesia regarded the IOC decision as legitimate. Moreover, in one area—sports—where she has had a good record of multiracial cooperation, Rhodesia has suffered punishment by the rest of the world. In assessing the impact of the IOC decision on Rhodesian politics, Ian Mills, political reporter for the *Rhodesia Herald,* noted on August 25, 1972, that "the pro-settlement cause in Rhodesia has been damaged by the Olympic fiasco and has forced a hardening of opinion in the opposite camp." The ultraconservative United Front party attacked the Smith régime for committing a "positive act of contempt against Rhodesia and her independence" by allowing Rhodesian athletes to parade under a foreign

flag and anthem. This view was echoed by the equally conservative
Rhodesia National party.[17]

Ironically, the sentiments of these two parties were exactly the same
as those of the one major African government which decided to keep its
Olympic team in Munich if Rhodesia competed—Nigeria. Explaining the
Nigerian decision, made before the IOC vote, the government-owned
newspaper, the *Morning Post* (Lagos), stated: "It might appear that
Rhodesia has scored a success. But in fact it is Africa which has scored
a success by getting Rhodesia literally to lick her vomit. She has been
made to acknowledge that she is not strictly independent and this
compelled acknowledgement is a humiliation for Rhodesia."[18]

In preparation for the 1976 Olympic Games in Montreal, the International Olympic Committee sent three investigators from Brazil, Pakistan, and Canada to Rhodesia in April 1974, to determine whether the
Rhodesia National Olympic Committee complied with the IOC rules.
The report of the investigation was considered at the meeting of the
IOC in Lausanne, Switzerland, in May 1975, and found the RNOC
compliant with IOC rules and independent of government control. The
national sports federations in Rhodesia did not have racially discrimina-
tory clauses in their constitutions and were also free of government
control. The three investigators found, however, that there was virtually
no multiracial school sports in Rhodesia and no guarantee of equality of
training facilities and installations for blacks and whites. The IOC,
under continuing pressure from African countries, voted 41-26 to withdraw its recognition of the RNOC and exclude it from the 1976 Olympic
Games. The UN Sanctions Committee welcomed the IOC decision,
noting that it supported the whole conception and intent of the mandatory
sanctions.[19]

Conclusion

On May 18, 1970, the *Bulawayo Chronicle* editorialized as to the role
of sport in the effort to isolate Rhodesia and predicted what would
happen: "The overall strategy of Southern Africa's enemies is to discredit the Governments of this part of the world and their policies, to
isolate them and then to destroy them. Sport is being used effectively
and tellingly as an instrument in this offensive. Unwillingness to play
against us will increase. Visits to this part of the world by overseas teams
will become fewer and fewer, and Southern African sportsmen will
become more and more unwelcome as participants in events overseas."
This prediction was valid as it related to Rhodesia; with the few excep-

tions of hockey, rugby and golf, Rhodesia's international sporting contacts have been progressively reduced.

In any event, if countries were as diligent in applying sanctions in the economic area as they were in the sporting area, Rhodesia's viability would have been seriously endangered long ago. Two major differences between the areas are that sports are, by their very nature, public, open activities, and hence Rhodesian involvement is easily detectable. Also, the application of sanctions against Rhodesian sports involves very little economic cost on the part of the sanctioning countries. Indeed, it may be a very good way for a country to demonstrate its fidelity toward sanctions and generate good publicity at very little actual cost to itself.

AGRICULTURE

Many of Rhodesia's international linkages in agriculture are with other countries within the southern Africa region. According to the Rhodesian Ministry of Health, close liaison between neighboring territories is vital in the control and eradication of such problems as locusts, typhoid, and the tsetse fly.[20] The Agricultural Research Council of Central Africa, notable for its work in this area, was established in 1960, with funding from Great Britain and retained as a statutory body operating for the benefit of Rhodesia, Malawi, and Zambia after the dissolution of the Federation. In March 1967, for political reasons, Zambia withdrew from the council, which led to British withdrawal of financial support, and the council was dissolved. Rhodesia, South Africa, and Mozambique, however, cooperated in an inter-territorial committee for tsetse fly control.

In 1971, Zambia, Kenya, and Botswana formally signed an agreement breaking away from the Red Locust Control Services to join the International Red Locust Control Organization. The Zambian government found it necessary to discontinue membership in an organization which included "racist-ruled" countries.[21] As of 1973, the remaining members were Angola, Rhodesia, Mozambique, and South Africa.

An important organization promoting regional cooperation at the technical level on matters relating to soil conservation and land-use is the Southern African Regional Commission for the Conservation and Utilization of the Soil (SARCCUS). Formed in 1950, its members included Angola, Botswana, Lesotho, Malawi, Mozambique, South Africa, South West Africa, Rhodesia, Sao Tome and Principe, and Swaziland. After the Portuguese coup of April 1974, the Portuguese territories ceased to participate. Zambia never joined.

EDUCATION

Links between Rhodesian and British universities were severed after Rhodesia's declaration of republican status in 1970. In March 1970, the University of London announced that it would not issue degrees to the students at the multiracial University College of Rhodesia after November 1972, and the University of Birmingham decided to withdraw its sponsorship of the medical school of the University College. The government of Rhodesia then granted the University College full university status with the authority to issue its own degrees from January 1, 1971. As of January 1975, the University of Rhodesia was still a member of the Association of Commonwealth Universities although there were often protests over the attendance of University officials at the Association's conferences. For example, Vice-Chancellor Robert Craig, denied admittance into Nigeria en route to the 1971 conference in Ghana, subsequently decided not to attend the conference because of the demonstrations being planned against him in Ghana.

The number of Rhodesians attending South African universities totaled 1,886 in 1972—nearly twice the number of full-time students at the University of Rhodesia. There were twelve South Africans enrolled at the University of Rhodesia. One reason for the large number of Rhodesians attending South African universities is that the University of Rhodesia did not have faculties of engineering until 1974. Regular annual statistics on the number of Rhodesians studying outside the country are not published. The 1969 Census, however, did show 3,277 Rhodesians (non-African) absent from Rhodesia for educational reasons; 83 percent of these were studying in South Africa.[22]

The Rhodesian government does publish the number of visitors arriving in Rhodesia for educational purposes. From 1964 through 1967, the annual average was 5,714; from 1968 through 1974, the average increased to 7,764, and in 1975 and 1976, the average dropped sharply to 5,082.[23] Despite the lack of specific statistics as to the country of origin of the students studying in Rhodesia, Malawi and Zambia undoubtedly account for a large proportion of the alien students using Rhodesian facilities. Malawian European and Asian communities send many of their children to Rhodesian schools, and many Malawians—both government officials and citizens—make use of the facilities of the multiracial Ranche House College in Salisbury. When Rhodesia's border with Zambia was closed in January 1973, there was some concern over the movement of Zambian school children across the border and the remittance of school fees to Rhodesian schools. In these cases, the Zambian government did not interrupt normal procedures.[24]

INTERNATIONAL MEETINGS

Rhodesians attempting to travel abroad to attend professional or social meetings, have met indiscriminate failure and success. Failures have been: in 1972, the British Foreign Office declared that it woud not permit a "Miss Rhodesia" to enter Britain to compete for the "Miss World" beauty title regardless of the passport she carried; in the same year, an engineer representing Rhodesia was denied admittance into Australia to attend the meeting of the International Commission of Large Dams despite his British passport; in 1973, five nurses representing the Rhodesia Nurses' Association were told that they would not be allowed into Mexico to attend the Congress of the International Council of Nurses despite the humanitarian nature of the trip and the meeting. Yet Rhodesian delegates successfully attended International Chamber of Commerce conferences in Vienna (1971), Rio de Janeiro (1973), and Madrid (1975). Likewise, Rhodesian delegates attended the 1973 Lions International Convention in Miami. In 1975, Prime Minister Smith was awarded the Lions Club International Distinguished Award—the second highest award that that organization can make.

Occasionally Rhodesia hosts international meetings. Two of the most important meetings hosted in recent years were the International Geological Symposium in August 1971, which drew 236 delegates from all over the world, and the International Dental Congress in July 1973. Refused permission to meet in Malawi, the International Conference of Bishops of the United Methodist Church changed its venue to Rhodesia in January 1974.

In 1971, the United Nations Educational, Scientific, and Cultural Organization (UNESCO) suspended its "consultative status" with forty-two international organizations which had branches, affiliates or operations in South Africa, Rhodesia, and Portuguese Africa—despite the fact that most of the work of the organizations suspended was non-political—including the International Association for Religious Freedom, Rotary International, World Federation of Catholic Youth, International Council of Nurses, International Chamber of Commerce, and the International Grotius Foundation for the Propagation of International Law.[25] Thus in the effort to isolate southern Africa, and especially Rhodesia, even nonpolitical, social organizations and activities are not immune to some form of sanctions.

GENERAL ENTERTAINMENT

Sanctions complicate existing problems Rhodesia has in booking world famous entertainers and groups into local theatres and auditoriums. Charles Stoneman, theatre critic for the *Rhodesia Herald*, explained to the author on August 27, 1971, that Rhodesia cannot provide a large enough audience and consequent financial support to draw "big-name" entertainers to Rhodesia. Sanctions are used as an excuse in some instances to explain the inability of Rhodesian promoters to sign top entertainers for Rhodesian tours. Most of the entertainers that Rhodesia hosts are booked through South Africa—sometimes after they actually arrive in South Africa.

Nevertheless, according to Stoneman, since UDI both classical and contemporary entertainers have performed in Rhodesia, including Danny Kaye, Trini Lopez, Frank Sinatra, Jr., the Vienna Boys Choir, classical pianists Gina Bachauer, Alicia de Larrocha, and Peter Katin, and the West German Heutling and Koeckert quartets.

Aside from reducing the sense of cultural isolation, sometimes performers make public statements, which boost European public morale. For example, referring to the exclusion of Rhodesia's Olympic team from the Munich games, Danish entertainer Victor Borge stated to the *Sunday Mail*, August 27, 1972: "I think the Rhodesian team's expulsion is disgusting . . . nothing short of blackmail by black states;" and Eartha Kitt, a black American singer, remarked to the *Rhodesia Herald*, May 30, 1972: "Although the picture [in Rhodesia] may not be as healthy as someone like myself would like to see, I see smiles on the faces of people here. And I did not see that in South Africa."

Many of the entertainers who appear in Rhodesia are British. The British Musicians' Union forbids members from performing in either South Africa or Rhodesia. In 1972, it warned British pop groups performing in Rhodesia that they could be banned from playing almost anywhere in the world. British Actors' Equity, on the other hand, allows its members to work in South Africa and Rhodesia on the understanding that they do so as individuals responsible for their own contracts.

There is not too much difficulty supplying films for the several cinemas and drive-in theatres in Salisbury—with many top American films shown within a few months after their release in the United States.

This includes some films which have been banned in South Africa. According to Stoneman, South African distributors have always provided Rhodesia with motion pictures, and this arrangement continued after sanctions.

BROADCASTING

The chairman of Rhodesia Television Limited (RTV) spoke in 1971, of the "considerable difficulties we continue to experience in obtaining suitable programmes, due to the imposition of economic sanctions."[26] The *Rhodesia Herald,* in a review of the broadcasting industry on May 24, 1973, reported that television has been a particular target of the sanctions campaign. Nevertheless, since the imposition of sanctions, RTV, a one channel service broadcasting about six hours a day, expanded existing service beyond Salisbury and Bulawayo to Gwelo in 1970, and Umtali in 1972. It is estimated that more than 90 percent of the European population has access to television service.

Prior to 1976, Rhodesia was the only country other than Zambia and the Malagasy Republic, in southern Africa to have television service. Without television until 1976, South Africa had not been able to assist Rhodesia as much as it did in, for example, supplying motion pictures, however, the South African Broadcasting Corporation (SABC) is nonetheless of help to Rhodesian broadcasting. The president of Rhodesia, Clifford Dupont, said at the opening of a new broadcasting center in Salisbury in 1970: "I am informed that there is never an occasion when the SABC is not prepared to extend generous co-operation in the technical and programme fields."[27]

Rhodesia receives mostly American television programs and series, such as Bewitched, Rockford Files, The Hollywood Palace, Mannix, Hogan's Heroes, Love American Style, Cannon, Kojak, Medical Center, and Mary Tyler Moore. As of 1976, many series and motion pictures shown on RTV were also currently being shown on American television—although the particular episodes being shown in Rhodesia *may* have been from previous years. Other series broadcast in Rhodesia were being shown on American independent and UHF stations, resulting in a good selection for Rhodesian viewers. The motion pictures that were shown included Cat on a Hot Tin Roof, Carousel, Lovers and Other Strangers, Zorba the Greek, Ben Hur, Kelly's Heroes, On Her Majesty's Secret Service, What's Up Doc, and Topaz.

The Rhodesian government sometimes takes a dimmer view of the quality of the imported television programs. Opening the new service in Umtali, the minister of information, immigration, and tourism commented in a report in the *Sunday Mail*, December 19, 1972, that much imported material was produced by people "ideologically at total variance with us in this country and who prostitute the medium in order to infect the audiences of the world with their pernicious propaganda." He noted that sanctions denied Rhodesia the wide range of canned programs essential to the proper maintenance of a TV service and made it very difficult to select programs "suitable and acceptable to Rhodesian audiences." However, it is undeniable that imported broadcasting, as well as live entertainment, has helped alleviate the sense of isolation in Rhodesia.

8

Conclusions

U NTIL 1974, the Rhodesian economy prospered in the face of United Kingdom and United Nations sanctions—sanctions which had failed to achieve their declared goal of causing enough internal political change to terminate the "illegal rebellion" by the Smith régime. Not only did sanctions fail to achieve their major goal, but they may have been a contributory factor to the deterioration of a situation which they were designed to alleviate. As documented in Chapter 2, in terms of human rights and self-determination, the position of the African population of Rhodesia eroded in the nine years after UDI. Meanwhile, the Rhodesian Front party of Ian Smith consolidated its support and, as of 1974, had never been stronger.

But in 1974, the overthrow of the Portuguese government and the desire of subsequent governments to disengage Portugal from Africa signalled a radical shift in the balance of power in the southern African region. The guerrilla war waged against the Smith régime by black nationalists was intensified as a result of the willingness of an independent Mozambique to provide staging areas, sanctuaries, and support for the Rhodesian guerrillas. Prior to 1974, Rhodesian security forces backed by South African police contained the guerrilla war with minimal cost to the Rhodesian economy. Withdrawal of the police in 1975, the closure of the Mozambique border in 1976, and the growing militancy of Zambia in 1977, required a substantial diversion of Rhodesian resources from domestic production to the war effort. The 1977–78 estimates of expenditure published in the *Rhodesia Herald,* July 1, 1977, revealed that the war effort was consuming over 25 percent of the government budget—or more than R$400,000 per day—an increase of 44 percent over the previous year. According to the Johannesburg *Star,*

August 27, 1977, between December 1972 and August 1977, 375 security force members were killed in action (41 percent in the first eight months of 1977), and 3,174 "terrorists" were killed (31 percent in the first eight months of 1977). Virtually every able-bodied European male became subject to military duty, and large numbers of women volunteered for supporting duties. The resulting shortage of skilled manpower in domestic production was aggravated by record net European migration losses in 1976 and 1977. For the first time since 1966, the gross domestic product declined in 1975 by 1.1 percent; it fell another 3.4 percent in 1976, and the Standard Bank of Rhodesia estimated a further decline in 1977 of between 4 and 5 percent in real terms (1965 prices). The bank further noted a "severe slump in business morale."[1]

By 1977, the Smith régime not only had accepted the principle of majority rule but was prepared to examine a joint Anglo-American proposal to install a majority-ruled government in Rhodesia by the end of 1978. The combined effects of sanctions, Mozambique hostility, and the guerrilla war accomplished what the sanctions program alone could not do—induce the Smith régime to consider yielding political power to the African nationalists.

As noted at the outset of this book, scholars who have studied the use of sanctions to secure various policy objectives in the international system have generally concluded that they are ineffective and may be counterproductive. Study of the Rhodesian case confirms their conclusions. This does not suggest, however, that sanctions by themselves have failed to achieve secondary goals or that they have not had any adverse effects on Rhodesia. An Africa Bureau study found that sanctions kept Rhodesia in a state of complete diplomatic isolation, forced the régime to struggle for economic survival at ever rising costs to itself, maintained international concern over the Rhodesian issue, and sustained the world view of the unacceptability of the régime.[2] These are mainly successes of a symbolic or punitive nature and were insufficient to end the rebellion or end the situation which the UN Security Council found to be a "threat to international peace and security."

On a tactical level, the failure of sanctions was a failure to isolate Rhodesia from international relations. The prohibitions contained in the sanctions applied by both the United Kingdom and the United Nations involve the isolation of Rhodesia from all international contacts except those concerning humanitarian needs and communications. The purpose of this book has been to identify, explain, and determine how, and under what circumstances Rhodesia has been able to maintain and/or establish her international relationships.

Clearly, from the evidence presented, Rhodesia has managed to avoid international isolation. But isolation is not an absolute variable in the sense of it either existing or not existing. It is an especially difficult concept to measure in the case of Rhodesia. Comparisons cannot be made to what Rhodesia's international relations might have been in the absence of sanctions. Nor is it entirely appropriate to compare Rhodesia's international position before and after the application of sanctions. Rhodesia's international identity was changed unilaterally by her declaration of independence. Prior to UDI, she was a "self-governing territory" of the United Kingdom; after UDI, she was a "self-proclaimed independent state." Many indices of inward or outward orientation or isolation of countries are thus not fully applicable to Rhodesia (e.g., the number of diplomats sent and received, and the number of international memberships). Moreover, Rhodesia was a separate political entity for less than two years prior to UDI. From 1953 to 1963, she had been part of the Federation of Rhodesia and Nyasaland, and separate statistics were not kept for Rhodesia in many areas such as foreign trade.

Charles Taylor and Michael Hudson employ three indices to measure a country's external dependence:

1. Concentration of commodities within a country's exports.

2. Concentration in the number of countries to which a country sends these exports.

3. Total foreign trade as a percentage of gross national product, and foreign mail as a percentage of total mail.

Of course, since UDI, statistics are not available to compute the first two indices. It is reasonable to suppose that since Rhodesia's economy has diversified since UDI, and the reliance on tobacco, Rhodesia's major pre-UDI export, as an earner of foreign exchange has diminished, Rhodesia's export trade has become far less concentrated. Since South Africa's role as a major trading partner has greatly increased, the concentration of countries to which Rhodesia sends her exports also probably increased. Statistics are available through 1972 for the third set of indices. Taylor and Hudson explain that "these series are designed to show whether the country has an inward or outward orientation and the degree of that orientation."[3] Table 8.1 presents statistics which indicate

Table 8.1
Measures of Outward Orientation of Rhodesia
1964–1972

Year	Foreign Mail as Percentage of Total Mail	Year	Foreign Trade as Percentage of G.N.P.*
1964–65	39.26	1964	71.84
1965–66	37.20	1965	75.72
1966–67	36.79	1966	49.58
1967–68	34.24	1967	47.13
1968–69	32.48	1968	45.60
1969–70	29.84	1969	43.13
1970–71	28.46	1970	46.13
1971–72	27.81	1971	46.62
1972–73	26.63	1972	45.03

Sources: Rhodesia, *Annual Reports* of the postmaster-general and the Posts and Tele-communications Corporation, 1964–73; Rhodesia, Central Statistical Office, *Monthly Digest of Statistics,* February 1974, pp. 40, 44.
* G.N.P. calculated at market prices.

that Rhodesia has developed a more inward orientation since UDI; they show that the foreign component in Rhodesia's total mail gradually declined since UDI and that foreign trade as a percentage of gross national product sharply declined in the first year after UDI and remained steady thereafter. Compared to 125 other countries in 1965, however, Rhodesia had a very high outward orientation to begin with— ranking 14th.

In any overall discussion of the degree to which sanctions have isolated Rhodesia, the essential question is: Has Rhodesia's isolation from international relations been sufficient to provoke an internal political change satisfactory to those parties imposing the sanctions? The answer is clearly in the negative. Avoiding isolation generates both material and symbolic benefits for Rhodesia; economic deprivation is averted, public morale is enhanced, and subjective feelings of legitimacy are stimulated. The Rhodesian government claimed that international relationships and contacts would also bring objective recognition of Rhodesia's legitimacy. Rhodesian Minister of External Affairs Lord Graham told the Legislative Assembly, July 6, 1966: "just as in the past it used to be said that the flag followed trade, so to-day I am quite certain that recognition will not be long in following trade also." President Dupont, in referring to the expansion of exports in 1967, told the Legislative Assembly, April 19, 1967, that "such a demonstration of increasing economic strength is the surest way of attaining recognition of Rhodesia's independent status." The government was incorrect, however, to assume that maintenance and development of international relationships would bring or would lead to recognition and the acquisition of legitimacy from other countries. It has not.

ANALYTICAL PERSPECTIVES

In order to specifically identify and explain how Rhodesia has been able to maintain and/or establish international relationships and avoid isolation, it is necessary to re-examine the hypotheses and generalizations presented in the Introduction in light of the evidence recorded in the subsequent chapters. The three levels of analysis or perspectives identified from which this question could be examined are the global, the regional, and the national.

The Global Perspective

The simplistic theory of sanctions suggests that if a target state's international trade is concentrated in a few trading partners and in a few commodities, its vulnerability to sanctions should be great. What this theory overlooks is the nature of the trading process itself. If the target state has enough time and can effectively communicate, then it might be able to arrange to continue trading with the same countries it traded with before the application of sanctions, by having the goods involved transshipped through intermediary countries in order to disguise their point of origin or point of ultimate destination. Indeed, the transshipment can be arranged on paper without the goods being physically moved to the intermediary country. Who could have foreseen, for example, the importance of Gabon and Liechtenstein when the sanctions were being formulated for application against Rhodesia, yet both of these countries, along with many others, are used to facilitate movement of goods to and from Rhodesia.

The generalization that "the effectiveness of an individual sanction-measure will be diminished when that effectiveness specifically depends upon universal adherence and compliance" is also simplistic. The central geopolitical fact concerning Rhodesia is that she is land-locked and must depend upon contiguous states for access to the sea. Rhodesia's entire communications and transportation system is dependent upon Mozambique and South Africa. All other things being equal, if these two states applied sanctions, Rhodesia could not survive. It may be, as was the case with Zambia for a number of years after sanctions were im-

posed, that states contiguous to the target find it most difficult to apply
sanctions.

Another feature of the global system is that there is no workable
international agency to apply the sanctions, establish surveillance, and
coordinate enforcement. The United Nations does not have agents stationed all over the world to do these tasks. The UN must rely upon its
member-states to administer and enforce the sanctions. But there are
large international organizations that do have agents stationed all over
the world to help arrange the evasion of sanctions. Large multinational
corporations, banks, trading companies, commodity brokers, and shipping lines, all help to make the arrangements to buy and sell goods for
Rhodesian interests. Moreover, it is extraordinarily difficult in many
instances to detect the complex transactions and, when detected, to
assign responsibility in order that a member-state may prosecute the
violators.

The Regional Perspective

"The effectiveness of the sanctions against Rhodesia will be lessened
when they cannot be applied against the entire region." It has always
been the contention of the great majority of African states that sanctions against Rhodesia would not prove successful unless they were also
applied against Portugal and South Africa and were strictly supervised
by force. Indeed, this is the essence of paragraph 4 of GA/RES/2383
(XXIII) passed by the UN General Assembly on November 7, 1968,
by the vote of 86–9 with 19 abstentions.

When sanctions were being devised, inadequate consideration was
given to the fact that Rhodesia was an integral part of a regional grouping of states with regular interactions, mutual dependencies, and common goals. The central core of the system includes South Africa (with
South West Africa), Portugal (through Angola and Mozambique until
1974), Rhodesia, and Malawi. Despite different political and social systems, the government of these countries shared a common outlook on such
matters as the permanence of the white communities within the region,
the nature of the Communist threat to the region, and the hypocrisy and
double standards involved in the approaches taken toward the racial
problems within the region by those outside the region. Including Malawi
in the central core, in view of President Banda's dislike of white racial
supremacy, may seem controversial. The degree of intimacy in relations between Rhodesia and Malawi is greater than that which would
be warranted by mere economic dependency. Outside the central core,

several states exist in the periphery which, while not sympathetic to the political policies of the core states, are nonetheless functionally dependent upon the core; included among these states are independent Mozambique, Botswana, Lesotho, Swaziland, and Zambia. Were sanctions to be placed against South Africa, in addition to Rhodesia, there is little doubt that the economies of these peripheral states, plus Malawi, would be grievously affected. Moreover, South Africa is a major industrial state and possesses materials important to the functioning of other national economies. In such a situation, sanctions against South Africa could prove far more disruptive of world trading patterns than those applied against Rhodesia. Yet, without sanctions applied on a regional level, Rhodesia can use the facilities of the other states in the region to gain access to the world outside the region and thus frustrate attempts to isolate her. The Somalian ambassador to the UN predicted in the Security Council on November 17, 1965 (S/PV.1263) that "there is little doubt that the racial and political policies in Mozambique, South Africa and Southern Rhodesia will cause those countries to draw together in closer economic and political alliance. Under these circumstances, effective economic sanctions against Southern Rhodesia will prove impossible."

While the ambassador's pessimism has proved quite valid, it should be noted that the core of the regional system is not necessarily stable or without internal strains, and there are limits to the degree to which Rhodesia can integrate herself into the core. Formal integration is precluded by Rhodesia's "illegal" status—a status recognized by the other core states. This means that Rhodesia cannot participate in such schemes as the regional tourism council (SARTOC) or any potential regional common market. Moreover, while relations between Rhodesia and the other core states have been generally cordial since UDI, there have been strains. Rhodesia's closure of the border with Zambia was not endorsed by South Africa or Portugal, Rhodesian anxiety over the military situation in Mozambique did not please the Portuguese government in 1972, and the flood of cheap Rhodesian manufactured goods into South Africa drew complaints from South African businessmen. In addition, the Rhodesian government has failed to achieve a constitutional settlement with the United Kingdom, a settlement eagerly desired by the other core states.

After Portugal's exit from the core, South Africa especially desired a Rhodesian settlement. Realizing the increased vulnerability of the core to guerrilla attacks and the dangers posed by Communist assistance to independent Angola and Mozambique, South Africa in 1974, renewed its efforts to promote *détente* with black Africa. A Rhodesian settlement was a necessary, but not sufficient, prerequisite for *détente* to have any chance of success. Strains developed between Rhodesia and South Africa over the form and substance of South Africa's *détente* policy and the withdrawal of the South African police from Rhodesia. South African policy toward Rhodesia shifted from one of "benevolent neutrality" and at times "acceptance," to one which ranged between "strict neutrality" and "impatience with the status quo." Certainly, by 1977, "entente cordiale" was no longer an appropriate description of the relations between the core states.

Furthermore, the Rhodesian issue contributed to the increased alienation of Zambia and Mozambique from the core. Those countries, at tremendous economic cost to themselves, closed their borders with Rhodesia. These actions increased the physical isolation of Malawi from the core as well.

Disintegration of the regional core as reflected by the disengagement of Portugal, the growing neutrality of South Africa toward Rhodesia, and the increased alienation of peripheral states like Mozambique and Zambia, greatly enhanced the impact and effectiveness of the sanctions on Rhodesia.

The National Perspective

"The effectiveness of sanctions will be lessened when national governments are unable or unwilling to bring under control transnational relations involving Rhodesia." Andrew M. Scott has observed that "most states are either unwilling or unable to control fully the movement or funds, persons, ideas, information, and material across national borders."[4] This lack of control and the resulting permeability of national frontiers to flows of communications, goods, money, and people is quite evident in the case of Rhodesia. Governments may be unwilling to control these flows for a variety of reasons. Some governments may not have the legal authority to maintain control. For example, the United States government does not have the constitutional authority to prevent U.S. citizens from visiting Rhodesia, nor does it have the legal authority to censor written and oral communications which might promote the Rhodesian viewpoint at the expense of maintaining public respect for the sanctions. The Federal Republic of Germany does not have the legal authority to void existing contracts with Rhodesian businesses. France and Japan would have constitutional problems with communications sanctions; Sweden and Austria reported similar problems in restricting travel of their citizens to Rhodesia to the UN Sanctions

Committee; and Italy claimed not to have the authority to interrupt postal correspondence of its citizens to Rhodesia. Furthermore, maintenance of such control may violate traditional national norms such as the Swiss policy of neutrality and the United States tradition of "freedom of movement and speech" between countries.

As noted in Chapter 7, governmental and political control of sports is often resisted—especially if it concerns the international olympic principles. In some cases, transnational interests and governmental interests may coincide with the governments publicly declaring compliance with the sanctions while allowing, or encouraging, the noncompliance of transnational actors under their jurisdiction. Circumstantial evidence to support this contention is contained in the annual reports of the UN Sanctions Committee which document the lack of response by some governments to committee evidence that a breach of sanctions may have occurred. In March 1966, the South African government did not supply oil to Rhodesia but allowed oil companies and private citizens to do so instead. In this instance, transnational actors accomplished an economic transaction which might have proved politically embarrassing had it been conducted on a government-to-government level.

Many states may simply be unable to monitor transnational flows across their borders in order to detect and stop sanctions violations. In Chapter 4, Charles Burton Marshall was quoted as stating that effective policing of sanctions requires "much administrative and technical perseverance," and Ambassador Schaufele noted that "some nations plead that they are unable to allot the resources and money" necessary to carry out chemical analyses of imported minerals to determine their origin. In cases such as tourism, there may be no record that the transaction took place, making any attempt at control impossible. There are factors, however, which make the supervision of the sanctions a bit less formidable.

Regardless of the type of international relationship involved, the single most important factor in frustrating the relationship is *publicity*. For most governmental and transnational actors public image is important and to be publicly accused of contravening the Rhodesian sanctions is detrimental to that image. This finding is strong enough to propose the hypothesis that: "The effectiveness of sanctions in preventing the maintenance or development of any given international relation by Rhodesia is directly related to the degree to which that relationship generates publicity."

National governments are not the only source of information and publicity regarding the evasion of sanctions. Ironically, as transnational actors have been essential to Rhodesia in the evasion of sanctions, they have also provided vital information to governments and the United Nations relating to those evasions. The *Sunday Times* (London), the Anti-Apartheid League of the Netherlands, various church groups, trade unions, the Carnegie Endowment for International Peace (United States), and various pro-United Nations interest groups, among others, have been most helpful providing information regarding sanction-busting operations. As the target state can use transnational actors for their benefit, so can the countries applying the sanctions. The value of transnational actors was given belated recognition by the UN Security Council, in S/RES/333 (1973), which recommended that nongovernmental organizations and individuals be encouraged to report to the appropriate bodies reliable information regarding sanction-breaking operations.

Another hypothesis relating to the national perspective is: "The effectiveness of sanctions will be lessened when the enforcement of sanctions conflicts with other national interests perceived to be more important than the aims and goals of the sanctions policy." British Foreign Minister George Brown told the UN Security Council on December 8, 1966 (S/PV.1331), that if the program of sanctions is to succeed, "all Members . . . must put their international responsibilities first, but I can think of no case where these international responsibilities would conflict with real national interests." Robert C. Good, in describing British policy immediately after UDI, aptly noted that "bad estimates became the stock-in-trade of policy-makers in London."[5] In Salisbury, Prime Minister Ian Smith issued a white paper on April 26, 1965, assessing the likely consequences of an unilateral declaration of independence. In contrast to the British estimation, the white paper asserted that: "Although initially it would involve some inconveniences, it is certain that Rhodesia would obtain elsewhere all those imports which today it gets from Britain and the Commonwealth and that a great proportion of the country's exports could be marketed in those other countries with which Rhodesia has trading relations. There is no sentiment attached to money. Rhodesia has the potential, and if it produces goods of the right quality and at the right price, countries will continue to trade with it. This happens universally."[6]

At first glance, the white paper's assertions seem to have been proven correct; certainly this book has examined an abundance of reasons why governmental and transnational actors want to trade with Rhodesia. Brown's statement implicitly assumes that international responsibilities are unambiguous and acknowledged by all member-states of the UN; it explicitly assumes that national interests, such as national security and economic well-being, do not conflict seriously with those responsibilities.

The most conspicuously successful sanctions have been the political sanctions—involving nonrecognition and withdrawal of consular facilities from Salisbury and termination of Rhodesian memberships in international organizations. International visibility of these sanctions is high, and cost of implementation is low. The degree of control is also high, because political recognition and the establishment of diplomatic relations are sole prerogatives of sovereign governments.

The least successful sanctions against Rhodesia have been the economic restrictions—especially those involving international trade. The following outline culled from Chapter 4, highlights some of the purely economic reasons for trading with Rhodesia:

1. Minerals found in Rhodesia are strategic, in demand, and not easily substituted (e.g., chrome). Agricultural products—especially beef and maize—are also in demand.

2. The quality of exports is high; for example: cotton (low soil stains, moisture, and trash; good fiber length and color); tobacco (low nicotine, high sugar, low pesticides); chrome ore (good lumps, high chromic oxide content); asbestos (good fiber length); and lithium (low iron content).

3. Productivity and quality control are high (e.g., cotton is mostly handpicked; research provides high yield for many agricultural products such as maize seed).

4. Rhodesia sells at low prices due to discount forced by sanctions and because of access to cheap labor and low-cost power. Rhodesia, likewise, buys high.

5. Profits for middlemen and brokers are high.

6. Contract dependability. Rhodesia meets export commitments and is a dependable supplier. Sanction-busters receive preferential treatment.

7. Financial integrity. Rhodesia pays her bills, is a good risk, and has a reputation for fair dealing.

8. Rhodesia is discreet about transactions—good security, protects identity of customers, and avoids publicity.

9. Vertical integration. Secondary producers may be tied into Rhodesian primary production, the cost of changing source of supplies

may be high, and unique physical properties of Rhodesian goods may make conversion technically difficult.

10. Rhodesia offers lower transportation costs and quick service to contiguous states and to other states in Africa compared to suppliers in Europe.

11. Trading linkages prior to UDI were maintained after UDI due to habit, convenience, or personal relationships with Rhodesians.

Galtung notes that "the diversity of motives for not making sanctions complete is impressive. Such diversity is a factor on which a skilful government in a receiving nation can base policies designed to demoralize the sending nation."[7] Before discussing this factor *vis-à-vis* the next hypothesis, it would be useful to take a second glance at the Rhodesian white paper cited above.

At second glance, a weakness in the Rhodesian estimation is the use of the word "initially." The Rhodesian government always believed that economic sanctions would be a short-term affair. Indeed, the prevailing myth about sanctions in Rhodesia was that they would eventually dissipate. Governor of the Reserve Bank of Rhodesia Noel Bruce stated: "It is not anticipated that sanctions will be any more effective in the future than in the past. Experience has shown that measures of this nature tend to lose their effectiveness with the effluxion of time."[8] Minister of Finance John Wrathall stated that Rhodesia can ride sanctions out until they wither away; they had been eroded to some extent and will erode to a greater extent.[9] The one formal, political event these men might point to in order to substantiate their forecasts is the U.S. action of lifting the boycott on certain Rhodesian exports through implementaton of the Byrd Amendment. The most important consideration, however, is that no country followed this initiative by formally lifting or repealing any sanctions measures. On the contrary, after repeated attempts in the U.S. Congress, the Byrd Amendment was, in essence, repealed in 1977, and the UN Security Council continued to pass resolutions dealing with sanctions and their enforcement. London was evidently not the only place where "bad estimates" were made.

By 1974, more somber judgments about the tenacity of sanctions were being made in Salisbury. In his budget statement to the House of Assembly on August 29, 1974, the minister of finance referred several times to the "intensification of sanctions" and warned the business community about complacency and the need for the "greatest discretion in the conduct of external trade." In the budget statement presented in the

CONCLUSIONS   249

following year to the House, on July 10, 1975, the minister of finance admitted that "sanctions surveillance, if anything, has been stepped up."

The final hypothesis relating to the national perspective is: "The sanctioned state will pursue policies designed to induce both national governments and transnational actors to think that the application of sanctions is not in their best self-interest." This hypothesis shifts the perspective to the target of the sanctions and focuses on the kinds of policies which it can pursue in order to induce, persuade, or encourage noncompliance wth the sanctions or, to use Galtung's phrase, "demoralize the sending nation."

Doxey notes that "the ideological orientation of the target may prove an additional strength in its ability to resist sanctions." Ideological loyalties may preclude the achievement of universal application.[10] The Rhodesian government portrays itself as staunchly anticommunist and committed to the preservation of western civilization in Africa. Both the anticommunist theme and friendship for the United States were reflected in Smith's offer to provide help to the U.S. in the Vietnam War in February 1966. Such a position complicates efforts by the U.S. government to wage economic warfare against a small country professing friendship and ideological harmony. As noted in Chapter 4, this was a major argument of those congressmen supporting passage of the Byrd Amendment. Professions of loyalty by Rhodesians to the Queen for several years after UDI and emphasis on identification with their "kith and kin" in the United Kingdom may have been partly designed to erode support for the sanctions within that country. Chapter 3 details how Rhodesian foreign policy is geared, in part, to undermine the legitimacy and credibility of the premises upon which the sanctions are based. Rhodesia has tried to establish a pattern of conduct in its foreign relations that can in no way be construed as hostile or threatening. Its policy stresses tolerance for all forms of established governments. The Rhodesian government encourages the formation of "Friends of Rhodesia Societies" throughout the non-Communist world and is conscious of the value of favorable publicity in countries like the U.S.

While trying to persuade governments and their citizens that the application of sanctions against a friendly country is not in their best political self-interest, Rhodesia also stresses the economic costs that are involved. With respect to the trade in chrome ore, Smith stated in the *Sunday Mail,* September 12, 1971, that he suspected Communist countries were buying quite a lot of the ore. In this instance, not only is the United States denying herself access to a strategic mineral, but is actually losing it to her major world adversary and is, in turn, becoming dependent on that adversary for supplies of the mineral. The Rhodesian government enjoys pointing out these kinds of ironies arising from the application of sanctions. The Rhodesian government also states that the costs incurred in implementing the sanctions burden not only governments, but also their citizens. For example, according to the Smith régime, while Rhodesian trade played a relatively small part in Britain's economy, ending the sanctions could help ameliorate both Britain's balance of payments and unemployment problems. "The burden is not borne by [the Labour Cabinet] but by the ordinary man-in-the-street who has never been consulted about sanctions on Rhodesia."[11]

Another policy which Rhodesia can and does follow in order to try to persuade other countries not to apply sanctions is to remind them of the costs which they will incur by being subjected to Rhodesian countersanctions. In 1965, this approach took the form of an outright threat to repatriate nondigenous labor if sanctions were imposed. After the sanctions were adopted, in keeping with its policy of avoiding to appear threatening, the Rhodesian government explained that its countersanctions were always imposed reluctantly in response to the initial sanctions. For example, commenting on Rhodesian blockage of interest and capital repayments on debts and investment income due to American and British interests, Smith noted that it was the American and British governments who first froze Rhodesian funds. "Rhodesia's reputation for honouring her debts is beyond reproach, but I am sure you will agree that it would be quite unreasonable for Rhodesia to tolerate the action taken by the American Government without introducing reciprocal arrangements of the same kind."[12] Of course, as noted in Chapter 4, the countersanctions actually helped Rhodesia since she had a large net outflow of capital repayments and interest payments on liabilities.

Another Perspective

It might be well to explore another perspective which could yield information to explain Rhodesia's international relations during the period of sanctions.

It is argued that failure to isolate Rhodesia may be due, in part, to flaws in the sanctioning process itself. Aside from the possible counterproductive aspects of sanctions *vis-à-vis* the target state's internal political cohesion, there are numerous weaknesses in the sanctions process which impede enforcement and reduce efficacy. For instance, communications services—postal, telegraph, telephone, telex—exempted from the sanctions against Rhodesia weakened the overall program and are essential in Rhodesia's maintenance and development of international contacts.

The operative purposes of the Rhodesian sanctions policy are muddled and unclear, with different actors seeking different objectives. Moreover, some key actors, such as the United Kingdom, changed their objectives as time passed, and their original objectives remain unrealized. Also, it is unclear exactly what conditions would have to be satisfied before sanctions could be terminated. Likewise, there is some doubt as to exactly how sanctions could be terminated.

The method of implementation—involving the escalation of the sanctions along three continua: bilateral to multilateral; voluntary to mandatory; and selective to comprehensive—over a period of 18 months, allowed Rhodesia valuable time to develop new international contacts and plan measures to counter international isolation. This suggests another hypothesis: "The effectiveness of sanctions, in the absence of force, will be inversely related to the amount of time required to apply the entire array of sanction measures available."

Finally, sematic ambiguities exist in various words and phrases of the sanctions resolutions (e.g., "promotion" and "humanitarian"). In the absence of authoritative interpretation, each sanctioner may define these terms as broadly or as narrowly as it wishes.

SOME IMPLICATIONS

On August 2, 1963, the U.S. ambassador to the United Nations, Adlai Stevenson, in referring to possible sanctions against South Africa, noted in the Security Council (S/PV.1052) that "the result of the adoption of such measures, particularly if compliance is not widespread and sincere, would create doubts about the validity of, and diminish respect for, the authority of the United Nations and the efficacy of the sanction process envisioned in the Charter." Seven years later, the U.S. ambassador to the UN, Charles W. Yost, in referring to the extension of sanctions against Rhodesia, warned that impossible burdens must not be placed upon the UN, and care must be taken not to demand of it more than it can deliver. "To do so will only emphasize its shortcomings, bring it into contempt, and lessen that public confidence and support on which its future growth and reinforcement depend."[13]

The efficacy of the sanctions against Rhodesia is important to the general perception of the United Nations as an instrument able to promote world peace and security. Sanctions have been neither speedy nor particularly effective in achieving termination of UDI. Conditions have been described—some unique to Rhodesia, some inherently a part of the present international political system—which impede the sanctioning effort and cast doubts about the efficacy of sanctions in any future application by the United Nations.

Yet Rhodesia really has not become more viable in the years that sanctions have been in effect. Initial prosperity after UDI was due in large measure to the basic soundness of the Rhodesian economy at that time and the ability to tap the country's reserves such as excess industrial capacity, import-substitution, increased productivity, and mineral exploitation. But these reserves are not unlimited. A rapidly expanding African population and a marked increase in the guerrilla war dampen optimism about the future of the present political structures in Rhodesia. Sanctions hinder the ability of the Rhodesian government to cope with these two problems—a fact acknowledged by the Rhodesian government. The Rhodesian economy has been remarkably resilient in the face of the enormous costs which must be expended to evade the sanctions, but there is a question as to how long this resiliency can continue in the face of not only the sanctions but the population and guerrilla problems. Prime Minister Ian Smith, provided one answer on November 25, 1971, to the House of Assembly: "Things seem to be doing pretty well, and I cannot, by any stretch of the imagination, say that if we had failed to reach agreement this would have prejudiced Rhodesia's position this year, or next year. But, it is our assessment that in ten or twenty years time the position would not be so good for our children." Smith's assessment was correct in the short-term, 1971–74, but was incorrect in the long-term. He could not foresee that Rhodesia's economic viability would be called into question as early as 1976, because of a disintegration of will and determination—not in Salisbury, but rather in Lisbon. The Portuguese coup of April 1974, and all its ramifications for Southern Africa was the single most important factor in persuading Smith to accept the principle of majority rule.

The tenacity with which the idea of Rhodesian sanctions has been maintained—at least on the governmental level—is impressive. As noted above, sanctions have not withered away. For most of the member-states of the United Nations, the effort against Rhodesia is an ideological and symbolic struggle which is not easily forgotten. As the Finnish delegate to the UN noted in the Security Council on June 13, 1969 (S/PV.1476), while the illegal régime continues to survive in an economic sense, it survives as an outcast with no hope of ever gaining recognition. "Thus, what has been achieved so far by the United Nations in the question of

Southern Rhodesia is surely an impressive demonstration on behalf of the equality of races and the rights of man." In 1974, UN Secretary-General Kurt Waldheim observed that the question of Southern Rhodesia will go down in history as the first case in which the measures provided for in Article 41 of the UN Charter were implemented. Although the authority was there, practical experience in applying sanctions was completely lacking. It is understandable that it has taken time to develop the sanctions procedure and gradually perfect the machinery by use.[14]

It may be that sanctions are long-term means of influence whose symbolic achievements become apparent before their political achievements. In terms of political achievements, sanctions must be regarded as marginal instruments of influence best employed in conjunction with other means of influence such as armed force—especially if political results are desired in the short-run.

Whether or not the sanctions program against Rhodesia will diminish respect for the United Nations is speculative. But when African majority rule is eventually established in Rhodesia—and even if this is achieved mainly through guerrilla warfare—the United Nations will still be able to claim success for its sanctions program as having been a contributory factor.

Notes

CHAPTER 1—Rhodesia's International Status Prior to UDI

1. See Charles Burton Marshall, *Crisis Over Rhodesia: A Skeptical View* (Baltimore: The John Hopkins Press, 1967), pp. 9–16, for details of company rule in Rhodesia and pp. 16–33 for details of relations between the United Kingdom and Rhodesia since 1923. A thorough treatment of these relations may be found in Claire Palley, *The Constitutional History and Law of Southern Rhodesia 1888–1965* (Oxford: Clarendon Press, 1966).

2. After the Referendum of 1922, Rhodesia was renamed Southern Rhodesia. The government of Southern Rhodesia reassumed the name Rhodesia early in 1965 (before UDI). "Rhodesia" is the prevalent usage; United Nations documents and British constitutional documents retain the use of "Southern Rhodesia." African nationalists use the term "Zimbabwe" when referring to Rhodesia.

3. Marshall, *Crisis Over Rhodesia*, p. 19.

4. Rhodesia, Appellate Division of the High Court of Rhodesia, Judgment No. A.D. 1/68, cited as the Madzimbamuto judgment, 1968, p. 9.

5. Frank Clements, *Rhodesia: A Study of the Deterioration of a White Society* (New York: Praeger, 1969), p. 108.

6. Rhodesia, *Report of the Constitutional Commission 1968*, W. R. Whaley, Chairman (Salisbury: The Government Printer, 1968), p. 7.

7. See Kenneth W. Dam, *The GATT: Law and International Economic Organization* (Chicago: University of Chicago Press, 1970), pp. 109, 346.

8. Rhodesia, Ministry of External Affairs, *Annual Report for the Year ended 31st December, 1964* (Salisbury: The Government Printer, 1965), pp. 1–2.

9. Cited by Justice J. A. Macdonald in Rhodesia, Appellate Division of the High Court of Rhodesia, Judgment No. A.D.138/68, cited as the Ndhlovu judgment, 1968, p. 37.

10. Great Britain, Parliament, "Southern Rhodesia: Documents relating to the negotiations between the United Kingdom and Southern Rhodesian Governments, November 1963–November 1965," Cmnd. 2807, 1965, p. 59.

11. Palley, *Constitutional History and Law,* p. 727.

12. Rhodesia, Ministry of External Affairs, *Annual Report,* p. 2.

13. Rhodesia, Ministry of Commerce and Industry, *First Annual Report of The Secretary for the period ended 31st December, 1964* (Salisbury: The Government Printer, 1965), pp. 2, 13.

14. Information on the South African loans may be found in Eschel M. Rhoodie, *The Third Africa* (Cape Town: Twin Circle, 1968), pp. 146–47; and P. Smit and E. J. van der Merwe, "Economic Co-operation in Southern Africa," *Journal for Geography* (Stellenbosch) 3 (September 1968):287.

15. Great Britain, Parliament, *Parliamentary Debates* (Commons), vol. 770 (October 22, 1968), col. 1096; hereafter cited as Great Britain, *Hansard* (Commons). Palley, *Constitutional History and Law,* p. 731, notes that Southern Rhodesia was treated as a dominion in that the convention that United Kingdom military forces should not be stationed in her territory without the consent of the Southern Rhodesian Government had been observed.

16. For the European attitudes toward the dissolution of the federation see Sir Roy Welensky, *Welensky's 4000 Days* (London: Collins, 1964).

17. Great Britain, Cmnd. 2807, pp. 113–14.

18. *Ibid.,* p. 11.

CHAPTER 2—The Nature and Purposes of Rhodesian Sanctions

1. Johan Galtung, "On the Effects of International Economic Sanctions with Examples from the Case of Rhodesia," *World Politics* 19 (April 1967):379.

2. Roger Fisher, *International Conflict for Beginners* (New York: Harper & Row, 1969), pp. 27–28.

3. Galtung, "On the Effects of International Economic Sanctions with Examples from the Case of Rhodesia," *World Politics* 19 (April 1967):381, 388.

4. Peter Wallensteen, "Characteristics of Economic Sanctions," in *A Multi-Method Introduction to International Politics,* ed. William D. Coplin and C. W. Kegley (Chicago: Markham, 1971), pp. 129–30.

5. Margaret P. Doxey, *Economic Sanctions and International Enforcement* (New York: Oxford University Press, 1971), p. 14.

6. *Ibid.,* p. 1.

7. Galtung, "On the Effects of International Economic Sanctions with Examples from the Case of Rhodesia," *World Politics* 19 (April 1967):411–12.

8. Anna P. Schreiber, "Economic Coercion as an Instrument of Foreign Policy," *World Politics* 25 (April 1973):413.

9. George W. Ball, *The Discipline of Power: Essentials of a Modern World Structure* (Boston: Little, Brown, 1968), p. 245; testimony of Dean Acheson before the U.S. Congress, House Committee on Foreign Affairs, *Rhodesia and United States Foreign Policy, Hearings* before the Subcommittee on Africa, 91st Cong., 1st sess., 1969, pp. 124–73.

10. Galtung, "On the Effects of International Economic Sanctions with Examples from the Case of Rhodesia," *World Politics* 19 (April 1967):388.

11. T. R. C. Curtin and David Murray, *Economic Sanctions and Rhodesia* (London: Institute of Economic Affairs, 1967), p. 12.

12. Fisher, *International Conflict for Beginners*, p. 28; see also his chapter entitled "The Ineffectiveness of Inflicted Pain," pp. 29–37.

13. Harold Wilson, *A Personal Record: The Labour Government 1964–1970* (Boston: Little, Brown, 1971), p. 148.

14. Wallensteen, "Characteristics of Economic Sanctions," p. 143.

15. George W. Baer, "Sanctions and Security: The League of Nations and the Italian-Ethiopian War, 1935–1936," *International Organization* 27 (Spring 1973):179.

16. Doxey, *Economic Sanctions*, p. 26.

17. Galtung, "On the Effects of International Economic Sanctions with Examples from the Case of Rhodesia," *World Politics* 19 (April 1967):407.

18. *Ibid.*, pp. 384–87.

19. Figures calculated from Rhodesia, Central Statistical Office, *Annual Statement of External Trade*, 1965.

20. Robert B. Sutcliffe, *Sanctions Against Rhodesia* (London: Africa Bureau, 1966), p. 2.

21. For discussions of the Rhodesian issue at the United Nations, see J. Leo Cefkin, "The Rhodesian Question at the United Nations," *International Organization* 22 (Summer 1968):649–69; L. C. Green, "Southern Rhodesian Independence," *Archiv des Volkerrechts* 14 (August 1969):155–91; A. G. Mezerik, ed., *Rhodesia and the United Nations* (New York: International Review Service, 1966); and, *A Principle in Torment: The United Nations and Southern Rhodesia* (New York: United Nations Office of Public Information, 1969).

22. Great Britain, *Hansard* (Commons), vol. 720 (November 11, 1965), col. 361.

23. James Barber, "The Impact of the Rhodesian Crisis on the Commonwealth," *Journal of Commonwealth Political Studies* 7 (July 1969):83–95.

24. See the statements of the French Ambassador to the UN, Roger Seydoux, UN, Security Council, *Debates*, S/PV.1277, April 9, 1966, pp. 51–52.

25. Statement by French Ambassador to the UN, Claude Chayet, *UN Monthly Chronicle* 7 (April 1970):32–33.

26. Statement by British Ambassador to the UN, Lord Caradon, *ibid.*, p. 32.

27. Wilson, *A Personal Record*, p. 196.

28. British Information Service, *Rhodesia: Cost to Britain*, Policy Statement 35/67, March 16, 1967; Rhodesia, Ministry of Information, Immigration and Tourism, *Sanctions: The Cost to Britain* (Salisbury: The Government Printer, November 1967).

29. Arthur Bottomley, former Labor party minister, charged that because the Conservative party would not support the government on an all-embracing economic sanctions policy in 1965, the government was forced to introduce sanctions piecemeal. Great Britain, *Hansard* (Commons), vol. 845 (November 9, 1972), col. 1234.

30. Fisher, *International Conflict for Beginners*, p. 35.

31. Statement by Harold Wilson, Great Britain, *Hansard* (Commons), vol. 720 (November 11, 1965), cols. 356, 359.

32. Fredrik Hoffmann, "The Functions of Economic Sanctions: A Comparative Analysis," *Journal of Peace Research* 4 (1967):149.

33. Wilson, *A Personal Record*, p. 181.

34. Great Britain, *Hansard* (Commons), vol. 720 (November 12, 1965), col. 584.

35. *Ibid.*, col. 549; see also cols. 587 and 589.

36. Wilson, *A Personal Record*, pp. 182–83.

37. Great Britain, *Hansard* (Commons), vol. 720 (November 15, 1965), col. 632.

38. *Ibid.*, col. 748. Some scholars claim that rewards are a special type of sanctions—positive sanctions. In this study, while rewards are recognized as a means by which one state can induce another state to do what it wishes, rewards are considered to be conceptually different from sanctions in that they do not involve elements of deprivation. The termination of sanctions can be viewed as a reward and the negation or cancellation of rewards can be viewed as a sanction. For another point of view, see David A. Baldwin, "The Power of Positive Sanctions," *World Politics* 24 (October 1971):20–38.

39. Great Britain, *Hansard* (Commons), vol. 838 (June 15, 1972), col. 1763.

40. *Ibid.*, vol. 845 (November 9, 1972), col. 1213.

41. *Ibid.*, vol. 898 (October 31, 1975), cols. 1953–54, 2034.

42. *Ibid.*, vol 863 (November 8, 1973), col. 1250.

43. UN, Security Council, *Debates*, S/PV.1907, April 6, 1976, pp. 13–15.

44. U.S., Department of State, Bureau of Public Affairs, "Southern Africa and the United States: An Agenda for Cooperation," speech by Secretary Henry A. Kissinger in Lusaka, Zambia, April 27, 1976.

45. Doxey, *Economic Sanctions*, p. 12.

46. Ralph Zacklin, "Challenge of Rhodesia: Toward an International Public Policy," *International Conciliation*, no. 575 (November 1969):6.

47. UN, Security Council, *Debates*, S/PV.1408, March 26, 1968, p. 2.

48. *Ibid.*, S/PV.1428, May 29, 1968, p. 4.

49. *Ibid.*, S/PV.1333, December 12, 1966, p. 4.

50. *Ibid.*, S/PV.1476, June 13, 1969, p. 6 (Finland); S/PV.1714, May 17, 1973, p. 18 (Austria); S/PV.1712, May 14, 1973, p. 18 (Yugoslavia).

51. Rhodesia, Parliament, "Anglo-Rhodesian Relations: Proposals for a Settlement," Cmnd. R.R.46–1971, 1971, p. 9.

52. Rosalyn Higgins, "International Law, Rhodesia and the U.N.," *The World Today* 23 (1967):103.

53. U.S. Congress, Senate Committee on Foreign Relations, *Sanctions Against Rhodesia-Chrome, Hearings* before the Subcommittee on African Affairs, 92nd Cong., 1st sess., 1971, p. 21.

54. U.S. Congress, House Committee on Foreign Affairs, *Sanctions as an Instrumentality of the United Nations—Rhodesia as a Case Study, Hearings* before the Subcommittee on International Organizations and Movements, 92nd Cong., 2nd sess., 1972, p. 126.

55. See Zacklin, "Challenge of Rhodesia," pp. 1–72; Higgins, "International Law," pp. 94–106; and other references in Chapter 4 where some of these considerations are noted in describing Rhodesia's attempt to undermine the legitimacy of the sanctions policy.

56. UN, Office of Public Information, Press Release WS/757, April 9, 1976, p. 3.

57. "Rhodesia," *Survey of British and Commonwealth Affairs* 2 (August 2, 1968):718.

58. *Manchester Guardian,* Weekly Airmail Edition, May 27, 1972, p. 9.

CHAPTER 3—Political and Diplomatic Relations

1. Rhodesia, Ministry of Information, *Speech by Prime Minister Ian Smith on the Occasion of the Opening of the Bloemfontein (South Africa) Agricultural Show* (Salisbury: The Government Printer, March 24, 1971), p. 8.

2. Statement by Desmond Lardner-Burke, minister of law and order, in Rhodesia, *Hansard,* vol. 62 (November 25, 1965), col. 1943.

3. Rhodesia, *Speech by Ian Smith on Opening of Bloemfontein Show,* p. 8.

4. Margaret P. Doxey, *Economic Sanctions and International Enforcement* (New York: Oxford University Press, 1971), p. 101.

5. Great Britain, *Hansard* (Commons), vol. 845 (November 9, 1972), col. 1206.

6. Rhodesia, Appellate Division of the High Court of Rhodesia, Judgment No. A.D.138/68, cited as the Ndhlovu judgment, 1968, p. 42.

7. For a refutation of the Rhodesian arguments see Rosalyn Higgins, "International Law, Rhodesia and the U.N.," *The World Today* 23 (1967):94–106; Myres S. McDougal and W. M. Reisman, "Rhodesia and the United Nations: The Lawfulness of International Concern," *American Journal of International Law* 62 (January 1968):1–19; and Ralph Zacklin, "Challenges of Rhodesia: Toward an International Public Policy," *International Conciliation* 575 (November 1969): 1–72. For a defense of the Rhodesian arguments see Michael Stephen, "Natural Justice at the United Nations: The Rhodesia Case," *American Journal of International Law* 67 (July 1973):488–90; testimony of Dean Acheson before the U.S. Congress, House Committee on Foreign Affairs, *Rhodesia and the United States Foreign Policy, Hearings* before the Subcommittee on Africa, 91st Cong., 1st sess., 1969, pp. 124–73; and Charles Burton Marshall, *Crisis Over Rhodesia: A Skeptical View* (Baltimore: The John Hopkins Press, 1967). One broad question which arises from the debate is: Are the traditional prerogatives of sovereignty, including the notions of "domestic jurisdiction" and "threat to the peace," being transformed or transcended by an emerging new stress by members of the international community on the promotion and assurance of "human rights" in all areas of the world? For a discussion of the question see Vernon Van Dyke, *Human Rights, the United States, and World Community* (New York: Oxford University Press, 1970).

8. *Star* (Johannesburg), September 9, 1972. All reference to this newspaper is to the International Airmail Weekly edition unless otherwise noted.

9. *Rhodesia Herald,* July 2, 1975.

10. *Africa,* June 1975, p. 93.

11. Rhodesia, *Hansard,* vol. 77 (June 16, 1970), col. 589.

12. Rhodesia, Appellate Division of the High Court of Rhodesia, Judgment No. A.D. 1/68, cited as the Madzimbamuto judgment, 1968, p. 21.

13. *Ibid.,* pp. 39–40, 43–44, 46, 89.

14. Rhodesia, High Court, Ndhlovu judgment, p. 22.

15. *To the Point* (South Africa), June 17, 1972, p. 23.

16. Great Britain, British Information Services, *Rhodesia,* Policy Statement 6/70 (March 3, 1970), pp. 3–4.

17. Christopher Munro, acting Malawi government representative, private interview, Salisbury, Rhodesia, July 22, 1976.

18. For an excellent discussion of the political and diplomatic networks in Southern Africa see Kenneth W. Grundy, *Confrontation and Accommodation in Southern Africa: The Limits of Independence* (Berkeley: University of California Press, 1973), pp. 83–117. Grundy notes that secret, covert diplomatic linkages exist in Southern Africa as well as unofficial contacts—sometimes involving the use of transnational actors as intermediaries.

19. U.S. Congress, House Committee on Foreign Affairs, *Implications for U.S. International Legal Obligations of the Presence of the Rhodesian Information Office in the United States, Hearings* before the Subcommittee on Africa, 93rd Cong., 1st sess., 1973, pp. 64–65; hereafter cited as: U.S., *Hearings on the Rhodesian Information Office,* 1973.

20. *Rhodesia Herald,* October 14, 1972.

21. Officer of the Department of Information of Malawi, private interview on a "not for attribution basis," Blantyre, Malawi, August 13, 1971.

22. *Africa,* September 1975, p. 59 and *Rhodesia Herald,* June 24, 1975.

23. *Star* (Johannesburg), December 2, 1972.

24. Rhodesia, *Hansard,* vol. 64 (July 6, 1966), cols. 581–82.

25. *Ibid.,* vol. 68 (August 1, 1967), col. 372.

26. Rhodesia, Ministry of External Affairs, *Annual Report for the Year ended 31st December, 1964* (Salisbury: The Government Printer, 1965), pp. 17–18.

27. Information for this section on the RIO is compiled from: U.S., *Hearings on the Rhodesian Information Office,* 1973, pp. 1–87.

28. Statement quoted in: *Africa Report* 19 (March–April 1972):37–39.

29. Rhodesia, Ministry of Information, *Ròdesia-Rhodesia* (Salisbury: The Government Printer, July 1966), p. 1.

30. James Barber, *South Africa's Foreign Policy 1945–1970* (London: Oxford University Press, 1973), p. 246.

31. *Rhodesia Herald,* March 10, 1973.

32. Charles W. Petersen, "The Military Balance in Southern Africa," in *Southern Africa in Perspective: Essays in Regional Politics,* ed. by Christian P. Potholm and Richard Dale (New York: The Free Press, 1972), p. 313; Alan Rake, "Black Guerrillas in Rhodesia," *Africa Report* 13 (December 1968):24.

33. *Star* (Johannesburg), August 10, 1974.

34. *Rhodesia Herald,* December 5 and 23, 1972.

35. *Rhodesia Herald,* April 9, 1973.

36. See reports in *Star* (Johannesburg), September 1, 1973; *Sunday Times* (London), June 11, 1972; *Manchester Guardian,* September 12, 1973.

37. UN, SCOR, 32nd Yr., Spec. Supp. No. 2, Vol. II, Doc. S/12265, 1977, p. 217.

38. See the following for discussions of South African–Rhodesian relations: Gail-Maryse Cockram, *Vorster's Foreign Policy* (Pretoria: Academica, 1970), pp. 173–86; J. E. Spence, *Republic Under Pressure: A Study of South African Foreign Policy* (London: Oxford University Press, 1965); Amry Vandenbosch, *South*

Africa and the World: The Foreign Policy of Apartheid (Lexington: University of Kentucky Press, 1970); James Barber, *South Africa's Foreign Policy 1945–1970* (London: Oxford University Press, 1973); Christopher R. Hill, "UDI and South African Foreign Policy," *Journal of Commonwealth Political Studies* 7 (July 1969):96–103; Sam C. Nolutshungu, *South Africa in Africa: A Study in Ideology and Foreign Policy* (New York: Africana, 1975), pp. 174–90.

39. UN Security Council, *Letter Dated 26 January 1973 from the Representative of South Africa to the President of the Security Council,* Doc. S/10870, 1973.

40. UN Security Council, *Letter Dated 15 November 1965 from the Representative of South Africa to the Secretary-General,* Doc. S/6935, 1965.

41. *Sunday Mail,* October 27, 1968.

42. F. R. Metrowich, *Rhodesia: Birth of a Nation* (Pretoria: Africa Institute of South Africa, 1969), p. 152; interview with Metrowich.

43. Richard Hall, *The High Price of Principles: Kaunda and the White South* (London: Hodder and Stoughton, 1969), p. 231.

44. *Rhodesia Herald,* November 23, 1971 and *New York Times,* November 23, 1971.

45. UN Security Council, *Letter from South Africa,* Doc. S/10870, 1973.

46. *Rhodesia Herald,* January 30, 1973. It is interesting to note that these criticisms were republished in the Rhodesian newspapers.

47. See John D'Oliveira, "Report from South Africa," *Rhodesia Herald,* September 1, 1975.

48. South Africa, *Hansard* (Assembly), April 22, 1976, col. 5205.

49. *Sunday Mail,* November 3, 1974.

50. *Star* (Johannesburg), March 22, 1975 and May 17, 1975.

51. *Rhodesia Herald,* September 3, 4, 20, 1975.

52. *Ibid.,* October 10, 16, 1975; August 1, 1975; June 20, 1975.

53. UN, Security Council, *Letter Dated 27 April 1966 from the Minister for Foreign Affairs of Portugal to the Secretary-General,* Doc. S/7271, 1966.

54. Portugal, Secretaria de Estado da Informação e Turismo, "The Forthright Intention of Serving the Portuguese Nation," speech delivered by the prime minister, Professor Marcello Caetano, before the National Assembly on 27 November 1968, p. 11.

55. Prime Minister Harold Wilson said that he received information that Dr. Salazar had pressed Smith in the strongest terms to settle; see Harold Wilson, *A Personal Record: The Labour Government 1964–1970* (Boston: Little, Brown & Co., 1971), pp. 317–18. For Caetano's statement on his efforts, see *New York Times,* May 24, 1970.

56. UN, SCOR, 32nd Yr., Spec. Supp. No. 2, Vol. I, Doc. S/12265, 1977, p. 22.

57. For general discussions of Malawi's foreign policy, see James Mayall, "Malawi's Foreign Policy," *World Today* 26 (October 1970):435–45; James R. Hooker, "The Unpopular Art of Survival: A Guide to the Foreign Policy of Malawi," *American Universities Field Staff Reports* (Central and Southern Africa Series) 14 (December 1970):1–19; Samuel W. Speck, Jr., "Malawi and the Southern African Complex," in *Southern Africa in Perspective: Essays in Regional Politics,* ed. by Christian P. Potholm and Richard Dale (New York: The Free Press, 1972), pp. 207–18; Carolyn McMaster, *Malawi: Foreign Policy and Development* (New York: St. Martin's Press, 1974).

58. Malawi, Department of Information, *H. Kamuzu Banda, Address to the Heads of State at the O.A.U. Conference in Cairo* (Blantyre, July 1964), pp. 10–12.

59. *Sunday Mail,* September 12, 1971.

60. Malawi, Parliament, *Proceedings of Parliament,* Third Session (January 11, 1966), pp. 286–88. Hereafter cited as Malawi, *Hansard.*

61. *Star* (Johannesburg), June 14, 1975.

62. UN, SCOR, 22nd Yr., Supp. for January to March 1967, Doc. S/7781, 1967, pp. 117–18. For an interesting discussion of the Swiss dilemma regarding the UN sanctions, see Boleslaw A. Boczek, "Permanent Neutrality and Collective Security: The Case of Switzerland and the United Nations Sanctions Against Rhodesia," *Case Western Reserve Journal of International Law* 1 (Spring 1969): 75–104.

63. J. Albert Coetzee, *The Sovereignty of Rhodesia and the Law of Nations* (Pretoria: Transvaal Publishing Co., 1970), p. 42.

64. D. J. Devine, "Status of Rhodesia in International Law," *Acta Juridica* (1967):42.

65. D. J. Devine, "Does South Africa Recognize Rhodesian Independence?" *South African Law Journal* 86 (November 1969):443.

66. *To the Point* (South Africa), January 29, 1972, p. 50.

67. Devine, "Does South Africa Recognize Rhodesian Independence?" *South African Law Journal* 86 (November 1969):442.

CHAPTER 4—Economic Relations

1. Exports as a percentage of gross output in 1965 for agriculture was 40.8 percent; for mining, 91.6 percent; for manufacturing, 32.2 percent. Rhodesia, *Report by J. L. Sadie on Planning for the Economic Development of Rhodesia* (Salisbury: The Government Printer, 1967), p. 9. Employment figures calculated from Rhodesia, Ministry of Finance, *Economic Survey of Rhodesia for 1965* (Salisbury: The Government Printer, 1966), pp. 55–56.

2. A. M. Hawkins, "The Rhodesian Economy Under Sanctions," *Rhodesian Journal of Economics* 1 (August 1967):57–58.

3. Rhodesia, *Hansard,* vol. 81 (July 13, 1972), col. 962.

4. Karl Keyter, Salisbury correspondent, *Financial Mail* (South Africa), private interview, Salisbury, Rhodesia, August 17–18, 1971.

5. Rhodesia, Ministry of Finance, *Economic Survey of Rhodesia 1975* (Salisbury: The Government Printer, 1976), p. 8.

6. *Rhodesia Herald,* November 12, 1975.

7. All statistics used in this section were taken from Rhodesia, Central Statistical Office, *Monthly Digest of Statistics,* April 1977, and the 1976 Budget Message of the Minister of Finance in Rhodesia, *Hansard,* vol. 93 (July 15, 1976).

8. This section was based on Neal J. Dickinson, "Don't Rely too much on Manufacturing," *Rhodesia Herald,* November 4, 1971.

9. John Robertson, "How Has It Been Done?" *Rhodesia Herald,* January 11, 1973.

10. Rhodesia, Central Statistical Office, *Monthly Digest of Statistics,* April 1977, p. 7.

11. U.S. Bureau of Mines, *Minerals Yearbook 1974,* Vol. I: *Metals, Minerals, and Fuels* (Washington: Government Printing Office, 1976); Vol. III: *Area Reports: International,* p. 1195. See also George Kay, *Rhodesia: A Human Geography* (New York: Africana Publishing Co., 1970), pp. 130–42.

12. Rhodesia, Central Statistical Office, *Annual Statement of External Trade, 1965.* Henceforth, all 1964–65 import and export trade statistics will originate from this source. U.S. Bureau of Mines, *Minerals Yearbook 1971,* Vol. I: *Metals, Minerals, and Fuels* (Washington: Government Printing Office, 1973), p. 825.

13. *Rhodesia Herald,* April 10, 1973.

14. *Ibid.,* September 26, 1972.

15. *Ibid.,* June 20, 1973.

16. *Ibid.,* February 4, 1972. The actual production figure in pounds is a rough estimate; see the discussion in Kay, *Rhodesia: A Human Geography,* pp. 112, 116.

17. Official of the Cotton Promotion Council of Rhodesia, private interview on a "not for attribution basis," Salisbury, Rhodesia, July 9, 1971.

18. *Rhodesia Herald,* February 17, 1972; September 23, 1971.

19. *Sunday Mail,* December 7, 1975.

20. *Rhodesia Herald,* February 16, 1973.

21. Kenneth Young, *Rhodesia and Independence: A Study in British Colonial Policy* (London: J. M. Dent and Sons, 1969), p. 336. The *Rhodesia Herald,* May 2, 1973, mentioned a figure of R$15 million currently frozen.

22. Annual budget statement for 1967, by the minister of finance in Rhodesia, *Hansard,* vol. 68 (July 20, 1967), cols. 24–25, 36.

23. *Rhodesia Herald,* June 13, 1973.

24. *Star* (Johannesburg), December 4, 1971.

25. J. E. Spence, "South African Foreign Policy: The 'Outward Movement'," in *Southern Africa in Perspective: Essays in Regional Politics,* ed. Christian P. Potholm and Richard Dale (New York: The Free Press, 1972), p. 53.

26. R. B. Sutcliffe, "The Political Economy of Rhodesian Sanctions," *Journal of Commonwealth Political Studies* 7 (July 1969):124.

27. The survey is discussed in D. S. Pearson, "Industrial Development in Rhodesia," *Rhodesian Journal of Economics* 2 (March 1968):12–14, 23.

28. Giovanni Arrighi, *The Political Economy of Rhodesia* (The Hague: Mouton and Co., 1967), pp. 47–48.

29. Figures cited from U.S. Congress, House Committee on Foreign Affairs, *Policy Towards Africa for the Seventies, Hearings* before the Subcommittee on Africa, 91st Cong., 1st sess., 1970, p. 176.

30. Edwin S. Munger, "Rhodesia: Republic in Gestation," *American Universities Field Staff Reports,* Central and Southern Africa Series, 13 (October 1969):4.

31. *Rhodesia Herald,* April 6, 1973.

32. *Ibid.,* March 26, 1972, and January 25, 1973.

33. *Ibid.,* May 12, 1972.

34. This report was culled from UN, Security Council, *Eighth Report,* S/11927/Add.1/Annex II, February 6, 1976, pp. 133–50; and *Sunday Times* (London), April 14, 1974.

35. "Rhodesia Since UDI—Economic Prizes, Political Penalties," Supplement to *Financial Mail* (South Africa), April 30, 1971, p. 32.

36. *Rhodesian Commentary* 4 (October 1970):1–2.

37. Karl Keyter, private interview, August 17–18, 1971.

38. *Rhodesia Herald,* November 6, 1975; the amount *legally* repatriated from South Africa in 1974 was listed as R$6.0 m.

39. See *Rhodesia Herald,* October 2 and 16, 1975.

40. Statement of the Chamber of Mines of Rhodesia, *Rhodesia Herald,* January 18, 1973.

41. Rhodesia, Central Statistical Office, *Monthly Digest of Statistics,* March 1973, p. 41; and, UN, SCOR, 31st Yr., Spec. Supp. No. 2, Vol. II, S/11927/Rev.1, 1976, p. 126.

42. Guy Arnold and Alan Baldwin, *Rhodesia: Token Sanctions or Total Economic Warfare* (London: The Africa Bureau, 1972), p. 32.

43. In 1965, Rhodesia had trading links involving goods worth in excess of R$2000 with over 119 countries according to the *Annual Statement of External Trade, 1965.* The 1972 figures are from Export Credit Insurance Corporation of Rhodesia, *Annual Report 1972.*

44. Rhodesia, Ministry of Commerce and Industry, *Annual Report of the Secretary for the year ended 31st December, 1971* (Salisbury: The Government Printer, 1972), p. 8.

45. Rhodesia, Ministry of Finance, *Economic Survey of Rhodesia 1976* (Salisbury: The Government Printer, 1977), p. 1.

46. Rhodesia, Ministry of Commerce and Industry, *Annual Report 1971,* p. 4.

47. Theodore Bull, *Rhodesia: Crisis of Color* (Chicago: Quadrangle Press, 1968), pp. 102–103; P. B. Harris, "Rhodesia: Sanctions, Economics and Politics," *Rhodesian Journal of Economics* 2 (September 1968):17.

48. Lionel Disler, "The Effects of the Rand Devaluation on Rhodesia," *Rhodesian Journal of Economics* 6 (March 1972):20–23.

49. UN, Security Council, *Debates,* S/PV.1890, March 16, 1976.

50. "Mozambique: Sanctions Against Rhodesia," *Bulletin of the Africa Institute of South Africa,* nos. 5 & 6 (1976):213.

51. UN, Security Council, *Fourth Report,* S/10229/Add.1, June 16, 1971, p. 137.

52. UN, SCOR, 32nd Yr., Spec. Supp. No. 2, Vol. II, S/12265, 1977, p. 23.

53. Arnold and Baldwin, *Rhodesia: Token Sanctions,* p. 24.

54. Rhodesia, Ministry of Commerce and Industry, *Annual Report 1971,* p. 4. In April 1976, Rhodesia put import controls on a wide range of manufactured or secondary goods imported from Malawi.

55. Malawi, National Statistical Office, *Balance of Payments (1969)* (Zomba: Government Printer, 1970), p. 6.

56. UN, Security Council, *Note Dated 15 February 1967 from Malawi to the Secretary-General,* S/7751, February 15, 1967.

57. Malawi, National Statistical Office, *Annual Statement of External Trade 1972* (Zomba: Government Printer, 1973). These annual statements, for various years, are the source for the information on trade between Rhodesia and Malawi in specific products noted in this section.

58. UN, SCOR, 32nd Yr., Spec. Supp. No. 2, Vol. II, S/12265, 1977, pp. 188–91.

59. UN, Security Council, *Note Dated 27 February 1967 from Botswana to the Secretary-General,* S/7813, March 9, 1967, pp. 5–6.

60. UN, Security Council, *Letter Dated 28 April 1970 from Botswana to the Secretary-General,* S/9770, April 28, 1970.

61. UN, Security Council, *Note from Botswana,* S/7813, p. 2.

62. *Ibid.,* pp. 4–5.

63. Hawkins, "The Rhodesian Economy Under Sanctions," *Rhodesian Journal of Economics* 1 (August 1967):51. Two sources which describe Rhodesian-Zambian interdependence in detail are Richard Hall, *The High Price of Principles: Kaunda and the White South* (London: Hodder and Stoughton, 1969); Robert C. Good, *U.D.I.: The International Politics of the Rhodesian Rebellion* (Princeton: Princeton University Press, 1973), pp. 86–123, 161–66.

64. UN, Security Council, *Report by the Secretary-General Concerning the Situation in Southern Rhodesia,* S/8786/Add.2, October 10, 1968, p. 5.

65. Central African Power Corporation, *Annual Report and Accounts for the year ended 30th June 1970,* pp. 1–3.

66. *Rhodesia Herald,* February 5, 1973.

67. UN, Office of Public Information, Press Release, WS/773, July 30, 1976, p. 6.

68. *Africa,* May 1976, p. 17.

69. James R. Hooker, "Zambia since Independence: Yesterday's Hopes," *American Universities Field Staff Reports,* Central and Southern Africa Series 15 (December 1971):4–7; *Sunday Times* (London), October 14, 1973.

70. *Star* (Johannesburg), April 15, 1972. See also: Hall, *The High Price of Principles,* p. 162.

71. This is a combination of paraphrasing and direct quotation of several notes from the government of the Federal Republic of Germany to the UN Secretary-General. All relevant materials will be found in UN, Security Council, *Fourth Report,* S/10229/Add.1, June 16, 1971, pp. 128–33.

72. L. C. Green, "Southern Rhodesian Independence," *Archiv des Volkerrechts* 14 (August 1969):201, 203.

73. UN, Security Council, *Fourth Report,* S/10229/Add.1, June 16, 1971, p. 140.

74. *Ibid.,* S/10229, pp. 15–17.

75. Material for this section was compiled from the various annual reports of the Sanctions Committee of the UN Security Council including the Ninth Report released in August 1977 as UN, SCOR, 32nd Yr., Spec. Supp. No. 2, Vol. III, S/12265, 1977, pp. 1–47.

76. W. J. Levy, Inc., *The Economics and Logistics of an Embargo on Oil and Petroleum Products for Rhodesia,* Report for the Office of the United Nations Secretary-General, February 12, 1966 (New York: W. J. Levy, Inc., 1966), pars. 12, 26, 38–39, 77–78.

77. *Ibid.,* par. 23, 84.

78. Young, *Rhodesia and Independence,* p. 368. See also Frank Kearns, "Why Oil Sanctions Failed," *Africa Report* 11 (April 1966):24.

79. UN, General Assembly, *Southern Rhodesia Working Paper prepared by the Secretariat,* A/7200/Add. 1, September 30, 1968, pp. 32–33.

80. W. J. Levy, Inc., *The Economics and Logistics of an Embargo on Oil,* par. 12.

81. UN, Security Council, *Fourth Report*, S/10229/Add.2, July 13, 1971, pp. 147–66.

82. Guy Arnold, *Sanctions Against Rhodesia, 1965 to 1972* (London: The Africa Bureau, 1972), p. 19. The following oil companies operate in Rhodesia presumably under local control: Shell, British Petroleum (BP), Total, Caltex, and Mobil.

83. Munger, "Rhodesia: Republic in Gestation," *American Universities Field Staff Reports*, p. 2.

84. *Star* (Johannesburg), March 18, 1972.

85. UN, Security Council, *Fourth Report*, S/10229/Add.1, June 16, 1971, pp. 98–100; *Fifth Report*, S/10852/Add.1, December 31, 1972, pp. 53–55; *Seventh Report*, S/11594/Add.2/Annex II, April 2, 1975, pp. 35–36, 79.

86. Arnold, *Sanctions Against Rhodesia*, p. 24.

87. S/RES/333 implements pars. 10–22 from UN, Security Council, *Second Special Report Concerning Southern Rhodesia*, S/10920, April 15, 1973.

88. U.S. Congress, House Committee on Foreign Affairs, *Rhodesia and United States Foreign Policy, Hearings* before the Subcommittee on Africa, 91st Cong., 1st sess., 1969, p. 103.

89. U.S. Congress, House Committee on Foreign Affairs, *Sanctions as an Instrumentality of the United Nations—Rhodesia as a Case Study, Hearings* before the Subcommittee on International Organizations and Movements, 92nd Cong., 2nd sess., 1972, pp. 10, 20.

90. See *Rhodesia Herald*, February 10 and November 9, 1972.

91. Rhodesian Promotion Council, *Annual Report 1975–76*, p. 6.

92. *Rhodesia Herald*, August 12, 1971.

93. U.S., *Hearings on the Rhodesian Information Office*, 1973, p. 84.

94. *Rhodesian Commentary* 6 (May 1972):5.

95. J. T. Gilbert, "Finance for Exports," *Rhodesian Journal of Economics* 6 (December 1972):60.

96. Official of the Cotton Promotion Council of Rhodesia, private interview on a "not for attribution basis," Salisbury, Rhodesia, July 9, 1971.

97. See Anthony Lake, *The "Tar Baby" Option: American Policy Toward Southern Rhodesia* (New York: Columbia University Press, 1976).

98. John Donahey, director of public relations, Foote Mineral Company, private interview, Exton, Pennsylvania, May 25, 1972.

99. *Congressional Quarterly Weekly Report*, November 20, 1971, p. 2379.

100. U.S., *Federal Register*, vol. 37 (January 25, 1972), pp. 1108–109.

101. U.S. Congress, Senate Committee on Foreign Relations, *U.S. Sanctions Against Rhodesia—Chrome, Hearings* before the Subcommittee on African Affairs, 92nd Cong., 1st sess., 1971, p. 6.

102. Charles Coles Diggs, et al. v. George P. Shultz, Secretary of Treasury, No. 72-1642 (U.S. Ct. App. 1972), p. 9.

103. Testimony of Senator Gale McGee before U.S., *Sanctions as an Instrumentality of the United Nations, Hearings*, p. 137.

104. David D. Newsom, assistant secretary of state for African affairs, private interviews, Washington, D.C., November 16, 1972, and Villanova, Pa., April 4, 1973.

105. McGee testimony, p. 134.

106. U.S. Congress, House Committee on International Relations, *The Rhodesian Sanctions Bill, Joint Hearings* before the Subcommittees on Africa and International Organization, 95th Cong., 1st sess., 1977, p. 54.

107. For a review of this prior support see "Controversy Over Present U.S. Policy Toward Rhodesia," *Congressional Digest* 46 (March 1967); and Raymond Arsenault, "White on Chrome: Southern Congressmen and Rhodesia 1962–1971," *Issue* 2 (Winter 1972):46–57.

108. John Donahey, private interview, May 25, 1972.

109. U.S. Congress, Senate Committee on Foreign Relations, *Importation of Rhodesian Chrome, Hearings* before the Subcommittee on African Affairs, 93rd Cong., 1st sess., 1973, p. 91.

110. U.S., *Hearings on the Rhodesian Information Office,* 1973, p. 39.

111. *Ibid.,* p. 33.

112. This section is based on Kenneth Towsey, deputy secretary, Rhodesia Ministry for Foreign Affairs, and director, Rhodesian Information Office, Washington, D.C., private interviews, Washington, D.C., 1971–73.

113. U.S., *The Rhodesian Sanctions Bill, Joint Hearings,* pp. 44, 48.

114. U.S. Congress, House Committee on International Relations, H.Rept. No. 95–59 to accompany H.R.1746, 95th Cong., 1st sess., March 7, 1977, p. 6.

115. U.S., *Federal Register,* vol. 42 (April 5, 1977), p. 18074.

116. U.S., *Importation of Rhodesian Chrome, Hearings,* pp. 69, 71.

117. J. A. Lombard, "Economic Co-operation in Southern Africa," *Rhodesian Journal of Economics* 3 (September 1969):11.

118. *Rhodesia Herald,* March 3, 1972.

119. *Ibid.,* August 30, 1971.

120. These problems are not to be discussed here, see instead O. P. F. Horwood, "Regional Trade Co-operation in Southern Africa," *Rhodesian Journal of Economics* 4 (June 1970):1–9; Eschel M. Rhoodie, "Southern Africa: Towards a New Commonwealth?" in *Southern Africa in Perspective: Essays in Regional Politics,* ed. Christian P. Potholm and Richard Dale (New York: The Free Press, 1972), pp. 276–97.

121. Rhoodie, "Southern Africa: Towards a New Commonwealth?" in *Southern Africa in Perspective: Essays in Regional Politics,* p. 287.

122. Horwood, "Regional Trade Co-operation in Southern Africa," *Rhodesian Journal of Economics* 4 (June 1970):1.

CHAPTER 5—Communication and Transportation

1. *U.S. Department of State Bulletin* 62 (April 13, 1970): 503, 506.

2. Rhodesia, *Report of the Postmaster-General 1965/66,* p. 2; Rhodesia, *Report of the Postmaster-General 1968/69,* p. 2; *Rhodesia Telephone Directory,* 1971 and 1974.

3. Rhodesia, Posts and Telecommunications Corporation, *Annual Report 1974/75,* p. 9.

4. Rhodesia, Posts and Telecommunications Corporation, *Annual Report 1971/72,* p. 11; *Annual Report 1974/75,* p. 11; and "Mozambique: Sanctions

Against Rhodesia," *Bulletin of the Africa Institute of South Africa,* nos. 5 & 6 (1976):214.

5. Figures compiled from the relevant *Annual Reports* of the Rhodesia Postmaster-General and from the *Annual Report 1974/75* of the Posts and Telecommunications Corporation of Rhodesia.

6. UN, Security Council, Sanctions Committee, *Special Report,* S/AC.15/ WP.177/Add.3/Rev. 1, November 14, 1975, pp. 6, 8, 9.

7. Edmund H. Dale, "Some Geographical Aspects of African Land-Locked States," *Annals of American Association of Geographers* (September 1968):496.

8. *Rhodesia Herald,* March 10, 1976; *Financial Times* (London), May 11, 1976.

9. M. L. Rule, "The Report of the Beit Bridge Rail Link Commission," *Rhodesian Journal of Economics* 1 (August 1967):61–68.

10. *Financial Mail* (South Africa), May 23, 1975, pp. 663–64; *Rhodesia Herald,* August 9, 1975, and March 9, 1976.

11. *Rhodesia Herald,* June 8, 1975, and June 11, 1975.

12. *Star* (Johannesburg), July 13, 1974; *Rhodesia Herald,* March 16, 1976.

13. UN, Security Council, *Note from Botswana to the Secretary-General,* S/7813, March 9, 1967, p. 14.

14. *Star* (Johannesburg), September 21, 1974.

15. *Financial Times* (London), May 11, and 26, 1976.

16. Simon Katzenellenbogen, "Zambia and Rhodesia: Prisoners of the Past. A Note on the History of Railway Politics in Central Africa," *African Affairs* 73 (January 1974):63–66.

17. R. T. R. Hawkins, "Transport in Relation to Exports," *Rhodesian Journal of Economics* 6 (December 1972):50.

18. Details of Zambia's demands may be found in Rhodesia Railways, *Third Annual Report for the year ended 30th June 1970,* pp. 13–14.

19. *Sunday Mail,* January 14, 1973.

20. *Standard Bank Review,* March 1973, p. 17, and May 1973, p. 14. See also UN, Security Council, *Report of the Security Council Special Mission,* S/ 10896, March 5, 1973.

21. *Standard Bank Review,* March 1974, p. 43.

22. *Rhodesia Herald,* August 21, 1975.

23. Rhodesia, Central Statistical Office, *Monthly Digest of Statistics,* July 1976.

24. *Star* (Johannesburg), March 20, 1976, and *Rhodesia Herald,* July 20, 1976.

25. UN, Security Council, *Report by the Secretary-General Concerning the Situation in Southern Rhodesia,* S/8786, Annex II, August 28, 1968, p. 49.

26. UN, SCOR, 32nd Yr., Spec. Supp. No. 2, Vol. II, Doc. S/12265, 1977, p. 190.

27. Malawi, *Malawi Statistical Yearbook 1974,* p. 125.

28. *Malawi Directory of Trade and Commerce 1972* (Blantyre: N. P. Kamkwalala, 1972), p. 3.

29. *Ibid.,* April 9, 1976, and August 23, 1976.

30. *Ibid.,* August 12, 1972.

31. Rhodesia Railways, *Third Annual Report 1970,* pp. 12, 31.

32. UN, Security Council, *Sixth Report,* S/11178/Add.1, January 9, 1974, pp. 77–79.

33. See also Anthony Lake, *The "Tar Baby" Option: American Policy Toward Southern Rhodesia* (New York: Columbia University Press, 1976), pp. 174–80.

34. Air Rhodesia Corporation, *Fourth Annual Report for the year ended 30th June 1971;* UN, Security Council, *Seventh Report,* S/11594/Add.2 (Part II), April 2, 1975, pp. 9–48. The explanation of the Turkish government for the interline agreement between its airlines and Air Rhodesia is an interesting example of transnational linkages with political consequences for a government which is ignorant of the linkage: "The highly technical nature of these agreements and the fact that they usually never reach governmental level for conclusion but are done by exchanges of letters between companies can explain their being overlooked until recently." *Ibid.,* p. 40.

35. UN, Security Council, *Special Report,* S/AC.15/WP.177/Add.3/Rev.1, November 14, 1975, pp. 3, 7, 13.

36. UN, Security Council, *Third Report,* S/9844, June 15, 1970, p. 17.

37. UN, Security Council, *Report of the Secretary-General,* S/8786, Annex II, August 28, 1968, p. 49; and, UN, SCOR, 32nd Yr., Spec. Supp. No. 2, Vol. II, S/12265, 1977, p. 189.

38. "Mozambique: Sanctions Against Rhodesia," p. 213.

39. UN, Security Council, *Fourth Report,* S/10229/Add.1, June 16, 1971, pp. 123–25.

40. This section based on UN, Security Council, *Sixth Report,* S/11178/Add.1, January 9, 1974, pp. 68–76, and *Sunday Mail,* April 22, 1973.

41. U.S., *Hearings on the Rhodesian Information Office,* 1973, p. 85.

42. *Rhodesian Financial Gazette,* May 26, 1972.

43. For details on these transactions see UN, Security Council, *Sixth Report,* S/11178/Add.1, January 9, 1974, pp. 96–128, and UN, SCOR, 32nd Yr., Spec. Supp. No. 2, Vol. II, S/12265, 1977, pp. 196–202.

44. *Rhodesian Commentary* 5 (November 1971):7.

45. Figures computed from Rhodesia National Tourist Board, *Annual Report for the year ended 31st December 1971* (Salisbury: The Government Printer, 1972).

CHAPTER 6—Tourism, Labor, and Migration

1. Rhodesia National Tourist Board, *Annual Report for the year ended 31st December, 1969* (Salisbury: The Government Printer, 1970), p. 18; *Rhodesia Herald,* February 23, 1973.

2. Rhodesia National Tourist Board, *Annual Report for the year ended 31st December, 1970* (Salisbury: The Government Printer, 1971), p. 19. The Swiss government told the UN Secretary-General in 1972 that there was no RNTB office in Basle. UN, Security Council, *Sixth Report,* S/11178/Add.1, January 9, 1974, pp. 87–88.

3. Rhodesia National Tourist Board, *Annual Report 1970,* pp. 18–19; *Annual Report for the year ended 31st December, 1971* (Salisbury: The Government Printer, 1972), p. 15.

4. *Rhodesia Herald*, April 20, 1972.

5. U.S., *Hearings on the Rhodesian Information Office*, 1973, pp. 82–83.

6. UN, Office of Public Information, Press Release, SC/3619, May 27, 1975.

7. Rhodesia, Central Statistical Office, *Monthly Digest of Statistics*, July 1976 and April 1977. This trend continued into 1977.

8. Rhodesia, Central Statistical Office, *Census of Population 1969* (Salisbury: The Government Printer), p. 78.

9. "Rhodesia," *Survey of British and Commonwealth Affairs* 2 (August 2, 1968):718.

10. Statistics calculated from South Africa, Department of Statistics, *Bulletin of Statistics*, December 1970, December 1973, December 1975, June 1976.

11. "Mozambique: Sanctions Against Rhodesia," *Bulletin of the Africa Institute of South Africa*, nos. 5 & 6 (1976):213.

12. Malawi, National Statistical Office, *Tourist Report 1970* and *1971*.

13. UN, Security Council, *Report of the Secretary-General*, S/8786, Annex II, August 28, 1968, p. 49.

14. UN, SCOR, 32nd Yr., Spec. Supp. No. 2, Vol. II, S/12265, 1977, p. 189.

15. *Star* (Johannesburg), April 6, 1974.

16. UN, Security Council, *Report of the Secretary-General*, S/8786, Annex II, August 28, 1968, p. 52.

17. UN, SCOR, 32nd Yr., Spec. Supp. No. 2, Vol. II, S/12265, 1977, p. 193.

18. Malawi, Department of Tourism, *Tourist Topic*, August 1970, No. 26/70.

19. *Ibid.*, No. 28/70.

20. *Ibid.*, January 1971, No. 2/71; February 1971, No. 12/71.

21. Alex Inglesby, director, Rhodesia National Tourist Board, private interview, Salisbury, Rhodesia, August 17, 1971.

22. *Tourist Topic*, April 1971, No. 16/71.

23. A. H. Mell, senior tourism officer, Malawi, Department of Tourism, private interview, Blantyre, Malawi, August 13, 1971.

24. Rhodesia, Ministry of Information, press statement, May 24, 1971.

25. Rhodesia, Central Statistical Office, *Monthly Digest of Statistics*, January 1974; *Industry and Commerce of Rhodesia 1976* (Salisbury: Thoms, 1976), p. 78.

26. Rhodesia, Central Statistical Office, *Monthly Digest of Statistics*, January 1974. 1972 was the last year that such figures were released by the Rhodesian government.

27. *Sunday Mail*, January 30, 1972.

28. *Southern Africa Data* (Pretoria: The Africa Institute, 1970), p. 10.

29. Rhodesia, *Census of Population 1969*, p. 15. The number of foreign-born Africans living in Rhodesia exceeds the total number of Europeans living there by about 100,000.

30. Rhodesia, Ministry of Labour and Social Welfare, *Report of the Secretary for the year ended 31st December 1972* (Salisbury: The Government Printer, 1973), p. 4.

31. "Migration" is used in this book to denote a movement of people from one country to another country with the aim of establishing a new residency without any plan to return to the original country. Migration is discussed in the third major section of this chapter in reference to non-African peoples. "Labor" is used in this study to denote a movement of people from one country to an-

other country for a short-term aim—to seek employment. Labor is discussed in this section in reference to African peoples. Some whites may enter Rhodesia for a short period of time for employment, but separate statistics on these people are not available; they are included in the discussion on migration.

32. *Malawi Statistical Yearbook 1974*, pp. 77–79. The earnings from migrant contract labor more than offset Malawi's foreign trade deficit (exports-imports) of MK20.1 million in 1973.

33. Duncan G. Clarke, *Contract Workers and Underdevelopment in Rhodesia* (Gwelo: Mambo Press, 1974), pp. 8, 16–17, 65–66.

34. Rhodesia African Labour Supply Commission, *Chairman's Report for the year ended 31st December, 1971*, p. 2. The RALSC did raise its minimum wage by 25 percent effective January 1, 1972.

35. *Rhodesia Herald*, February 16, 1966; *Sunday Mail*, October 21, 1973.

36. South Africa, Parliament, *Parliamentary Debates* (House of Assembly), Weekly Edition (June 9–13, 1975), col. 1131.

37. South Africa, Mine Labour Organizations (WENELA) Limited, *Reports for the Years Ended 31st December, 1972, 1973, 1974, 1975*.

38. *Rhodesia Herald*, January 6, 1976; October 14, 1976; December 23, 1976.

39. Great Britain, Parliament, "Southern Rhodesia: Documents relating to the negotiations between the United Kingdom and Southern Rhodesian Governments, November 1963–November 1965," Cmnd. 2807, 1965, p. 85.

40. Rhodesia, *Report by J. L. Sadie on Planning for the Economic Development of Rhodesia* (Salisbury: The Government Printer, 1967), pp. 2–4. For an economic criticism of this approach to stimulating African employment opportunities, see Duncan G. Clarke, "The Assumed Employment Generating Capacity of European Immigration in Rhodesia," *Rhodesian Journal of Economics* 4 (June 1970):33–42.

41. Rhodesia, *Hansard*, vol. 90 (July 22, 1975), col. 1186.

42. *To the Point* (South Africa), January 15, 1972, p. 55.

43. *Sunday Mail*, April 14, 1974. Asian and colored migration was not a significant factor and, for this reason, was not included in Table 6.5.

44. Rhodesia, Central Statistical Office, *Monthly Migration and Tourist Statistics for June, 1976*, p. 17.

45. *Rhodesian Commentary* 4 (November 1970):2; *Rhodesia Herald*, October 23, 1971.

CHAPTER 7—Social Relations

1. The term "athletics" refers to track and field sporting events; in the United States, the term is often given a broader definition.

2. *Encyclopaedia Rhodesia* (Salisbury: The College Press, 1973), p. 339.

3. UN, SCOR, 32nd Yr., Spec. Supp. No. 2, Vol. I, Doc. S/12265, 1977, pp. 17–18.

4. *Sunday Mail*, July 23, 1972.

5. *Rhodesia Herald*, November 26, 1971. Most of this section is based on George Kerr, secretary-treasurer, Football Association of Rhodesia, private inter-

view, Salisbury, Rhodesia, August 17, 1971. The specific dates mentioned hereafter in this chapter refer to materials appearing in the *Rhodesia Herald* and *Sunday Mail* for those dates.

6. *Rhodesia Herald*, March 26, 1970.

7. *Rhodesia Herald*, September 2, 1975.

8. *Sunday Mail*, May 7, 1967.

9. John Cheffers, *A Wilderness of Spite or Rhodesia Denied* (New York: Vantage Press, 1972), p. 15; see also pp. 15–19 and 126–48 for a thorough documentation of the Rhodesian experience with the 1968 Olympic games. Cheffers, an Australian, was the national track and field coach of Rhodesia's ill-fated 1968 Olympic team. Eric Shore, president, Rhodesian Amateur Athletic Union, private interview, Salisbury, Rhodesia, August 20, 1971, was also helpful.

10. *Rhodesia Herald*, May 16, 1970.

11. UN, Security Council, *Fifth Report*, S/10852, December 22, 1972, pp. 22–23.

12. UN, General Assembly, *Document*, A/AC.109/375, June 30, 1971.

13. *Rhodesia Herald*, September 11, 1971.

14. *Sunday Mail*, September 19, 1971.

15. *Rhodesia Herald*, August 10, 1972.

16. *New York Times*, August 24, 1972.

17. *Rhodesia Herald*, August 24, 1972.

18. *New York Times*, August 20, 1972.

19. UN, Office of Public Information, Press Release SC/3629, June 12, 1975.

20. *Rhodesia Herald*, February 8, 1973.

21. *Rhodesian Financial Gazette*, December 31, 1971.

22. Rhodesia, Central Statistical Office, *Census of Population 1969* (Salisbury: The Government Printer), p. 202.

23. Rhodesia, Central Statistical Office, *Monthly Digest of Statistics*, April 1977, p. 2.

24. *Sunday Mail*, January 21, 1973, and July 8, 1973.

25. *New York Times*, January 23, 1972.

26. *Sunday Mail*, October 31, 1971.

27. *Rhodesian Commentary* 4 (October 1970):2.

CHAPTER 8—Conclusions

1. *Rhodesia Herald*, June 9, 1977.

2. Guy Arnold and Alan Baldwin, *Rhodesia: Token Sanctions or Total Economic Warfare* (London: The Africa Bureau, 1972), p. 2.

3. Charles L. Taylor and M. C. Hudson, *World Handbook of Political and Social Indicators* (New Haven: Yale University Press, 1972), p. 349.

4. Andrew M. Scott, *The Functioning of the International Political System* (New York: Macmillan, 1967), p. 199.

5. Robert C. Good, *U.D.I.: The International Politics of the Rhodesian Rebellion* (Princeton: Princeton University Press, 1973), p. 27.

6. Rhodesia, Prime Minister's Office, *The Economic Aspects of a Declaration of Independence* (Salisbury: The Government Printer, 1965).

7. Johan Galtung, "On the Effects of International Economic Sanctions With Examples from the Case of Rhodesia," *World Politics* 19 (April 1967):382.

8. *To the Point* (South Africa), June 17, 1972, p. 21.

9. *Rhodesia Herald,* February 19, 1972, and July 31, 1972. It is possible that these statements were motivated by a desire to maintain public morale rather than to make a valid prediction.

10. Margaret P. Doxey, *Economic Sanctions and International Enforcement* (New York: Oxford University Press, 1971), p. 101.

11. Rhodesia, Ministry of Information, Immigration, and Tourism, *Sanctions: The Cost to Britain* (Salisbury: The Government Printer, November 1967), p. 3.

12. *Ibid.,* pp. 2–3; Rhodesia, Ministry of Information, *An Address to the All-Africa Christian Crusade Congress in Salisbury on 17th January, 1969 by the Prime Minister* (Salisbury: The Government Printer, 1969), p. 8.

13. *The Department of State Bulletin* 62 (April 13, 1970):507.

14. *Objective: Justice* 6 (January–March 1974):28.

Bibliography

BOOKS AND REPORTS

Arnold, Guy. *Sanctions Against Rhodesia, 1965 to 1972.* London: The Africa Bureau, 1972.

Arnold, Guy, and Baldwin, Alan. *Rhodesia: Token Sanctions or Economic Warfare.* London: The Africa Bureau, 1972.

Arrighi, Giovanni. *The Political Economy of Rhodesia.* The Hague: Mouton, 1967.

Ball, George W. *The Discipline of Power: Essentials of a Modern World Structure.* Boston: Little, Brown, 1968.

Barber, James. *South Africa's Foreign Policy 1945–1970.* London: Oxford University Press, 1973.

Behrman, Jack N. *National Interests and the Multinational Enterprise.* Englewood Cliffs, N.J.: Prentice-Hall, 1970.

Bull, Theodore. *Rhodesia: Crisis of Color.* Chicago: Quadrangle, 1968.

Cheffers, John. *A Wilderness of Spite or Rhodesia Denied.* New York: Vantage, 1972.

Clarke, Duncan G. *Contract Workers and Underdevelopment in Rhodesia.* Gwelo: Mambo Press, 1974.

Clements, Frank. *Rhodesia: A Study of the Deterioration of a White Society.* New York: Praeger, 1969.

Cockram, Gail-Maryse. *Vorster's Foreign Policy.* Pretoria: Academica, 1970.

Coetzee, J. Albert. *The Sovereignty of Rhodesia and the Law of Nations.* Pretoria: Transvaal, 1970.

Curtin, T. R. C. and Murray, David. *Economic Sanctions and Rhodesia.* London: Institute of Economic Affairs, 1967.

Dam, Kenneth W. *The GATT: Law and International Economic Organization.* Chicago: University of Chicago Press, 1970.

Doxey, Margaret P. *Economic Sanctions and International Enforcement.* New York: Oxford University Press, 1971.

275

Encyclopaedia Rhodesia. Salisbury: The College Press, 1973.

Fisher, Roger. *International Conflict for Beginners*. New York: Harper & Row, 1969.

Good, Robert C. *U.D.I.: The International Politics of the Rhodesian Rebellion*. Princeton: Princeton University Press, 1973.

Grundy, Kenneth W. *Confrontation and Accommodation in Southern Africa: The Limits of Independence*. Berkeley: University of California Press, 1973.

Hall, Richard. *The High Price of Principles: Kaunda and the White South*. London: Hodder and Stoughton, 1969.

International Politics of Regions, The. Edited by Louis Cantori and Stephen Spiegel. Englewood Cliffs, N.J.: Prentice-Hall, 1970.

Kay, George. *Rhodesia: A Human Geography*. New York: Africana, 1970.

Lake, Anthony. *The "Tar Baby" Option: American Policy Toward Southern Rhodesia*. New York: Columbia University Press, 1976.

Levy, W. J., Inc. *The Economics and Logistics of an Embargo on Oil and Petroleum Products for Rhodesia*. Report for the Office of the United Nations Secretary-General, February 12, 1966. New York: W. J. Levy, 1966.

McMaster, Carolyn. *Malawi: Foreign Policy and Development*. New York: St. Martin's Press, 1974.

Marshall, Charles B. *Crisis Over Rhodesia: A Skeptical View*. Baltimore: The Johns Hopkins Press, 1967.

Metrowich, F. R. *Rhodesia: Birth of a Nation*. Pretoria: Africa Institute of South Africa, 1969.

Nolutshungu, Sam C. *South Africa in Africa: A Study in Ideology and Foreign Policy*. New York: Africana, 1975.

Palley, Claire. *The Constitutional History and Law of Southern Rhodesia 1888–1965*. Oxford: Clarendon Press, 1966.

Petersen, Charles W. "The Military Balance in Southern Africa." In *Southern Africa in Perspective: Essays in Regional Politics*, pp. 298–317. Edited by Christian P. Potholm and Richard Dale. New York: The Free Press, 1972.

Rhodesia and the United Nations. Edited by A. G. Mezerik. New York: International Review Service, 1966.

Rhoodie, Eschel M. "Southern Africa: Towards a New Commonwealth?" In *Southern Africa in Perspective: Essays in Regional Politics*, pp. 276–97. Edited by Christian P. Potholm and Richard Dale. New York: The Free Press, 1972.

———. *The Third Africa*. Cape Town: Twin Circle, 1968.

Scott, Andrew M. *The Functioning of the International Political System*. New York: Macmillan, 1967.

Speck, Samuel W., Jr. "Malawi and the Southern African Complex." In *Southern Africa in Perspective: Essays in Regional Politics*, pp. 207–18.

Edited by Christian P. Potholm and Richard Dale. New York: The Free Press, 1972.

Spence, J. E. *Republic Under Pressure: A Study of South African Foreign Policy.* London: Oxford University Press, 1965.

————. "South African Foreign Policy: The 'Outward Movement'." In *Southern Africa in Perspective: Essays in Regional Politics,* pp. 46–58. Edited by Christian P. Potholm and Richard Dale. New York: The Free Press, 1972.

Sutcliffe, Robert B. *Sanctions Against Rhodesia.* London: Africa Bureau, 1966.

Taylor, Charles L., and Hudson, M. C. *World Handbook of Political and Social Indicators.* New Haven: Yale University Press, 1972.

Van Dyke, Vernon. *Human Rights, the United States, and World Community.* New York: Oxford University Press, 1970.

Vandenbosch, Amry. *South Africa and the World: The Foreign Policy of Apartheid.* Lexington: University of Kentucky Press, 1970.

Wallensteen, Peter. "Characteristics of Economic Sanctions." In *A Multi-Method Introduction to International Politics,* pp. 128–54. Edited by William D. Coplin and C. W. Kegley, Jr. Chicago: Markham, 1971.

Welensky, Sir Roy. *Welensky's 4000 Days.* London: Collins, 1964.

Wilson, Harold. *A Personal Record: The Labour Government 1964–1970.* Boston: Little, Brown, 1971.

Young, Kenneth. *Rhodesia and Independence: A Study in British Colonial Policy.* London: Dent, 1969.

JOURNAL ARTICLES

Arsenault, Raymond. "White on Chrome: Southern Congressmen and Rhodesia 1962–1971." *Issue* 2 (Winter 1972):46–57.

Baer, George W. "Sanctions and Security: The League of Nations and the Italian-Ethiopian War, 1935–1936." *International Organization* 27 (Spring 1973):165–79.

Baldwin, David A. "The Power of Positive Sanctions." *World Politics* 24 (October 1971):20–38.

Barber, James. "The Impact of the Rhodesian Crisis on the Commonwealth." *Journal of Commonwealth Political Studies* 7 (July 1969):83–95.

Barnekov, C. C. "Sanctions and the Rhodesian Economy." *Rhodesian Journal of Economics* 3 (March 1969):44–75.

Boczek, Boleslaw A. "Permanent Neutrality and Collective Security: The Case of Switzerland and the United Nations Sanctions Against Rhodesia." *Case Western Reserve Journal of International Law* 1 (Spring 1969):75–104.

Bowman, Larry. "The Subordinate State System of Southern Africa." *International Studies Quarterly* 12 (September 1968):231–61.

Cefkin, J. Leo. "The Rhodesian Question at the United Nations." *International Organization* 22 (Summer 1968):649–69.

Clarke, Duncan G. "The Assumed Employment Generating Capacity of European Immigration in Rhodesia." *Rhodesian Journal of Economics* 4 (June 1970):33–42.

"Controversy Over Present U.S. Policy Toward Rhodesia." *Congressional Digest* 46 (March 1967):65–96.

Dale, Edmund H. "Some Geographical Aspects of African Land-Locked States." *Annuals of American Association of Geographers* (September 1968):485–505.

Devine, D. J. "Does South Africa Recognize Rhodesian Independence?" *South African Law Journal* 86 (November 1969):438–43.

———. "Status of Rhodesia in International Law." *Acta Juridica* (1967): 39–47.

Disler, Lionel. "The Effects of the Rand Devaluation on Rhodesia." *Rhodesian Journal of Economics* 6 (March 1972):20–23.

Galtung, Johan. "On the Effects of International Economic Sanctions with Examples from the Case of Rhodesia." *World Politics* 19 (April 1967): 378–416.

Gilbert, J. T. "Finance for Exports." *Rhodesian Journal of Economics* 6 (December 1972):58–63.

Green, L. C. "Southern Rhodesian Independence." *Archiv des Volkerrechts* 14 (August 1969):155–91.

Harris, P. B. "Rhodesia: Sanctions, Economics and Politics." *Rhodesian Journal of Economics* 2 (September 1968):5–20.

Hawkins, A. M. "The Rhodesian Economy Under Sanctions." *Rhodesian Journal of Economics* 1 (August 1967):44–60.

Hawkins, R. T. R. "Transport in Relation to Exports." *Rhodesian Journal of Economics* 6 (December 1972):50–57.

Higgins, Rosalyn. "International Law, Rhodesia and the U.N." *The World Today* 23 (1967): 94–106.

Hill, Christopher R. "UDI and South African Foreign Policy." *Journal of Commonwealth Political Studies* 7 (July 1969):96–103.

Hoffmann, Fredrik. "The Functions of Economic Sanctions: A Comparative Analysis." *Journal of Peace Research* 4 (1967):140–59.

Hooker, James R. "The Unpopular Art of Survival: A Guide to the Foreign Policy of Malawi." *American Universities Field Staff Reports* (Central and Southern Africa Series) 14 (December 1970):1–19.

———. "Zambia Since Independence: Yesterday's Hopes." *American Universities Field Staff Reports* (Central and Southern Africa Series) 15 (December 1971):1–12.

Horwood, O. P. F. "Regional Trade Co-operation in Southern Africa." *Rhodesian Journal of Economics* 4 (June 1970):1–9.

Kaiser, Karl. "The Interaction of Regional Subsystems." *World Politics* 21 (October 1968):84–107.

Katzenellenbogen, Simon. "Zambia and Rhodesia: Prisoners of the Past. A Note on the History of Railway Politics in Central Africa." *African Affairs* 73 (January 1974):63–66.

Kearns, Frank. "Why Oil Sanctions Failed." *Africa Report* 11 (April 1966): 24.

Lombard, J. A. "Economic Co-operation in Southern Africa." *Rhodesian Journal of Economics* 3 (September 1969):7–15.

McDougal, Myres S., and Reisman, W. M. "Rhodesia and the United Nations: The Lawfulness of International Concern." *American Journal of International Law* 62 (January 1968):1–19.

McKinnell, Robert. "Sanctions and the Rhodesian Economy." *Journal of Modern African Studies* 7 (December 1969):559–81.

Mayall, James. "Malawi's Foreign Policy." *World Today* 26 (October 1970): 435–45.

"Mozambique: Sanctions Against Rhodesia." *Bulletin of the Africa Institute of South Africa* 5 & 6 (1976):212–14.

Munger, Edwin S. "Rhodesia: Republic in Gestation." *American Universities Field Staff Reports* (Central and Southern Africa Series) 13 (October 1969): 1–30.

Nye, Joseph S., Jr. and Keohane, Robert O. "Transnational Relations and World Politics." *International Organization* 25 (Summer 1971):329–49, 721–58.

Pearson, D. S. "Industrial Development in Rhodesia." *Rhodesian Journal of Economics* 2 (March 1968):12–14, 23.

Rake, Alan. "Black Guerrillas in Rhodesia." *Africa Report* 13 (December 1968): 23–5.

Rule, M. L. "The Report of the Beit Bridge Rail Link Commission." *Rhodesian Journal of Economics* 1 (August 1967):61–68.

Schreiber, Anna P. "Economic Coercion as an Instrument of Foreign Policy." *World Politics* 25 (April 1973):387–413.

Smit, P., and van der Merwe, E. J. "Economic Co-operation in Southern Africa." *Journal for Geography* (Stellenbosch) 3 (September 1968): 279–94.

Stephen, Michael. "Natural Justice at the United Nations: The Rhodesia Case." *American Journal of International Law* 67 (July 1973):488–90.

Sutcliffe, R. B. "The Political Economy of Rhodesian Sanctions." *Journal of Commonwealth Political Studies* 7 (July 1969):113–25.

Zacklin, Ralph. "Challenge of Rhodesia: Toward an International Public Policy." *International Conciliation*, no. 575 (November 1969):1–72.

NEWSPAPERS AND MAGAZINES

Africa, June, September 1975; May 1976.
Bulawayo Chronicle, 1966–71.

Congressional Quarterly Weekly Report, 20 November 1971.

Department of State Bulletin, 62 (April 13, 1970):503, 507.

Dickinson, Neal J. "Don't Rely Too Much on Manufacturing." *Rhodesia Herald,* 4 November 1971.

Financial Times (London), 11, 26 May 1976.

Manchester Guardian, Weekly Airmail Edition, 27 May 1972; 27 August 1973; 27 April 1974.

New York Times, 1965–73.

Objective: Justice 6 (January–March 1974):28.

Property and Finance (Rhodesia), October 1966.

Rand Daily Mail (Johannesburg), 15 February and 18 March 1966.

"Rhodesia." *Survey of British and Commonwealth Affairs* 2 (August 2, 1968):718.

"Rhodesia: Entering a New Era of Development." *Journal of Commerce* (New York). Special Supplement. 19 June 1972.

"Rhodesia Since UDI—Economic Prizes, Political Penalties." *Financial Mail* (South Africa). Special Supplement. 30 April 1971.

Rhodesia Herald, 1964–77.

Rhodesian Commentary 4–7 (October 1970–November 1973).

Rhodesian Financial Gazette, 1970–75.

Robertson, John. "How Has It Been Done?" *Rhodesia Herald,* 11 January 1973.

Standard Bank Review, March, May 1973; March 1974.

Star (Johannesburg), International Airmail Weekly, 1971–76.

Sunday Mail (Salisbury), 1967–76.

Sunday Times (London), 11 June 1972; 26 August 1973; 2 September 1973; 14 October 1973; 14 April 1974.

Times (London), 21 January 1971.

To the Point (South Africa), 15, 29 January 1972; 17 June 1972.

U.N. Monthly Chronicle 7 (April 1970):15–33.

U.S. News and World Report, 29 November 1971.

INTERVIEWS

Black, Colin. Rhodesian sportsman and sports promoter, Salisbury, Rhodesia. 30 August 1971.

Dawson, R. Rhodesia Secretary of Labor, Salisbury, Rhodesia. 30 July 1976.

Donahey, John. Director of Public Relations, Foote Mineral Company, Exton, Pennsylvania. 25 May 1972.

Inglesby, Alex. Director, Rhodesia National Tourist Board, Salisbury, Rhodesia. 17 August 1971.

Kerr, George. Secretary-Treasurer, Football Association of Rhodesia, Salisbury, Rhodesia. 17 August 1971.

Keyter, Karl. Salisbury Correspondent, *Financial Mail* (South Africa), Salisbury, Rhodesia. 17–18 August 1971.

Mell, A. H. Senior Tourism Officer, Malawi, Department of Tourism, Blantyre, Malawi. 13 August 1971.

Munro, Christopher. Acting Malawi Government Representative in Rhodesia, Salisbury, Rhodesia. 22 July 1976.

Newsom, David D. Assistant Secretary of State for African Affairs, Washington, D.C. 16 November 1972; Villanova, Pennsylvania. 4 April 1973.

Officer of the Department of Information of Malawi, Blantyre, Malawi. 13 August 1971.

Official of the Cotton Promotion Council of Rhodesia, Salisbury, Rhodesia. 9 July 1971.

Shore, Eric. President, Rhodesian Amateur Athletic Union, Salisbury, Rhodesia. 20 August 1971.

Stoneman, Charles. Theatre Critic, *Rhodesia Herald,* Salisbury, Rhodesia. 27 August 1971.

Towsey, Kenneth. Deputy Secretary, Rhodesia Ministry of Foreign Affairs; Director, Rhodesian Information Office, Washington, D.C. Several interviews, 1971–74.

Tull, Thomas S. British High Commissioner to Malawi, 1967–71, Philadelphia, Pennsylvania. Public answers to questions after a speech to the World Affairs Council of Philadelphia, 10 November 1971.

Van der Byl, P. K. Rhodesia Minister of Defense and Foreign Affairs, Salisbury, Rhodesia. 2 August 1976.

MISCELLANEOUS

Central African Power Corporation. *Annual Report and Accounts for the year ended 30th June 1970.*

Export Credit Insurance Corporation of Rhodesia. *Annual Report 1972.*

Industry and Commerce of Rhodesia 1976. Salisbury: Thoms Commercial Publication, 1976.

Malawi Directory of Trade and Commerce 1972. Blantyre: N. P. Kamkwalala, 1972.

Rhodesia Telephone Directory. 1971 and 1974.

Rhodesian Promotion Council. *Annual Report 1971–72* and *Annual Report 1975–76.*

Southern Africa Data. Pretoria: The Africa Institute, 1970.

Travel Information Manual, July 1976.

PUBLIC DOCUMENTS

Great Britain

British Information Services. *Rhodesia.* Policy Statement 6/70. 3 March 1970.

British Information Services. *Rhodesia: Cost to Britain.* Policy Statement 35/67. 16 March 1967.

Parliament. *Parliamentary Debates* (Commons), vols. 720–898 (11 November 1965–31 October 1975); cited as *Hansard*.

Parliament. "Southern Rhodesia: Documents relating to the negotiations between the United Kingdom and Southern Rhodesian Governments, November 1963–November 1965." Cmnd. 2807, November 1965.

Malawi

Department of Information. *H. Kamuzu Banda, Address to the Heads of State at the O.A.U. Conference in Cairo.* Blantyre: Malawi Department of Information, July 1964.

Department of Tourism. *Tourist Topic.* No. 26/70–16/71, August 1970–April 1971.

Malawi Statistical Yearbook 1974.

National Statistical Office. *Annual Statement of External Trade 1972.* Zomba: The Government Printer, 1973.

National Statistical Office. *Balance of Payments (1969).* Zomba: Government Printer, 1973.

National Statistical Office. *Tourist Report 1970* and *Tourist Report 1971.*

Parliament. *Proceedings of Parliament* (9 November 1965–67 October 1975); cited as *Hansard*.

Rhodesia

Air Rhodesia Corporation. *Fourth Annual Report for the year ended 30th June 1971*

Appellate Division of the High Court of Rhodesia. Judgment A.D. 1/68, cited as the Madzimbamuto Judgment, 1968.

Appellate Division of the High Court of Rhodesia. Judgment A.D. 138/68, cited as the Ndhlovu Judgment, 1968.

Central Statistical Office. *Annual Statement of External Trade 1965.*

———. *Census of the Population 1969.* Salisbury: The Government Printer.

———. *Monthly Digest of Statistics.* March 1973–April 1977.

———. *Monthly Migration and Tourist Statistics for June, 1976.*

———. *National Accounts and Balance of Payments 1974.* Salisbury: The Government Printer, 1975.

Ministry of Commerce and Industry. *First Annual Report of The Secretary for the period ended 31st December, 1964.* Salisbury: The Government Printer, 1965.

———. *Annual Report of the Secretary for year ended 31st December, 1971.* Salisbury: The Government Printer, 1972.

Ministry of External Affairs. *Annual Report for the year ended 31st December, 1964.* Salisbury: The Government Printer, 1965.

Ministry of Finance. *Economic Survey of Rhodesia for 1965* through *1976.* Salisbury: The Government Printer.

Ministry of Information. *An Address to the All-Africa Christian Crusade Congress in Salisbury on 17th January, 1969 by the Prime Minister.* Salisbury: The Government Printer, 1969.
————. *Press Statement.* 24 May 1971.
————. *Ròdesia-Rhodesia.* Salisbury: The Government Printer, 1966.
————. *Speech by Prime Minister Ian Smith on the Occasion of the Opening of the Bloemfontein (South Africa) Agricultural Show.* Salisbury: The Government Printer, 24 March 1971.
————. Immigration and Tourism. *Sanctions: The Cost to Britain.* Salisbury: The Government Printer, November 1967.
Ministry of Labour and Social Welfare. *Report of the Secretary for the year ended 31st December 1972.* Salisbury: The Government Printer, 1973.
Parliament. "Anglo-Rhodesian Relations: Proposals for a Settlement." Cmnd.R.R.46–1971, November 1971.
————. *Parliamentary Debates* (Legislative Assembly/House of Assembly), vols. 62–93 (25 November 1965–15 July 1976); cited as *Hansard.*
Posts and Telecommunications Corporation. *Annual Report 1971/72* and *Annual Report 1974/75.*
Prime Minister's Office. *The Economic Aspects of a Declaration of Independence.* Salisbury: The Government Printer, 1965.
Report by J. L. Sadie on Planning for the Economic Development of Rhodesia. Salisbury: The Government Printer, 1967.
Report of the Constitutional Commission 1968. W. R. Whaley, Chairman. Salisbury: The Government Printer, 1968.
Rhodesia African Labour Supply Commission. *Chairman's Report for the year ended 31st December, 1971.*
Rhodesia National Tourist Board. *Annual Report for the year ended 30th June 1966; Annual Reports for the years ended 31st December, 1969, 1970, 1971.* Salisbury: The Government Printer.
Rhodesia Railways. *Third Annual Report for the year ended 30th June 1970.*

United Nations

General Assembly. *Document* (A/AC.109/375), 30 June 1971.
————. *Southern Rhodesia Working Paper prepared by the Secretariat* (A/7200/Add.1), 30 September 1968.
Office of Public Information. *A Principle in Torment: The United Nations and Southern Rhodesia,* 1969.
————. Press Releases. (SC/3619), 27 May 1975. (SC/3629), 12 June 1975. (WS/757), 9 April 1976. (WS/773), 30 July 1976.
Security Council. *Annual Reports of the Committee Established in Pursuance of Resolution 253 (1968) Concerning the Question of Southern Rhodesia* (cited as the U.N. Sanctions Committee). *Third Report* (S/9844), 15 June 1970. *Fourth Report* (S/10229/Add.1), 16 June 1971. *Fifth Report* (S/10852/Add.1), 31 December 1972. *Sixth Report* (S/11178/

Add.1), 9 January 1974. *Seventh Report* (S/11594/Add.2/Annex II),
2 April 1975. *Eighth Report* (S/11927/Add.1/Annex II), 6 February
1976. *Ninth Report* (S/12265), cited in SCOR, 32nd Yr., Special Supplement No. 2.

———. *Debates* (S/PV.1052–1907), 2 August 1963–6 April 1976.

———. *Letter Dated 15 November 1965 from the Representative of South
Africa to the Secretary-General* (S/6935), 15 November 1965.

———. *Letter Dated 27 April 1966 from the Minister for Foreign Affairs
of Portugal to the Secretary-General* (S/7271), 28 April 1966.

———. *Letter Dated 28 April 1970 from Botswana to the Secretary-General*
(S/9770), 28 April 1970.

———. *Letter Dated 26 January 1973 from the Representative of South
Africa to the President of the Security Council* (S/10870), 26 January
1973.

———. *Note Dated 15 February 1967 from Malawi to the Secretary-General*
(S/7751), 15 February 1967.

———. *Note Dated 27 February 1967 from Botswana to the Secretary-
General* (S/7813), 9 March 1967.

———. *Official Records* (cited as SCOR). Twenty-Second Year. Supplement
for January to March 1967 (S/7781). 1967. Thirty-First Year. Special
Supplement No. 2 Vol. II (S/11927/Rev.1). 1976. Thirty-Second Year.
Special Supplement No. 2. Vols. I–III (S/12265). 1977.

———. *Report by the Secretary-General Concerning the Situation in
Southern Rhodesia* (S/8786/Annex II), 28 August 1968; (S/8786/
Add.2), 10 October 1968.

———. *Report of the Security Council Special Mission Established under
Resolution 326 (1973)* (S/10896), 5 March 1973.

———. Sanctions Committee. *Special Report* (S/AC.15/WP.177/Add.3/
Rev.1), 14 November 1975.

———. *Second Special Report Concerning Southern Rhodesia* (S/10920),
15 April 1973.

United States

Bureau of Mines. *Minerals Yearbook 1971*. Washington: Government Printing Office, 1973.

Bureau of Mines. *Minerals Yearbook 1974*. Washington: Government Printing Office, 1976.

Charles Coles Diggs, et al. v. George P. Shultz, Secretary of Treasury, No.
72–1642 (U.S. Ct. App. 1972).

Congress. *Congressional Record,* 10 January 1966–16 June 1977.

———. House. Committee on Foreign Affairs. *Implications for U.S. International Legal Obligations of the Presence of the Rhodesian Information
Office in the United States, Hearings* before the Subcommittee on Africa,
93rd Cong., 1st sess., 1973.

———. House. Committee on Foreign Affairs. *Policy Towards Africa for the Seventies, Hearings* before the Subcommittee on Africa, 91st Cong., 1st sess., 1970.

———. House. Committee on Foreign Affairs. *Rhodesia and the United States Foreign Policy, Hearings* before the Subcommittee on Africa, 91st Cong., 1st sess., 1969.

———. House. Committee on Foreign Affairs. *Sanctions as an Instrumentality of the United Nations—Rhodesia as a Case Study, Hearings* before the Subcommittee on International Organizations and Movements, 92nd Cong., 2nd sess., 1972.

———. House. Committee on International Relations. *House Report No. 95–59* to accompany *House Report 1746.* 95th Cong., 1st sess., 7 March 1977.

———. House. Committee on International Relations. *The Rhodesian Sanctions Bill, Joint Hearings* before the Subcommittees on Africa and International Organization, 95th Cong., 1st sess., 1977.

———. Senate. Committee on Foreign Relations. *Importation of Rhodesian Chrome, Hearings* before the Subcommittee on African Affairs, 93rd Cong., 1st sess., 1973.

———. Senate. Committee on Foreign Relations. *Sanctions Against Rhodesia-Chrome, Hearings* before the Subcommittee on African Affairs, 92nd Cong., 1st sess., 1971.

Department of State. Bureau of Public Affairs. "Southern Africa and the United States: An Agenda for Cooperation." Speech by Secretary Henry A. Kissinger in Lusaka, Zambia. 27 April 1976.

Federal Register. Vol. 37 (25 January 1972); Vol. 42 (5 April 1977).

Miscellaneous

Portugal. Secretaria de Estado de Informação e Tourismo. "The Forthright Intention of Serving the Portuguese Nation." (Speech delivered by the Prime Minister, Professor Marcello Caetano, before the National Assembly on November 27, 1968).

South Africa. Department of Statistics. Bulletin of Statistics. December 1970; December 1973; December 1975; June 1976; March 1977.

South Africa. Mine Labour Organizations (WENELA) Limited. *Reports for the Years Ended 31st December 1972–75.*

South Africa. Parliament. *Parliamentary Debates* (House of Assembly), Weekly Edition (9–13 June 1975, 22 April 1976); cited as *Hansard.*

Index

SANCTIONS
The Case of Rhodesia

was set in 10-point Linotype Times Roman and leaded two points
with display type in handset Times Roman,
printed letterpress in black ink on 55-pound Glatco Offset
by Joe Mann Associates, Inc.;
Smyth-sewn and bound over boards in Columbia Bayside Linen
by Maple-Vail Book Manufacturing Group, Inc.;
and published by

SYRACUSE UNIVERSITY PRESS
SYRACUSE, NEW YORK 13210